Fourth Edition

Red, White, and Black

The Peoples of Early North America

Gary B. Nash
University of California, Los Angeles

Prentice Hall, Upper Saddle River, New Jersey 07458

Library of Congress Cataloging-in-Publication Data

Nash, Gary B.
    Red, white, and black : the peoples of early North America / Gary B.
Nash — 4th ed.
      p.   cm.
    Includes bibliographical references and index.
    ISBN 0–13–956756–9
    1. United States—History—Colonial period, ca. 1600–1775.
2. America—Discovery and exploration.   3. United States—Race
relations. I. Title.
    E188.N37   2000
    973.2—dc21   99–27631
                                                 CIP

Production Editor: Barbara DeVries
Executive Editor: Todd Armstrong
Assistant Editor: Emsal Hasan
Cover Designer: Karen Salzbach
Cover Design Director: Jayne Conte
Cover Image: "Die Einwohner von Boston werfen den englisch oftindischen
    thee ins Meer am 18 December 1773." Historische genealogischer Calender
    fur 1784, Leipsig.
Manufacturing Buyer: Lynn Pearlman
Editorial Assistant: Holly Jo Brown
Cartographer: CartoGraphics
Indexer: Richard Genova

This book was set 10/12 New Baskerville by Pub-Set, Inc.,
and was printed by Courier Companies, Inc.
The cover was printed by Phoenix Color Corp.

© 2000, 1992, 1982, 1974 by Prentice-Hall, Inc.
Upper Saddle River, New Jersey 07458

Printed in the United States of America

10 9 8 7 6 5 4 3 2

ISBN 0-13-956756-9

PRENTICE-HALL INTERNATIONAL (UK) LIMITED, *London*
PRENTICE-HALL OF AUSTRALIA PTY. LIMITED, *Sydney*
PRENTICE-HALL CANADA INC., *Toronto*
PRENTICE-HALL HISPANOAMERICANA, S.A., *Mexico*
PRENTICE-HALL OF INDIA PRIVATE LIMITED, *New Delhi*
PRENTICE-HALL OF JAPAN, INC., *Tokyo*
PEARSON EDUCATION ASIA PTE. LTD., *Singapore*
EDITORA PRENTICE-HALL DO BRASIL, LTDA., *Rio de Janeiro*

Contents

Acknowledgments

The pages that follow began to take form in my mind several decades ago when I participated in redesigning the introductory course in American history at the University of California, Los Angeles. This effort was directed at making American history more understandable to an ethnically, socially, and intellectually diverse undergraduate audience by studying it as the process of change that occurred when people of widely varying cultural backgrounds interacted over a period of four centuries. Although this does not sound like a startling innovation, I discovered that it required me to read broadly in areas that had largely escaped my notice during fifteen years of studying and teaching colonial American history—anthropology, ethnohistory, African history, and Latin American history. To say that they "escaped my notice" is to put the point obliquely, for one of the thrusts of this book is that we read, think, and write selectively and in ways that reflect our cultural biases. Nothing more than changing my "angle of vision" was required to make it apparent that early American history and the early history of the American peoples were two different subjects and that the latter was comprehensible only by vastly widening the scope of my reading and thinking about the subject.

In revising this book for this fourth edition I have been ably assisted by Samantha Holtkamp. Edie Sparks and Kelly Lytle also provided help. For their valuable reviews of the third edition that led to important changes, I gratefully acknowledge Debra E. Barth, *San Jose City College*, Kirsten Fischer, *University of South Florida*, Michael G. Hall, *University of Texas-Austin*, Keith Lawrence, *Brigham Young University*, and Philip Weeks, *Kent State University*.

Introduction

"God is English." Thus John Aylmer, a pious English clergyman, exhorted his parishioners in 1558, attempting to fill them with piety and patriotism.[1] That thought, though never stated so directly, has echoed ever since through our history books. As schoolchildren, as college students, and as presumably informed citizens, most of us have been brought up on what has passed for the greatest success story of human history, the epic tale of how a proud, brave offshoot of the English-speaking people tried to reverse the laws of history by demonstrating what the human spirit, liberated from the shackles of tradition, myth, and oppressive authority, could do in a newly discovered corner of the earth. For most Americans, colonial history begins with Sir Walter Raleigh and John Smith and proceeds through William Bradford and John Winthrop to Jonathan Edwards and Benjamin Franklin. It ends with the Revolution, where wilderness-conquering settlers pitted themselves against a mother country that had grown tyrannical and won their independence against the odds.

This is ethnocentric history, as has been charged frequently and vociferously in recent decades, both by revisionist white historians and by those

---

[1]Quoted in Carl Bridenbaugh, *Vexed and Troubled Englishmen, 1590–1642,* (New York: Oxford University Press, Inc., 1968), p. 13.

1

whose citizenship is American but whose ancestral roots are in Africa, Asia, Mexico, or the native cultures of North America. Just as Eurocentrism made it difficult for the early colonizers and explorers to believe that a continental land mass as large as North America could exist in the oceans between Europe and Asia, historians in this country have found it difficult to understand that the colonial period of our history is the story of a minority of English colonizers interacting with a majority of Iroquois, Delawares, Narragansetts, Pequots, Mahicans, Catawbas, Tuscaroras, Creeks, Cherokees, Choctaws, Ibos, Mandingos, Fulas, Yorubas, Ashantis, Germans, French, Spaniards, Swedes, Welsh, and Scots-Irish, to mention only some of the cultural strains present on the continent.

In recent years, American historians have provided correctives to white-oriented, male-dominated, hero-worshipping history. At first they devoted their efforts to restocking the pantheon of national heroes with new figures whose skin is not so pale. Pedestals, for example, were erected for Crispus Attucks, the half-Indian, half-black fisherman of Boston who fell first at the Boston massacre; for Ely Parker, the Seneca general who helped the North win the Civil War and later served his friend, Ulysses Grant, when the latter attained the presidency; and for Cesar Chávez, the leader of the United Farm Workers, who brought major gains to the agricultural workers in this country.

Historical revisionism often begins in this tentative way, turning a monochromatic cast of characters into a polychromatic one with the story line unchanged. Nearly thirty years ago, Vine Deloria, Jr., an outspoken Indian leader, charged that much of the "new" history "takes a basic 'manifest destiny' white interpretation of history and lovingly plugs a few feathers, woolly heads, and sombreros into the famous events of American history."[2] But historians have moved beyond this crude form of multicultural history.

When first drafting this book in 1972, I took Deloria's criticism to heart, believing that a fuller and deeper understanding of the colonial underpinnings of American history must examine the interaction of many peoples, at all levels of society, from a wide range of cultural backgrounds over a period of several centuries. For the colonial and revolutionary period this means exploring not only how the English and other Europeans "discovered" North America and transplanted their cultures there, but also how societies that had been in North America and Africa for thousands of years were actively and intimately involved in the process of forging a new, multistranded culture in what would become the United States. Africans were not merely enslaved. Native Americans were not merely driven from the land. As Ralph Ellison, the African-American writer, has reasoned: "Can a people . . . live and develop for over three hundred years by simply *reacting*?

---

[2]Vine Deloria, Jr., *We Talk, You Listen: New Tribes, New Turf* (New York: The Macmillan Co., 1970), p. 39.

Are American Negroes simply the creation of white men, or have they at least helped to create themselves out of what they found around them?"[3] To include Africans and Indians in our history in this way, simply as victims of the more powerful Europeans, is hardly better than excluding them altogether. It is to render voiceless, nameless, and faceless people who powerfully affected the course of our historical development as a society and as a nation.

Breaking through the notion of Indians and Africans being kneaded like dough according to the whims of the invading Europeans was one of the main goals of this book from the start. During the last two decades, when this book has been revised for new editions, resourceful and talented anthropologists and historians—a host of them—have provided rich studies that add depth and complexity to this initial formulation. A body of historical literature now shows irrefutably how Africans and Native Americans were critically important participants in the making of American history. Wherever has fallen the focus of these scholarly inquiries—the French penetration of the Great Lakes region, the Spanish occupation of Florida and New Mexico, the English interaction with the Iroquois or Catawba, the English enslavement of Africans in South Carolina, Virginia, Barbados, and Jamaica—a consistent picture has emerged of the complex, intercultural birthing of the "new world." It is a new world for conquerors and conquered alike. It is the story of transformation for all involved, regardless of enormous inequalities in status, where European and Indian worlds blurred at the edges and merged, where Africans and Europeans made a new world together.

Every historian and anthropologist engaged in breaking old molds in the service of a more faithful recounting of how North American societies emerged has had to abandon the old master narrative of "primitive" and "civilized" peoples careening toward each other after 1492 on a collision course, surely one of the greatest collisions of human history. Much utility still remains in pointing out differences in technological levels—for example, the Europeans' ability to navigate across the Atlantic and to process iron and thereby to manufacture guns. But placing too much emphasis on technological advancement creates a mental trap in which Europeans are imagined as the principal agents of history, the African and Indian peoples as the passive victims, and the outcomes seemingly inevitable. Inevitability is a victor's story, one that robs history of its contingency and unexpected outcomes. This book presents historical outcomes as part of a tangled and unpredictable human process where very little is inexorable or foreordained.

Africans, Indians, and Europeans all developed various societies that functioned, for better or worse, in their respective environments. None thought of themselves as inferior people. "Savages we call them," wrote

---

[3]Ralph Ellison, *Shadow and Act* (New York: New American Library, 1964), p. 301.

Benjamin Franklin more than two centuries ago, "because their Manners differ from ours, which we think the Perfection of Civility; they think the same of theirs."[4] To imagine Indians simply as victims of European aggression is to bury from sight the rich and instructive story of how Narragansetts, Iroquois, Delawares, Pamunkeys, Cherokees, Creeks, and many other nations, which had been changing for centuries before Europeans touched foot on the continent, responded creatively and powerfully to the newcomers from across the ocean and in this way reshaped themselves while reshaping the course of European settlement.

This book adopts a cultural approach to our early history. It looks at the land mass we know as "North America" as a place where a number of different societies converged during a particular period of history—between about 1550 and 1790, to use the European system of measuring time. In the most general terms we can define these cultural groups as Indian, African, and European, though, as we will see, this oversimplification is itself a Eurocentric device for classifying cultures. In other words, this book is not about early American history as usually defined—as the English colonization of thirteen colonies along the continent's eastern seaboard—but about the history of the *peoples* of North America during the two centuries leading toward the American Revolution.

Each of these three cultural groups was exceedingly diverse. In their cultural characteristics Iroquois were as different from Natchez as English from Egyptians; Hausas and Yorubas were as distinct as Pequots and Creeks. Nor did the subgroups in each of these cultural blocs act in concert. The French, English, and Spanish fought wars with each other, contending for power and advantage in the seventeenth and eighteenth centuries, just as Hurons and Iroquois or Creeks and Cherokees sought the upper hand in their respective regions. Our task is to discover what happened when peoples from different continents, diverse among themselves, came into contact with each other at particular points in history. Social and cultural *process* and *change* are of primary concern: how societies were affected and how their destinies changed by the experience of contact with other societies. Anthropologists call this process "transculturation"; historians call it "social change." Whatever the terms, this book explores a dynamic process of interaction that shaped the history of American Indians, Europeans, and Africans in North America in the seventeenth and eighteenth centuries.

It is important to consider that when scholars speak of "cultural groups" or "societies," they are referring to abstractions. A *society* is a group of people organized together so that their needs—the sustaining of life at the most basic level—can be met. *Culture* is a broad term that embraces all the specific characteristics of a society as they are functionally related to

[4]"Remarks Concerning the Savages of North America" (1784), in *The Writings of Benjamin Franklin,* ed. Albert H. Smyth (New York: The Macmillan Co., 1907), X: 97.

each other—technology; modes of dress and diet; economic, social, and political organization; religion; language; art; values; methods of child-rearing;
and so forth. Simply stated, "culture" means a way of life, the framework
within which any group of people—a society—comprehends the world
around it. But "culture" and "society" are also terms that imply standards or norms of behavior. This is what is meant by "cultural traits" or
"group behavior."

Employing such terms runs the danger of losing sight of the individual human beings, none of them exactly alike, who make up a society. Culture is a mental construct that scholars employ for the sake of convenience,
so that highly varied and complex individual behavior can be broadly classified and compared. Because we are Americans, belonging to the same
nation, speaking (or learning to speak) the same language, living under the
same laws, participating in the same economic and political system, does not
mean that we are all alike. Otherwise there would be no generation gap,
no differences in aesthetic taste, no gendered values, no racial tension, no
political conflict. Nonetheless, taken collectively, Americans typically organize their lives differently than do people in other parts of the world. While
we must be aware of the problems of a cultural approach to history, it at
least provides a way of understanding the interaction of the great mass of
individuals of widely varying backgrounds who found themselves cohabiting
one part of the "New World" several centuries ago.

One other cautionary note is necessary. Though I often speak of racial
groups and racial interaction, these terms do not refer to genetically different groups of people. For more than a century anthropologists poured their
intellect and energy into attempts to classify all the peoples of the world,
from the pygmies of Borneo to the Aleuts in Alaska, according to genetic
differences. Noses were measured, cranial cavities examined, body hair
noted, lips described, and hair and eye color classified in an attempt to define scientifically the various physiological types of humankind. Much was at
stake in this effort. If physiological characteristics, with skin color prominent
among them, could be "scientifically" determined, it would be possible to
rank degrees of "cultural development" or achievement on a scale reaching
from "savagery" to "civilization." It should come as no surprise that this
massive effort of Western white anthropologists resulted in the conclusion
that the superiority of the Caucasian peoples of the world could be "scientifically" proven.

Today, genetic sciences have wiped away this long effort to establish a
hierarchy of human types. Modern science finds that race is not biologically
determined. It is socially and historically constructed. No objective foundation exists for the idea that a person belongs to one biological "race" or another or that a particular number of distinct races exists. It is now apparent
that Europeans in the New World fashioned different codes of race relations
based on their own needs and attitudes concerning how people should be

classified, treated, and separated. "Negro" in Brazil and in the United States, for example, came to have different meanings that reflected conditions and values, as well as degrees of social mingling, not genetic differences. As Sidney Mintz wisely reminds us, "The 'reality' of race is thus as much a social as a biological reality, the inheritance of physical traits serving as the raw material for social sorting devices, by which both stigmata and privileges may be systematically allocated."[5] This social sorting is highly arbitrary—down to the present day when, for example, the U.S. Census Bureau for many decades obliged every resident to choose one racial category as if no people whatsoever existed with mixed racial inheritance.

Thus we gain little insight into the historical process by distinguishing cultural groups at the biological or physiological level. We are not considering genetically different groups but human populations from different parts of the world, groups of people with cultural differences. Most of all, we will be inquiring into the way these peoples, brought into contact with each other, changed over the course of several centuries—and changed in a manner that would shape the course of American history for generations to come.

---

[5]Sidney Mintz, "Toward an Afro-American History," *Journal of World History* (published in Switzerland), 13 (1971): 318.

1

Before Columbus

The history of the American peoples begins not in 1492 but hundreds of centuries before the birth of Christ. It was then, according to archaeologists and geologists, that humans first discovered what much later would be called North America. Thus American history can begin with some basic questions: Who were the first inhabitants of the "New World"? Where did they come from? What were they like? How had their societies changed over the millennia that preceded the arrival of Europeans? Can their history be reconstructed from the mists of prehistoric time?

Almost all the material evidence suggesting answers to these questions comes from ancient sites of early life in North America. By unearthing pots, tools, ornaments, and other objects, and establishing the age of skeletal remains of the "first Americans," archaeologists have dated the arrival of man in America to about 35,000 B.C., at about the time that humans began to settle Japan and Scandinavia.

Most Native American peoples have their own creation stories about their origins in North America itself. However, paleo-anthropologists generally agree that these first inhabitants of the continent were men and women from Asia. Game-hunting nomadic peoples from the inhospitable environment of Siberia, they migrated across the Bering Straits to Alaska in search of more reliable sources of food. Geologists have determined that Siberia and Alaska were connected by a land bridge only during the two long periods when massive glaciers covered the northern latitudes, locking up most of the world's moisture and leaving the floor of the Bering Sea exposed. These two long periods were from roughly 36,000 to 32,000 years ago and again from 25,000 to 14,000 years ago. At other times the melting glaciers raised the level of water in the Bering Straits, inundating the land bridge and blocking foot traffic to North America. So when Europeans found a way to reach North America in ships 500 years ago, they encountered a people whose ancestors had come on foot many thousands of years before. The main migration apparently occurred between 25,000 and 14,000 years ago, although our knowledge of this is very tentative and hotly debated as anthropologists discover new early human living sites.

Although most anthropologists agree that the migration was of Asian peoples, particularly those of Mongoloid stock from northeast Asia, the skeletal remains of these migrants also reveal non-Asian characteristics. It is probable that they represent a potpourri of different populations in Asia, Africa, and Europe, which had been mixing for thousands of years. But whatever the prior infusion of genes from peoples of other areas, these first Americans were Asiatic in geographical origin.

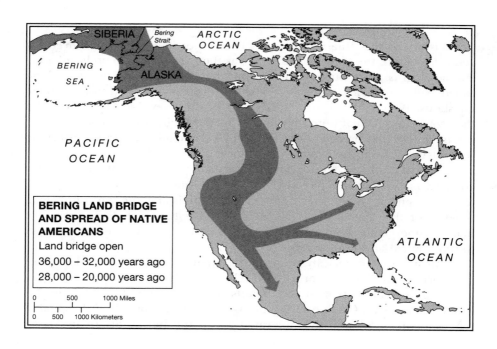

CULTURAL EVOLUTION

Once on the North American continent, these early wanderers began trekking southward and then eastward, following vegetation and game. Hundreds of generations passed before these nomads reached the Pacific Northwest. The migratory movement, taking thousands of years, ultimately brought them to the tip of South America and the east coast of North America. American history traditionally emphasizes the "westward movement," but for hundreds of generations in North America the frontier moved southward and eastward. The distances were immense—15,000 miles from the Asian homeland to Tierra del Fuego, the southernmost limit of South America, and 6,000 miles from Siberia to the eastern edge of North America. By roughly 9000 B.C. the first Americans were widely dispersed across the Western Hemisphere.

During the centuries spanned by these long migrations, one band in search of new food sources would split off from another. This process, repeated many times in many areas, marked the emergence of separate societies, numbering in the hundreds on the continent by the time the Europeans arrived. Cultural differences over thousands of years became more distinct as people in widely different ecological regions organized their lives and related to the land in ways dictated by their natural habitats. Much later Europeans would indiscriminately lump together a wide variety of native cultures under a single rubric "Indian." But in reality myriad ways of life had developed by the time Europeans found their way to the very old "New World." If Europeans had been able to drop down on native villages from the Atlantic to the Pacific coasts and from Alaska to the Gulf of Mexico in 1492 they would have found "Indians" living in Kwakiutl rectangular plank houses on the northwest coast, in Gothic domed thatched houses in Wichita grasslands, in earth lodges in Pawnee prairie country, and in barrel-roofed rectangular houses in Algonkian villages in the Northeast woodlands. Different societies had developed a great variety of techniques for providing basic shelter because they lived in areas where building materials and weather conditions varied widely. The same diversity marked the ornaments and clothes they fashioned, the tools they employed, and the natural foods they gathered.

This diversity of native culture is also evident in the languages they spoke. Linguistic scholars divide Indian languages, at the point when Europeans first arrived in North America, into twelve linguistic stocks, each as distinct from the others as Semitic languages are from Indo-European languages. Within each of these twelve linguistic stocks, a great many separate languages and dialects were spoken, each as different as English from Russian. In all, about 2,000 languages were spoken by the native Americans—a greater linguistic diversity than in any other part of the world.

How can we account for this striking diversity of Indian cultures? The explanation lies in an understanding of environmental conditions and the way in which bands of people lived in relatively self-contained communities for centuries, adapting to their natural surroundings and molding their culture in ways that allowed for survival in their region. As elsewhere in the prehistoric world, human beings were basically seed gatherers and game hunters. They were dependent for life on a food supply over which they had little control. They struggled to master their environment but were frequently at its mercy. Thus, to take a single example, as great geologic changes occurred in North America about 8000 B.C., vast areas from Utah to the highlands of Middle America were turned from grasslands into desert. Big game and plants requiring plentiful water could not survive these changes, and Indian societies in these areas either had to move on to find new sources of food or modify their cultures to the new conditions.

Another way of understanding the process of cultural change and the proliferation of culture groups is to focus on agriculture—the domestication of plant life. Like all living organisms, human beings depend ultimately on plants to survive. For both man and animals plants are the source of life-sustaining fuel. The ultimate source of this energy is the sun. But in tapping this solar energy humans and animals had to rely on plants because they are the only organisms capable of producing significant amounts of organic material through the photosynthetic process. Plant food was—and still is—the strategic element in the chain of life. It nurtured humans and it sustained the animals that provided them with their second source of food.

When humans learned to control the life of plants—*agriculture* is the term we give to the process—they took a revolutionary step toward controlling their environment. The domestication of plants began to emancipate human beings from oppression by the physical world. To learn how to harvest, plant, and nurture a seed was to assume some of nature's functions and to gain partial control over what had been uncontrollable. In the wake of this acquisition of partial control over nature's forces came vast cultural changes.

Dating the advent of agriculture in the New World is difficult, but archaeologists estimate it at about 5000 B.C. Agriculture had already developed in Southwestern Asia and Africa and spread to Europe at about the time peoples in the Tehuacán Valley of central Mexico were first planting maize and squash. Where agriculture occurred first, a much debated subject, is not as important as the fact that the "agricultural revolution" began independently in several widely separated parts of the world, all of which were later subordinated by European colonizers.

When the production of domesticated plant food replaced the gathering of wild plant food, dramatic changes occurred in the life of societies. First, plant domestication gradually allowed settled village life to replace nomadic existence. Second, it spurred population growth, for even putting as little as 1 percent of the land under cultivation produced enormous increases in the food supply. This in turn caused large groups to split off to form separate societies. Third, the cultivation of plants reduced the amount of time and energy needed to obtain a food supply and thus created more favorable conditions for social, political, and religious development; aesthetic expression; and technological innovation. Last, it led in most areas to a sexual division of labor, with men clearing the land and engaging in the hunt for game while women planted, cultivated, and harvested crops.

Thus the agricultural revolution began to reshape the cultural outlines of native societies. Population growth and the beginnings of sedentary village life were accompanied by more complex social and political organization. Bands evolved into tribes, and tribes evolved into larger political entities. Tasks became more specialized, and a more complex social structure took form. In some societies the religious specialist became the dominant figure, just as in other parts of the world where the agricultural revolution had occurred. The religious figure organized the common followers, directed their work, and exacted tribute as well as worship from them; in return he was counted on to protect the community from hostile forces.

REGIONAL CULTURES

When Europeans first reached the "New World," Native Americans were in widely different phases of this agricultural revolution, and therefore their cultures were marked by striking differences. A glimpse at several of the societies with which Europeans first came into contact in the early sixteenth century will illustrate the point.

In the Southwest region of North America, Hohokam and Anasazi societies had been engaged in agricultural production and a sedentary village life for several thousand years before the Spanish arrived in the 1540s. By about 700 to 900 A.D. descendants of these people began to abandon the ancient pit houses dug in cliffs and to construct rectangular rooms arranged in apartment-like structures. By about 1200 A.D. "Pueblo" people, as the Spanish called them, had developed planned villages composed of large terraced buildings, each with many rooms. These apartment-house villages were often constructed on defensive sites—on ledges of massive rock, on flat summits, or on steep-sided mesas, locations that would afford the Anasazi protection from their northern enemies. The largest of them, at Pueblo Bonito, in Chaco Canyon, contained about 800 rooms and may have housed as many as 1,200 persons. No larger apartment-house type construction would be seen on the continent until the late nineteenth century in New York City.

By the time of Spanish arrival, descendants of the Anasazi were also using irrigation canals, check-dams, and hillside terracing as techniques for bringing water to what had for centuries been an arid, agriculturally marginal area. At the same time, the ceramic industry became more elaborate, cotton replaced yucca fiber as the main clothing material, and basket weaving became more artistic. In its technological solution to the water problem, its artistic efforts, its agricultural practices, and its village life, Pueblo society on the eve of Spanish arrival was not radically different from peasant communities in most of the Euro-Asian world. Don Juan de Oñate reported home in 1599 after reaching the Pueblo villages on the Rio Grande that the Indians "live very much the same as we do, in houses with two and three terraces. . . ."[1]

Far to the north, on the Pacific coast of the Northwest, native people organized their societies around cedar and salmon. Tlingit, Haida, Kwakiutl, and Salish people lived in villages of several hundred, drawing their sustenance from salmon and other spawning fish. Their plank houses of red cedar displayed elaborately carved pillars and were guarded by gigantic totem poles that depicted animals with supernatural power such as the bear, sea otter, bald eagle, raven, killer whale, frog, and wolf. Early European explorers, who reached this region much later than most other parts of the hemisphere, were amazed at the architectural and artistic skills of the Northwest Indians. "What must astonish most," wrote one French explorer in the late eighteenth century, "is to see painting everywhere, everywhere sculpture, among a nation of hunters."[2]

Carving and painting soft wood from deep cedar forests surrounding their villages, native people of the Northwest defined their place in the cosmos with ceremonial face masks. Often the masks represented animals, birds, and fish—reminders of magical ancestral spirits that inhabited the four interconnected zones of their cosmos: the Sky World, the Undersea World, the Mortal World, and the Spirit World.

Ceremonial masks had a pivotal place in the Potlatch, a great winter gathering where through song, dance, and ritual Northwest Indian peoples sought to give meaning to their existence and reaffirm their goal of achieving balance and harmony in their world. In the Potlatch ceremonial dances, native leaders expressed their family lineage and their chiefly authority in the tribe. By giving away many of their possessions, chiefs satisfied tribe members and thus maintained their legitimacy. Such largesse mystified and often disturbed Europeans. Attempts by American and Canadian authorities to suppress Potlatch ceremonies in the late nineteenth century never succeeded.

Far to the east, other Indian cultures evolved over thousands of years. From the great plains of the mid-continent to the Atlantic tidewater region,

---

[1]Quoted in Thomas D. Matijasic, "Reflected Values: Sixteenth-Century Europeans View the Indians of North America," *American Indian Culture and Research Journal,* 11 (1987): 45.

[2]Quoted in Paul S. Boyer, et al., *The Enduring Vision: A History of the American People* (Lexington, Mass.: D.C. Heath, 1993), p. 6.

a variety of tribes belonging to four main language groups—Algonquian, Iroquoian, Muskhogean, and Siouan—grew in strength. Their existence in eastern North America, which has been traced as far back as about 9,000 B.C., was based on a mixture of agriculture, food gathering, game hunting, and fishing. Like other tribal groups that had been touched by the agricultural revolution, they gradually adopted semi-fixed settlements and developed a trading network linking together a vast region.

Among the most impressive of these societies were the so-called Mound builders of the Ohio River Valley, who constructed gigantic sculptured earthworks in geometric designs, sometimes in the shapes of huge humans, birds, or writhing serpents. When colonial settlers first crossed the Appalachians, after almost a century and a half in North America, they were astounded at these monumental constructions, some reaching as high as seventy feet. Their stereotype of eastern Indians as forest primitives did not allow them to believe that these were built by primitive native peoples, so they postulated that survivors of the sunken islands of Atlantis or descendants of the Egyptians and Phoenicians had wandered far from their homelands, built these mysterious monuments, and then disappeared.

Archaeologists and anthropologists now conclude that the Mound builders were the ancestors of the Creeks, Choctaws, and Natchez. Their societies evolved slowly over the centuries and by the advent of Christianity had developed considerable complexity. In southern Ohio alone about ten thousand mounds, used as burial sites, have been pinpointed. Archaeologists have excavated another one thousand earth-walled enclosures, including one enormous fortification with a circumference of about three and one-half miles, enclosing about one hundred acres, or the equivalent of fifty modern city blocks. Archaeologists know that the Mound builders participated in a vast trading network that linked together hundreds of Indian villages across the continent because they can trace a great variety of items found in the mound tombs to widely separated parts of the continent: large ceremonial blades chipped from obsidian rock formations in what is now Yellowstone National Park; embossed breastplates, ornaments, and weapons fashioned from copper nuggets from the Great Lakes region; decorative objects cut from sheets of mica from the southern Appalachians; conch shells from the Atlantic seaboard, and ornaments made from shark and alligator teeth and shells from the Gulf of Mexico.

By about 500 A.D. the Mound builder culture was declining, perhaps because of attacks from other tribes or because severe climatic changes undermined agriculture. To the west another culture, based on intensive agriculture, was beginning to flourish. Its center was beneath present-day East St. Louis, and it radiated out to encompass most of the Mississippi watershed from Wisconsin to Louisiana and from Oklahoma to Tennessee. Hundreds of villages were included in its orbit. By about 700 A.D. this Mississippian culture, as it is known to archaeologists, began to send its influence eastward to transform the life of most of the less technologically advanced woodland tribes. Like the Mound builders of the Ohio region, these tribes built gigantic mounds as burial and ceremonial places. The largest of them, rising in four terraces to a height of one hundred feet, has a rectangular base covering nearly fifteen acres and containing 22 million cubic feet of earth. It is larger at its base than the Great Pyramid of Egypt. Built between 900 and 1100 A.D., this huge earthwork faced the site of a palisaded Indian city which contained more than one hundred small artificial mounds marking burial sites. Spread among them was a dense settlement, called "America's first metropolis" by one archaeologist. This Mississippi Valley city, known as Cahokia, is estimated to have had a population of 30,000 to 40,000.

The finely crafted ornaments and tools recovered by archaeologists at Cahokia include elaborate ceramics, finely sculptured stonework, carefully embossed and engraved copper and mica sheets, and one funeral blanket for an important chief fashioned from 20,000 shell beads. These artifacts indicate that Cahokia was truly an urban center, with clustered housing, markets, and specialists in toolmaking, hide dressing, potting, jewelry making, weaving, and salt making.

By about 1300, two hundred years before Europeans arrived on the Atlantic seaboard, the Mound builder and Mississippian cultures had passed their prime and, for reasons not yet clear, were becoming extinct. But their influence had already passed eastward to transform the woodlands societies along the Atlantic coastal plain. Although the widely scattered and relatively fragmented tribes that were settled from Nova Scotia to Florida never matched the earlier societies of mid-continent in architectural design, earthwork sculpturing, or artistic expression, they were far from the forest primitives that Europeans pictured. Changed by contact with the Hopewell and Mississippi cultures of the Ohio and Mississippi river valleys, they added agriculture to the skills they had already acquired in exploiting a wide variety of natural plants for food, medicine, dyes, flavoring, and smoking. In the mixed natural economies that resulted, they utilized all the resources around them—open land, forests, streams, shore, and ocean.

For the most part, these people of the Northeast woodlands, on whose lands European fishermen began camping to dry their codfish in the late fifteenth century, lived in villages, especially after they had been influenced by the agricultural traditions of the Ohio and Mississippi Valley societies. Locating their cornfields near fishing grounds and learning to fertilize the young plants with the heads of fish, they settled into a more sedentary pattern of life. Domed wigwams of birch and elm, copied in the early years by Europeans, were clustered together in villages that were often palisaded. The birch-bark canoes, light enough to be carried by a single adult from stream to stream, gave them a means of trading and communicating over a vast territory. The extent of development among these Eastern woodlands societies on the eve of European contact is indicated by the archaeological evidence of a Huron town in the Great Lakes region which contained more than one hundred large structures housing a total population of between four and six thousand. Settlements of this size were larger than the average European village of the sixteenth century and larger than all but a handful of European colonial towns in America a century and a half after the first settlers arrived.

Along the Atlantic seaboard, from the St. Lawrence Bay to Florida, Europeans encountered scores of local tribes of the Eastern woodlands. Each maintained cultural elements peculiar to its people, although they shared in common many things such as agricultural techniques, the sexual division of labor, pottery design, social organization, and toolmaking. But the most important common denominator among them was that each had mastered the local habitat in a way that sustained life and ensured the perpetuation of their people. In the far north were Abenakis, Penobscots, Passamaquoddys, and others, who lived by the products of the sea and supplemented their diet with maple sugar and a few foodstuffs. Farther south, in what was to become New England, were Massachusetts, Wampanoags, Pequots, Narragansetts, Niantics, Mahicans, and others—small tribes occupying fairly local areas and joined together only by occasional trade. South of them, in the mid-Atlantic area were Lenni Lenape, Susquehannock, Nanticoke, Pamunkey, Shawnee, Tuscarora, Catawba, and other peoples, who subsisted on a mixture of agriculture, shellfish, game, and wild foods. They, too, were settled in villages and lived a semi-sedentary life.

One of the most heavily populated regions of the Atlantic coast was the Southeast, where rich and complex cultures, some of them joined in loose confederacies, were located. Belonging to several language groups, these peoples traced their ancestry back at least 8,000 years. Some of the most elaborate pottery-making in the eastern half of the continent occurred in the Southeast, beginning about 2000 B.C. Hopewell burial mound techniques also influenced these cultures, and a few hundred years before Hernando de Soto marched through the area in the 1540s, grandiose ceremonial centers, whose construction involved earthmoving on a vast scale, had become a distinct feature of this area. In touch with Mississippian culture, the tribes of the Southeast evolved elaborate ceramic and basketweaving techniques, long-distance trade, and in some cases, as with the Natchez, hierarchical and authoritarian social and political organizations. These people included the powerful Creeks and Yamasees in the Georgia and Alabama regions, the Apalachees in Florida and along the Gulf of Mexico, the Choctaws, Chickasaws, and Natchez of the lower Mississippi Valley, the Cherokees of the southern Appalachians, and several dozen smaller tribes scattered along the southeast coast.

THE IROQUOIS

Among the Eastern woodlands societies, the one that loomed largest in the European–Indian encounters in North America was the Iroquois. Their territory stretched from the Adirondack Mountains to the Great Lakes and

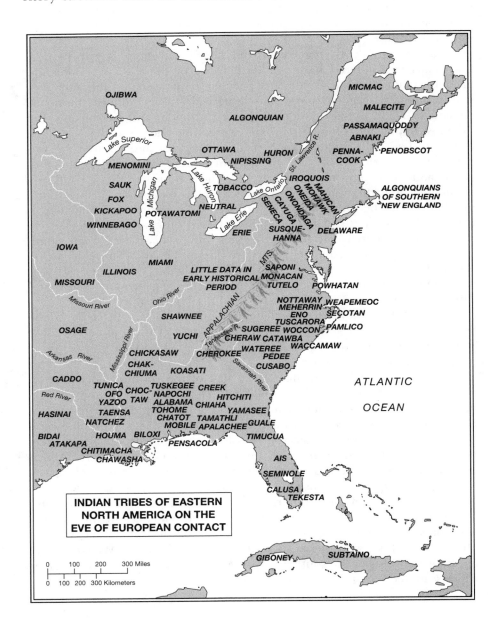

INDIAN TRIBES OF EASTERN
NORTH AMERICA ON THE
EVE OF EUROPEAN CONTACT

from what is now northern New York to Pennsylvania. Five tribes—the Mohawks ("People of the Flint"), Oneidas ("People of the Stone"), Onondagas ("People of the Mountain"), Cayugas ("People at the Landing"), and Senecas ("Great Hill People")—composed what Europeans later called the League of the Iroquois. The Iroquois confederation was a vast extension of the kinship group that characterized the Northeastern woodlands pattern of family settlement and embraced perhaps 10,000 people at the beginning of the seventeenth century. Situated athwart major Indian trade routes in the Northeast and positioned between French and English zones of settlement, the Iroquois were intensely caught up with the onrush of Europeans, which is also to say that the settlers, whether Dutch, French, or English, were caught up with the Iroquois as well.

Not long before the arrival of Europeans, the loosely organized and strife-ridden Iroquois strengthened themselves by creating a more cohesive political confederacy. By learning to suppress intra-Iroquois blood feuds, villages gained stability, population increased, and the Iroquois developed political mechanisms for solving their internal problems and presenting a more unified front in negotiating with their Algonquian neighbors for the use of hunting territories to the north or in admitting dependent tribes to settle on their territory. This facilitated the development of a coordinated Iroquois policy for dealing with the European newcomers.

Work in the palisaded villages of Iroquoia, some of which bustled with more than a thousand people, was performed communally and land was owned not by individuals but by all in common. An individual family might till their own patch of land, but it was understood that this usage of land in no way implied private ownership. Likewise, hunting was a communal enterprise. Though individual hunters differed in their ability to stalk and kill deer, the collective bounty of the hunting party was brought back to the village and divided among all. Similarly, several families occupied a longhouse, but the house itself, like all else in the community, was regarded as common property. For the Iroquois the concept of private ownership of property— the idea that each person should own his own land or house—would have struck at the heart of the most important theme in their value system—the reciprocal and communal principle. "No hospitals [poorhouses] are needed among them," wrote a French Jesuit in 1657, "because there are neither mendicants nor paupers as long as there are any rich people among them. Their kindness, humanity and courtesy not only makes them liberal with what they have, but causes them to possess hardly anything except in common. A whole village must be without corn, before any individual can be obliged to endure privation."[3] One historian has called this "upside-down

---

[3]Reuben Gold Thwaites, ed., *The Jesuit Relations and Allied Documents: Travels and Explorations of the Jesuit Missionaries in New France, 1610–1791* (Cleveland: Burrows Brothers, 1899), XLIII: 271.

capitalism" where the goal was "not to accumulate goods but to be in a position to provide them to others."[4]

Village settlement was organized by extended kinship groups. Contrary to European practice, the Iroquois family was matrilineal, with family membership determined through the female rather than male line. Thus a typical family was composed of an old woman, her daughters with their husbands and children and her unmarried granddaughters and grandsons. Sons and grandsons remained with their kinship group until they married; then they joined the family of their wife or the family of their mother's brother. If this puzzled Europeans, so did the Iroquois woman's prerogative of divorce; if she desired it, she merely set her husband's possessions outside the longhouse door. Thus Iroquois society was organized around the matrilineal "fireside." In turn, several matrilineal kinship groups, related by a blood connection on the mother's side, as between sisters, formed an *ohwachira*, or a group of related families. These *ohwachiras* were grouped together in clans. A village might be made up of a dozen or more clans. Villages or clans combined to create a nation (or "kinship state," as it has been called) of Senecas or Mohawks.[5]

Iroquois society was not only matrilineal in social organization but invested the women of the community with a share of the political power unmatched in European societies. Political authority in the villages derived from the *ohwachiras*, headed by the "matrons"—the senior women of the community. These women named the men representing the clans at village and tribal councils and appointed the forty-nine sachems or chiefs who met periodically at Onondaga as the ruling council for the confederated Five Nations. These civil chiefs were generally middle-aged or elderly men who had earlier gained fame as warriors but now "forsook the warpath for the council fire."[6]

The political power of the women extended beyond the appointment of male representatives to the various ruling councils. When individual clans met, in a manner resembling the later New England town meeting, the senior women were fully in attendance, caucusing behind the circle of men who did the public speaking and lobbying with them. To an outsider it might appear that the men ruled, because it was they who did the public speaking and formally reached decisions. But their power was shared with the women. If the men of the village or tribal council moved too far from the will of the women who had appointed them, they could be removed, or

[4]Daniel K. Richter, *The Ordeal of the Longhouse: The Peoples of the Iroquois League in the Era of European Colonization* (Chapel Hill, NC: University of North Carolina Press, 1992), p. 22.

[5]William N. Fenton, "The Iroquois in History," in *North American Indians in Historical Perspective*, eds. Eleanor Burke Leacock and Nancy Oestreich Lurie (New York: Random House, Inc., 1971), p. 139.

[6]*Ibid.* p. 138.

"dehorned." Only so long as they could achieve a consensus with the women who had placed them in office were they secure in their positions.

The division of power between male and female was further extended by the role of the women in the tribal economy. While men were responsible for hunting and fishing, the women were the primary agriculturists of the village. In tending the crops they became equally important in sustaining the community. Moreover, when the men were away on hunting expeditions, often for a period of weeks, women were left entirely in charge of the daily life of the community. To a large extent, the village "was the woman's domain" while "the forest belonged to the men."[7]

Even in military affairs women played an important role, for they supplied the moccasins and food for warring expeditions. A decision to withhold these supplies was tantamount to vetoing a military foray. Clan matrons often initiated war by calling on the Iroquois warriors to bring them enemy captives to replace fallen clan members. Thus power was shared between the sexes, and the European idea of male dominance and female subordination in all things was conspicuously absent in Iroquois society.

In raising children Iroquois parents were more permissive than their European counterparts. They did not believe in harsh physical punishment. They encouraged their young to imitate adult behavior and were tolerant of fumbling early attempts. In the first months of a baby's life the mother nursed and protected the child and at the same time hardened it by baths in cold water. Weaning was not ordinarily begun until the age of three or four. Rather than beginning strict regimens of toilet training at an early age, Iroquois parents allowed the child to proceed at its own pace in achieving control over natural functions. Early interest in the anatomy of the body and in sexual experimentation was accepted as normal. All this was in sharp contrast to European child-rearing techniques, which stressed the importance of accustoming the child to authority from an early age and backed this up by taking the child from the breast at about two years, by toilet training at an early age, by making frequent use of physical punishment, by condemning early sexual curiosity, and by emphasizing obedience and respect for authority as central virtues. Iroquois parents would have regarded as misguided the advice of John Robinson, the Pilgrims' pastor, to the parents of his congregation: "Surely there is in all children . . . a stubbornness, and stoutness of mind arising from natural pride, which must, in the first place, be broken and beaten down; that so the foundation of their education being laid in humility and tractableness, other virtues may, in their time, be built thereon. . . . For the beating, and keeping down of this stubbornness parents must provide carefully . . . that the children's ills and willfulness be restrained and repressed. . . . Children should not know, if it

[7]Richter, *Ordeal of the Longhouse*, p. 23.

could be kept from them, that they have a will of their own, but in their parents' keeping."[8]

The approach to authority also differed for adult members of the society. Iroquois society, like most Indian societies of North America, had little of the complicated machinery that Europeans developed to direct the lives of its members. No laws and ordinances, sheriffs and constables, judges and juries, or courts or jails—the apparatus of authority in European societies—were to be found in the Northeast Woodlands prior to European arrival. Yet boundaries of acceptable behavior were firmly set. Though priding themselves on the autonomous individual, the Iroquois maintained a strict sense of right and wrong. Rather than relying on formal instruments of authority, however, they governed behavior by inculcating a strong sense of tradition and attachment to the group through communally performed rituals. It was this sense of duty, bolstered by a fear of gossip and a strongly held belief in the power of evil spirits to punish wrongdoers, that curbed antisocial behavior and produced a general domestic peacefulness among the Iroquois. In European society a crime or unethical act might be dealt with by investigation, arrest, prosecution, sentencing, and imprisonment, involving at various steps along the way the authority of a number of people and institutional devices. In Indian society a simpler system operated to transform the aberrant individual. He or she who stole another's food or showed cowardice in war was "shamed" and ostracized until the culprit had atoned for his actions and demonstrated that he had morally purified himself.

It is a mistake to romanticize Iroquois culture or judge it superior to the culture of the European invader. To do so is only to invoke the same categories of "superior" and "inferior" that Europeans used to justify the violence they unleashed when they arrived in the New World and to forget that exercises in ranking cultures depend almost entirely on the criteria employed. Instead of grading cultures, almost always an exercise of expansionist societies attempting to subjugate other people, we best understand Iroquois society, like English or French society, as a total social system that had evolved over a long period of time before Europeans arrived. In dynamic relationship with their environment and with neighboring peoples, the Iroquois had become more populous, more sedentary in their mode of settlement, more skilled in agricultural techniques, more elaborate in their art forms. They had also emerged as one of the strongest, most politically unified, and aggressive societies in the Northeast woodlands. Even after the formation of the League of the Iroquois, which had as one of its objectives the abatement of intertribal warfare, an impressive amount of fighting seems to have occurred between the Five Nations and surrounding Algonquian

---

[8]Quoted in John Demos, *A Little Commonwealth: Family Life in Plymouth Colony* (New York: Oxford University Press, Inc., 1970), pp. 134–35.

peoples. Many of these conflicts involved a quest for glory, and some of them may have been initiated to test the newly forged alliance of the five tribes against lesser tribes which could be brought under Iroquoian domination. Whatever the reasons, the Iroquois on the eve of European arrival were feared and sometimes hated by their neighbors for their skill and cruelty in warfare.

PRE-CONTACT POPULATION

On the eve of European contact, how many Native Americans inhabited North America? Anthropologists and historians have argued for decades about pre-conquest population levels and have searched for methods that might provide reliable estimates. But only recently have scholars conceded that most estimates made in the past have been affected by the estimator's conception of Native American societies. When Indian culture is viewed as "savage," characterized by nomadic hunters and gatherers, it is difficult to think in terms of large populations in North America. But if these societies are seen as sedentary, agriculturist, and complex in their social organization, then larger numbers seem possible.

Until recently, the accepted population of Native Americans north of Mexico in the immediate pre-contact period was about one million, with about ten million in the Americas as a whole. This estimate, made in 1910 by the noted anthropologist James Mooney, has been sharply challenged, primarily on the basis of research demonstrating that Mooney greatly underestimated the demographic disaster that occurred when Native Americans came into contact with European diseases. Mooney based his estimates on rough tabulations of Indians made in various areas several decades or more after initial contact. But he failed to recognize the precipitous population decline, approaching 90 percent in many regions, that occurred very rapidly when pathogens carried by Europeans infected Native Americans and spread like wildfire through their villages. Today's scholars believe that the pre-contact population north of Mexico was at least 3 million, and some estimates run as high as 10 million. For the western hemisphere the population may have been 60 to 70 million when Columbus reached it in 1492. Perhaps 700,000 lived along the Atlantic coastal plain and in the piedmont region accessible to the early European colonizers. Historical demographers will debate native population levels for many decades, weighing archaeological evidence, estimating the lethal effects of European diseases, and arguing over the carrying capacity of various Indian economic systems. But regardless of the twists and turns of this fascinating debate, we are left with the startling realization that Europeans were not coming to a "virgin wilderness," as some called it, but were invading a land which in some areas was as densely populated as their homelands.

THE NATIVE AMERICAN WORLD VIEW

While Native American and European cultures were not nearly so different as the concepts of "savagery" and "civilization" imply, societies on the eastern and western sides of the Atlantic had developed distinct—and sometimes radically different—systems of values in the centuries that preceded contact. Lurking behind the physical confrontations that would take place when European and Native American met were vastly different ways of looking at the world. These latent conflicts can be seen in contrasting European and Indian views of man's relationship to his environment, the concept of property, and personal identity.

In the European view the natural world was filled with resources for man to use. "Subdue the earth," Christians read in the book of Genesis, "and have dominion over every living thing that moves on the earth." God still ruled the cosmos, of course, and men could not control supernatural forces, manifesting themselves in earthquakes, hurricanes, drought, and flood. But a scientific revolution was underway in the early modern period, giving humans more confidence that they could comprehend the natural world—and thus eventually control it. For Europeans the secular and the sacred were distinct, and the human relationship to the natural environment fell mostly into the secular sphere.

Native Americans recognized no such separation of secular and sacred. Every part of the natural world was sacred, and the world was inhabited by a great variety of "beings," each pulsating with spiritual power and all linked together to form a sacred whole. "Plants, animals, rocks, and stars," explains Murray Wax, "are thus seen not as objects governed by laws of nature but as 'fellows' with whom the individual or band may have a more or less advantageous relationship."[9] Consequently, if one offended the land by stripping it of its cover, the spiritual power in the land—called "manitou" by some woodlands tribes—would strike back. If one overfished or destroyed game beyond one's needs, the spiritual power inherent in fish and animals would take revenge because humans had broken the mutual trust and reciprocity that governed relations between all beings—human and nonhuman. To exploit the land or to treat with disrespect any part of the natural world was to cut oneself off from the spiritual power dwelling in all things and "was thus equivalent to repudiating the vital force in Nature."[10] To neglect reciprocal obligations in Nature's domain was to court sickness, hunger, injury, or even death.

[9]"Religion and Magic," in *Introduction to Cultural Anthropology: Essays in the Scope and Method of the Science of Man,* James A. Clifton, ed. (Boston: Houghton Mifflin Company, 1968), p. 235.
[10]Calvin Martin, *Keepers of the Game: Indian–Animal Relationships and the Fur Trade* (Berkeley and Los Angeles: University of California Press, 1978), p. 34.

Because they regarded the land as a resource to be exploited for man's gain, Europeans had no discomfort in treating land as a commodity to be privately held. Private ownership of property became one of the fundamental bases upon which European culture rested. Fences were the symbols of exclusively held property, inheritance became the mechanism for transmitting these "assets" from one generation to another within the same family, and courts provided the institutional apparatus for settling property disputes. In a largely agricultural society property was the basis of political power. In fact, political rights in England derived from the ownership of a specified quantity of land. In addition, the social structure was largely defined by the distribution of property, with those possessing great quantities of it standing at the apex of the social pyramid and the mass of propertyless individuals forming the broad base.

For Native Americans this view of land as a privately held asset was incomprehensible. Tribes recognized territorial boundaries, but within these limits the land was held in common. Land was not a commodity but a part of nature that the Creator entrusted to the living. John Heckewelder, a Moravian missionary who lived with the Delawares in the eighteenth century, explained their belief that the Creator "made the Earth and all that it contains for the common good of mankind; when he stocked the country that he gave them with plenty of game, it was not for the benefit of a few, but of all; Every thing was given in common to the sons of men. Whatever liveth on the land, whatsoever groweth out of the earth, and all that is in the rivers and waters . . . was given jointly to all and every one is entitled to his share. From this principle hospitality flows as from its source."[11]

In personal identity Indian and European values also differed sharply. Europeans were acquisitive, competitive, and over a long period of time had been enhancing the role of the individual. Most Europeans celebrated the wider choices and greater opportunities for the individual to improve his or her status—by industriousness, valor, or even personal sacrifice leading to martyrdom. Personal ambition, in fact, played a large role in the migration of Europeans across the Atlantic in the sixteenth and seventeenth centuries. In contrast, the cultural traditions of Native Americans emphasized the collectivity—the band, lineage, or village—rather than the individual. Because they held land and other natural resources in common and their society was less stratified than in Europe, Indians looked askance at the accumulative spirit and personal ambition of the newcomers. "In contrast to the exalted position of man in Judeo-Christian tradition," writes Calvin Martin, the Native American "cosmology conferred upon the Indian a rather humble

[11]John Heckewelder, *Account of the History, Manners, and Customs of the Indian Nations* (Philadelphia: American Philosophical Society, 1819), p. 85, reprinted in Wilcomb Washburn, *The Indian and the White Man* (Garden City, N.Y.: Doubleday & Company, Inc., 1964), p. 63.

stature."[12] Hence, in Indian society the ideal of the autonomous individual was carefully restrained by the overriding commitment to clan and tribe. Rivalry flourished in Iroquois society as much as in Europe, but the tribal ethos channeled rivalries into conferring benefits upon the longhouse or the entire village.

In spite of these differences it was not inevitable that the confrontation of European colonizers and Native Americans should lead to mortal combat. Inevitability is not a satisfactory explanation for any human event because it implies that man's destiny is beyond human control and thus relieves individuals and societies of responsibility for their actions. As old as the tales told by conquerors, the narrative structure of inevitability is a winner's rationalization for historical clashes; a mode of explanation rarely advanced by the losing side. We shall see that the clash of cultures took many forms in the New World, with nothing predetermined but with everything dependent upon the complex interweaving of many factors in particular places and at specific times.

---

[12]Martin, *Keepers of the Game,* p. 74.

2

Europeans Reach North America

From the fifteenth to the twentieth centuries one of the dominant themes of history has been the militant expansion of European peoples and European culture into other continents. Only in the last half century has this process been reversed, as colonized people have struggled to regain their autonomy through wars of national and cultural liberation. For Western historians this global expansion has been closely equated with the spread of "civilization," the carrying of an allegedly superior European culture to so-called backward areas of the world. As various cultures were engulfed by colonizing Europeans, the notion grew in the western mind that the growing outreach of European civilization put "progress" at the disposal of "primitive" peoples.

Yet assuming the cultural superiority of Europeans at the time they reached the western hemisphere is a highly loaded notion. For centuries, the categorizing of "superior" and "inferior" cultures has been done by the conquering nations, with great emphasis placed on technological advances, such as metal working, and on literacy. These have been promoted as key benchmarks for describing and ranking cultures. Certainly literacy was an important element in the growth of European economies, the spread of urbanization, and the rise of technological and scientific innovations in Europe in the early modern period. But the contrast in economic growth and technological development between Europe on the one hand and Africa and the Americas on the other is explained by a wide range of factors. Literacy, in fact, was more widespread in the Middle East and North Africa in the fifteenth and sixteenth centuries than in Europe, yet Europe underwent more rapid economic development in the sixteenth century.

In exploring converging cultures in the Americas, it is best to leave aside crude comparisons, for example between a literate Europe and a nonliterate Africa or pre-Columbian America. This kind of mindset, leading toward claims of cultural superiority, masks the complex interaction of peoples from different parts of the world whose lives converged in the Americas.

What is important to know about European achievements in the age of Columbus is that, after a long period of recovery from the bubonic plague that devastated western Europe and parts of Africa in the 1340s, monarchs began to assert their political authority over feudal lords and unify their realms. This creation of power at the center of European societies placed the normal powers of the state—to tax, wage war, and administer the law—far more in the hands of ambitious monarchs. This new concentration of power was essential to the European expansionist impulse that was ripening in the second half of the fifteenth century. Also feeding this impulse was a mighty cultural revival known as the Renaissance. Beginning in Italy and spreading northward following revived commerce through Europe, the Renaissance ushered in a new, more secular age, encouraged freedom of thought, and emphasized human abilities. It reached its peak in the late fifteenth century when a dramatic series of European oceanic explorations began. Since the seventh century Islamic culture had been the most dynamic and expansionist force in the Afro-Eurasian world, penetrating Africa deeply and extending into Europe as far west as Cordoba, Spain. But now Christian and Jewish Europeans were to assume center stage in an epoch of trans-oceanic expansion.

SPANISH AND PORTUGUESE EXPANSION INTO THE AMERICAS

When he made landfall on the tiny island of San Salvador in the Bahamas in 1492, Columbus thought he had reached the East Indies. This was precisely his quest—to find an all-water route to the Orient so that European traders, who trafficked in the indispensable spices that made European food palatable, could avoid paying tribute to the Middle Eastern middlemen who skimmed the profits off overland trading ventures. Burning with desire to liberate Jerusalem from Muslim rule and believing he had reached Old Testament lands, Columbus sent ashore for reconnaissance Luis de Torres, a converted Jew who knew Hebrew, Arabic, and Chaldaic—the biblical languages necessary for communication among Old Testament people.

In attempting to find a water route to the oldest parts of the Old World, Columbus had stumbled upon what was a new world only in the European mind. But this fortuitous error sparked the imagination of the Europeans—one of their most valuable qualities—and fueled a revival of enterprise and overseas expansion that lasted for more than four hundred years. Moreover, Columbus's four voyages set in motion a gigantic mixing of populations from different parts of the world, shifted Europe's commercial center of gravity from the Mediterranean to the Atlantic, and planted the seeds of the first global empires that spanned entire oceans.

It is customary to focus on the navigational and geographical importance of Columbus's voyages, but his sea wanderings would have been written off as an expensive failure, once it was realized that he had not found the illusive water route to India, had it not been for the discovery of gold on Hispaniola in 1493. Without the gold and other precious metals, the new-found land would have been only an obstacle on the water road to the Far East.

While his discovery was accidental, Columbus was still an archetypical figure of European expansion. Thoroughly medieval in his patterns of thought, he was also ambitious, adventuresome, full of practical knowledge, ready to translate an idea, however ridiculed, into action, and audacious enough to maintain his course even when his sailors were ready to mutiny in despair of ever seeing dry land again. Capitalizing on advances in marine and mapmaking technology and on earlier Portuguese oceanic explorations into the Atlantic "sea of darkness," as they called it, and down the west coast of Africa all the way to the southern tip, Columbus, like the Vikings five hundred years before him, discovered that the ocean west of Europe had its limits.

Once the Spanish found gold and silver, a wholesale rush of enterprising young men from the lesser nobility in Spain began the transatlantic adventure. By the 1550s they had explored, and claimed, if not always conquered, the Isthmus of Panama, Mexico, most of South America except Brazil and the far southern plains, and the southerly reaches of North America from California on the Pacific Coast to "La Florida" on the Atlantic Coast. Led by military figures such as Cortés, Pizarro, Ponce de León, de Soto, and Coronado, they established the authority of Spain and the Catholic Church over an area that dwarfed their homeland in size and population. By the end of the sixteenth century the Spanish had conquered the major centers of native population and established a thriving transatlantic trade, and were carrying African slaves by the thousands to their colonies and supervising the extraction of gold and silver in fabulous quantities from the lands under their domination.

From the 1490s to the 1590s, the colonization of the Americas was dominated by Spain. Its only rival was Portugal, whose energies first went into colonizing the Atlantic islands—Azores, Madeira, and Canaries—that lay off the coast of Portugal and northwest Africa, and establishing centers of trade on the east and west African coasts. Not until the 1550s did Portugal stake out a claim in Brazil, destined to become the center of its New World activities. By the end of the century sugar production claimed the labor of most of some 25,000 Portuguese colonists and perhaps an equal number of African slaves in Brazil.

Closely tied to the economic strivings of Europe's emerging nation-states were the religious goals of colonization. Both Catholics and Protestants looked upon the occupation of the New World as a religious crusade. Spain had been involved for centuries in conflict with the "infidel" Muslims; in fact, not until the year Columbus reached Hispaniola did Christian Spain complete the expulsion of the Moors. Conquest of the New World not only fulfilled national dreams of glory but also offered the challenge of converting to Christianity a continent filled with "heathen" people who had been seduced by Satan.

The religious motive was complicated by the Catholic–Protestant division within Christianity. For Europeans heathens were heathens; but whether their conversion would be to Catholicism or to Protestantism depended on which European nation achieved domination over them. That Christians could be so bitterly divided, engaging in religious wars for several centuries and inflicting mass destruction in the name of God, may seem puzzling to those raised in a secular society. But the intensity of this conflict within Christian Europe becomes more understandable when we remember that for men and women of this age—as in the centuries before—religion was the organizing principle of life. Because science and technology had not yet advanced far enough to control natural forces, man's mastery of the environment was slight and people attributed what could not be understood or governed to supernatural forces, especially the intervening hand of God. With faith, not reason, dominating life, people of different religious commitments defended their ideology passionately and attacked those with variant views.

These "isms"—Protestantism and Catholicism—can be understood as prescribed codes of living, as ways of ordering and imparting meaning to one's world and one's place in it. Such ideological commitments did not differ markedly from the "isms" of today—socialism, communism, democracy—in terms of their power to compel allegiance. These, too, are systems of values and beliefs, ways of organizing societies. They, too, give meaning to what people do and provide them with a sense of identity. Twentieth-century wars, fought with far greater ferocity and technological ruthlessness than the religious wars of the early modern era, provide a way of understanding why Christians and Muslims or Catholics and Protestants would fight so relentlessly to spread their particular faith to the native inhabitants of the lands they were invading. Moreover, the religious bitterness and wars that continue today—from the Middle East to Sri Lanka to Bosnia—remind us that religion still inspires deadly conflict.

The Spanish Conquest and the Atlantic Exchange

For a quarter century after Columbus's first voyage in 1492, the Spanish colonizing efforts in the western hemisphere were confined to occupying the Caribbean islands of Cuba, Puerto Rico, and Hispaniola. Then, in two bold and bloody strokes, beginning in 1519, the Spanish overwhelmed the ancient civilizations of the Aztecs and the Incas. Hernán Cortés's march from coastal Veracruz over rugged mountains brought 600 soldiers into the Valley of Mexico where for two years they fenced with Montezuma's people. Then in 1521, Cortés attacked the huge Aztec capital—Tenochtitlan (modern-day Mexico City). The Spanish soldiers were astounded to find themselves confronting an urban population of 100,000 or more contained within a city replete with floating gardens, elaborate causeways and aqueducts, and monumental temples. The Aztecs were equally astounded at the intruders with much hair on their faces and accompanied by huge animals—large, ferocious dogs and huge "deer" more powerful than any animal the Aztecs had seen that carried metal-clad warriors on their backs and traveled faster than the fleetest Aztec. Aided by dissident natives oppressed by Montezuma's tyranny, the Spanish brought the great Aztec ruler to his knees after a siege of 75 days. Over the next several decades they extended their dominion over the Mayan people of the Yucatan and Guatemala.

In a second conquest, in 1531–32, Francisco Pizarro marched from Panama through the jungles of Ecuador and into the towering mountains of Peru with a mere 168 men to overwhelm the densely settled Incas. Like the Aztecs, the Incas suffered from internal divisions. Capitalizing on this, Pizarro toppled the gold- and silver-rich Inca empire with a momentous victory at the capital city of Cuzco. From there, Spanish soldiers marched farther afield, plundering Inca cities and establishing their authority over native peoples in Bolivia, Chile, New Grenada (Colombia), and Argentina. By 1550, with only a few thousand soldiers, the Spanish had overwhelmed the major centers of native population throughout the Caribbean, Mexico, Central America, and the west coast of South America, creating an empire larger than any in the Western world since the fall of Rome one thousand years before.

The astounding Spanish victories were accomplished in part by enlisting the support of subject peoples who hated their cruel Aztec and Inca rulers. Spanish military conquest was also facilitated by bringing across the ocean two animals unknown in the Americas—mastiffs and horses—and an arsenal derived from metalworking capabilities—body armor and muskets. Yet the deadliest of all European weapons and the Spaniards' greatest ally was disease. Nearly every intruder from across the Atlantic, whether two- or four-legged, brought ashore pathogens that tore through the native peoples with a rapidity that was as gratifying to the Spanish as it was demoralizing to the indigenous people. This was part of an Atlantic exchange of people, animals, plants, and germs that would transform nearly every society on both sides of the Atlantic, though with very different results.

The secret advantage to Europeans, unbeknownst to them, was that the millions of native peoples in the Americas had lived for many millennia isolated from epidemic diseases known in other regions of the world. The closing of the Bering Land Bridge thousands of years before had provided a "cold filter" through which no raging diseases could penetrate. Nor did native peoples have herd animals, which in Eurasia and Africa lived in close contact with humans, where they acted as hosts and conduits of infectious diseases. If native peoples did not quite live in a disease-free paradise, they were spared the killer pestilence that for hundreds of generations had severely punished Africans, Europeans, and Asians. These bacteriological infections—smallpox, diphtheria, measles, whooping cough, scarlet fever, and others—were steady killers in most parts of the world, especially in densely populated regions. Yet infected populations had gradually built up immunities against them that enabled many to survive virulent infections. Indian peoples of the Americas had no such immunities. Defenseless once exposed to the killer pathogens and parasites, they fell like wheat before a scythe. Whole tribes could be nearly wiped out in a few decades, leaving vast areas depopulated. On the island of Hispaniola, where an estimated one million Tainos were present in 1492 to witness the arrival of Columbus, smallpox arrived in 1518. In what amounted to a biological holocaust, only about 1,000 Tainos were left a few decades later.

Indeed, Cortés's victory in 1521 was hugely aided by a terrible onslaught of smallpox in 1520–21 that may have halved the Aztec population just before the Spanish attack on Tenochtitlan. "Smallpox was the captain of the men of death in the war, typhus fever the first lieutenant, and measles the second lieutenant," writes the first historian to appreciate the role played by disease in the Spanish conquest and colonization of the southern hemisphere. "More terrible than the conquistadors on horseback, more deadly than sword and gunpowder, they made the conquest . . . a walkover compared with what it would have been without their aid." The killer diseases "were the forerunners of civilization, the companions of Christianity, the friends of the invader."[1] A murderous outbreak of smallpox in the 1520s similarly paved the way for Spanish conquest of the Inca.

The hammer blows unleashed by infectious diseases were so catastrophic for native people that they could hardly comprehend how their gods had failed them. Rampant disease caused mass agony, paralyzed community life, shattered leadership elites, and terrorized survivors. One of the first chroniclers of the Spanish conquest of Mexico described how smallpox, covering the bodies of horrified Aztecs, caused "great havoc." "They could

[1]P. M. Ashburn, *The Ranks of Death: A Medical History of the Conquest of America* (New York: Coward-McCann, 1947), p. 98.

not walk," wrote Fray Bernardino de Sahagún, "they only lay in their resting places and beds. They could not move; they could not stir; they could not change position, not lie on one side; nor face down, nor on their backs. And if they stirred, much did they cry out. Great was its destruction."[2]

Much more than microbes crossed the Atlantic with European explorers, conquerors, and settlers. With them came animal and plant life that transformed the landscape and altered ecosystems. Back across the Atlantic, more slowly, went plant and animal species that were equally transformative in Europe. Westward-bound ships brought wheat, barley, rye, and other grains; fruits such as peaches, pears, oranges, lemons, melons, and grapes; and vegetables such as radish, onions, and salad greens. All of these, unknown in the Americas, perpetuated European cuisine and gradually changed Indian diets. But much more important were the herd animals of the Europeans: burros, cattle, goats, horses, pigs, and sheep. The burro pulling a wheeled cart could move ten times as much corn or cordwood as a human beast of burden. The horse could carry a messenger twice the speed of the fleetest runner. Still more transformative was livestock. Cattle, sheep, and pigs flourished, grazing in the vast grasslands of the Americas and safe from the large carnivores that attacked them in the Old World. They reproduced so rapidly that feral livestock swarmed across the countryside, often increasing tenfold in three or four years. Indeed they flourished so well that in time they ate themselves out of their favorable environment, stripping away plant life and leading to topsoil erosion and desertification.

Pigs were even harder on the environment. Reproducing at staggering rates, they tore into the manioc tubers and sweet potatoes in the Caribbean islands where Columbus first introduced eight of them in 1493, devoured guavas and pineapples, ravaged lizards and baby birds—in short, stripped the land clean. Similar swine explosions occurred on the mainland of Mexico and Central America, where along with cattle they omnivorously devastated the grasslands. Meat was never lacking for European intruders (nor was leather or milk); all were there for the taking because Old World hoofed animals took to the savannas and meadows of the New World, as Alfred Crosby puts it, "like Adam and Eve returning to Eden."[3]

Spaniards—and later, other Europeans—naturally brought the flora and fauna that they prized most to the Americas. But also traveling with them were flora and fauna the newcomers would gladly have left behind. Weed seeds could never be strained out of bags of fruit and vegetable seed,

[2]Bernardino de Sahagún, *General History of the Things of New Spain*, trans. and edited by Arthur J. O. Anderson and Charles E. Dibble, quoted in Alfred W. Crosby, "Metamorphosis of the Americas," in Herman J. Viola and Carolyn Margolis, eds., *Seeds of Change* (Washington, D.C.: Smithsonian Institution Press, 1991), p. 73.

[3]Crosby, "Metamorphosis of the Americas," in Herman J. Viola and Carolyn Margolis, eds. *Seeds of Change.*

and once planted they proved hard to control. Hence, the New World acquired invasive weeds, including clover, that crowded out native flora. Rats were pesky stowaways impossible to keep off ships bound across the Atlantic. Notorious carriers of disease deadly to humans, they did their part in punishing the European colonizers, though native people bore the brunt of their vicious bites. Reproducing nearly as fast as pigs, they decimated native small animals and added a new dimension to the human struggle for life.

Whereas westbound ships transiting the Atlantic brought more misery than munificence to Native Americans—death-dealing epidemic diseases greatly outweighing the acquisition of horses and certain new foods—eastbound ships crossing the Atlantic mainly brought benefits to Europeans. Yaws and syphilis, apparently not known in Europe until about 1500, were New World afflictions that created misery in the Old World, but never remotely on the scale of the scathing smallpox epidemics. Table foods such as peanuts, pumpkins, pineapples, squash, and beans enriched the European diet. So did turkeys and guinea pigs. Llamas and alpacas produced wool for warmth. But by far the most important was the spread in Europe of Indian maize and potatoes. The spread was gradual because it took generations to understand the fundamental advantage the potato had over Old World grains. For example, across the north European plain, from the North Sea to the Ural Mountains, farmers slowly learned that by substituting potatoes for rye—the only grain that would thrive in the short and often rainy summers—they could quadruple their yield in calories per acre. Columbus had been dead for several hundred years before potato and corn production took hold in Europe. But when this occurred, the change allowed for population growth and strengthened the sinew of Europe's diet. The same phenomenon occurred with the introduction of corn in southern Europe and Africa and later in China.

ENGLAND ENTERS THE COLONIAL RACE

By the time England awoke to the promise of the New World, the two Iberian powers were firmly entrenched there. England was the most backward of the European nations facing the Atlantic in exploring and colonizing the Americas. Only the voyages of John Cabot (who was in reality the Genoa-born Giovanni Caboto) gave England any title to a place in the New World sweepstakes. Moreover, Cabot's voyages in the 1490s were never followed up. Even the buccaneering expeditions of John Hawkins in the 1560s must be dismissed as unimportant in the expansion of Europe into America because Hawkins was primarily involved in piracy—raiding Spanish trade in the Caribbean with the backing of Catholic-hating English merchants, who hoped to induce their government to sponsor their occasional attempts to challenge the New World monopoly of Spain and Portugal. England's only significant contact with North America had been in connection with the Newfoundland fisheries where, since the 1520s, English fishing fleets had competed with the French, Portuguese, and Spanish for the valuable cod— a vital protein source in the diet of most Europeans.

But England too sought New World colonies, for colonies provided new markets, new sources of raw materials, and, if they contained gold and silver, added to the total supply of specie by which the strength of nations was measured. By the end of the sixteenth century, England was eager to establish a foothold on the North American coast, for Spain and Portugal already dominated the South American continent and parts of the Caribbean and had claimed the southern portions of the North American landmass as well. If the English did not move soon, it would be too late. By the same token, Spain intended to resist English incursions into its sphere of influence by attacking any English settlement that dared to exist on the Atlantic coast of North America. The first known map of the tiny English settlement of Jamestown, Virginia, drawn by an Irish Catholic sailor on an English ship that delivered colonists to the Chesapeake settlement, was smuggled back to Spain. It was highly prized because it provided the necessary information for a surprise attack on this first English foothold on the North American coast.

English entry into the colonial race had origins not only in the lure of New World resources but also in the ideological war that raged in Europe throughout the last half of the sixteenth century. All the western European powers facing the Atlantic, with the exception of the Scandinavian countries, were involved in this struggle between those who professed Catholicism and those who adhered to Protestantism. This national and religious conflict continued issues and interests first raised in the Reformation and Counter-Reformation.

During much of the sixteenth century England swayed back and forth between religious ideologies, living first under the Protestant regimes of Henry VIII (1509–47) and his sickly son, Edward VI (1547–53), and then under the Catholic reign of his daughter Mary Tudor (1553–58), who had married Philip II of Spain—the chief pillar of Catholic power in Europe. When Mary Tudor died and Henry's second daughter, Elizabeth, took the throne in 1558, she returned England to Protestantism. Like her father, Elizabeth favored Protestantism primarily as an expression of national independence. Always, however, the religious question hung above her head. Philip II of Spain, her brother-in-law, regarded her as a Protestant heretic and plotted against her incessantly.

In 1587 the smoldering conflict between Catholic Spain and Protestant England broke into open conflict. The English braced themselves for the seaborne attack expected from the Spanish armada, regarded as the most powerful navy in the world. The battle that ensued is known simply as the Spanish Armada. In the spring of 1588 the Spanish fleet set sail for England, reaching its destination late in July. For two weeks a battle raged at sea. To the amazement of most of Europe the English, aided by the Dutch, prevailed. The Spanish defeat did not establish English superiority at sea or bring England any overseas territory in recognition of its victory. It did not even propel England into the overseas colonial race. But it did prevent a crushing Catholic victory in Europe and temporarily ended Spanish dreams of European hegemony. The Armada brought a temporary stalemate in the wars of religion and made clear for a generation—until 1618, when the beginning of the Thirty Years War again threw Europe into open religious conflict— that religious uniformity could not be imposed by force. England was free to pursue its own destiny, free from the domination of other European powers.

With the way clear for overseas expansion, the "westward fever" began to catch hold in England at the end of the sixteenth century. One inconsequential effort had already been made—the planting of a small settlement on Roanoke Island, off the coast of North Carolina, in the 1580s. But after the Armada the English gentry and merchants began to sense the profits beckoning from the New World. Their capital and experience would be indispensable in the decades ahead.

Urging their countrymen on were two Richard Hakluyts, uncle and nephew. In the last quarter of the 1500s they explained the advantages of settling the remote regions on the other side of the Atlantic. Glory, profit, and adventure awaited everybody: for the nobility at court colonization promised an empire in the New World and a source of new baronies, fiefdoms, and feudal estates; for the merchant there were new markets and a landmass filled with exotic produce that could be marketed at home; for the clergymen there awaited a continent filled with "savages" to be converted for the greater glory of Christ; for the commoner there beckoned a field of adventure and limitless economic opportunity; for the impoverished laborer there was the prospect of starting life anew amidst boundless land. The Hakluyts publicized the idea that the time was ripe for planting English stock across the Atlantic. Shakespeare contributed his bit to the national excitement by writing a play, *The Tempest,* about those who crossed the ocean to further the greatness of their country.

English participation in the age of exploration and colonization began with a generation of adventurous seadogs and gentlemen such as Walter Raleigh, Francis Drake, Humphrey Gilbert, and Richard Grenville. With limited capital and minimal support from the Crown, they attempted much and ended mostly in failure. History books give their exploits much room because they were the first to try. But England could not become a serious colonial power in the New World until the government, as in Spain and Portugal, gave active support to colonizing schemes, and, more important, until the merchant community and the rising middle class in England began plowing capital into overseas colonizing experiments. Thus all the early efforts came to little or nothing—the voyages of Hawkins in the 1560s on the Spanish Main; the Roanoke voyages of 1585 to 1588, which ended in

Theodore DeBry, a Flemish painter, traveled to London to meet John White, who did a water color of this Indian village of Secotan when he was part of the Roanoke expedition in 1587. DeBry's rendition of White's water color is faithful in most particulars, including the depiction of corn in various stages of cultivation. When DeBry's engravings of the New World were published in the late 1580s, Europeans got their first full view (though often distorted) of what they would meet on the other side of the Atlantic. (*Grand Voyages,* published 1590)

failure; the Sagadahoc settlement on the coast of Maine in 1607, which lasted only a year; and even the settlement of Jamestown, Virginia, in 1607, which limped along for several decades.

To the difficulties of generating adequate financial and political support was added the reality that whether they focused on the North American continent or the Caribbean islands, English colonizers confronted rival claims of other European nations—claims that in many cases were backed up by actual occupation of territory. By the early seventeenth century Portugal and Spain already had about 150,000 colonists in their overseas possessions. Although most of them were in Peru and Mexico, where the Spanish established major population centers at Potosi, Mexico City, and Cartagena, they had also planted frontier outposts in southwestern North America and at various points along the Atlantic coast from Florida to the Chesapeake Bay. Spanish claims extended as far north as Newfoundland.

Englishmen were also approaching a continent occupied by the French. Since 1524, when Giovanni da Verrazano had explored the eastern edge of North America, the French had dreamed of finding cities of gold and the Northwest Passage to China. The French could settle, however, only where the Spanish had no use for the land. Thus, after abortive attempts to plant colonies in Florida and Brazil, which the Spanish and Portuguese wiped from the map, the French contented themselves with developing the northerly expanses of Canada.

EARLY SPANISH INCURSIONS IN NORTH AMERICA

When the English first tried to plant themselves at Roanoke Island off the North Carolina coast in 1585, they entered a region where the Spanish had been active for three-quarters of a century. The effects of Spanish–Indian contact along the southern Atlantic coast had rippled through the region for many decades. In this zone of intercultural contact, Indians would have regarded the English as a new branch of arriving Europeans rather than the first bearers of a strange new culture.

Spanish incursions into southeastern North America were very different than the main areas of their colonizing zeal—silver-rich Mexico and Peru and even secondary efforts in Chile, New Granada, Cuba, and Jamaica. In the North American Southeast, the Spanish came mainly as explorers, plunderers, and traders. The Spanish had great difficulty in controlling this vast region and in fact met with a series of costly failures. Meeting many different chiefdoms, most of them warlike, rather than a centralized empire such as the Aztecs, the Spanish never truly dominated the Southeast.

Spanish explorers had been charting the southeastern and Gulf regions of North America since the early sixteenth century, beginning with Juan Ponce de León's expeditions to Florida in 1515 and 1521. By the latter date the Florida tribes must have been fully aware of the dangers inherent in contact with Europeans, for in that year Lucas Vasquez de Ayllón, a Spanish imperial officer and member of the Royal Council of Hispaniola, lured some sixty Indians aboard his ships and whisked them away into slavery in the West Indies. "By such means," wrote a contemporary writer, Peter Martyr, "they sowed hatred and warfare throughout that peaceful and friendly region, separating children from their parents and wives from their husbands."[4]

For the next half century, Spaniards planted small, fragile settlements on the southeastern coast of the continent, engaged in minor trade with the Indians of the region, and established missions manned briefly by Jesuit and then Franciscan fathers. But many attempts to bring the entire Gulf region under their control failed. From 1539 to 1542 Hernán de Soto led a plundering and ill-fated expedition deep into the country of the Creek people, several hundred miles from the coast. Hoping to find a new silver-rich Peru—where he had helped defeat the Incas a few years before—de Soto instead died miserably. Only half of his soldiers and African slaves survived tenacious Indian attacks and limped back to Mexico.

Again the Spaniards drove northward from Mexico, under Tristan de Luna in 1559 and under Juan Pardo in 1566–68, in attempts to establish their authority in the Southeast. Everywhere they went, the Spanish enslaved Indians, used them as provisions carriers, and lived off the land. But while Spanish weaponry and man-eating mastiffs terrorized Indians and infectious diseases did their deadly work, the military expeditions never succeeded in completely pacifying the numerous chiefdoms.

In 1565 the Spanish made a more concerted effort to establish themselves in the eastern part of North America. Inspired by the construction of a French fort at the mouth of the St. John's River in that year, they founded St. Augustine, now the oldest continuously inhabited town in the continental United States. After evicting the French, the Spanish established St. Augustine as a military outpost and a mission town coordinating Spanish religious efforts on the southeastern missionary frontier. On occasion, as in 1597, the various coastal tribes concerted themselves in an attempt to wipe out the Spanish missions and trading posts on the Atlantic coast and drive the Spaniards back to Florida. But the Franciscans kept returning as if God had meant for them to settle all the Indians of the region within the sound of the mission bell. Reaching the Indian's soul, the Spanish friar proved more effective than the Spanish soldier.

Crucifix and mission bell outperformed sword and gun among the Guale, Apalachee, and Timucua. Respecting tribal customs such as polygamy and matrilineality, the priests had converted most of the Florida Indians by

[4]Quoted in John R. Swanton, *Early History of the Creek Indians and their Neighbors,* Smithsonian Institution, Bureau of American Ethnology, Bulletin 73 (Washington, D.C.: Government Printing Office, 1922), p. 33.

the 1640s. But the Spanish blackrobes could stop neither smallpox nor influenza. Ghastly numbers of Indians succumbed to European diseases. This partly explains the short-lived revolts of the Apalachee in 1647 and the Timucua in 1656, away from the area of St. Augustine.

Meanwhile, New Mexico became a second region of missionary activity. Francisco Vásquez de Coronado had explored the area in 1540–42, and half a century later, the Spanish mounted their first big incursion into the ancient homelands of the Pueblo people along the Rio Grande. Thrusting northward along the Rio Grande from the Spanish mining region in northern Mexico, Don Juan de Oñate's expedition, with 83 wagons and 129 men, reached the heart of the Pueblo region in 1598, where 60,000 native people lived in about 60 villages. Santa Fé, founded only three years after Jamestown, became the administrative center of Spanish colonization thereafter.

With little gold and silver to exploit, the Spanish northern borderlands were chiefly interesting to Franciscan missionaries. The Spanish established small presidios, or garrisons, in this far-flung territory of the Southwest, and they commandeered the labor of some Indians while mixing with Indian women. But the primary institution of New Mexico was the Franciscan mission, which in many cases served also as presidio and administrative center. Hence the Spanish presence in New Mexico was numerically insignificant. Even as late as 1680 probably no more than 1,000 Spaniards lived in New Mexico. By 1800 the number had grown only to about 20,000 in the Southwest, and of these the vast majority were the descendants of native people who had mingled with Spanish soldiers. With no fur trade to conduct, or minerals to extract, and with no fertile lands beckoning incoming immigrant farmers, the Spanish pattern of settlement contrasted sharply with that of the English on the eastern side of the continent. The Spanish incursion was primarily a religious intervention, although, in the long run, some of its effects paralleled those of the massive encroachment of land-hungry farmers and town builders far to the east.

Sharp differences also marked the Spanish missionaries' own methods. In early Florida, and much later in California, they tried to gather Indians within mission complexes where priests could closely supervise every aspect of life. The California missions took root in areas where Indian peoples were widely scattered and led a semi-nomadic existence, so this scheme bore some of the marks of forced agricultural labor. To the Spanish priests, supremely indifferent to physical deprivation, this semi-incarceration of native people was essential to the primary goal, for they viewed religious conversion "as a broadly civilizing process" and thus attempted to bring about a "full social and cultural reorientation of native life."[5] In New Mexico, however, Pueblo people had lived in settled villages along the Rio Grande for centuries, practicing agriculture extensively. Here the Spanish missionaries

[5]Charles Gibson, *Spain in America* (New York: Harper & Row, 1966), p. 196.

made no attempt to gather native people within the mission walls but instead built their churches on the edges of settled towns. This led to a division of life "between a town-oriented secular aspect and a church-oriented religious aspect."[6]

The lack of a mutually advantageous economic tie such as united French and Algonkians in New France tended to place the full emphasis in Spanish–Indian relations on religious conversion. This often involved a determined effort by the colonizers to effect a wholesale cultural change among the Indians, and tension was inherent from the outset. This can be seen in the persistent mid-seventeenth-century outbreaks of violence against the Franciscan missionaries of Florida by Guale, Apalachee, and Timucua Indians. Similarly, in New Mexico, where Franciscans attempted to graft Catholicism onto Pueblo culture, native people often staunchly resisted the imposition of the Spanish Catholic worldview. The Franciscans' work among the Pueblo people along the Rio Grande in New Mexico "was less an effort to transfer individuals from an Indian-type community to Spanish-type community than it was to remake Indian communities into tightly knit, church-centered social units with Indian leadership still operative."[7] Under this program, the Jesuits were able to convert thousands of Pueblos in the mission churches they built on the edges of ancient native villages in the early 1600s.

However, in the 1670s, when the Franciscans went beyond attempting to overlay Pueblo culture with a thin veneer of Catholicism, they met with fierce resistance. Spanish priests began to restrict traditional Pueblo religious activities—forbidding native dances, destroying masks and prayer sticks, and imprisoning and flogging Pueblo priests and medicine men. In every pueblo north of El Paso, native people answered this attempt to undermine traditional culture by a concerted effort to drive the Franciscans out of the region altogether.

Called Popé's Rebellion after the Pueblo medicine man who coordinated it, the revolt was a holy war against the attempt of foreigners to forcibly undermine the Pueblo religion and way of life. The Pueblo rebels destroyed every church in New Mexico; killed twenty-one of forty priests and several hundred Spanish settlers; laid waste to Spanish ranches, fields, and government buildings; and drove the remaining Spaniards out of Pueblo country. Over the ruins of the Spanish plaza in Santa Fe they rebuilt their kiva, the deep chamber where Pueblos engaged in activities. Indians of the Rio Grande willingly borrowed the material culture of the Spanish, but their well-integrated communities fought tenaciously against

---

[6]*Ibid.,* p. 197.

[7]Edward H. Spicer, *Cycles of Conquest: The Impact of Spain, Mexico and the United States on the Indians of the Southwest, 1553–1960* (Tucson: University of Arizona Press, 1962), p. 287.

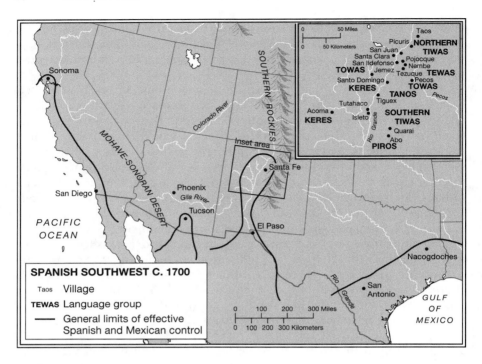

SPANISH SOUTHWEST C. 1700

Taos   Village
TEWAS   Language group
—   General limits of effective
      Spanish and Mexican control

attempts to impose a religion and culture meant to obliterate the Pueblos' ancient cultural identity.

Although the Spanish attempted to reassert their control after Popé's Rebellion, they faced repeated resistance by Pueblos in the 1690s. Not until the early 1700s could the Spanish begin to establish control along the Rio Grande, and then only by declaring a cultural truce with eased demands for Pueblo labor tribute and certain Pueblo rituals permitted in return for nominal acceptance of Christianity. Spanish authority was not fully established until about 1740, and by that time, the deadly work of European diseases had cut the native population at least by half. By 1800 only one-sixth of the pre-contact Indian population existed in New Mexico. Though faced with less resistance, Spanish missionaries found they had fewer and fewer native people to convert to Catholicism.

In California the Spaniards made a brief and intermittent contact with the native population beginning in 1542, but the first permanent settlements did not appear until 1769. In that year Spanish forces landed at San Diego. Promptly constructing a presidio, or fort, they founded the Mission San Diego de Alcalá, the first of twenty-one Spanish missions eventually erected in California. During the two centuries that preceded the founding of the San Diego mission, Spanish influence on native cultures in most parts of California was negligible. The native population at the time of contact numbered some 300,000 persons, and this number diminished slowly during the first two centuries of intermittent contact. Most Indian communities were organized by lineage of clan, though the Chumash and Gabrielinos along the southern coast lived in towns with more centralized political organizations. Indian culture in these southern coastal towns may have changed during the years prior to the first Spanish settlements, but Spanish influence in other areas was negligible.

During the late 1700s Spanish intrusion into the lands of various California Indian societies disrupted community stability and drastically altered native lifestyles. The missions that dotted the coast between San Diego and San Francisco drew their recruits from small dispersed villages, not the settled villages of New Mexico. Spanish encroachment forced many Indians to abandon their hunting and gathering practices and lineage-based political systems to take their places in the rigidly hierarchical ranking system that existed within the missions. The missionaries turned many natives into sedentary horticulturists and craftspersons, while a few were recruited as *vaqueros,* or cowboys, to tend the large herds of cattle and horses on the outlying mission estates. During the late eighteenth and early nineteenth centuries the Indian population within reach of the mission system declined dramatically as periodic epidemics of smallpox, measles, dysentery, pleurisy, pneumonia, and syphilis took their ghastly toll.

THE FRENCH PENETRATION OF NORTH AMERICA

The French, like the Spanish, were a force in the New World before the English arrived. Their activities in the late sixteenth and early seventeenth centuries were confined to harrying Spanish and Portuguese shipping, trading surreptitiously with Iberian settlers in the Caribbean and South America, and planting tiny fishing and trading settlements on the North American mainland.

French fisherman had been working the coasts of Newfoundland and Nova Scotia since the early sixteenth century. The development of a sporadic fur trade with the Indians of the area began in 1534 with Cartier's exploration of the Gulf of St. Lawrence. These efforts convinced the French that the St. Lawrence River area could be profitable, even if the climate was inhospitable. Realizing that only the St. Lawrence and Hudson rivers provided access by water into the interior of the northern parts of the continent, the French wisely chose to plant their first settlements near the mouth of the St. Lawrence in 1603. From there they pushed forward their quest for another form of New World gold—the skins of fur-bearing animals.

By the end of the sixteenth century the French were most numerous among the hundreds of European fishing ships that came annually to Canadian waters. When French settlements at the mouth of the Rio de Janeiro and on the southeastern coast of North America were wiped out by the Portuguese and Spanish, respectively, in 1560 and 1565, the French decided to concentrate to the north, where their commercial activities would be free from Spanish and Portuguese molestation.

As valuable as fishing was, the fur trade turned out to be vastly more profitable. Nothing more was required than to bring trade goods desired by Indians across the Atlantic, anchor a few ships in a sheltered bay of the St. Lawrence, and wait for Indian traders to arrive with pelts. Military conquest was unnecessary and in fact would only adversely affect trade with the Indians. Even large settlements were not required, for the fur trade involved a simple barter relationship.

In time, the French decided to plant permanent settlements in North America because without a colonial population base their trading posts would be subject to the predatory raids of the Dutch, English, or any other colonizing nation. Thus the French planted a colony in 1604 at Port Royal, Nova Scotia, and in 1608 established a second settlement at Québec. This attempt to solidify claims to the northern part of the continent was enough to induce the English, a thousand miles to the south, to mount a campaign of extermination against the French. Although England and France were not at war, the governor of Virginia, Sir Thomas Dale, commissioned a seasoned explorer and Atlantic seadog, Samuel Argall, to attack the French settlements in 1613. Just a few months after he had abducted Pocahontas in Virginia, Argall wiped out the French settlement at Port Royal.

For the next few decades the French struggled to plant tiny settlements in the face of growing English opposition centered in New England. But France was preoccupied with the Thirty Years War in Europe and could spare neither men nor money for overseas development. By 1643, after almost half a century of colonization, there were still fewer than four hundred Frenchmen in New France. Most of them were Indian traders or Jesuit priests, who had come in considerable numbers to convert the Indians. As one royal governor of Canada later remarked, only two kinds of business existed in New France—the conversion of souls and the conversion of beaver.

Under the leadership of Samuel de Champlain, backed by the Company of New France, New France was established on a more permanent footing. By offering free land the company lured settlers from France to establish a permanent agricultural society. By 1660, about two thousand Frenchmen lived in the colony (as compared with twenty times that number in New England), huddled in small towns along the St. Lawrence River.

While the Dutch, English, and Spanish typically used military force or guile to wrest land and political submission from their Indian neighbors, the French in the north forged relations of a much different kind with Indian societies of the St. Lawrence River valley and the upper Great Lakes region. For the French, the Indians were absolutely vital. The French were so few in number that they could not have entertained the slightest hope of survival without the friendship of the native peoples surrounding them. In 1640, after four decades of colonizing activity, the entire French population in North America was about 270, hardly equal to any of the number of New England towns. Even a generation later, in 1663, the French population had increased only to 3,000, not much more than that of several Huron towns on the upper Great Lakes.

A high proportion of these French settlers were male, which added to the dependency on Indian neighbors. In contrast to the English and Dutch settlements, where the sex ratio among Europeans was far more balanced, Frenchmen freely took Indian mistresses, concubines, and wives. They exhibited no embarrassment at this mixing of blood and were hard put to understand English qualms about interracial relations. The French Catholic church was more permissive in this regard also. In Nova Scotia, where French women were uncommonly scarce, intermarriage was so common that one authority believes that by 1676 virtually all French families had Indian blood in their veins. In the more settled areas of the St. Lawrence River valley, where the Algonkian tribes were less sedentary and Jesuit priests raised some objections to racial mixing, interracial fornication rather than interracial marriage was more customary. The Jesuits frowned on church marriages between the two cultures, but they could do nothing about the sexual urges of their parishioners. "In the Night time," wrote Baron de Lahontan, "all of them, barring the Jesuits, roll from House to House to debauch the Women Savages." Farther west at the trading posts, "miscegenation between the *coureurs de bois* and the Indian women was the rule rather than the exception."[8]

The practice of racial intermixture became official government policy in the 1660s when Colbert, Louis XVI's architect of imperial reorganization, called for a full-fledged integration of the races. Colbert ordered the French settlers "to civilize the Algonquins . . . and the other savages who have embraced Christianity, and dispose them to come and settle them in community with the French, live with them, and bring up their children in their manners and customs." In spite of opposition from the Catholic Church, Colbert also encouraged intermarriage and urged the governor of New France to bring about a mingling of the cultures "in order that, having but one law and one master, they may form only one people and one blood."[9] It was a policy contrived to bring the Indians under French control, not by destroying or weakening the indigenous population, but by assimilating it. A half century later, two lettered Virginians, William Byrd and Robert Beverly, pondered this "Modern Policy" adopted by France in Canada and lamented that English "false delicacy" in the early years on the Chesapeake

[8]Alfred G. Bailey, *The Conflict of European and Eastern Algonkian Cultures, 1504–1700: A Study in Canadian Civilization* (Sackville, N.B.: The Tribune Press, 1937), p. 112.
[9]Quoted in *ibid.*, p. 107.

had kept them from making a "prudent Alliance" through intermarriage, as the French had done.[10]

It is true that racial mingling almost always linked French men and Indian women and that the offspring of these liaisons followed the mother. This meant that Indian blood was rarely added to the French gene pool. But despite this evidence of French ethnocentrism, frequent intermixing brought contacts of the most intimate nature between the two peoples, and this intimacy could not help but bring about greater mutual understanding. For Indian leaders marriage would seal alliances with the French. For the undermanned and "underwomaned" French colonists, intimate relations with native peoples of the St. Lawrence region made good sense.

Equally important in establishing relatively nonviolent relations was the fact that virtually every man in early New France was there either to trade furs or to evangelize among the Indians. Both tasks required Indian cooperation; only rarely could either be accomplished through coercion. Thus French traders traveled hundreds of miles into the remote Great Lakes regions of the Hurons, establishing trading posts, learning the language and customs of the tribes, and finding Indian consorts. In the English and Dutch settlements the Indian trader was the exception rather than the rule, since the vast majority of the settlers after the first few years were farmers engaging in an activity to which the Indians had nothing to offer once the colonizers understood native techniques of cultivating indigenous crops.

Those who were not traders in New France were generally Jesuit priests. They established missions, martyred themselves in hostile Indian country, and worked for the greater glory of their God by converting Indians to Catholicism. Fur trading and missionary work often went hand in hand, with missions established at important river junctions where the fur trade took place. Jesuits trekked northward to the farthest shores of the Gulf of St. Lawrence and westward as far as Lake Huron. Their main efforts were concentrated among some 15–20,000 Hurons who were settled in the Great Lakes region in towns of several thousand.

The Jesuits were more willing than the Puritans to accept that Indian beliefs in a supreme being, in the immortality of the soul, and in supernatural forces could be revised sufficiently to find acceptance from their Christian God. Whereas the Puritans insisted that Indians of the New England area renounce their way of life and abandon their religious beliefs as a starting point in accepting Christianity, the Jesuits studied the Indian structure of belief and attempted to change it slowly. Jesuits did not contest Indian belief that the manitous—great spirits—smiled upon a successful hunt or military victory; rather they tried to persuade Indians that thanks should go

---

[10]William K. Boyd, ed., *William Byrd's Histories of the Dividing Line Betwixt Virginia and North Carolina* (Raleigh: North Carolina Historical Commission, 1929), pp. 3–4; Robert Beverly, *The History and Present State of Virginia*, ed. Louis B. Wright (Chapel Hill: University of North Carolina Press, 1947), pp. 38–39.

to the power of Christ. "Indians were not so much being converted to Christianity," writes one historian, "as Christ was being converted into a manitou."[11] The statement of Father Ragueneau in 1647, which the Puritan clergy would have deplored, reveals the ethnocentrism of the French—but an ethnocentrism tempered by respect and affection. "One must be very careful before condemning a thousand things among their customs, which greatly affend minds brought up and nourished in another world. It is easy to call irreligion what is merely stupidity, and to take for diabolical working something that is nothing more than human. . . ."[12]

This greater flexibility in approaching native culture on its own terms, even while demeaning it, led to a far greater degree of cultural interaction in New France than in New England. The meager Puritan missionary activity focused on the weakest tribes, those that had lost or were losing their political autonomy and cultural self-sufficiency. Weakened by disease and warfare and demoralized by the rapid growth of the English population, small tribes abandoned some of their traditional ways and attempted to refashion themselves in the white man's image. Living in "praying villages," they conformed to English clothing styles, work habits, and forms of worship. In contrast, some of the greatest successes of the Jesuits in New France were among the most powerful Indian societies, although the priests never made much headway among the Iroquois. Like the English Protestant clergy, the French Catholic *recollects* believed that the true conversion to Christianity ultimately required giving up "savage" ways. But the Jesuits adopted a more gradualist approach and worked within a colonizing society that did not pursue a militant policy of establishing political domination over native people.

The different nature of the French–Indian relations is also revealed in the Gallic attitude toward Indian sovereignty. In all European–Indian contacts the concept of sovereignty was used to connote political authority and can be regarded as a kind of litmus test of the balance of power between the two cultures. All Europeans regarded native peoples as inferior and all pursued sovereignty as the ultimate goal, for if native peoples recognized the authority of European law and kingly authority they were, in effect, surrendering their political independence. Whenever Indians surrendered sovereignty, subjugation was not far behind. When the New Englanders fought the Pequots in 1637 the goal was to exterminate or at least bring under English jurisdiction a powerful tribe that refused to accept Puritan sway in this region. Similarly, as soon as the Chesapeake colonists were strong enough, they forced the Indians to recognize their sovereignty, a process that began with John Smith's attempts to exact tribute from the tribes

---

[11]Richard White, *The Middle Ground: Indians, Empires, and Republics in the Great Lakes Region, 1650–1815* (New York: Cambridge University Press, 1991), p. 26.

[12]Quoted in W. J. Eccles, *The Canadian Frontier, 1534–1760,* (New York: Holt, Rinehart, and Winston, 1969), p. 48.

of the Powhatan Confederacy. But in New France, the governing council was debating as late as 1664 whether or not an Algonkian Indian who had raped the wife of a French settler should be prosecuted in the French court of justice—a telltale argument revealing that French sovereignty had not yet been established.

Of course, declaring sovereignty and implementing it were different matters. All European colonizers, having judged their strength sufficient to pronounce their sovereignty, still faced the job of imposing it. In New France in 1664 French authorities decided to consult with the chiefs of nearby tribes about the rape. The Indian spokesman pointed out that friendly relations had been maintained for decades in spite of individual acts of crime and violence on both sides, and said that each side must do its best to control its members. The French agreed that the Indian offender should not be prosecuted. A half century later, in 1714, when the Indians declared that the French had no right to jail or punish them for drunkenness, since they were not subject to the laws of the colony and the liquor, not the drinker of it, was responsible for breaches of conduct, the French acquiesced because "the matter is extremely delicate." Assenting to the Indians' claim of jurisdiction over wrongdoers, the French passed laws prohibiting the sale of alcohol to the Indians. When crimes were committed by Indians under the influence of alcohol, the French courts attempted to discover the illegal supplier, prosecute him for violating French law, and charge him with damages committed by the drunken Indian. This was not the English way.

The French policy did not always reflect greater understanding of the Indians or acceptance of their culture. First and foremost it was a policy born of weakness. "The French were unable to impose their law on the Indians, and for one good reason;" writes one historian "to have attempted to do so with any degree of vigor would have alienated the Indians, and this the French could not afford to do."[13] But from this policy founded on weakness came the most lastingly intimate, if not fully amicable, relations between Europeans and Native Americans on the continent. By regulating their own subjects in relations with Indians and by continuing to recognize the sovereignty of the Algonkians, the French coexisted fruitfully with native societies to a degree unprecedented elsewhere in North America. That their settlements were so small and competed so little for cleared land doubtless helped in this regard.

In spite of the relatively pacific character of French–Algonkian relations, the Indians were not spared the ravages that beset other native societies after European arrival. Epidemic diseases were not a matter of policy or national character, and they struck the Hurons as mortally in 1649 as they had the Indians of New England three decades earlier. Nor could the French, however good their intentions, avert the attacks on their Huron

[13]*Ibid.*, pp. 78–79.

allies by the Iroquois after the European rivalry for the fur trade began. Once the beaver supply dwindled in the traditional Iroquois hunting grounds, the Five Nations seized the role of middlemen between the Albany traders and the Huron and Ottawa tribes of the Great Lakes region. When this could not be accomplished through diplomacy, as in the late 1640s, the Iroquois resorted to war. Within a few years they had decimated the Hurons and other tribes living around Lake Erie. War raged intermittently thereafter, as the Iroquois exploited the remaining beaver in their newly conquered territories and perfected the art of hijacking fleets of fur-laden canoes from the northern Ottawa country as they headed for French markets in Montreal.

Although Catholicism and French values helped shape the relationship with Indian societies, economic and demographic factors were sometimes more important. This is amply demonstrated by French relations with the Natchez of the lower Mississippi region in the early eighteenth century, which stand in stark contrast to the French experience in Canada. The Natchez were a highly stratified and ritualistic people, the southernmost descendants of the ancient Mound builders. In their social hierarchy, theocratic authority, hereditary class system, and celebration of war they more closely approximated European culture than any other group in eastern North America. After de Soto had passed through the country in 1542, they experienced little contact with Europeans until the arrival of Robert La Salle, the French explorer, who laid claim to the lower Mississippi valley for France in 1682. For another three decades, until the French established a small trading post on the Mississippi River in 1713, the Natchez had only occasional contact with French missionaries and French and English traders.

When the French began a permanent fortification in Natchez country in the second decade of the eighteenth century—part of their plan to seize control of the interior of the continent—they brought soldiers, women, and African slaves with them. Trade with the Natchez was only incidental to French purposes. When the Indians killed five traders in retaliation for the ill treatment they had received, the French executed several minor chiefs. When tension flared again in 1722, the French governor burned three Natchez villages to the ground and demanded that the Natchez emperor, Tattooed Serpent, send him the head of one of the minor chiefs, though this violated tribal custom, by which all chiefs were immune from the death penalty.

The draconic policy of the French led to further hostilities. In 1729, when the French demanded land cessions without compensation, including the site of an important Indian village, the Natchez mounted an offensive to eliminate their oppressors. By this time the French had found the Natchez useless for their purposes in the lower Mississippi and felt no qualms about attempting to intimidate them. Though the Natchez overpowered the French at Fort Rosalie in 1729, killing several hundred of the French and taking prisoner many women, children, and black and Indian slaves, they beat back the French only temporarily. Reinforcements arrived in 1731, and with the aid of Choctaw allies the French stormed the Natchez strongholds with cannon. Killing more than 1,000 Natchez, the French burned many captives at the stake and sold some 400 into slavery in St. Dominigue. The surviving Natchez, scattering into small bands, sought refuge among other southeastern tribes. By the end of the year the Natchez nation, once nearly 5,000 strong, had ceased to exist as a sovereign people. Finding no way of utilizing the Indians to their own advantage, the French worked toward the elimination of these ancient sun-worshiping people with a thoroughness that would have aroused the envy of the English in New England, the Dutch in New Amsterdam, or the Spanish in Mexico.

ENGLISH IMAGES OF THE NATIVE AMERICANS

Englishmen approaching the North America coast had to reckon with Spain and France, whose established claims dictated that the English look to the middle part of the Atlantic seaboard for a toehold on the continent. Well aware of the Spanish presence, the English would build their forts facing the sea, to fend off Spanish attacks, rather than facing inland where the Indian danger lay. It was the prudent work of those who knew they were intruding on territory claimed by Spain.

But it was another people, the indigenous inhabitants of the land, that claimed English attention most forcefully. What did men like Gilbert and Raleigh know about the native occupiers of the land as they approached the forbidding coast of North America in the 1580s? How would they be received by these people whom Columbus, thinking he had reached India, mistakenly called Indians? How would Englishmen obtain the use or possession of land these Indians occupied? And how were ideas about the nature of Indian peoples influenced by the thorny question of obtaining sovereignty over the land? And how would the Indians' long experience with Spanish and French traders, missionaries, plunderers, and settlers affect the native disposition toward the English?

No doubt the first English colonizers experienced the apprehensions that regardless of time or place fill the minds of those who are attempting to penetrate the unknown. But they were far from uninformed about the Indian people of the New World. Beginning with Columbus's description of the New World, published in several European capitals in 1493 and 1494, a mass of reports, stories, and promotional accounts had been circulating among sailors, merchants, geographers, politicians, and churchmen who were participating in the early voyages of discovery, trade, and settlement. These became the basis for an understanding of the Americas by any adventurer approaching the eastern edge of land in the western Atlantic Ocean.

From this considerable literature, the early colonists most likely held a split image of the natives of North America. On the one hand they had reason to believe that the Indians were a gentle people who would be receptive to those who came not to harm them but to live and trade with them. Columbus had written of the "great amity towards us" that he encountered in San Salvador in 1492 and described the Arawak Indians there as "a loving people without covetousness," who "were greatly pleased and became so entirely our friends that it was a wonder to see." The Indians "brought us parrots and cotton thread in balls, and spears and many other things, and we exchanged for them other things, such as small glass beads and hawks' bells, which we gave to them."[14] Verrazano, the first European to navigate the eastern edge of the continent, wrote with similar optimism from the Bay of New York in 1524. The natives were graceful of limb, tawny colored, with black alert eyes, and "dressed in birds' feathers of various colors, and they came toward us joyfully, uttering loud cries of wonderment, and showing us the safest place to beach the boat."[15]

From this time on, accounts of natives of the New World included many such enthusiastic descriptions of native people and their eagerness to receive European explorers and settlers. This positive side of the image of the Indians not only reflected the friendly reception Europeans apparently received in Newfoundland, parts of Florida, and elsewhere in the Caribbean and South America, but also represented a part of the vision of the New World as an earthly paradise—a Garden of Eden where war-torn, impoverished Europeans could find a new life amidst nature's bounty. That Columbus thought he had found the Gihon, one of the Biblical rivers flowing from Eden, when he reached the Orinoco River in 1498 is vivid testimony to this strain in the European mentality.

Another reason existed for drawing a favorable image of the North American natives. The English, like other European colonizers, hoped that trade with native peoples would become a major source of profit on the other side of the Atlantic. Indeed, the early English voyages were not primarily intended for the purpose of large-scale settlement and agricultural production. Trade with the Indians, the search for gold and silver, and discovery of the Northwest Passage were the principal goals. So a special incentive existed for seeing the Indian as something more than a "savage." Only a friendly Indian could be a trading Indian. If trade was the key to overseas development, then it is not surprising that English promoters would suggest that the Indian might be receptive and generous—a person who could be wooed and won to the advantages of trade.

---

[14]Quoted in Wilcomb E. Washburn, ed., *The Indian and the White Man* (Garden City, N.Y.: Doubleday & Co., Inc., 1964), p. 4.
[15]Lawrence C. Wroth, *The Voyages of Giovanni da Verrazano, 1524–1528* (New Haven: Yale University Press, 1970), p. 137.

However, a counterimage of the Indian also lodged itself in the minds of Englishmen approaching the coast of North America. This negative view pictured a savage, hostile, beastlike person and even a people cursed by God because they were descended from the ancient Israelites. Spanish and French literature of colonization bristled with such depictions. As early as the first decade of the sixteenth century, Sebastian Cabot had paraded in England three Eskimos taken captive on his voyage to the Arctic in 1502. A contemporary described the natives as flesh-eating, primitive specimens, who "spake such speech that no man coulde understand them, and in their demeanour like to bruite beasts."[16] A flood of pamphlets in the second half of the sixteenth century described the natives in terms that could have caused little optimism concerning the reception Europeans would receive. These accounts portrayed the Indians as crafty, brutal, loathsome half-men whose cannibalistic instincts were revealed, as one pamphleteer wrote in 1578, by the fact that "there is no flesh or fishe, which they finde dead, (smell it never so filthily) but they will eate it, as they finde it, without any other dressing [cooking]."[17] Other accounts depicted the natives as bestial, living in sexual abandon, and in general moved entirely by passion rather than reason.

Apart from tales of travel and adventure in the New World, the English had a more striking reason for imagining that all would not be friendship and amiable trading when they encountered the native occupants of the North American coast. For years they had read accounts of the Spanish experience with Indian peoples in Mexico and Peru—and the story was not a pretty one. Chief among these Spanish accounts was the work of the Dominican friar Bartholomé de Las Casas, whose *Brevissima Relación de la Destrucción de las Indias* was translated into English and published in 1583. Englishmen could delight in Las Casas's gory descriptions of Spanish cruelty and genocide, for such stories confirmed all the worst things that the Protestant English believed about the Catholic Spaniards with whom they were about to go to war. The Hakluyts eagerly contributed to the "Black Legend" concerning the Spanish colonizers, labeling them "hell-hounds and wolves."

Such accounts, useful in fueling anti-Spanish and anti-Catholic prejudices, also suggested that when Europeans met "primitive" people, slaughter was inevitable. Moreover, Las Casas was rebutted by a host of Spanish writers who justified Spanish behavior by insisting that the Indians had precipitated bloodletting and, because of their unalterably bestial nature, could be dealt with in no other way. However useful accounts of Spanish cruelty might have been for Protestant pamphleteers, Englishmen embarking for the New World

[16]Richard Hakluyt, *Divers Voyages touching the discoveries of America, and the Ilands adjacent unto the Same* (1582), Hakluyt Society *Publications*, 1st Ser., 7 (London: The Hakluyt Society, 1850): 23.

[17]Vilhjalmur Stefansson, ed., *The Three Voyages of Martin Frobisher* (London: The Argonaut Press, 1938), 2: 23.

must have wondered whether the same experience awaited them. The English knew from their own invasions of Ireland and the Netherlands in the late sixteenth century that indigenous peoples did not ordinarily welcome those who came to dominate them. However tractable and amenable to trade the Indian might appear in some of the English literature, the image of a hostile savage who awaited Christian adventurers could never be blotted from the English mind. Few Englishmen doubted that they enjoyed the same technological superiority as the Spanish. If they desired, they could presumably lay waste the country they were entering. The English experience with the Irish, in whose country military officers like Gilbert and Raleigh had gained experience in the subjugation of "lesser breeds" for several decades, suggested that the English were fully capable of every cruelty contrived by the Spanish. To imagine the Indian as a savage beast was therefore a way of predicting the future, preparing for it, and justifying what one would do, even before one caused it to happen.

Another factor nourishing negative images of the Indian related directly to the native possession of land coveted by Europeans. For Englishmen, as for other Europeans, the Indian occupation of the land presented problems of law, morality, and practicality. As early as the 1580s, George Peckham, an early Catholic promoter of colonization, had admitted that some Englishmen doubted their right to take possession of the land of others. In 1609 the thought was raised again by another promoter of colonization, Robert Gray, who asked rhetorically, "By what right or warrant can we enter into the land of these Savages, take away their rightful inheritance from them, and plant ourselves in their places, being unwronged or unprovoked by them?"[18] It was an appropriate question to ask, for Englishmen, like other Europeans, had organized their society around the concept of private ownership of land and regarded this concept as important evidence of their superior culture. They were not blind to the fact that they were entering the land of another people, who, by prior possession, could lay sole claim to the entire continent.

The problem could be partially resolved by arguing that Englishmen did not intend to take the Indians' land but wanted only to share with them what seemed a superabundance of territory. In return, they would extend to the Indians the advantages of a richer culture, a more advanced civilization, and, most importantly, the Christian religion. It was this argument that the governing council in Virginia used in 1610 when it advertised in England that the settlers "by way of marchandizing and trade, doe buy of them [the Indians] the pearles of earth, and sell to them the pearles of heaven."[19] It did not matter that the Chesapeake tribes had indicated no desire to

[18]*A Good Speed to Virginia* (1609), quoted in Wesley Frank Craven, "Indian Policy in Early Virginia," *William and Mary Quarterly*, 3rd Ser., 1 (1944): 65.
[19]*A True Declaration of the Estate of the Colonie in Virginia . . .* (1610), in *Tracts and Other Papers, Relating Principally to the Origin, Settlement, and Progress of the Colonies in North America . . .*, Peter Force, comp. (Washington, D.C., 1884), 3: No. 1, p. 6.

exchange their land for such Christian instruction as a ragged band of Englishmen could provide.

Another, more portentous way of answering the question of English rights to the land was to deny the humanity of the Indians. Thus, Robert Gray asked rhetorically if Englishmen were entitled to "plant ourselves in their places" and then answered by arguing that the Indians' inhumanity disqualified them from the right to possess land. "Although the Lord hath given the earth to children of men," he wrote, "the greater part of it [is] possessed and wrongfully usurped by wild beasts, and unreasonable creatures, or by brutish savages, which by reason of their godles ignorance, and blasphemous Idolatrie, are worse than those beasts which are of most wilde and savage nature."[20] This line of reasoning was filled with danger for the Indian. While many leaders of colonization would avow, as one of them put it, that "every foote of Land which we shall take unto our use, we will bargayne and buy of them," others would find it more convenient to suggest that Indians, merely by being "Godless" and "savage," as defined by English invaders, had disqualified themselves from rightful ownership of the land.[21] In this sense much was to be gained by projecting deeply negative images of native peoples. The darker the image—the more it defined aboriginal peoples in nonhuman terms—the stronger was the European claim to the land of the New World. Defining the Indian as a "savage" or "brutish beast" or "tawny serpent" did not give Europeans the power to dispossess Indians of their land. But it gave them the moral force to do so if and when physical force became available. The Spanish, Portuguese, Dutch, French, and English did not differ much in this regard.

A pamphlet published in London as the first English expedition was preparing to embark for Roanoke Island illustrates the tension between the positive and the negative English images of the Indian. Written by Sir George Peckham, who had accompanied Humphrey Gilbert on a voyage to Newfoundland in 1583, *A True Report, of the late discoveries, . . . of the Newfound Landes* clearly expressed the emerging formula for English colonization: formal expressions of goodwill, explanations of mutual benefits to be derived from contact between English and Indian peoples and yet, lurking beneath the surface, dark images and the anticipation of violence. Peckham's pamphlet began with an elaborate defense of the rights of maritime nations to "trade and trafficke" with "savage" nations and assured Englishmen that such enterprises would be "profitable to the adventurers in particular, beneficial to the Savages, and a matter to be attained without any great daunger or difficultie." Some of the natives, he allowed, would be "fearefull by

---

[20]*A Good Speed to Virginia* (1609), quoted in Gary B. Nash, "The Image of the Indian in the Southern Colonial Mind," *William and Mary Quarterly*, 3rd Ser., 29 (1972): 210.

[21]William Strachey, *The Historie of Travell into Virginia Britania* (1612), eds. Louis B. Wright and Virginia Freund, Hakluyt Society *Publications*, 2nd Ser., 103 (London: The Hakluyt Society, 1953): 26.

nature" and disquieted by the "straunge apparrell, Armour, and weapons" of the English, but "courtesie and myldness," along with a generous bounty of "prittie merchaundizes and trifles as looking Glasses, Bells, Beades, Brace-letts, Chaines, or collers of Bewgle, Christall, Amber, Jett, or Glasse" would soon win them over and "induce their Barbarous natures to a likeing and mutuall society with us."[22]

Following this explanation of how he hoped the English might act, and how the Indians might respond, Peckham revealed what he must have considered the more likely course of events.

> But if after these good and fayre meanes used, the Savages neverthe-less will not be heerewithall satisfied, but barbarously wyll goe about to practise violence either in repelling the Christians from theyr Portes and safe Landinges or in withstanding them afterwardes to enjoye the rights for which both painfully and lawfully they have adventured themselves thether; Then in such a case I holde it no breache of equitye for the Christians to defende themselves, to pursue revenge with force, and to doo whatsoever is necessary for attayning of theyr safety; For it is allowable by all Lawes in such distresses, to resist vio-lence with violence.[23]

With earlier statements of the gentle and receptive qualities of the Indians almost beyond recall, Peckham reminded his countrymen of their responsi-bility to employ all necessary means to bring the Indians from "falsehood to truth, from darkness to light, from the highway of death, to the path of life, from superstitious idolatry, to sincere christianity, from the devill to Christ, from hell to Heaven."

Thus two conflicting images of the Indian wrestled for ascendance in the English mind as the first attempts to challenge the Spanish and French in North America began. At times the English tended to see the native as a backward but receptive person with whom amicable and profitable relations might be established. But the negative image, filled with visions of violence and bloodshed, reverberated even more strongly in the minds of those who were sailing toward land already occupied by people of a different culture.

[22]David Beers Quinn, ed., *The Voyages and Colonizing Enterprises of Sir Humphrey Gilbert,* Hakluyt Society *Publications,* 2nd Ser., 84 (London: The Hakluyt Society, 1940): 450–52.
[23]*Ibid.,* p. 453.

3

Cultures Meet
on the Chesapeake

The first encounters between English settlers and the native peoples of North America occurred in the temperate zone of the Chesapeake Bay and the lands just southward of this waterway. For a third of a century, from 1585 to 1620, this was the only region in which the adventuring English intruded on ancient homelands of American Indians. Though the number of settlers involved was very small, only a few thousand, the impact was very great—both on the English and Algonquian peoples of this region. The latter had already met—and repulsed—Europeans who had made brief incursions in the Chesapeake area in the 1560s. But the Spaniards (who soon went away) proved much easier to deal with than the English, who were determined to maintain a foothold on the continent once they arrived. The course of Anglo–Indian relations on the Chesapeake shaped English sensibilities and strategies for many decades and in faraway regions.

THE FAILED COLONY AT ROANOKE

England's first real attempt to establish colonies in the New World came in 1585, when Walter Raleigh, a favorite at the court of Queen Elizabeth, organized a major expedition of ships and men. A year before, Raleigh had dispatched two ships on a reconnaissance voyage to the lower latitudes of the North American coast, for the English at this time still knew little about the climate and natural resources of the area between French-claimed territory in the St. Lawrence region and Spanish-held Florida. Relying on a Portuguese pilot who had accompanied an earlier Spanish voyage along the coast, Raleigh's ship captains made landfall on the Outer Banks of the Carolina coast and established contacts with the local Indians on Roanoke Island. Two Indians were induced to return to England. Displayed in London, they were invaluable in the publicity campaign that Raleigh launched for a large expedition in 1585.

The second Roanoke voyage marked the first extended encounter between Indians and the English-speaking, Protestant variety of European. Some 600 men in 7 ships sailed from Plymouth in April 1585 and reached the Outer Banks that summer. About 100 of the men were left on Roanoke Island with promises that a relief expedition would return the next spring. Indians of the Chesapeake region then learned who and what these Englishmen were. Likewise, the accounts of the Roanoke experience later published in London helped plant ideas in the minds of other Englishmen coming to America of the people they were likely to encounter.

Though differing in detail, all accounts agree that the Indians of the Carolina coast were receptive to the English in 1585. Arthur Barrow, a member of the first expedition, wrote that "we were entertained with all love, and kindness, and with as much bounties after their manner, as they could possibly devise. We found the people most gentle, loving and faithful, void of all guile, and treason." Barrow remarked that the Indians were "much grieved" when their hospitality was shunned by the suspicious English.[1] Other accounts, while less complimentary to the Indians, also averred that the indigenous people were eager to learn about the artifacts of English culture. Though wary, they extended their hospitality. Since the English came in small numbers, the Indians probably did not regard them as much of a threat. No conflict occurred until the English discovered a silver cup missing and dispatched a punitive expedition to a nearby Indian village. When the Indians denied taking the cup, the English, deciding to make a show of force, burned the village to the ground, and destroyed the Indians' supply of corn. After that, relations deteriorated.

Aware of their numerical disadvantage and convinced that the local Indian leader was organizing mainland tribes against them, the English employed force in large doses to convince the local Indians of their invulnerability. As one member of the expedition admitted, "Some of our companie towardes the ende of the yeare, shewed themselves too fierce, in slaying some of the people, in some towns, upon causes that on our part, might

[1]David Beers Quinn, ed., *The Roanoke Voyages, 1584–1590,* Hakluyt Society *Publications,* 104 (London: The Hakluyt Society, 1955): 108.

easily enough have been borne withall."[2] Given this course of events, the coastal tribes must have concluded that the English were untrustworthy, quick to resort to arms, and dangerously unpredictable.

The 1585 Roanoke settlers scanned the horizon for sight of the relief expedition in the early summer of 1586. But the ships that finally appeared belonged to Sir Francis Drake, who had been conducting predatory raids on the Spanish Main and only incidentally dropped in on the Roanoke colony. Discouraged at the failure of the relief expedition to appear, and short of food, the colonizers clambered aboard Drake's ships for a ride home. About six weeks later the relief expedition arrived, only to find the colony abandoned. From the relief ship, fewer than twenty men were left to guard the fort that had been erected on Roanoke Island. But they were nowhere to be found when another relief expedition arrived in 1587 with 110 adventurers, led by John White. These were to become the famous "Lost Colonists," for when the next relief expedition finally reached Roanoke in 1590 (earlier attempts at sending out ships having been thwarted by the Spanish Armada) no trace could be found of the colonists. Given the previous hostility between settlers and Indians, it is likely that they had succumbed to the attacks of local tribes.

The Roanoke voyages were never large nor fully capitalized enough to have led to permanent and self-sustaining colonies. They served only as a symbol of the English challenge to Spain in North America. They were also useful in accumulating knowledge about the region that was to become the focus of English overseas colonization. In terms of the first sustained contact between English and Native American cultures, they were a resounding failure. "What was lost in this famous lost colony," writes one historian, "was more than the band of colonists who have never been traced. What was also lost and never quite recovered in subsequent ventures was the dream of Englishmen and Indian living side by side in peace and liberty."[3]

For two decades after the Roanoke experiment, Englishmen launched no new colonial adventures. A few English sea captains, representing merchants who dabbled in the West Indies trade, looked in on the coast of North America and attempted to barter with the Indians. They reported that their relations were generally friendly. But no further English attempts at colonization came until after the death in 1603 of Queen Elizabeth. Though much had been done during her reign to propagandize overseas colonizing and to obtain for it the backing of the Crown and the mercantile wealth of the nation, North America, so far as it was an arena of European colonization, still belonged to the Spanish and French.

---

[2]*Ibid.*, 381–82.
[3]Edmund S. Morgan, "Slavery and Freedom: The American Paradox," *Journal of American History*, 59 (1972–73): 16.

THE REESTABLISHMENT OF VIRGINIA

The English founded their first permanent settlement in the Americas at Jamestown, Virginia, in 1607. But it was not a colony at all, at least not in the sense of being a political unit governed by the mother country. Rather it was a business enterprise, the property of the Virginia Company of London, made up of stockholders and a governing board of directors that answered directly to James I. Its primary purpose was to return a profit to its shareholders—merchants, political figures at the royal court, and others who had invested capital in the hope that the English could duplicate the remarkable success of the Spanish and Portuguese in Mexico, Peru, and Brazil.

The King's charter to the Virginia Company of London began with the suggestion that the company concern itself with bringing the Christian religion to such people "as yet live in darkness and miserable ignorance of the true knowledge and worship of God." Christianizing the Indians of the Chesapeake area no doubt concerned many Englishmen, in a rivalry with Spain for the uncommitted peoples of the earth. (A recent analogy was the ideological struggle for the uncommitted people of the Third World by communist and capitalist countries after World War II.) But far more important in the minds of those who subscribed to shares in the Virginia Company was the desire to receive a return on their investment. Captain John Smith, who was to become a central figure in the drama unfolding in Virginia, later wrote: "We did admire how it was possible such wise men could so torment themselves and us with such strange absurdities and impossibilities: making Religion their colour, when all their aime was nothing but present profit. . . . For I am not so simple to think that any other motive than wealth will ever erect in Virginia a Commonweale."[4]

How would the Virginia Company enrich its stockholders? Nobody was quite sure, but it was assumed that profits in the New World would come in a variety of ways: through the discovery of gold and other minerals; by trade with the Indians; by production of pitch, tar, potash, and other products of the forest needed by the English navy; through the development of a fishing industry; and, best of all, by discovering the illusive passage through the American continent to Cathay. Some of these objectives had been realized in other English joint-stock ventures in Russia, in the Middle East, and in the Far East. Why not in North America?

Once sufficient capital was obtained, the principal problems were to recruit laborers who would go to the colony as employees of the Virginia Company and to establish the kind of administration and authority that would channel their energies toward the desired goals. Both of these problems proved thorny in the early years.

---

[4]Edward Arber and A.G. Bradley, eds., *Travels and Works of Captain John Smith* (Edinburgh: J. Grant, 1910), 2: 928.

The tiny fleet that set sail for Virginia in December 1606 carried about 120 colonists under the command of Captain Christopher Newport. Sixteen weeks later, after stopping in the West Indies for water and provisions, they made landfall on the Chesapeake Bay. Men and provisions went ashore, and a few weeks later the ships disappeared over the horizon, leaving the small band of Englishmen alone in an unknown land.

What followed in the next nine months, before Captain Newport returned with supplies and additional settlers, is a dismal tale of human weakness and misfortune. The sea-weary men explored the area, built a fort and shelters within it, planted crops, and organized a bit of fishing. But the colonists spent much of their time dividing into factions and organizing plots against each other. The supplies quickly dwindled, and the men were soon on starvation rations. Some deserted to the Indian villages where food was plentiful. Dysentery, caused by the brackish water of the drought-stricken Jamestown area, plagued the settlement. One of the members of the resident council of governors was expelled by his exasperated colleagues. A second was sentenced to execution as a spy for the Spanish, who were thought to be planning the elimination of the colony. A third was saved from hanging only by the arrival of the reprovisioning ships from England. When Newport returned in January 1608, only thirty-eight of the original settlers were still alive. Three days later fire destroyed most of the crude buildings in Jamestown and most of the freshly unloaded supplies.

Twice in 1608 and once in 1609 the Virginia Company of London sent out ships with new settlers and supplies. But the "starving time" continued and, as one of the leaders later wrote, "dissentions and jarrs were daily sowne amongst them [the settlers], so that they choaked the seed and blasted the fruits of all men's labors."[5] Although the Virginia Company sent more than 900 settlers to the colony in the first three years, by the winter of 1609–10 only sixty survivors remained, and some among them had resorted to cannibalism in their distress. In London, while the directors of the Virginia Company circulated promotional pamphlets such as *Good Speed to Virginia* and *Virginia Richly Valued*, street talk rumored that the colony was a dismal failure, and investors glumly counted the money they had wasted on this ill-starred enterprise. Men asked what had gone wrong with the plan to establish English presence in North America.

One of the flaws in the plans of English promoters of colonization was miscalculating the resources of the North American coast. Most investors and participants in the colony were hoping to duplicate the Spanish experience in Mexico and Peru. They dreamed of dragging from the earth the precious minerals that would make them wealthy. They hoped to utilize a native labor force or at least to profit from trade with the Indians. But Virginia was

[5]John Rolfe, *A Relation of the State of Virginia* (1616), quoted in Perry Miller, "Religion and Society in the Early Literature: The Religious Impulse in the Founding of Virginia," *William and Mary Quarterly*, 3d Ser., 6 (1949): 29.

not Mexico or Peru. Its earth contained neither gold nor silver, and thus all the frantic digging that was done in the early months and all the loading of ships with mica-speckled dirt, which the colonists thought must be gold, brought only a depletion of energy and shattered dreams. "Our gilded refiners, with their golden promises," wrote John Smith, "made all men their slaves in hope of recompence. There was no talke, no hope, nor worke, but dig gold, wash gold, refine gold, load gold [in order to load] a drunken ship with so much gilded [mica-filled] durt."[6]

Doubling the disappointment was their inability to utilize the labor of the Indians of the region. Most Englishmen who came to Virginia in the first years probably assumed that they could exploit the Indians of the New World. Upon their backs they would build a prosperous society. Cortés had conquered the mighty Aztec empire with a few hundred men and then turned the labor of thousands of Indians to Spanish advantage. Pizarro had done the same in Peru. Why should it not be so in Virginia?

But in the Chesapeake region the English found that the indigenous people were not so densely settled and could not be so easily subjugated. Smith later wrote that the Spaniards were fortunate enough to colonize "in those parts where there were infinite numbers of people who had manured the ground so that food was provided at all times."[7] Moreover, the Spanish got the "spoil and pillage" of the well-developed regions they colonized because they brought with them a military force capable of overpowering the native society. But the English settled in Virginia where there was no wealthy Indian empire to conquer. Nor could some 15,000 Indians of the Chesapeake region be molded into a labor force at the Europeans' command, for the English brought with them neither an army of conquistadors nor an army of priests to convert Indians to the European religion. Unable to exploit or utilize the native population, the Virginia settlers found the New World paradise far from utopian.

A third flaw in the English plan of settlement originated in the composition of the early settlers at Jamestown. Of those who arrived, many were gentlemen-adventurers ill equipped to undertake the rugged work of colony building, who proved to be only a drain on the tiny settlement's resources. By the same token there were far too few laborers and farmers—men who could cut trees, build houses, and till the soil. John Smith complained that a small number of adventure-seeking gentlemen would have been well enough; but "to have more to wait and play than worke, or more commanders and officers than industrious labourers" was foolishness, "for in Virginia a plaine Souldier that can use a pickaxe and spade, is better than five Knights."[8] Those who had been bred to a life of labor were not much better.

---

[6]Arber and Bradley, eds., *Works of Smith*, 1: 104.
[7]Quoted in Sigmund Diamond, "From Organization to Society: Virginia in the Seventeenth Century," *American Journal of Sociology*, 63 (1958): 460.
[8]*Ibid.*, 461.

"A more damned crew hell never vomited," growled the president of the Company. His opinion was echoed by one of Virginia's first historians, who described the original colonizers as "unruly Sparks, packed off by their Friends, to escape worse Destinies at home . . . , poor Gentlemen, broken Tradesmen, Rakes and Libertines, Footmen, and such Others, as were much fitter to spoil or ruin a Commonwealth, than to help to raise or maintain one."[9] This bizarre selection of colonists created manpower problems and also led to chronic social tension. Men of high social standing were regarded in England as essential to the strength and stability of society. But in a wilderness settlement on the edge of a vast, unknown continent, they only created resentment, unwilling to work themselves and unable to command the respect of those under them.

The most revealing example of the social tension in early Virginia is the case of Captain John Smith. Smith claimed no aristocratic blood; his father was a simple west country tenant farmer. Concluding at sixteen that life as a merchant's apprentice held nothing for him, Smith embarked on war as a career. Before reaching his mid-twenties he had traveled and fought his way across Europe and back as a professional mercenary in the employ of various local warlords. He fought duels in Transylvania, battled the Turks on the plains of western Hungary, was captured and enslaved for several years in Istanbul, escaped into Russia, and worked his way back to England by way of North Africa. His military experience, his skill as a cartographer, and his toughness suggested to Virginia's organizers that Smith would be a good man to have along when the going got rough.

Even on the ocean voyage Smith fell out with some of the leaders of the expedition, men with gentry blood flowing in their veins, and they clapped him in irons on the *Susan Constant.* When the secret orders were opened upon arrival on the Chesapeake, Smith discovered that he had been named a member of the Virginia governing council. This aroused further resentment. Smith had little patience with men who claimed that their social origins excused them from manual labor, and he did not hesitate to say so. As it happened, he was one of the few who possessed the courage and ability to explore and map the region around Jamestown, establish contact with the Indians, negotiate with them, and attempt rational organization of the colony's slender human resources. His exertions, however, alienated the gentlemen councilors around him, who saw his aggressiveness and disdain for their social superiority as a calculated attempt to gain control of the colony and to depose them in the process. They attempted to eliminate Smith as a dangerous influence at Jamestown, but by September 1608 Smith

[9]George Sandys to John Ferrar, 1623, in Susan M. Kingsbury, ed., *The Records of the Virginia Company of London* (Washington, D.C.: Government Printing Office, 1906–35), 4: 23; William Stith, *The History of the First Discovery and Settlement of Virginia* (New York: Joseph Sabin, 1865), p. 103.

had outlasted most of his enemies, and for a year he ruled the colony as president of the council.

REORGANIZATION AND TOBACCO

After three years of failure, the Virginia Company directors in London recruited ordinary farmers instead of soldiers of fortune. Under a new system of recruitment, about 1,200 new emigrants came to Virginia in 1610 and 1611 with promises of free land at the end of seven years' labor for the company. But even with new manpower the Virginia Company could not develop staple crops or find a way of returning a profit to its investors. By 1616 death and re-emigration to England had reduced the population to 350. Again the company raised the ante for going to the Chesapeake. This time they offered 100 acres of land outright to anyone who would journey to the colony. Instead of pledging limited servitude for the chance to become sole possessor of land, an Englishman trapped at the lower rungs of society at home could now become an independent landowner in no more time than it took to reach a ship carrying him to the Chesapeake. Now the company operated simply as an organization for the promotion and sale of land. Its aim was to encourage as many English settlers as possible to come to Virginia to pursue their fortunes independently. In time, if the colony proved itself valuable, its vast land resources could be sold profitably. Other concessions were made. In 1619 the company allowed the election of a representative assembly, which would participate in governing the colony and thus bind the colonists emotionally to the land. In the same year the company shipped a boatload of unmarried women to the colony in order to improve morale and touch off a small population explosion.

In response to these concessions more than 4,500 colonists arrived between 1619 and 1624. They no longer came as employees of the Virginia Company of London or as individuals to be governed entirely at the discretion of the resident council and the governing council in London. Through its failures, the company had learned that only by promising immediate ownership of land and by allowing a degree of local government could it hope to keep the colony alive and growing. After almost two decades, London entrepreneurs adjusted their original plans to match the realities of the New World.

The new inducements to settlement helped lift the colony out of the depths of social disorder and unprofitability of the early years. But crucial to Virginia's revival was the discovery that tobacco grew exceptionally well in the bottomlands of the Chesapeake region. Widely used in the seventeenth century as a mild narcotic, tobacco had first been brought to Portugal from Florida in the 1560s, a dubious gift of the New World to the

Old. But it was Francis Drake's boatload of the "jovial weed," procured in the West Indies in 1586 and then popularized among the upper class by Raleigh, that converted the plant from medicinal purposes to a social addiction. By the early seventeenth century the smoking craze swept England. Youngbloods developed various tricks and affectations as a part of the smoking cult: the "Ring," the "Whiffle," the "Gulp," and the "Retention" became a part of a new social habit. Even the opposition of King James could not arrest the popularity of smoking. Sounding like a modern physician, James anonymously published *Counterblast to Tobacco,* in which he described smoking as "a custom loathsome to the eye, hateful to the nose, harmful to the brain, dangerous to the lungs, and in the black stinking fumes thereof, nearest resembling the horrible stygian smoke of the pit that is bottomless." This was to no avail. English society, as well as Europeans everywhere, cried for more New World tobacco leaf, oblivious to the dangers lurking in its delights. At first the West Indies supplied the bulk of the crop, but experiments with tobacco culture in Virginia proved phenomenally successful. Virginia shipped its first crop to England in 1617; seven years later it exported 200,000 pounds of leaf, and by 1638 the crop exceeded three million pounds. Tobacco became to the Chesapeake region what sugar was to the West Indies and silver to Mexico and Peru.

Tobacco, of course, would not grow by itself, and as the demand grew, English planters on the Chesapeake sought a source of cheap labor. In the Spanish and Portuguese colonies the settlers had incorporated the native populations into a forced labor system that approximated slavery. But the English lacked the power in the early years to enslave the local tribes. So the tobacco planters looked to England for their labor supply—and particularly to the most depressed segment of the population, made up of young men and women willing to sell their labor for four to seven years in exchange for passage across the Atlantic and a chance, after they had served their time, to become independent landowners and tobacco planters. England was full of such people, for population growth and the enclosure of land had created an army of unemployed. "Our country [is] overspread," wrote a magistrate in Kent, "not only with unpunished swarms of idle rogues and counterfeit soldiers but also with numbers of poor and weak but unpitied servitors."[10]

Such impoverished immigrants were called *indentured servants* because they had committed themselves to serve a master for a specific period of time. They differed from the earlier employees of the Virginia Company only in that they had contracted their labor to an individual rather than to a company. Put to work in the tobacco fields, an indentured servant could tend about 1,000 to 2,000 tobacco plants, which could be expected to yield

[10]Quoted in Peter Clark, "The Migrant in Kentish Towns, 1580–1640," in Peter Clark and Paul Slack, eds., *Crisis and Order in English Towns, 1500–1700* (Toronto: University of Toronto Press, 1972), p. 117.

tobacco worth about £100 to £150 a year. Few men in England could generate an equivalent income for a year's labor.

After tobacco proved successful, Virginia landowners clamored for indentured servants in order to bring more land under cultivation. Brought to the colony by the shipload, these servants were auctioned at the dock to the highest bidder. The more servants a landowner could purchase, the greater the crop he could produce; larger crops brought more capital with which to purchase more land and additional servants. Thus, Edmund Morgan writes, "Virginia differed from later American boom areas in that success depended not on acquiring the right piece of land but on acquiring men.... Men rushed to stake out claims to men, stole them, lured them, fought over them—and bought and sold them, bidding up the prices to four, five, and six times the initial cost."[11]

Life for these indentured servants was nightmarish. If malarial fevers of the swampy Chesapeake area and malnutrition did not kill them within a few years, then the work routine imposed by masters, who treated them like cattle, usually did. Virginia's servants became the personal property of a small group of tough, ambitious planters in whom political and social power was so concentrated that they would brook no restraints on their behavior. What might happen to a man who challenged this system became apparent to an ordinary immigrant named Richard Barnes in 1624. His tongue loosened by alcohol in a local tavern, Barnes uttered some "base and detracting" words against the resident governor. For this it was ordered that he "be disarmed [and] have his armes broken and his tongue bored through with an awl [and] shall pass through a guard of 40 men and shalbe butted [with muskets] by every one of them and att the head of the troope kicked downe and footed out of the fort; that he shalbe banished out of James Citye and the Island, that he shall not be capable of any priviledge of freedome of the countrey ... [hereafter]."[12]

Barnes was not an indentured servant but a freeman; indentured servants who defied the will of the ruling group of tobacco planters found life could be even more hazardous. Servitude in early Virginia was different from early chattel slavery only in degree. Unrestrained by the courts, which in the mother country protected the rights of servants against unduly oppressive masters, servant owners treated their bondsmen as pieces of property. John Rolfe, one of the leading figures of the colony, reported in 1619 that the "buying of men and boys" and even the gambling at cards for servants in Virginia "was held in England a thing most intolerable." Six years later, an English merchant refused to take a boatload of indentured servants to Virginia because, as he explained, "servants were sold here up and down

[11]Edmund S. Morgan, *American Slavery, American Freedom: The Ordeal of Colonial Virginia* (New York: W.W. Norton & Co., 1975), pp. 114–15.
[12]*Ibid.*, p. 124.

like horses." What occurred in "boomtime Virginia" was "not only the fleeting ugliness of private enterprise operating temporarily without check, not only greed magnified by opportunity, producing fortunes for a few and misery for many," but also the beginning of "a system of labor that treated men as things."[13] No wonder, then, that of some 10,000 persons transported to Virginia between 1607 and 1622, only about 2,000 were still alive at the end of that period. "In steed of a plantacion," wrote one English critic, Virginia "will shortly gett the name of a slaughter house."[14]

ENGLISH–INDIAN RELATIONS

While Virginia's promoters adapted their plans to the realities of the Chesapeake environment, the settlers were not only devising means of exploiting the land and immigrant labor but also encountering the native people of the region. They simply could not develop the region's resources without directly confronting the original inhabitants of the land. From the time that the first Jamestown expeditions touched shore, Indians and Englishmen were in continuous contact in North America. Moreover, permanent settlement required acquisition of land by white settlers—land that was in the possession of native people. That single fact initiated a chain of events that governed the entire sociology of red–white relations.

Historians do not know exactly what Englishmen expected of the Algonquian occupiers of the land as they approached the Chesapeake Bay in the spring of 1607. Nor is it possible to be certain whether the Indian destruction of a Spanish Jesuit mission on the York River in 1571 bespoke a generalized hostility toward Europeans. But it is likely, given the English belief that the Roanoke colony had been reduced to a pile of bones by the Indians a generation earlier, and given the Indians' sporadic experience with Europeans as a militaristic people, that neither side was very optimistic about encountering each other. English pessimism must have intensified when Indians attacked the Jamestown expedition near Cape Henry, the most seaward point of land in the Chesapeake Bay region, where the first landfall was made. From this event on, the English proceeded with extreme caution, expecting violence and treachery from the Indians, even when they approached in outwardly friendly ways. When the one-armed Captain Newport led the first exploratory trip up the newly named James River, just weeks after a tiny settlement had been planted at Jamestown, he was confused by the friendly greeting. The Indians, a member of his group wrote, "are naturally given to trechery, howbeit we could not find it in our travell

[13]*Ibid.,* p. 129.
[14]Francis Jennings, *The Invasion of America: Indians, Colonialism and the Cant of Conquest* (Chapel Hill, N.C.: University of North Carolina Press, 1975), p. 79.

up the river, but rather a most kind and loving people."[15] This account describes how the Algonquians wined and dined the English, explaining that they were "at oddes" with other tribes, including the Chesapeake tribe that had attacked the English at Cape Henry.

It is now known that the Indians of the region were accurately describing their situation when they said they were "at oddes" with other tribes. Some forty small tribes lived in the Chesapeake Bay region. Powhatan was the paramount chief of about thirty of these, and in fact had forged the most centralized Algonquian polity in the south-eastern region. For years before the English arrived he had been consolidating his hold on the lesser tribes of the area, while warding off inland tribes of the Piedmont. In this situation Powhatan probably saw an alliance with the English as a means of extending his power in the tidewater area while simultaneously neutralizing the power of his western enemies. At the same time, his unpleasant experience with Europeans, including a clash just three years before with a passing English ship whose crew had been hospitably entertained but then had killed a local chief and kidnapped several Indians, no doubt made Powhatan wary of these newcomers. From the Powhatan viewpoint the newcomers "were potentially useful and potentially dangerous."[16]

John Smith and others quickly perceived the intertribal tensions as well as the linguistic differences among the Indians. But convincing themselves that some tribal leaders could find potential advantage in the arrival of the English was impossible. Perhaps because their position was so precarious, with dysentery, hunger, drought, and internal strife debilitating their tiny settlement, the English could only afford to regard all Indians as threatening. Hence, hostile and friendly Indians were seen as different only in their outward behavior. Inwardly they were identical—"savage," treacherous men who only waited for a chance to drive the English back into the sea from which they had come.

During the first months of contact, the confusion in the English mind surfaced again and again. In the autumn of 1607, during the "starving time," when food supplies were running perilously low and all but a handful of the Jamestown settlers had fallen too ill to work, the colony was saved by Powhatan. His men brought food to keep the struggling settlement alive until the sick recovered and the relief ship arrived. Many saw this as an example of Powhatan's covert hostility rather than as an attempt of the chief to serve his own interests through an alliance with the English. "It pleased God (in our extremity)," wrote John Smith, "To move the Indians to bring us Corne, ere it was halfe ripe, to refresh us, when we rather expected . . . they

---

[15]Philip L. Barbour, ed., *The Jamestown Voyages Under the First Charter, 1606–1609,* Hakluyt Society *Publications,* 2d Ser., 136 (London: The Hakluyt Society, 1969): 103–04.

[16]Helen C. Rountree, "The Powhatans and the English: A Case of Multiple Conflicting Agendas," in Rountree, ed. *Powhatan Foreign Relations, 1500–1722* (Charlottesville: University Press of Virginia, 1993), p. 178.

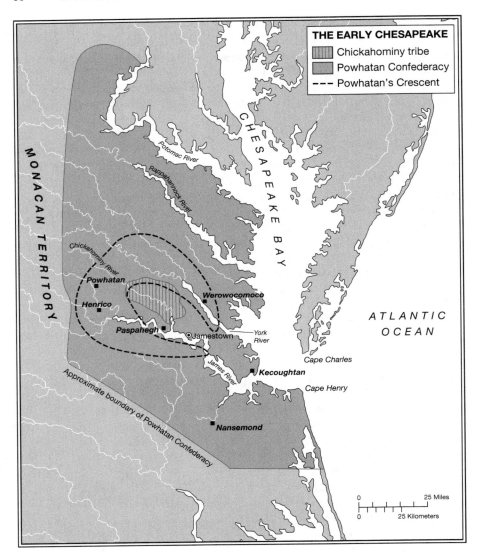

THE EARLY CHESAPEAKE

Chickahominy tribe
Powhatan Confederacy
Powhatan's Crescent

would destroy us."[17] As a man of military experience among "barbarian" people in other parts of the world, Smith was not willing to believe that the Indians, in aiding the colony, might have found the survival of the English in their own interest. Another leader of the colony could only attribute the Indians' generous behavior to the intervention of the white man's God. "If it had not pleased God to have put a terrour in the Savages heart," he wrote,

[17]Arber and Bradley, eds., *Works of Smith*, 1: 8–9.

"we had all perished by those wild and cruell Pagans, being in that weake estate as we were."[18]

In December 1607 Smith was captured during one of his exploratory incursions into Powhatan's country and marched to Werowocomoco, the seat of Powhatan's confederacy. Powhatan seems to have wanted to employ this opportunity to impress the English with his power, and thus arranged a mock execution ceremony for Smith. At the critical moment, as the executioners prepared to deliver the death blows, the chief's favorite daughter, Pocahontas, threw herself on Smith to save him. About twelve years old, Pocahontas had been a frequent visitor to Jamestown, undoubtedly as an emissary of her father, and was well known to Smith. But rather than understanding the rescue in symbolic terms, as Powhatan's way of indicating his strength but also his desire to forge a bond with the newcomers, Smith and other Virginians took Pocahontas's gesture as a spontaneous outburst of love for the English—an un-Indian-like act attributable to English superiority or perhaps to God's intervening hand. Hostility was on the English mind, sporadic hostility had already occurred, and Powhatan's deliverance of the English leader, at a time when the colony was almost defenseless, was thus not conceived as a conciliatory act.

In the aftermath of the incident, Pocahontas became a kind of ambassador from Powhatan to the struggling Jamestown colony, an agent who became fluent in the English language and kept her father informed on the state of the internally divided Englishmen. By late 1608, more colonists had arrived in Jamestown, and Smith, as the new president of council, adopted an aggressive stance, burning Indian canoes, fields, and villages in order to extort desperately needed Indian maize and to cow Powhatan and his lesser chiefs into submission. Aware that Virginia could not be resupplied from England every few months and that the colonists were unable to sustain themselves in their new environment, Smith sought a forced trade with Powhatan. But by now, Powhatan had determined to let the Englishmen starve, a policy made manifestly clear not only by his refusal to trade corn but by his withdrawal of Pocahontas. On penalty of death, Powhatan forbade his young daughter to enter the English settlement. "Captain Smith," warned Powhatan at a confrontation of the two leaders in January 1609, "some doubt I have of your coming hither, that makes me not so kindly seek to receive you as I would [like]. For many do inform me your coming is not for trade, but to invade my people and possess my country."[19]

Leading a colony where some men were deserting to the Indians while others starved, Smith raided Indian villages for provisions and slaughtered native people of both sexes and all ages. Colonists began to occupy Indian land in the James River valley. Powhatan retaliated by attacking the English

---

[18]Barbour, ed., *Jamestown Voyages*, 144–45.

[19]Quoted in Philip L. Barbour, *Pocahontas and Her World* (Boston: Houghton Mifflin Company, 1970), p. 46.

When John Smith published his *Generall Historie of Virginia* in 1624, London's Robert Vaughan provided sometimes fanciful illustrations of Smith's heroism. Here, in 1608, Smith seizes the gigantic Powhatan, chief of the Chesapeake Bay tribes, by the scalplock. In the background, English soldiers match firearms against Indian bows and arrows. Smith never bested Powhatan, but this early confrontation is accurate. (John Smith, *Generall Historie of Virginia*, London, 1624.)

wherever he could. Even the arrival of fresh supplies and several hundred new colonists in the summer of 1609 did not help, for the provisions were quickly exhausted, the men ravenously consuming more than they produced. When the relief ships departed in October 1609, with John Smith aboard one of them, Virginia embarked upon a winter of despair. Under the surveillance of Powhatan, who ambushed foraging colonists whenever he could, the death toll mounted. George Percy, Smith's successor, wrote that after the horses had been eaten, the dysentery-racked Virginians "were glad to make shift with [such] vermin as dogs, cats, rats, and mice." When these were exhausted, men resorted to "things which seem incredible, as to dig up corpses out of graves and to eat them—and some have licked up the blood which hath fallen from their weak fellows. And amongst the rest, this was most lamentable, that one of our colony murdered his wife, ripped the child out of her womb and threw it into the river, and after chopped the mother in pieces and salted her for his food, the same not being discovered before he had eaten part thereof."[20]

[20]Quoted in *ibid.*, pp. 64–65.

Powhatan's policy of withdrawing from trade with the encroachers had succeeded. By the spring of 1610 the Spanish ambassador to England, Alonso de Velasco, reported home that "the Indians hold the English surrounded in the strong place which they had erected there, having killed the larger part of them, and the others were left, so entirely without provisions that they thought it impossible to escape." Virginia could be easily erased from the map, Velasco counseled his government, "by sending out a few ships to finish what might be left in that place."[21] What the Spanish ambassador did not know was that two relief ships had reached Jamestown in May 1610 and found the situation so dismal that Sir Thomas Gates, arriving to assume the governorship of the colony, decided to embark the remaining sixty survivors, set sail for England, and admit that Englishmen had failed on the Chesapeake. On June 7, 1610, Gates ordered the forlorn settlement stripped of its meager possessions, loaded the handful of survivors aboard, and set sail down the James River for the open sea. The ships dropped anchor for the night after reaching the Chesapeake Capes and planned to start the return ocean voyage on the following day.

On the next morning three ships hove into sight. They carried 150 new recruits sent out by the Virginia Company and a new governor, Sir Thomas West, Lord De la Warr. Jamestown, at its moment of extinction, was reborn.

Newly armed and provisioned, the revitalized Jamestown colonists revived their militaristic Indian policy in what amounted to an on-again, off-again war between 1610 and 1613. The new attitude toward the Powhatan Confederacy was apparent in the orders issued in 1609 for governing the colony. Earlier, the Virginia Company had instructed, "In all your passages you must have great care not to offend the naturals, if you can eschew it."[22] Now the governor was ordered to effect a military occupation of the region between the James and York rivers; to make all tribes tributary to him rather than to Powhatan; to extract corn, furs, dyes, and labor from each tribe; and, if possible, to mold the natives into an agricultural labor force as the Spanish had done in their colonies. As the English settlement gained in strength, Smith's successors continued his policy of military foraging and intimidation. From 1610 to 1612 Powhatan attacked the colonists whenever opportunities presented themselves, and the English mounted fierce attacks that decimated three small tribes and destroyed two Indian villages. Much of the corn that sustained the colony in these years seems to have been extracted by force from Powhatan's villages, although tribes on the fringe of Powhatan's rule gladly traded maize for English shovels, hatchets, scissors, glass beads, and bells.

[21]Quoted in Grace Steele Woodward, *Pocahontas* (Norman, Okla.: University of Oklahoma Press, 1969), p. 120.

[22]E.G.R. Taylor, ed., *The Original Writing of Correspondence of the Two Richard Hakluyts*, Hakluyt Society *Publications*, 2d Ser., 77 (London: 1935): 494.

In 1613 the English kidnapped Pocahontas in a move designed to obtain a return of English prisoners and a quantity of weapons that the Indians had acquired over the years and, as Pocahontas's abductor, Captain Samuel Argall put it, to force payment of "a great quantitie of Corne."[23] Understanding that his daughter was not in harm's way, Powhatan made limited concessions to the English but refused to satisfy all the ransom conditions. In the following year, when the widower John Rolfe vowed to marry Pocahontas, Powhatan reluctantly assented to the first Anglo-Indian marriage in Virginia's history and signed a humiliating peace treaty. Pocahontas became the instrument of an uneasy truce between the two societies and returned to England with Rolfe and other members of Powhatan's Confederacy in 1616 in order to promote further colonization of the Chesapeake. She died on the eve of her return to Virginia in 1617, after helping to raise the money that pumped new lifeblood into the Virginia Company and consequently sent hundreds of new fortune-seekers to the Chesapeake as part of the population buildup that would lead to a renewal of hostilities five years after her death.

Notwithstanding misconceptions, suspicion, and violence on both sides, the English and the Powhatans lived in close contact during the first decade of English settlement, and cultural interchange and trade occurred on a broad scale. Although it has been a commonplace in the popular mind since the moment when Europeans and Native Americans first met that the Europeans were "advanced" and the Indians were "primitive," the technological differences between the two cultures were equaled or outweighed by the similarities between these two agricultural societies. The main technological advantages of the English were their ability to traverse large bodies of water in wooden ships and their superiority in fashioning iron implements and weapons. But the Indians quickly incorporated such iron-age items as kettles, fishhooks, traps, needles, knives, and guns into their material culture. In return they provided Englishmen with an understanding of how to use nets and weirs to catch the abundant fish and shellfish of the Chesapeake waters and introduced the intruders to a wide range of agricultural products unknown in Europe before 1492. Englishmen in Virginia learned from the natives how to cultivate tobacco, corn, beans, squash, pumpkins, and other food products. Algonquians also introduced the English to a wide range of medicinal herbs, dyes, and such important devices as the canoe.

Such cultural interaction proceeded even while hostility and sporadic violence was occurring in the early years. It was facilitated by Indians living among the English as day laborers, while a number of settlers fled to Indian villages rather than endure the autocratic English rulers and oppressive tobacco planters. This sojourning brought a knowledge and understanding of the other culture. Thus, even while the English pursued a policy of

[23]Quoted in Woodward, *Pocahontas,* p. 156.

intimidation in the early years, they recognized the resilience and strength of the Algonquians' culture. Smith marveled at the strength and agility of the Chesapeake tribesmen, at their talent for hunting and fishing, and admired their music and entertainment. He noted that they practiced civil government, that they adhered to religious traditions, and that many of their customs and institutions were not unlike those of the Europeans. "Although the countrie people be very barbarous," he wrote, "yet have they amongst them such government, as that their Magistrats for good commanding, and their people for due subjections, and obeying, excell many places that would be counted very civill." Other Englishmen, such as the Anglican minister Alexander Whitaker, who proselytized among the Indians, wrote that it was a mistake to suppose that the Indians were merely savage people, "for they are of body lustie, strong, and very nimble: they are a very understanding generation, quicke of apprehension, suddaine in their dispatches, subtile in their dealings, exquisite in their inventions, and industrious in their labour."[24] So, while both sides adjusted uneasily to the presence of the other, both were involved in cultural borrowing.

THE WAR OF 1622 AND ITS AFTERMATH

After the increase of population that accompanied the rapid growth of tobacco production, relations between the two peoples underwent a fundamental alteration. While giving Virginia an important money crop, the cultivation of tobacco created an enormous new demand for land. As more and more men pushed up the rivers that flowed into the Chesapeake Bay to carve out tobacco plantations, the Indians of the region perceived that what had previously been an abrasive and sometimes violent relationship might now become a disastrous one. Powhatan had retired in 1617, just as tobacco cultivation began to expand rapidly. His younger brother, Opechancanough, who assumed leadership of the tidewater tribes, concluded that he must embark upon a program of military renaissance and spiritual revitalization.

Opechancanough was battling not only against land-encroaching Englishmen but against the diseases they were spreading among the Indian population. The deadliest of all European weapons were the microorganisms brought ashore in nearly every immigrant. In the Chesapeake region minor epidemics had taken their toll in the 1580s and again in 1608. Between 1617 and 1619 another epidemic decimated the Powhatan tribes.

In leading a reorganization of his people, Opechancanough relied heavily on Nemattanew, a war captain and religious prophet whom the English

[24]Arber and Bradley, eds., *Works of Smith*, 1: 43–84; Whitaker, *Good News from Virginia* (1613), quoted in Roy H. Pearce, *The Savages of America: A Study of the Indian and the Idea of Civilization* (Baltimore: The Johns Hopkins University Press, 1953), p. 13.

called "Jack of the Feathers" for the "fantastick Manner" in which "he would often dress himself up with Feathers . . . as though he meant to flye."[25] A shadowy figure who came often to the English settlements, Nemattanew had convinced his tribesmen that he was immortal and that they would be immune to musket fire if they rubbed their bodies with a special ointment. In March 1622, as Opechancanough was piecing together plans for a unified attack on the Virginia settlements, the English murdered Nemattanew in retaliation for a settler death. Nemattanew's death triggered the famous Indian assault two weeks later that dealt the colony a staggering blow; but the highly combustible atmosphere generated by a half-dozen years of white expansion and pressure on Indian hunting lands was the fundamental cause of the attack.

Although it did not achieve its goal of ending English presence in the Chesapeake area, the Indian attack of 1622 and the famine that followed it wiped out nearly half of the white population. Included among the victims was Opechancanough's nephew by marriage, John Rolfe. It was the final straw for the Virginia Company of London, which declared bankruptcy and left the colony to the governance of the Crown.

The more important result was that those who survived the attack felt free to pursue a ruthless new Indian policy. Even though several leaders in the colony confided to men in England that the real cause of the Indian attack was "our owne perfidious dealing with them," it was generally agreed that henceforward the colonists would be free to hunt down the Indians wherever they could be found. Abandoning an obligation to "civilize" and Christianize the native, the Virginians adopted a no-holds-barred approach to "the Indian problem." One Virginian wrote revealingly after the attack:

> Our hands which before were tied with gentleness and faire usage, are now set at liberty by the treacherous violence of the Sauvages. . . . So that we, who hitherto have had possession of no more ground than their waste and our purchase at a valuable consideration to theire owne contentment gained; may now by right of Warre, and law of Nations, invade the Country, and destroy them who sought to destroy us; whereby wee shall enjoy their cultivated places, turning the laborious Mattacke into the victorious Sword . . . and possessing the fruits of others labours. Now their cleared grounds in all their villages (which are situate in the fruitfullest places of the land) shall be inhabited by us, whereas heretofore the grubbing of woods was the greatest labour.[26]

[25]J. Frederick Fausz, "The Powhatan Uprising of 1622: A Historical Study of Ethnocentrism and Cultural Conflict" (Ph.D. dissertation, College of William and Mary, 1977), pp. 346–49.

[26]Edward Waterhouse, "A Declaration of the State of the Colony and Affaires in Virginia . . ." (1662), in Kingsbury, ed., *Records of Virginia Company,* 3: 556–57.

In these sentences one can detect a note of grim satisfaction that the Indians had succeeded in wiping out one-third of the English population. John Smith, writing from England two years after the attack, noted that some men held that the attack "will be good for the Plantation, because now we have just cause to destroy them by all meanes possible." Another writer expressed the prevalent genocidal urge by reasoning that the Indians had done the colonists a favor by sweeping away the previous English reluctance to annihilate the Indians. He enumerated with relish the ways that the "savages" could be exterminated. "Victorie," he wrote, "may be gained many waies; by force, by surprize, by famine in burning their Corne, by destroying and burning their Boats, Canoes, and Houses, by breaking their fishing Weares [weirs], by assailing them in their huntings, whereby they get the greatest part of their sustenance in Winter, by pursuing and chasing them with our horses, and blood-Hounds to draw after them, and Mastives to teare them."[27]

Once the Virginians slaked their thirst for revenge, the only debatable point was whether the extermination of the tidewater Indian tribes would work to the benefit or disadvantage of the colony. One prominent planter offered "reasons why it is not fitting utterlye to make an exterpation of the Savages yett" and then assured his neighbors that he was not against genocide *per se* but opposed the destruction of a people who, if properly subjugated, could enrich all Virginians through their labor. But both subjugation and assimilation required more time and trouble than the Virginians were willing to spend. The simpler course, consistent with instructions from London to "root out [the Indians] from being any longer a people," was to follow a scorched earth policy, sending military expeditions each summer to destroy villages and crops.[28] In 1629 the council negotiated a peace treaty but then rejected it because a state of "perpetual enmity" would serve the colony better. The acculturation of the two people, even if possible, was not desirable.

For a number of years after the 1622 attack, the Virginians were too weak to carry out their genocidal urges on native peoples. But by 1640 Virginia had grown to about 8,000 settlers. By 1662 the population had swelled to 25,000 and the colony was shipping 7 million pounds of tobacco a year to England. Although the Crown appointed a royal governor to rule in conjunction with an appointed council and an elected House of Burgesses, the real power in the colony lay at the local level, where each tobacco planter operated autonomously with little regard for centralized authority. Men like Governor John Harvey, appointed in 1626, could complain that

[27] *Travels and Works of Smith*, 2: 578–79; Waterhouse, "State of the Colony," in Kingsbury, ed., *Records of Virginia Company*, 3: 557.
[28] John Martin, "The Manner Howe to Bringe the Indians into Subjection," in Kingsbury, ed., *Records of Virginia Company*, 3: 705–07.

these planters acted "rather for their owne endes than either seekinge the generall good or doinge right to particular men."[29] But he could do little to foster a spirit of community or curb the appetites of the land-hungry, profit-conscious tobacco planters. When he proposed a lasting peace with the Indians and that the Chesapeake tribes be left unmolested on the land they were occupying, the planters refused to cooperate. These were men who had clawed their way to the top of the rough-hewn frontier society. They eagerly conducted a fur trade with more distant tribes, but they had no intention of allowing the governor to interfere with their takeover of large tracts of land or their continuation of an aggressive Indian policy in the tidewater region. When Harvey tried again in 1635 to impose his will, Virginia's leaders plotted against him, provoked violence, and evicted him from the colony while sending petitions back to the mother country complaining of his arbitrary and unreasonable policies.

It was such tough, self-made, ambitious men as these, unhindered by religious or humanitarian concern for the Indians and unrestrained by government, that the Chesapeake tribes had to confront after 1630. They also had to face the rapidly shifting population balance—the drastic decline of their numbers by disease and war during the first quarter-century of English presence and the rapid increase of English colonists after 1624. These factors were beyond the control of the Chesapeake tribes. Even so, the natives continued to follow their traditional way of life. Years of contact with European culture had done little to convince them that they should remodel their religion, social and political organization, or values and beliefs on English patterns. Powhatan's people eagerly incorporated technological innovations and material objects of the newcomers into their culture, but they resisted or rejected the other aspects of European life.

Though greatly weakened by disease and war, many Algonquians were still determined to drive out the English intruders rather than adapt to an alien culture. Though far fewer in number than in 1622, Powhatan confederacy tribesmen attacked in April 1644 under the leadership of the aged Opechancanough. His warriors carried him into battle on a litter. That the young warriors were willing to risk an all-out attack, knowing the grim reprisals that would rain down on them if they were defeated, indicates "the stubborn resistance of the Indians to cultural annihilation."[30]

The Powhatan tribes were again the losers in the war of 1644, although they killed hundreds of colonists, about one-twelfth of the white population. They lost partially because the aid they expected from white Marylanders, whose relations with Virginia had always been abrasive, did not materialize.

---

[29]Quoted in Bernard Bailyn, "Politics and Social Structure in Virginia," in James Smith, ed., *Seventeenth-Century America: Essays in Colonial History* (Chapel Hill, N.C.: University of North Carolina Press, 1959), p. 97.

[30]Nancy Lurie, "Indian Cultural Adjustment to European Civilization," in *Seventeenth-Century America*, pp. 51–52.

Yet their determination apparently convinced the Virginians that Indians could rarely be cowed into submissiveness. Rather than risk future wars, the colonists altered the policy of the 1620s by signing a formal treaty in 1646 with the survivors of the Powhatan Confederacy. It drew a line between red and white territory and promised the Indians safety in their territory north of the York River. In return the Powhatan tribes agreed to render military assistance in the event of an attack by tribes outside the Chesapeake area and promised a yearly tribute of beaver skins to the Virginia colony in acknowledgement of their subject status. Powhatan's Confederacy died with this peace treaty.

When Virginians took a census in 1669, only 11 of the 28 tribes described by John Smith in 1608 and only about 2,900 of the 20,000 Indians present when the English arrived remained in the colony. The English victory in the clash of the two societies was mostly due to the continued immigration of new settlers to the colony during an era when disease drastically thinned the Indian ranks. Also important to the Indians' decline was their inability to unite against the incoming European peoples. They outnumbered the English during the first two decades of settlement and might have expected to be further aided by the fierce internal divisions that gripped the Virginia colony for years. But in times of military crisis the colonists were better able to unite, if only momentarily, than the tribes of the Chesapeake region.

A more indirect factor in the decay of Indian strength was the growing functionlessness of the Chesapeake tribes after the English no longer depended on the maize trade. This can be best understood by looking comparatively at the English and Spanish systems of colonization. In the Spanish colonies, the densely settled Indians had been utilized effectively as a subjugated labor force, both in the silver mines and in agriculture. The Spanish had unerringly located the native population centers in Mexico and Peru and made them the focal points of their colonizing efforts. The Indians supplied the bulk of the labor for Spanish extractive and productive enterprises in the early decades; hence it was not only desirable but necessary to assimilate them into the European culture. Moreover, the Spanish church had a vested interest in the Indians. It sent hundreds of missionaries to the colonies to obtain as many conversions as possible for the greater glory of the church. Also, because the Spanish immigrants were disproportionately male, Indian women served the function of mistress, concubine, and wife. Though regarded as inferior to Spanish women, thousands of them became the sexual partners, inside and outside marriage, of Spanish men and in this way were of the utmost importance to the colonizers. Of course none of these roles could be fulfilled until the native societies had been subordinated to Spanish authority. And the Spanish employed the most merciless forms of mass killing and terrorization to ensure their ascendancy in the first period of contact. Thereafter, Spanish colonizers regarded native peoples not primarily as a threat, though the possibility of native uprisings was always present, but as a population that could answer the economic, religious, and biological needs of the settlers. In spite of the catastrophic spread of European diseases, which reduced the Indian population by as much as 75 percent in the first century of contact, an impressive degree of acculturation and assimilation took place in the Spanish colonies.

In English Virginia none of these factors pertained except in the most limited way. The English brought no military force comparable to the conquistadors to subjugate the Chesapeake tribes and drive them into agricultural labor. The Anglican Church sent only a handful of clergymen to the colony, and they made only token efforts to mount a missionary campaign. Their power over local settlers so far as relations with the Indians was concerned was minimal. Nor was there any significant sexual conjoining of English males and native women, partly because of English squeamishness about women of another culture but probably even more because Indian women, living in tribes not subjugated by the English, had no inclination to consort with men of the intruding society. Interracial marriages were almost unknown in Virginia except in frontier areas where trappers and traders often made liaisons with native women.

Only in the maize and fur trade, where the Indian was food producer, trapper, and skin dresser, did the natives serve the needs of the white colonist. But the trade for corn lasted only until the colonists became self-sufficient by about 1616, and the fur trade was of negligible importance in the early Virginia settlements. What the colonists primarily wanted from the Indian was cleared land. Within the first generation of European settlement, neither side possessed the military capacity to subjugate the other. But for the English subjugation was unnecessary. With little to contribute to the goals of English colonization, native people were regarded mostly as an obstacle. In an almost perfect reversal of Spanish Indian policy the English in Virginia after 1622 worked to keep the two cultures apart. Like the Spanish policy, this plan was based on calculations of self-interest. Differences in the exploitable resources of the Spanish and English colonies, in the density of Indian population, in the demographic composition of the colonizing and colonized societies, and in the social backgrounds of the colonists, rather than differences in national character, in attitudes toward the indigenous people, or in national policy, were chiefly responsible for the pursuit of assimilation in Spanish America and the goal of racial separation in Virginia.

4

Cultures Meet in the Northeast

While Indians of the Powhatan confederacy were planning their attack on the white settlements of Virginia in 1622, Dutch and English colonizers were entering Indian territory hundreds of miles to the north. The commerce-minded Dutch got the first foothold in the northeastern Atlantic seaboard. Therefore, the religion-minded Pilgrims and Puritans who followed would have to reckon carefully with the Dutch presence and their trading relationships with native peoples.

Whether they were Dutch or English, the European newcomers came face to face with diverse Algonquian peoples, some of them composing largely autonomous small tribes and others, such as the Iroquois, that were populous, powerful, and organized into confederacies. Relationships among all these Indian societies, sometimes amicable and often hostile, went back hundreds of years. Into this maze of Indian relations, contending Europeans made their way filled with ambition and uncertainties.

THE DUTCH IN THE NORTHEAST

Hollanders had achieved independence from their own colonial masters, the Spanish, only in 1609. But even by then they had become the principal carriers of seaborne commerce in Western Europe and had begun interloping in the Spanish and Portuguese trade to the New World. Settlers, glad to get more favorable prices from the Dutch in the cloth and slave trade, traded illegally with them. Then, in a generation of spectacular achievement, the Dutch leaped to the front of the race for wealth in the Americas. In 1621 Dutch merchants and investors launched the Dutch West India Company, impressively capitalized and fully supported by the government. Its goals were commerce and conquest—to gain control of as much of the European–African–New World trade as possible and to plant colonies wherever the opportunity arose.

Success came quickly. Within a few decades the Dutch company had acquired so much power that it perhaps exerted more influence in the second quarter of the seventeenth century than do American megacorporations in the late twentieth century. In 1628 its fleet intercepted and captured the entire annual Spanish flotilla, homeward bound from the Caribbean. The Dutch scooped up enough gold in this single exploit—about fifteen million guilders—to pay a 50 percent dividend to the Company's shareholders with enough left over to finance a military campaign against the Portuguese settlements in northeastern Brazil. For the next half century the Dutch controlled shipping to the New World, reducing Spanish and Portuguese trade to insignificance.

At the same time, the Dutch began to take over the African slave trade of their competitors. By 1637, when they captured Elmina Castle, the center of Portuguese slaving activities on the Gold Coast, they had all but driven the Portuguese from the Atlantic slave trade. Soon they seized Spanish bases—Curaçao, Saba, St. Martin, and St. Eustatius. This was accompanied by assaults on Portuguese Brazil, culminating in 1630, when the Dutch overwhelmed the Portuguese and took control of their profitable sugar plantations on the northeast coast, the most important source of sugar for the kitchens of Europe. Other arms of the vast Dutch trading empire reached the East Indies, India, Ceylon, and Formosa.

The mighty Dutch also made their distinctive imprint on the North American mainland. Henry Hudson, sailing as an employee of the Dutch East India Company, initiated a trade in furs with the Indians in 1609. Five years later the Dutch established a trading post high on the Hudson River near Albany. Shortly after the chartering of the West India Company in 1621 they planted New Amsterdam on the present site of New York City. This became the center of Dutch colonization in North America for the next half century. As early as 1628, the small Dutch settlement was sending home 8,000 furs a year, linking their economy closely to their Indian neighbors.

The Indians engaging in trade with Dutchmen were the descendants of nomadic hunters who had come to the region some 8,000 years before. Living on the margin of the agricultural zone, their economy combined hunting, fishing, and agriculture, though the latter, by the time the Dutch arrived, was their primary subsistence activity. Utilizing their environment seasonally, they engaged in winter hunting, spring stream fishing, and autumn harvesting and hunting.

A sexual division of labor was marked among the Algonkian tribes. Men hunted and fished, but women were responsible for all phases of agriculture—planting, maintaining, and harvesting crops—as well as for fishing and gathering wild plant products. Since agriculture had become the most important component of the economy, a distinct imbalance had evolved in the productivity of the two sexes. This did not lead, as in the case of the Iroquois, to the adoption of a matrilineal kinship system or the conferring of a degree of political power upon women. In most of the Northeast kinship remained patrilineal, and men continued to dominate political and religious life.

Political leadership of Algonkian tribes in the Northeast was held by single individuals, called "sachems" or "sagamores." The sachem's role was to coordinate, at the village level, activities that concerned the group as a whole—hunting, trade, the administration of justice, and diplomacy. The sachem's authority depended heavily on maintaining the consent of his people. This, in turn, depended on the sachem's ability to communicate with the spiritual forces controlling the fate of the tribe. "Their authority is most precarious," wrote one Frenchman among the Abenaki, "if indeed, that may be called authority to which obedience is in no wise obligatory."[1] Sachems and sagamores were not chiefs or lords whose title was inherited and authority unquestioned, but "coordinators and ceremonial representatives for their people."[2]

In the pre-contact period the Algonquian-speaking people of the Northeast were more densely settled than in the Chesapeake region, probably numbering more than 125,000 between Maine and New York. Among them, the most numerous were the Abenaki, Pawtucket, Massachusett, Narragansett, Pequot, Wampanoag, Mahican, and Mohawk. All of these groups had been in contact with Europeans for many generations. Fishermen who dried their catches and engaged in minor trade had provided the northerly tribes with knowledge of European culture since the first quarter of the sixteenth century, and short-lived French and English attempts at settlement in the first decade of the seventeenth century gave them further understanding of the people from across the sea.

The Dutch radiated out in small numbers from New Amsterdam. They planted settlements to the north in the Connecticut River valley, to the south in the Delaware River valley and to the east on Long Island. Their numbers were not large, and in time they would be overwhelmed by the

---

[1]Reuben Gold Thwaites, ed., *The Jesuit Relations and Allied Documents, 1610–1791* (Cleveland: Burrows Brothers Company, 1896), II: 73.

[2]Neal Salisbury, *Manitou and Providence: Indians, Europeans, and the Making of New England, 1500–1643* (New York: Oxford University Press, 1982), p. 42.

more numerous English. But their power at sea was never to be underestimated, as Virginians found out as late as 1667, when Dutch raiders captured twenty tobacco ships in the James River, and in 1672 when they repeated this success. While the Dutch never settled more than 10,000 people in their Middle Atlantic colonies, they were able to exert a strong influence on English affairs. When three Anglo–Dutch wars erupted in Europe between 1650–1675, the colony at New Netherland became a target of English attack. It was captured by the English in 1664, recaptured by the Dutch in 1673, and then was almost immediately retaken by the English. This marked the end of Dutch political authority in North America.

For the Dutch, so long as the fur trade was thriving and represented the primary source of profit in New Netherland, relations with the Mahicans of the Albany area and the local tribes in the vicinity of New Amsterdam remained amicable. The Dutch did their utmost to preserve the Indians' goodwill because they were vastly outnumbered and dependent upon the Indian trade for profit. They needed the Indians far more than the Indians needed them. Unlike the Virginians on the Chesapeake or the Puritans in New England, the Dutch immigrated in small numbers, and their principal goal was not farming but the profitable bartering of European trade goods for the skins of the beaver, otter, and deer. From the Indian point of view there was little to fear from the Dutch presence, for these bearded Europeans were few in number, showed no voracious appetite for land, and eagerly traded commodities that Indians wanted and could obtain by trapping animals that existed abundantly in their territory.

As desirable as exchanging furs and skins for European trade goods seemed to Indian societies, it contained a hidden danger of utmost significance. Prior to the arrival of Europeans, Indians had hunted for subsistence, their modest needs ensuring the conservation of game. But once the skins of fur-bearing animals became incorporated into the international Atlantic market, Indians began hunting relentlessly to satisfy their trading partners. Under such conditions Indian hunters quickly exhausted the beaver supply in particular areas. When this occurred, as it did to Mahican suppliers of the Dutch during the first quarter of the seventeenth century, the fur merchants of the Dutch West India Company began to cultivate their enemies, the Mohawks, the easternmost of the Iroquois tribes whose territories stretched westward to the Great Lakes. The Mohawks eclipsed the Mahicans, became the major supplier of pelts to the Dutch, and were transformed into a formidable power in the Northeast.

The tendency of the Dutch fur trade to trigger or intensify intertribal hostilities became more pronounced in the second quarter of the seventeenth century. To the north of the Dutch settlements the French were also building a fur trade with the powerful Hurons, who commanded the territories north of the Great Lakes. In time, the depletion of furs in the tribal territories under Iroquois control enticed them into attacking the Hurons.

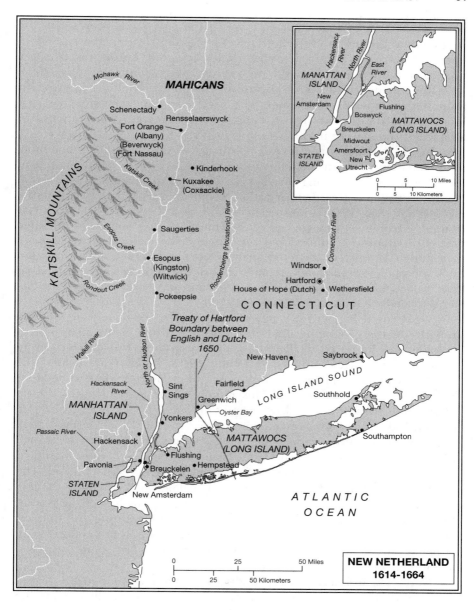

If successful, the Iroquois could divert the vast fur resources of the Canadian north from Montreal, the center of French trading activities, to Albany, the main Dutch trading post. Within the context of inter-European rivalry this was a commercial effort to make Amsterdam rather than Paris the major recipient of North American beaver skins. For the Dutch it could be accomplished entirely through diplomacy—the cultivation of ties with the Iroquois and the supply of firearms necessary to destroy the Hurons. Within the context of inter-Indian rivalry, diplomacy with Europeans began a process that often moved quickly to a second stage dominated by warfare. The Iroquois desire to obtain control of distant Huron hunting grounds, assuming the role of middlemen who received pelts from more westerly hunters and transported them eastward to the Dutch at Albany, intensified an ancient smoldering Iroquois–Huron hostility.

In the new world of European–Indian trade, it took only a few thousand Dutch and French intruders to wreak havoc on one populous Indian society while strengthening another. In the second quarter of the seventeenth century the great Huron nation, comprising 30,000 people or more, was severely weakened by European diseases and then nearly destroyed by Iroquois enemies seeking control of the Huron's beaver supply. At the same time the victorious Iroquois used the Dutch trade connection to increase their power. All this was triggered by tiny Dutch and French settlements and trading posts scattered along the waterways of the St. Lawrence and Hudson River valleys whose population, even after almost a half century of settlement, totaled no more than 3,000.

What could happen to smaller Indian tribes, which had neither the strength nor the geographical advantage to play a role in the all-important fur trade, was illustrated by the fate of the dozen or so Indian bands living in the vicinity of New Amsterdam in the 1640s. A few years before, the Dutch West India Company had begun recruiting more settlers to build up an agricultural base of society. This required land purchases from local Indian bands such as the Rockaways and Carnasees. Having sold their land, however, the Indians saw no reason to leave it until Dutch farmers took it up. Now agriculturists from both societies lived side by side in areas such as Long Island, Rockaway, and Staten Island. When Dutch cattle trampled Indian fields or the Indian dogs attacked Dutch cattle, tempers flared. The governor of the Dutch West India Company, Willem Kieft, added to the tension by taxing all local Indians to repair the sagging finances of the colony. The Indians resisted this attempt to exact tribute, venturing the opinion that Kieft "must be a very mean fellow to come and live in this country without being invited . . . and now wish to compel them to give them their corn for nothing."[3]

Dutch expansion and sharp trading with Indian bands in the region soon produced sporadic violence. When this involved loss of life among the Dutch, they demanded the surrender of the responsible Indians to their system of justice. As permanent settlers and agriculturists, the Dutch, like the Puritans in New England, sought unequivocal recognition of their sovereignty.

[3]Quoted in Allen W. Trelease, *Indian Affairs in Colonial New York: The Seventeenth Century* (Ithaca, N.Y.: Cornell University Press, 1960), p. 66.

By 1643, when local tribal chiefs refused to buckle under, the Dutch resorted to military force. Eighty Dutch soldiers led by John Underhill, who had slaughtered the Pequots at Mystic Fort six years before, fell upon two encampments of Wequasesgeeks, who had been granted refuge from their Indian enemies by the Dutch. The Dutch soldiers butchered women and children as well as men. Through this genocidal attack Governor Kieft made clear to all tribes within New Amsterdam's orbit that they must accept Dutch trading terms, pay tribute when required, and recognize Dutch authority.

Dutch–Indian relations in the New Amsterdam region did not differ significantly from English contacts with native societies on the Chesapeake. After the first few decades, little was to be gained from trade since the beaver in the area had been exhausted and the Dutch depended on their Albany traders to tap the rich fur resources of the interior. Nor did the local Indians serve any useful purpose as potential converts to the Dutch form of Christianity. The Dutch West India Company had little interest in sending over missionaries to convert the local Indians, who were looked upon as ignorant, brutish people separated from the Dutch by an unbridgeable gulf. Neither did the Dutch require Indian wives, for they were plentifully supplied with women from their homeland.

In this situation, with land settlement replacing trading as the dominant economic activity, the local tribes became only obstacles to Dutch expansion and Dutch authority. With the native people composed of separate small bands, it was all the easier for the Dutch to fix upon a military solution to the "Indian problem." Many Indians attempted to resist Dutch authority, but their strength was ebbing after decades of killer diseases and attritional warfare. When the English overpowered the Dutch in New Netherland in 1664, they encountered only demoralized remnants of an earlier Indian population.

By contrast Dutch–Indian relations at Albany were peaceful and profitable. Probably not more than one hundred Dutch resided there in the 1640s, but they neither attacked nor were attacked by the powerful Mohawks, for both peoples admirably served each other's needs. Even though they were greatly outnumbered, the Albany settlers did not hesitate to sell arms and ammunition to their Indian trade partners. By contrast, in New Amsterdam, where the colonists were far more numerous than the Indians and the Indians far more divided, the Dutch enforced strict regulations against the sale of firearms.

This policy is understandable when the competition for land in the New Amsterdam region is compared with the cooperative activities of Dutch and Mohawks in the Albany region. The Dutch provided firearms to the Mohawks knowing that they would be used to gain control over Huron tribesmen aligned with the French. Every gun in Indian hands contributed to the profitable flow of beaver skins to Amsterdam by way of the Hudson River rather than to Paris by way of the St. Lawrence River. Such a lucrative trade did not necessarily bring mutual respect and admiration between

Dutch and Mohawks. Thefts, attacks on animals, and trampled fields were also common in the mixing of the two societies. But as the most careful historian of Indian relations in seventeenth-century New Netherland has written, "Peace was maintained because both sides had everything to lose and nothing to gain by hostilities. . . . The two races regarded each other less often as corn thieves, trespassers, or Indian givers than as sources of economic prosperity; what they thought of each other personally was beside the point."[4]

When England, after a generation of civil conflict culminating in the restoration of Charles II in 1660, decided to make a second great effort in colonizing the West Indies and the North American mainland, the Dutch colony of New Netherland became a prime objective. To take it would remove the Hollanders entirely from the eastern seaboard and consolidate the English empire in North America.

To this end an English military expedition seized New Netherland in 1664. New Netherland became New York, and its Dutch inhabitants were obliged to incorporate themselves into the English colonial system. Though several generations would pass before the English made up even half the population of New York, political authority, trade, and military affairs were now securely contained within the British imperial system.

For the Indians of New York, the change of political authority meant little. Insofar as their relations with Europeans were concerned, Dutch and English were hardly distinguishable. Nothing in the takeover of the English could change the fact that disease and war had already decimated the Algonkian tribes on the lower Hudson. Nor were the English inclined to alter matters, as they had now taken over a European administration on which the local Indians had become pathetically dependent. The English undoubtedly counted it as their good fortune that they were the new masters in an area where the work of subjugating the indigenous population had already been accomplished. Nor were they more inclined than the Dutch to proselytize among the local tribes when more important commercial matters laid claim to their energies.

In the last third of the seventeenth century the small tribes of Manhattan, Long Island, and the lower Hudson River valley declined further. The Indian population dwindled as the natives struggled for existence through a mixture of hunting, fishing, farming, and day labor in white settlements. Their relationship to the Europeans became almost entirely servile. A Long Islander summed it up in 1670: "There is now but a few upon the Island, and those few no ways hurtful but rather serviceable to the English, and it is to be admired, how strangely they have decreast by the Hand of God, since the English first setling of those parts."[5]

---

[4]*Ibid.,* p. 115.
[5]Daniel Denton, *A Brief Description of New York* (1670), quoted in *ibid.,* p. 179.

Hostile Indians had become friendly Indians, but the friendliness was only the outward expression of internal social and political disorganization and the cultural dependency that accompanied it. In this state of demoralization alcohol became ever more important to the local tribes. But while serving as a painkiller for the eroded quality of life, it contributed further to the Indians' demise. Dutch authorities prohibited selling alcohol to Indians, "yet every one does it," remarked one observer in 1679.[6] Two years later a Minisink sachem bitterly remonstrated that alcohol had caused the death of sixty of his people in three years. The provincial council was several times obliged to affirm in the next decade that Indians in the colony "are free and not slaves" and should not be made lifetime servants against their will. This was poignant proof that the dwindling Indian population was losing not only its cultural autonomy but its physical freedom as well.

At Albany the advent of the English brought no significant change in Indian relations. The Iroquois continued to deal with merchants who were primarily Dutch, to negotiate through interpreters who were Dutch, and to receive European goods in return for their furs. The furs, of course, after passing through New York, traveled to English rather than Dutch markets, and the goods they received originated in a different part of the European world; but this was of little consequence to the Iroquois trappers. Far more important than the substitution of English for Dutch political administration was the fact that the fur trade itself had been in a state of long-term decline since about 1660. Nothing in the English conquest of the colony could reverse this trend because the decline was caused by the exhaustion of the beaver east of the Great Lakes and the difficulties of outwitting the French for control of the western beaver sources.

PURITANISM

If the Algonkian Indians of the Northeast were learning about the dangers of trade with small numbers of Dutch traders and settlers, they would realize by the 1630s that a different breed of European, intensely religious, was swarming to their ancient homelands. The most numerous of these English, they would learn, called themselves Protestants.

Puritanism was, among other things, a religious reform movement. Since the reign of Henry VIII, when England had turned toward Protestantism, Catholic–Protestant tensions had racked the country. When Elizabeth ascended the throne in 1558, she attempted to effect a religious compromise. But avowed anti-Catholics regarded the Church of England that flourished under her reign as at best a halfway house between a corrupt and a pure

[6]*Journal of Jaspar Danckaerts, 1679–1680,* ed. Bartlett B. James and J. Franklin Jameson (New York: Charles Scribner's Sons, 1913), p. 79.

church and at worst barely distinguishable from the Church of Rome with its liturgy, vestments, rituals, and oppressive bureaucracy. Some of them wanted greater purity in the church, a more radical cleansing of Catholic elements. Thus they became known as purifying radicals or Puritans.

Puritanism was also a political and social response to long-range changes that had been occurring in English society. Men and women of this era lived at a time when the traditional feudal society was giving way to what we now think of as a more modern social order. This brought the overturning of the traditional church, the growth of cities, the enclosure of land, an increase in trade, and the rise of a capitalistic society in which the individual had far more autonomy. The most visible social effects of these long-term trends were uprooted peasants cast off the land, an increase in vagabondage and poverty, and frightening increases in urban crime as people crowded into the cities, particularly into London, which grew from about 75,000 in 1550 to 200,000 in 1600 and to 325,000 in 1650.

The changes overtaking the English unsettled many while pleasing others. In the older medieval ethos people lived within a fixed system of hierarchies in church, government, economic organizations, and family. Life in an English rural village reflected this emphasis on rank and order. Every individual was contained within a web of relationships that conferred both rights and responsibilities on each member of the community. There was the manorial hierarchy with lord, steward, and tenants; the parish hierarchy with vicar, church wardens, and overseers of the poor; the hierarchy of the established church with archbishop, bishops, deans, canons, and visitors; and the hierarchy of economic enterprise with corporations, guilds, masters, journeymen, and apprentices.

But in the period of modernization individuals gradually worked themselves free of the authority of corporate groups. Little by little they made inroads on the religious authority, which dictated individual belief; on the political authority, which strictly governed civil behavior and defined political rights in a limited way; and on the economic authority, by which guilds and monopolies granted by the Crown closely regulated prices, wages, and conditions of work. Thus "protesters" or Protestants began challenging the authority of the Church of Rome; individual entrepreneurs challenged the right of the guilds to regulate work; individual enterprises challenged monopolies that excluded outsiders from areas of economic activity; and agricultural operators began buying small farmsteads and consolidating them into larger agricultural units, dislocating tenant farmers in the process.

To Puritans, the sight of individuals breaking free of traditional restraints was fearsome. In religion this could be applauded because it involved an attempt to place the individual in a more direct relationship with God, removing the traditional intermediaries—especially the Catholic Church. But Puritans deplored individualism in other areas of life because it left people to their own devices, where they promptly acted out the worst fantasies of social anarchy. Social order, respect for authority, morality—all seemed to be crumbling amidst the new social and economic order. Everywhere "idle and masterless men," as one social critic phrased it, roamed the land.

The concept of "every man alone," the individual operating freely in time and space, is at the core of our modern system of values and behavior. But to intellectuals, social critics, and religious leaders of the late sixteenth century this conjured up frightening visions of chaos. Individualism as a mode of behavior threatened the concept of community—of people bound together by obligations and responsibilities. Now, under a newer ethic, the individual rather than the group became the conceptual unit of thinking. To Puritans this conjured up a frightening vision of anticommunity.

Puritans intended to address this problem of the individual versus the community. Through a new discipline they hoped to create a regenerated social order. Their method was to prescribe an ethic that stressed work or industriousness as a primary way of serving God. One did not have to occupy a high station or follow a profession; one had only to work hard in whatever station one found oneself, be that lawyer, blacksmith, or common laborer. Each "calling" was equally worthy in God's sight and, if followed conscientiously, would lead the individual toward spiritual grace. One of the Puritan leaders wrote: "If thou beest a man that lives without a calling, though thou hast two thousands to spend, yet if thou has no calling, tending to publique good, thou art an uncleane beast. God sent you unto this world as unto a Workhouse, not a Playhouse."[7]

Puritans organized themselves into religious congregations where men and women labored together, disciplined themselves, and worked for mutual salvation. Each member not only worked for his or her own perfection but also scrutinized the behavior of others for signs of waywardness. Furthermore, the Puritans believed that to reform their society at large, they must assume responsibility—moral stewardship—over all those around them. In a chaotic and criminal world, God's "elect" must not only save themselves but must also assume the burdens of civil government so as to reform society at large. Others who could not find Christian truth in their hearts might have to be coerced and controlled, directed and dominated. Thus, all would be bound together in covenant to do God's work. In this sense Puritanism was a radical plan to bring about the conversion of the whole society. A mass movement with an ideological vision would rule the land—a radical departure from traditional thought, which held that kings ruled by divine right and delegated their authority to those below them.

The rise of Puritanism during Queen Elizabeth's reign, and the subsequent persecution of Puritans by her successor, James I, is a familiar story. Here it is enough to understand that despite their initial successes, Puritans

[7]Quoted in Perry Miller and Thomas H. Johnson, *The Puritans* (New York: American Book Company, 1938), pp. 325–26.

were increasingly harassed under King James. By the 1620s many were convinced that to reform English society, they would first have to carry out their crusade in another part of the world. Economic opportunity also beckoned abroad, at a time when many Puritans were feeling the effects of depression in England. But their ideological commitment marked them off from the colonizers in Virginia. These were men and women fired by a vision of building a Christian utopia, dedicated to organizing themselves around the concept of community, and possessed of the belief that industriousness and self-discipline were indispensable parts of worshiping their God. In Virginia, by contrast, the spirit of communalism and an ideological vision were conspicuously absent. Economic ambitions, rather than being contained and limited within a set of moral prescriptions, were pursued in and of themselves.

The Puritans were by no means the first Europeans to reach the shores of what they called New England. Fishermen of various European nationalities had been working the Newfoundland Banks and drying their catches on Cape Cod and the coast of Maine since the late sixteenth century. Hundreds of fishing ships had visited the New England coast and made contact with local Indians before 1607 when the English made their first attempt at colonization in the region. The small number of men alighting on the coast of Maine, beset with food shortages, fire, and inhospitable winds, lasted only briefly. Not until 1620 did a permanent settlement take root at Plymouth, Massachusetts, this time planted by several hundred English Pilgrims who had earlier fled to Holland. Slowly, in the 1620s, other fur-trading and fish-drying settlements took root along the coast. But none of these could compare with the great Puritan migration that began in 1630 when eleven ships and some seven hundred passengers set out from England. They were the vanguard of a movement that by 1640 had brought about 12,000 people to New England's shores.

THE ELUSIVE UTOPIA

Led by John Winthrop, a member of the English gentry, the Puritans set about building their "Citty on the Hill." They hoped to establish communities of pure Christians who collectively swore a covenant with God that they would work for his ends, knowing that in return he would watch over them. Puritan immigrants would bring individualistic impulses that had flowered in England under control as all worked for the common good. To accomplish this they agreed to employ what today we might regard as authoritarian means. No diversity of opinion concerning religious beliefs could be tolerated in the new communities. Government would be limited to those visibly filled with God's grace as determined by Puritans already in the church. Offenders, both civil and religious, would be rooted out and punished severely. Every aspect of life would be integrated in the quest for utopia. Participants in the experiment, at least initially, agreed to give up some of their freedoms in order to accomplish greater goals. They sought homogeneity, not diversity, and believed the good of the community outweighed protecting the rights of its individual members. The Puritans in England had formulated an ideology of rebellion, but now it would be employed as an ideology of control.

As in Virginia, the early months were difficult. More than two hundred of the first seven hundred immigrants perished, and a hundred more, chronically depressed by their first winter in the forbidding New England climate, returned to England the next spring. But Puritans kept coming. They began "hiving out" along the shores of Boston's Back Bay, along the rivers that emptied into it, south into what was to become Connecticut, and north along the rocky Massachusetts coast. Massachusetts quickly achieved a diversified and viable economic base, which had been so sorely lacking in early Virginia. This success can be explained not only by the militant work ethic and self-discipline shared by most of the settlers but also by the quality of leadership exercised by such men as Winthrop, John Cotton, John Eliot, Richard Mather, and Thomas Shepard, who were experienced in local government, law, and the uses of exhortation. The typical early leader in Virginia was a soldier of fortune or a roughneck adventurer whose instincts were almost entirely predatory. Massachusetts was led in the early years by university-trained ministers, experienced members of the English lesser gentry, and men compulsively determined to fulfill what they regarded as God's prophecy for New England.

Nevertheless, Massachusetts experienced dissension and conflict in the early decades, both within its communities and in contact with the natives of the region. Even on the voyage across the Atlantic some inkling that the sun would not always shine on the Puritan experiment appeared. In the middle of the voyage Winthrop felt compelled to remind the less submissive members of the expedition that respect for authority was a fundamental part of this new venture. Once on firm ground, and surrounded by boundless land, it proved difficult to squelch acquisitive instincts or to keep people closely bound in covenanted communities. Restless souls began moving away from the center of authority. Others, remaining at the center, agitated for a broader-based political system and a decentralization of authority that would give the individual towns the right to manage their own affairs. After only two years Winthrop wondered if the Puritans had not gone "from the snare to the pit." Thirteen years later he was still struggling to convince those around him that "if you stand for your natural corrupt liberties, and will do what is good in your own eyes, you will not endure the least weight of authority, but will murmur and oppose, and be always striving to shake off that yoke."[8]

[8]Quoted in Richard S. Dunn, *Puritans and Yankees: The Winthrop Dynasty of New England, 1630–1717* (Princeton, N.J.: Princeton University Press, 1962), p. 24.

Winthrop's troubles multiplied. In 1631, when Roger Williams arrived in New England, the established leaders faced a contentious and visionary man who defined religious orthodoxy in terms different from theirs. Williams preached that the Puritans were not truly pure because they would not separate completely from the Church of England. He argued that they interpreted the Bible incorrectly. Perhaps most discomfiting, he charged that the colonists were intruding on Indian soil and illegally depriving the natives of their rights. By 1635 Williams had resisted all who struggled to make him retreat from his views and defied the civil magistrates to try to punish him for his teachings. Convinced that Williams would split the colony into competing religious groups and destabilize authority through his religious perfectionism, the Massachusetts magistrates banished him from the colony and planned to ship him back to England. But Williams escaped and trekked southward, where he started a small settlement of his followers— the seed of the colony of Rhode Island.

Even as the magistrates banished Williams to his personal Eden, they were confronted with another preacher of unorthodoxy—Anne Hutchinson. Brilliant and charismatic, she had proven her value to the community as a midwife, healer, and spiritual counselor after arriving in 1634. But in the next two years she emerged as more than a counselor. She gathered many in the community for religious discussions and then began to dissect the previous Sunday's sermons, raising points of criticism concerning the theological interpretations of John Wilson, Boston's minister. Before long she was the center of a movement called Antinomianism—a variant interpretation of Puritan doctrine that stressed the mystical elements of God's grace and the futility of applying rules and regulations to govern the process by which each individual came to terms with his or her God. By 1636 Boston was divided into two camps and Anne Hutchinson was drawing to her circle not only those who believed in her theological views but most of the discontented in the community—merchants who were disgruntled with the government's price controls, young people who disliked the rigid rule of their elders in church and government, women chafing under male authority, and artisans who resented wage controls imposed to arrest the inflationary trend that had begun.

Determined to rid themselves of this second threat to conformity, the clergy and the magistrates tried Anne Hutchinson in 1636. After two long and symbolic interrogations, the Puritan leaders excommunicated her from the Boston church and banished her from the colony for preaching eighty-two erroneous theological opinions. The sentence read to her at the trial's end conveys the fear aroused in Boston and the determination of the magistrates to squelch further division within the community. "Forasmuch as you, Mrs. Hutchinson, have highly transgressed . . . and offended and troubled the Church with your Errors," intoned the judge, "and have drawn away many a poor soule, and have upheld your Revelations; and forasmuch as you have made a lye. . . . Therefor in the name of our Lord Jesus Christ . . . I doe cast you out . . . and deliver you up to Satan . . . and account you from this time forth to be a Hethen and a Publican . . . and I command you in the name of Jesus Christ and of this Church as a Leper to withdraw your selfe out of the Congregation."[9] With a number of her followers, Anne followed the route of Roger Williams to Rhode Island. The colony's leaders had demonstrated the lengths to which they were prepared to go to ensure homogeneity.

New England could not really remain homogeneous, no matter how many nonconformists were banished from its midst. Nor could the acquisitive instincts that ate at the concept of community be forever dampened. The work ethic brought material gains, and with worldly success individuals developed the ambition to reach still higher—precisely what the Puritan leaders feared would destroy the stable harmonious system they were trying to build. Population increase, geographical expansion, and trade with the outside world all worked against the idea of a closed corporate community suffused with religiosity. In spite of the leaders' admonitions that "the care of the public must oversway all private respects," Massachusetts, even in the early years, demonstrated the difficulty of setting down land-hungry immigrants in the New World and expecting them to restrain their appetites and individualistic urges. The centrifugal forces of the environment were more than a match for the centripetal forces of religious ideology.

PURITANS AND INDIANS

Given the Puritan ideal of community and the centrality of the idea of reforming the world in their image, it might be thought that the conflict and limited acculturation that characterized Anglo–Indian contacts on the Chesapeake would have been replaced in New England by less hostility and greater interaction. But this was not the case.

The series of English exploratory incursions and small-scale attempts at settlement in the early seventeenth century had to contend with the fact that the French and Dutch had already established permanent settlements and a trading network that extended from Nova Scotia to New Amsterdam. The French and Dutch had built the trade on a system of reciprocal relations with the natives of the region. None of the first English attempts at settlement fared well because the English adopted the more militaristic stance toward the Indians recommended by John Smith following his voyage to the New England coast in 1614. English expeditions attacked and kidnapped coastal Indians on a number of occasions. In 1614 one of Smith's captains

---

[9]Quoted in Emery Battis, *Saints and Sectaries: Anne Hutchinson and the Antinomian Controversy in the Massachusetts Bay Colony* (Chapel Hill: University of North Carolina Press, 1962), p. 246.

captured more than twenty Indians and sold them into slavery in Malaga, Spain. Such a predatory approach guaranteed that the English, when they began to arrive in the 1620s, would not be welcomed as a people with whom amicable relations could be expected.

It was not brute force or superior numbers, however, that paved the way for a permanent English presence in New England. Rather it was disease. In 1616 English fishermen stopped on the coast and triggered a "virgin soil epidemic"—the implantation of viruses into a population with no immunological defense. Tens of thousands of Indians died within a single year along the New England coast. Especially hard hit was the area from Massachusetts Bay to Plymouth Bay, where entire towns were swept away or abandoned. Five years later an Englishman moving through the area wrote that the Indians had "died on heapes, as they lay in their houses, and the living that were able to shift for themselves would runne away and let them dy, and let there Carkases ly above the ground without buriall. . . . And the bones and skulls upon the several places of their habitations, made such a spectacle . . . that as I travailed in that Forrest nere the Massachusetts [tribe], it seemed to mee a new found Golgotha."[10] Three-quarters or more of the native inhabitants of southern New England probably succumbed to the disease.

When the Pilgrims arrived at Plymouth in 1620, they disembarked in an area that had suffered catastrophic population losses just a few years before. This was crucial not only in opening up the land for them but also in greatly weakening the Indians' ability to resist the encroachers. It was the further good fortune of the English to encounter Squanto, a Wampanoag who had been kidnapped by an English ship captain in 1614. Squanto's abductor sold him in Spain, but somehow he had made his way to England where he joined an English captain on several trips to the New England coast. On the second of these trips Squanto found that most of his tribe had been killed by the plague, but he remained in the Cape Cod area and was there when the Pilgrims landed. Through Squanto's friendship the Pilgrims received important assistance in the early years.

A decade after the initial settlement, William Bradford, the leader of the Pilgrim colony, wrote that the English had come anticipating the "continual danger of the savage people, who are cruel, barbarous, and most treacherous"—characteristics that made "the very bowels of men to grate within them and make the weak to quake and tremble."[11] But given the record of kidnapping and broken trust the English had established in their periodic visits to the coast before 1620, the characterization better fit the English than the local tribes. The local Indians were probably deeply suspi-

---

[10]Thomas Morton, "New English Canaan," in *Tracts and Other Papers Relating Principally to the Origin, Settlement and Progress of the Colonies in North America*, Peter Force, comp. (Washington, D.C., 1836), II, No. 5: 19.

[11]William Bradford, *Of Plymouth Plantation, 1620–1647*, ed. Samuel Eliot Morison (New York: Alfred A. Knopf, Inc., 1966), p. 26.

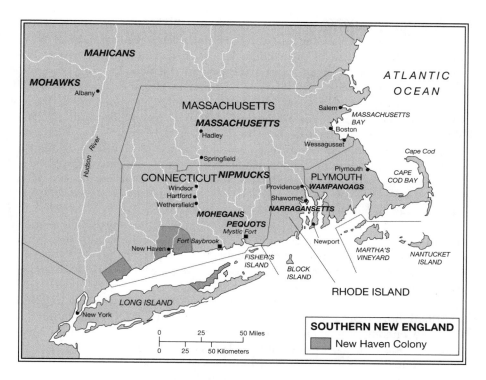

cious of the Pilgrims, but no incident of violence at Plymouth occurred until after the newcomers discovered the natives' underground cold-storage cellars and stole as much of the corn, placed there for winter use, as they could carry off. Even then the Indians chose to minimize contact with the settlers, though after death had reduced the Plymouth colony to about fifty persons in the spring of 1621 the vulnerability of the English invited Indian attack.

The need of the local Wampanoags for a military ally to aid them in their struggle with the neighboring Narragansetts probably explains why they tolerated English abuses and even signed a treaty in 1621 that formed the basis for trade and mutual assistance. The logic of the Wampanoag diplomacy was revealed when Miles Standish and other Pilgrims aided them in a dispute with their enemies in 1621. The Wampanoags regarded the treaty as an alliance of equals, but the English, regarding themselves as culturally superior, saw it as submission by the Indians to English domination.

This surface amity lasted only a year, however. In 1622 about sixty non-Pilgrim newcomers to the colony created serious friction. The new colonists settled themselves at Wessagusset, some distance from the Pilgrim colony, stole corn from the neighboring Massachusetts, and planned attacks on them when they refused to trade with the needy, but arrogant, newcomers. Under cover of a story that the Indians were conspiring against both white communities,

Standish, who had long harbored grudges against several insulting Massachusetts, led an offensive against the friendly Indians, killing eight of them and impaling the head of the sachem Wituwamet on top of the fort at Plymouth as a symbol of white power. Hearing of the deteriorating relations, John Robinson, formerly the Pilgrims' minister in Holland, wrote Governor Bradford in dismay, asking why the English indulged in needless violence. Were "civilized" men in the wilderness, asked Robinson, beginning to act like "savages," forgetting that they were supposed to represent order and piety? Singling out Miles Standish, the militia captain of Plymouth, Robinson wrote: "It is . . . a thing more glorious, in men's eyes, than pleasing in God's, or convenient for Christians, to be a terrour to poor barbarous people. And indeed I am afraid lest, by these occasions, others should be drawn to affect [this kind of behavior] in the world."[12]

As for the Indians, they "could not imagine, from whence these men should come," wrote Thomas Morton, a friend of the Indians, "or to what end, seeing them performe such unexpected actions." From that time on the English colonists were called "Wotowquenange, which in their language signifieth stabbers or Cutthroates."[13]

When the Puritan migration began in 1630, natives of the New England coast had more than a generation of experience with English ways. Little that they had encountered could have made them optimistic about future relations, although their own inter-cultural hostilities continued to make the settlers potentially valuable allies, and their desire for trade goods persisted. As for the Puritans, they were publicly committed to interracial harmony but privately preparing for the worst. The charter of the Massachusetts Bay Company claimed that the "principall ende of this plantacion" was to "wynn and incite the natives of [the] country, to the knowledg and obedience of the onlie true God and Savior of mankinde, and the Christian fayth."[14] But the instructions of the Company to John Winthrop revealed more accurately what was anticipated. According to these orders, all men were to be trained in the use of firearms; Indians were to be prohibited from entering the Puritan towns; and any colonists so reckless as to sell arms to the Indians or instruct them in their use were to be deported to England where they would be severely punished. While ordering that Indians must be fairly treated, the Company reflected the garrison mentality that settlers, once landed and settled, would strongly manifest. No missionary activity was to be initiated for thirteen years.

In the first few years of settlement the Indians did little to arouse Puritan wrath. Their sachems made overtures of friendship, supplied the colonists

---

[12]*Ibid.*, p. 375.
[13]Morton, p. 76, quoted in Neal E. Salisbury, *Manitou and Providence: Indians, Europeans, and the Making of New England, 1500–1643* (New York: Oxford University Press, 1982), p. 133.
[14]Nathaniel B. Shurtleff, *Records of the Governor and Company of the Massachusetts Bay in New England*, 5 vols. (Boston: W. White, 1853–54), I: 17.

with corn during the difficult first winter, and eagerly engaged in a minor trade. One Puritan leader recounted his surprise that during the first winter, when the Puritans "had scarce houses to shelter themselves, and no doores to hinder the Indians access to all they had in them, . . . where their whole substance, weake Wives and little ones lay open to their plunder; . . . yet had they none food or stuffe diminished, neither Children nor Wives hurt in the least measure, although the Indians came commonly to them at those times, much hungry belly (as they used to say) and were then in number and strength beyond the English by far."[15]

This state of coexistence lasted only a few years. Smallpox struck the eastern Massachusetts bands in 1633 and 1634, killing thousands as far north as Maine and as far south as the Connecticut River valley. For the colonists this was proof that God had intervened on the Puritans' behalf at a time when the land hunger of the settlers was causing friction over rights to land. The town records of Charlestown, for example, state that "without this remarkable and terrible stroke of God upon the natives, [we] would with much more difficulty have found room, and at far greater charge have obtained and purchased land."[16] As in Virginia, the need for land provided the incentive for steering away from rather than toward equitable relations between the societies. That the population buildup came so quickly in Puritan New England only hastened the impulse to regard Indians as objects to be removed rather than subjects to be assimilated.

THE QUESTION OF LAND

Puritan theories of land possession help to clarify this tendency to classify Indians in such a way that violence trumped assimilation or coexistence. Like other Europeans, Puritans claimed the land they were invading by right of discovery. This theory derived from the ancient claim that Christians were everywhere entitled to dispossess non-Christians of their land. A second European legal theory, called *vacuum domicilium*, bolstered Puritan claims that land not "occupied" or "settled" went by forfeit to those who attached themselves to it in a "civilized" manner. Before he set foot in the New World, John Winthrop wrote:

> As for the Natives in New England, they inclose noe Land, neither have any setled habytation, nor any tame Cattle to improve the Land by, and soe have noe other but a Naturall Right to those Countries, soe

[15]Edward Johnson, "Wonder-Working Providence," quoted in Salisbury, "Conquest of the 'Savage': Puritans, Puritan Missionaries, and Indians, 1620–1680" (Ph.D. dissertation, University of California, Los Angeles, 1972), pp. 63–64.
[16]Quoted in Alden T. Vaughan, *New England Frontier: Puritans and Indians, 1620–1675* (Boston: Little, Brown and Company, 1965), p. 104.

as if we leave them sufficient for their use, we may lawfully take the rest, there being more than enough for them and us.[17]

By this logic, entitlement to New England land required nothing more than the assertion that because their way of life did not conform to European norms, the Indians had forfeited all the land which they "roamed" rather than "settled." By European definition the land was *vacuum domicilium*—unoccupied. One early settler called New England a "vast and empty chaos."[18] To this mental picture of an unoccupied land the awful epidemic of 1616–18 had made an important contribution.

The slender power of the disease-ravaged coastal tribes of the Massachusetts Bay region and the legal principles invoked under the concept of *vacuum domicilium* situated the Puritans ideally to establish their beachhead in the New World. The remnants of the formerly populous Massachusett and Pawtucket peoples were in no position to resist and in fact willingly consented to the settlement of their lands by the Puritan vanguard that inhabited Naumkeag (renamed Salem) in 1629 and the 3,000 settlers who came in the next four years. In return for land, of which they now had a surplus, the Indians gained the protection of the English against their Micmac enemies to the north. Hence the Puritans quickly adopted the position that the local Indians were domesticated subjects, living in separate villages but answering to Puritan government and law.

Still in a very fluid stage, Puritan–Indian relations, by about 1634, began to revolve around the land question. Another epidemic in 1633 struck down many native people throughout a wide swath from the St. Lawrence River to Long Island. Once more the English saw the divine hand intervening on their behalf and Indians trembled at the power of the English God. This may have temporarily lessened the Indian sense of being overwhelmed by the steady influx of English colonists. But pressure on available land resources mounted rapidly.

The land question also became critical because in 1633 the radical separatist Roger Williams of Salem disputed the claim of the Massachusetts Bay leaders that their royal patent entitled them to occupy Indian land without first purchasing it from the natives. Williams had immersed himself in Indian culture shortly after his arrival in 1631—one of the few Englishmen to do so—and by the next year was absorbed in learning their language. Williams

---

[17]"Generall Considerations for the Plantation in New England . . . " (1629), in *Winthrop Papers*, 5 vols., ed. Allyn B. Forbes (Boston: Massachusetts Historical Society, 1929–47), 2: 118.

[18]Robert Cushman, "Reasons and Considerations Touching the Lawfulness of Removing out of England . . . ," in John Demos, ed. *Remarkable Providences: Readings on Early American History*, 2d ed. (Boston: Northeastern University Press, 1991), p. 7.

argued that the Puritans were illegally and sinfully grabbing Indian land and would have to answer for this before God and the English authorities. He also argued that the natives of the region used the land in rational and systematic ways. This directly challenged the Indians' random use of land supposed in the legal concept of *vacuum domicilium*. The Massachusetts magistrates indignantly dismissed these ideas and ceremoniously burned the pamphlet in which Williams advanced his arguments. Shortly thereafter, they banished him from the colony. Traveling to Rhode Island with some of his followers, Williams was offered land by a Narragansett sachem and found "among the savages," as he wrote, a place where he and his followers could peaceably worship God according to their consciences. Winthrop's response to Williams's argument was that "if we had no right to this lande, yet our God hathe right to it, and if he be pleased to give it us (takinge it from a people who had so long usurped upon him and abused his creatures) who shall controll him or his terms?"[19] By claiming that God directed all Puritan policy, Winthrop charged anyone who murmured dissent with opposing not only Puritan policy but God himself.

Understanding that seizing Indian land by right could be reckless, Puritans continued to purchase land from local tribes. But the purchases were often made to obtain a favorable legal settlement where rival groups of settlers claimed the same tract of land. In such cases a deed to the land in dispute from an Indian seller was the best way to convince a court of one's claim. Even in cases where intra-European rivalry necessitated the purchase of Indian land, the sale could be accomplished through a variety of stratagems designed to reduce the cost to the white settler. Turning livestock into cultivated Indian fields over a period of time was an effective way of convincing a tribe that their land was losing its value. Alcohol was sometimes used to reduce the negotiating skill of the Indian seller. Another method was to buy the land at a rock-bottom price from an Indian sachem who falsely claimed title to it and then take to court any disputing sachem who claimed ownership. Before an English court, with its white lawyers, judges, and juries, the Indian claimant rarely won his case. Perhaps most effective of all was fining an Indian for minor offenses of English law—walking on the Sabbath or illegally entering a town, for example—and then "rescuing" him from the debt he was unable to pay by discharging the fine in return for a tract of his land. None of these tactics worked in areas where Indian tribes were strong and unified. But they were effective among the decimated and divided tribes of southern New England.

---

[19]Quoted in "Generall Considerations for the Plantation in New England . . . " (1629), in *Winthrop Papers*, 5 vols., ed. Allyn B. Forbes (Boston: Massachusetts Historical Society, 1929–47), 2: 534n.

THE PEQUOT WAR

All the factors that operated in Virginia to produce friction between the two societies—English land hunger, a negative view of native culture, and inter-tribal Indian hostility—were present in New England. They were vastly augmented by another factor unknown on the Chesapeake—the Puritan sense of mission. For people of such high moral purpose, who lived daily with the anxiety that they might fail in what they saw as the last chance to save corrupt Western Protestantism, the Indian stood as a direct challenge to their "errand into the wilderness." The Puritans' mission was to tame and civilize their new environment, to convert wilderness into sacred space, and to build a pious commonwealth that would "shine like a beacon" back to decadent England. But how could order and discipline in holy communities be brought to the new environment unless its roaming original inhabitants were tamed and "civilized"? Governor William Bradford of Plymouth tellingly described the land he was entering as "a hideous and desolate wilderness full of wild beasts and wild men."[20] Land, beast, and man must all be brought under control. To do less was to allow chaos to reign when God's will was that Christian order be imposed. As Roy H. Pearce has explained, the Indian reminded the English of what they must not become. The native was the counterimage of civilized man, lacking in what was most valued by the Puritans—civility, Christian piety, purposefulness, and the work ethic. If such people could not be reconstructed as red Puritans, then white Puritans would have failed in regulating the corner of the earth to which God had directed them. God would surely answer such a failure with his wrath.[21]

In this providential view of history many Puritan leaders, if not ordinary settlers, felt an urgent need to master the "savagism" they encountered. However, mastering "savagism" did not require eliminating the "savages." From their writings it appears that Puritans would have preferred to convert the "heathen" to Christianity. But this could only be accomplished through great expenditure of time and effort. The Spanish and Portuguese had sent hundreds of missionaries along with the conquistadors and settlers. But the Puritans came only with their own ministers, and these men had more than enough to do to maintain piety, unity, and moral standards within the white communities. Proselytizing the natives of New England never received a high priority. Much was written about foiling Satan, who had "decoyed those miserable savages hither, in hopes that the gospel of the Lord Jesus Christ would never come here to destroy or disturb his absolute empire over them," but little was done to save the Native Americans from Satan.[22]

[20]Bradford, *Plymouth Plantation*, p. 62.
[21]Roy H. Pearce, *The Savages of America: A Study of the Indian and the Idea of Civilization* (Baltimore: The Johns Hopkins Press, 1953), pp. 3–24.
[22]Cotton Mather, *Magnalia Christi Americana: or, The Ecclesiastic History of New England* (New York: Russell & Russell, 1967), II: 556.

Rather than convert the "savages" of New England, the Puritans attempted to bring them under civil government, making them strictly accountable to the ordinances that governed white behavior in Massachusetts. Insofar as Indians were willing to subject themselves to the new white code of behavior, usually out of fear, the Puritans prevailed. They could keep a close eye on all Indians within the areas of white settlement and bring them to court for any offenses against white law. Many of the smaller bands of eastern Massachusetts, severely weakened by European disease or living in fear of strong and hostile neighbors, bent to the newcomers. But the question of control became a military problem when the Puritans encountered a tribe that was sufficiently strong to resist the loss of its cultural identity and political sovereignty.

Such were the Pequots—a strong and numerous people. By the 1630s they had built a trading network of tributary groups and viewed the Narragansetts as their main rival in southern New England. The Pequots worked hard to convince the neighboring Narragansetts that only by uniting against the English could either tribe survive. But their arguments went unheard. Following the advice of Roger Williams, the Narragansetts agreed to ally themselves with Massachusetts Bay, leaving the Pequots virtually alone in their determination to resist the English.

Hostilities between the Pequots and English were ostensibly triggered by the murder of two white ship captains and their crews. One of the mariners, John Stone, was hated among the English, for he had attempted to murder Governor Prence of Plymouth and had later been banished from Massachusetts for other misdeeds. Two years after Stone's death in 1634, John Oldham was found murdered on his pinnace off Block Island. Using these incidents as justification for a punitive expedition against the unsubmissive Pequots, a joint Connecticut–Massachusetts force marched into Pequot country and demanded the murderers (who, as it turned out, were not Pequots) as well as a thousand fathoms of wampum, an accepted unit of exchange, and some Pequot children as hostages.

The Pequots understood that the issue, ostensibly about the death of several English mariners, was much broader, involving an interlocking set of disputes over land, trade, and political control of the region. These were the real causes of the war that broke out shortly thereafter. At the center of the tensions were the English–Dutch trade rivalry and intertribal Indian hostilities. Since 1622 the Dutch in New Amsterdam had controlled the Indian trade of the region through their connections to both the Pequot and the Narragansett, the area's two strongest tribes. After the rapid expansion of the English in the early 1630s, the Dutch understood the threat to their trading empire. Hence, they purchased land on the lower Connecticut River—an area on which several English groups had their eyes—and built a trading post there to defend their regional economic monopoly. Some of the Pequots' discontented client tribes, however, were already breaking away, signing separate trade agreements with and ceding land to the English. Amidst such fragmentation, expansionist New England was ready, with the aid of its Narragansett allies, to drive the Dutch traders from southern New England and to subdue the Pequots who occupied some of the area's most fertile soil. The Pequots first tried to placate the English, though they were not prepared to subject themselves to English authority by making a huge wampum tribute. When Pequot attempts to negotiate the dispute failed, they chose to resist.

In the war that ensued, the English found the Pequots more than a match until they were able to surround a secondary Pequot village on the Mystic River in May 1637. The English and their Narragansett allies attacked before dawn, infiltrated the town, and set fire to the Pequot wigwams before

One year after the ferocious Pequot War of 1637, Londoners heard all about it, from the English point of view, in John Underhill's *Newes from America.* Underhill was one of the Puritan military leaders who led the attack on the Pequots at their Mystic River palisaded fort. This schematic drawing accurately depicts the attack on the fort. *(This item is reproduced by permission of the Huntington Library, San Marino, California)*

beating a fast retreat. In the melee about twenty Narragansetts suffered wounds at the hands of the English, who found it difficult to distinguish between Indian enemies and allies. Retreating from the flame-engulfed village, the English regrouped and waited for fleeing survivors from the inferno. Most of the victims were noncombatants since the Pequot warriors were gathered at another village about five miles away. Before the day was over the English slaughtered a large part of the Pequot tribe. Rounding up Pequots who escaped or were not at the fort, the English sold them to other tribes, shipped them to the West Indies for sale as slaves, and distributed about 250 captured women and children to serve as lifelong household servants in the towns of Massachusetts and Connecticut.

Religious zeal of Massachusetts and Connecticut leaders permeated their accounts of the war. One of New England's first historians, William Hubbard, wrote that dozens of captured Pequots were put on board the ship of Captain John Gallup, "which proved [to be] Charon's ferry-boat unto them, for it was found the quickest was to feed the fishes with 'em."[23] One of the militia captains wrote that at Mystic Fort "God . . . laughed [at] his Enemies and the Enemies of his People to Scorn, making them as a fiery Oven . . . [and] filling the Place with Dead Bodies." Governor William Bradford of Plymouth wrote that "it was a fearful sight to see them thus frying in the fire and the streams of blood quenching the same, and horrible was the stink and scent thereof; but the victory seemed a sweet sacrifice, and they gave the praise thereof to God, who had wrought so wonderfully for them, thus to enclose their enemies in their hands and given them so speedy a victory over so proud and insulting an enemy."[24] In 1638, at the Treaty of Hartford, the Pequot nation was declared dissolved. Two generations later Cotton Mather, a pillar of the Puritan ministry, reiterated: "in a little more than *one* hour, five or six hundred of these barbarians were dismissed from a world that was *burdened* with them."[25]

The genocidal behavior of the "civilized" Puritans demonstrated at Mystic Fort shocked the Narragansett "savages" who fought with the Puritans. According to one English officer, they came after the victory and "much rejoiced at our victories, and greatly admired the manner of Englishmen's fight . . . it is naught [bad or wicked] because it is too furious and slays too many men." It was a poignant comment on the different conduct and function

[23]William Hubbard, *A Narrative of the Troubles with the Indians in New England* (1677), quoted in Carolyn T. Foreman, *Indians Abroad, 1493–1938* (Norman: University of Oklahoma Press, 1943), p. 29. In Greek mythology, Charon ferried the recently deceased across the river Styx to their place in Hades.
[24]John Mason, "A Brief History of the Pequot War," *Massachusetts Historical Society Collections,* 2d Ser., 8 (Boston: 1826): 140–41. Bradford, *Plymouth Plantation,* p. 296.
[25]Cotton Mather, *Magnalia Christi Americana: or, The Ecclesiastic History of New England* (New York: Russell & Russell, 1967), II: 558.

of warfare in the two societies.[26] Indian war had traditionally been limited and sporadic—"far lesse bloudy and devouring than the cruell warres of Europe," as Roger Williams put it. Whereas the Indians "might fight seven years and not kill seven men," the English were schooled in terror tactics from their invasion of Ireland a generation before.[27]

By exterminating or enslaving the Pequots, Puritans proved their political and military ascendancy. Their victory also provided an antidote to the anxiety and disunity that had overtaken the colony. Coming on the heels of three years of intense internal discord centered around the challenges to the power of the magistrates by Roger Williams and Anne Hutchinson, the war refocused the attention of the elders and common people alike.

Victory over the Pequots decisively established English sovereignty over all the native peoples of southeastern New England except the Narragansetts and removed the one remaining obstacle to expansion into the Connecticut River valley. The tribes of southern New England, reduced to about one-quarter of their former population, adjusted as best they could to the realities of Puritan power. The fur trade kept the two societies in touch and provided the means by which English iron goods became incorporated into the material culture of the Indians. But the flourishing trade of the 1630s petered out by mid-century as the beaver supply in New England became depleted.

In spite of these trade contacts, most of the post-war remnant groups struggled to maintain their native way of life. Some of the weaker and more demoralized bands followed the handful of missionaries, finally spurred to action in 1643 by English critics who rightly charged that conversion had been ignored for more than a decade. After ten years of effort less than a thousand Indians of the region were settled in four villages of "praying Indians," and fewer than one hundred of these declared their conversion to the Puritan form of Christianity. Even among these, defections were numerous in the 1670s when war broke out again in Massachusetts. As in the case of Virginia, the natives incorporated certain implements and articles of clothing obtained in the European trade into their culture, but overwhelmingly, even after major military defeats, they preferred to resist acculturation if it meant adopting English religion, forms of government, styles of life, or methods of social and economic organization.

---

[26]John Underhill, "News from America," quoted in Salisbury, *Manitou and Providence,* p. 222.

[27]Williams' descriptions of English and Indian war are quoted in Colin Calloway, *New Worlds for All: Indians, Europeans and the Remaking of Eastern America* (Baltimore, Md.: Johns Hopkins University Press, 1997), p. 97.

For Puritans and non-Puritans migrating into New England in increasing numbers after mid-century, the Indians' usefulness was dwindling. To be sure, hundreds of enslaved Indians toiled in Puritan households; in coastal towns Indian men served on fishing boats; and many Indian women performed domestic labor. But the Indian population fell rapidly in the seventeenth century. The church took only a minor interest in the Indian, who in any event could rarely satisfy the qualifications that Puritans placed upon their own people for church membership. The Indian trade withered to relative unimportance, as fishing, lumbering, shipbuilding, and agriculture became the mainstays of the colonizers' economy. This withering of Indian utility within English society, combined with the special tendency of Puritans to doubt the Indians' capacity for meeting the cultural and religious standards required in the New Jerusalem, made close and reciprocal contacts between the two societies increasingly tenuous.

5

The Coastal Societies: Resistance, Accommodation, and Defeat

The Indian was rarely a passive agent in the first century of contact with European societies, as was dramatically apparent in the last quarter of the seventeenth century in Massachusetts and the first quarter of the eighteenth century in South Carolina. Indian tribes in both regions rose up to avoid becoming a colonized people. In other areas, such as Virginia and Pennsylvania, small tribes resisted encroachment by Europeans but, bereft of Indian allies and weakened by population decline, moved out of the path of colonial expansion or succumbed to confinement on reserved parcels of land.

Faced with the growing power of the Europeans, Indian societies improvised a variety of responses, ranging from resistance to accommodation to withdrawal. Each of these can be seen as an attempt to preserve corporate unity and cultural integrity. Rather than conceiving of these coastal native societies as brittle and static, and thus unable to adapt to the arrival of dynamic European culture, it is better to perceive them as malleable societies with which the colonists wished to mix, but only on certain terms.

The period from 1675 to 1725 was one of great stress for the coastal tribes but did not cause wholesale cultural disintegration as some historians have claimed. What seems most remarkable is that so many of the coastal societies that experienced the brunt of European population buildup fought with a determination that far exceeded their numbers. This can be seen by exploring the time of troubles for Indian peoples of the coastal plain in New England, in the new Quaker colony of Pennsylvania, and in the Chesapeake and the Carolinas.

METACOM'S WAR

Following the Pequot War of 1637 in New England, the Narragansetts, who had joined the English against the Pequots, tried to maintain as much of their autonomy as possible by keeping their distance from the English colonists. But the Narragansetts occupied precisely the territory toward which Puritan expansion into the Connecticut River Valley was moving. In 1643 the colonies of Massachusetts, Connecticut, and Plymouth, eager to forge an offensive league against the powerful Narragansetts (and also against the pestiferously deviant colony of Rhode Island), formed the New England Confederation. Military preparedness was the purported goal of the Confederation; military conquest was its true purpose. Strength was added to this Puritan front by alliances with the Mohegans, enemies of the Narragansetts. In 1643, when the Narragansett sachem Miantonomo sold a large tract of valuable land on Narragansett Bay to the arch-heretic Samuel Gorton, who was hated throughout Puritan New England for his outspoken criticism of Massachusetts policy, the New England Confederation arranged the murder of Miantonomo by his Mohegan enemies.

Threatened by the Puritans' growing power, the Narragansetts maneuvered for protection. In 1644 they decided "freely . . . and most humbly to submit, subject, and give ourselves, peoples, lands, rights, inheritances, and possessions . . . unto the protection, care, and government" of King Charles I "upon condition of His Majesties' royal protection." This was no admission of subjection to the Puritan colonists. Rather, the Narragansetts gained royal protection from "any of the natives in these parts" and pointedly declared that they could not "yield over ourselves unto any [in New England] that are subjects themselves in any case."[1] One year later the Puritans mobilized for war against the Narragansetts. Calculating the odds, the Narragansetts submitted to a treaty that saddled them with the cost of the mobilization and required a large cession of land. By such tactics the Puritans gradually eroded the land base of the Narragansetts, who, along with the Wampanoags, were the chief obstacle to territorial expansion.

While Puritans pushed southward and westward, their population growing to 25,000 by 1650 and 60,000 by 1675, a few men attempted to Christianize the remaining fragments of the eastern New England tribes. Led by John Eliot, Thomas Mayhew, and Daniel Gookin, the missionaries

---

[1]John R. Bartlett, ed. *Records of the Colony of Rhode Island* . . . (10 vols.; Providence, 1856–65), I: 134–35.

concentrated their efforts among Indian peoples whose numbers had been deeply diminished by epidemics and war, who had already lost much of their land, and who had already become economically dependent upon the colonizers. "The Algonquians who converted," it has been observed, "were those whose communal integrity had been compromised step-by-step—from the plague of 1616 to the treaties of political submission—and whose sources of collective identity and individual social stature had been destroyed."[2] Several thousand "praying Indians" gathered in fourteen villages, where they adopted English methods of agriculture, prayed to the English God, and adopted English hairstyles, dress, and customs.

Yet the praying Indians did not abandon traditional customs so much as they strove to find a new half-English life. That would allow for their survival within the expanding realm of Puritan settlers. One key advantage of the praying towns was greater power than possessed by non-missionized Indians in protecting their land from neighboring whites who hungrily eyed fertile Indian tracts. While the praying villages appeared to be halfway houses on the road to full assimilation into white society, the Puritans rarely acted as if accepting made-over Indians was part of their overall plan. This must have been apparent to acculturated Indians like the Christianized John Neesnummin, who was denied lodging in Boston when he visited there in 1708.

Other New England tribes, where stronger leaders and greater numbers prevailed, fended off the missionaries. "Each of the great sachems of the mid-seventeenth century—Massasoit, Metacom, Ninigret, Uncas—resisted the missionaries as threats to his tribe's survival."[3] Metacom, sachem of the Wampanoags, is said to have told John Eliot "that he cared no more for the white man's gospel than he did for the button on Eliot's coat."[4] But even the more cohesive tribes, which had maintained a degree of independence from the expanding Puritan society, were aware by the early 1670s that their position was precarious and worsening steadily. Their options were limited. They could submit to the English colonies by selling their land, putting themselves fully under Puritan government, and performing day labor within the white man's settlements. Or they could sell their land for whatever they could get and migrate westward, attempting to place themselves under the protection of the stronger Iroquois tribes at their backs. Or they could attempt what had never been successfully undertaken before anywhere on the continent—pan-Indian offensive against a people who greatly outnumbered them and possessed a far greater arsenal of weapons.

The Wampanoags chose the third alternative. In part this can be explained by the leadership of Metacom, or King Philip as the English called

[2]Neal Salisbury, "Red Puritans: The 'Praying Indians' of Massachusetts Bay and John Eliot," *William and Mary Quarterly*, 31 (1974), 50.

[3]*Ibid.*, p. 38.

[4]G. E. Thomas, "Puritans, Indians, and the Concept of Race," *New England Quarterly*, 48 (1975), 6.

him. Metacom was a son of Massasoit, the Wampanoag leader who had allied himself with the Plymouth settlers when they first arrived in 1620 and fought with them against other tribes throughout his life. Massasoit had died in 1661, and Metacom had watched his older brother, Wamsutta, preside over the deteriorating position of the Wampanoags. In 1662 Wamsutta died mysteriously after the Plymouth officials had interrogated him about rumors concerning an Indian conspiracy. For the next decade, Metacom brooded over the position of his people and was forced to accept one humiliating blow after another. The worst came in 1671 when he was compelled to surrender a large stock of guns and accept a treaty of submission in which he agreed not to sell any land without permission of the government of the Plymouth colony. From that time on he began building a league of Indian resistance, convinced that the steady loss of Wampanoag land and arms, combined with the corrosive effects of the Puritans' alcohol and the discriminatory character of the white man's government, could be reversed only by Indian initiative.

Metacom's ability to recruit support for his resistance movement is one indication that the Wampanoags, despite the setbacks of the previous decades, were far from a demoralized people. They lacked neither resources nor spirit to rebel. Still valuing their ancient cultural traditions, they sought new alliances with nearby tribes and embarked on a war to revitalize their culture.

The triggering incident of Metacom's War was the trial of three Wampanoags hauled before the Puritan courts for an act of tribal vengeance against a Christianized, Harvard-educated Indian, John Sassamon, who had served for a time as Metacom's assistant. Sassamon was a man caught between two cultures. Though he had fled white society some time after his Harvard experience, Sassamon was moved to inform the government at Plymouth in the spring of 1675 that the Wampanoags were preparing for a general attack on the English settlements. When he was found murdered shortly afterwards, the Plymouth officials listened to an Indian who claimed he had witnessed the murder and could identify the felons. Three Wampanoags swung at the end of English ropes in June 1675.

War did not break out immediately. In fact the haphazard and sporadic burning and looting that occurred during the next few weeks suggests that Metacom was attempting to restrain the more fiery young men of his tribe who were pushing hard for a war that would restore to their culture the honor that their fathers had compromised over the years. But the war came in full force on June 25, 1675—the day of a total lunar eclipse, which the Indians may have interpreted as a spiritual invitation to violence. The execution of the three Wampanoags had been the catalyst, but the underlying cause was the rising anger of the young Wampanoag males, who refused to accept submission to an alien culture. Rankling at the thought of how much had been sacrificed to accommodate the white invader, they girded themselves for battle. Revitalization of their culture through war was probably as important a goal as the defeat of the white encroacher.

In the first months of the war, Metacom's followers conducted daring hit-and-run attacks on villages in the Plymouth colony. These were accomplished without the assistance of the other tribes in New England—the Narragansetts, Nipmucs, and Mohegans. But when the English colonists failed to unify militarily for an immediate assault on the Wampanoags, and the Indian warriors easily evaded their pursuers, attacking the Puritan flanks and conducting guerrilla operations, many Indians decided that this was the opportunity they had long awaited. Tribe after tribe joined Metacom, and by late summer in 1675 towns all along the New England frontier felt the sting of Indian raids. Although the English retained the allegiance of the Niantics and Mohegans, many of whom fought side by side with the white New Englanders, most of the Pocomtucks and Pocassets—the latter inspired by the female leader Weetamoo, the widow of Wamsutta—joined Metacom's cause. Most important, the Narragansetts, who had attempted to stay officially neutral while apparently offering clandestine aid to the Wampanoags, were driven into the war in December 1675 when a Puritan army massacred hundreds of Narragansett women and children in an unfinished Indian fort. Even the Nipmucs, a tribe of local Indians near Springfield, who had silently nursed grievances for years but were thought by the colonists to be faithful allies, joined the offensive by late summer. A few months later the River Indians of the upper Hudson mobilized for an attack on the New Englanders. Their plans were aborted only when the governor of New York incited the Mohawks to attack them.

By the first November snowfall Indian forays had laid waste the entire upper Connecticut Valley, and the New England frontier was reeling under the attacks of the highly mobile Indian warriors. Fighting with smooth-bore muskets, they proved to be much better marksmen than colonial militiamen. By March 1676, Metacom's forces were attacking Medfield and Weymouth, less than twenty miles from Boston and Providence. Thoughts of English superiority began to fade as Indian ambushes punished the colonial forces. Draft resistance became epidemic by the spring of 1676, and eastern communities grumbled at the influx of refugees from the frontier towns. Food scarcities in the towns produced opportunities for profiteering among those who controlled supplies. Even in times of military crisis, it seemed, the centrifugal forces that had been eroding the Puritan concept of community for a generation were difficult to overcome.

In the spring of 1676 the Indian offensive waned, not as the result of colonial military victories but because of food shortages and disease among the Indians. In what became a war of attrition, they had more and more difficulty obtaining food supplies and weapons to replenish their depleted stores. At first, Metacom's warriors obtained some guns and ammunition from the Mohawks near Albany; but when the New York authorities cut this vital supply line and convinced the Mohawks to attack the Wampanoag winter encampment, Metacom's forces suffered a mortal blow.

Slowly, in the summer of 1676, groups of Indians began to head west to seek shelter among tribes there or to surrender. Puritan leaders executed most of the leaders who surrendered or were captured. But to pay for the costs of the war the New Englanders sold hundreds of other Indians into slavery, including Metacom's wife and son. One Massachusetts leader surrounded about 200 Indians in Maine after inviting them to parley under a flag of truce and then sold all but 8 of them into slavery. New England ships carried the enslaved Indians to Bermuda and Jamaica and even to Cadiz, Spain, where they were auctioned to buyers exactly as if they were Africans.

Puritan forces vanquished Metacom in a battle near the Wampanoag village where the war had begun, with an Indian soldier shooting Metacom in the back. Regarded by the Puritans as an agent of Satan—"a hellhound, fiend, serpent, caitiff and dog," as one leader put it—soldiers carried his head triumphantly back to the English settlements.[5] By the end of autumn the war was over, although "hunting redskins became for the time being a popular sport in New England, especially since prisoners were worth good money, and the personal danger to the hunters was now very slight."[6]

At the end of the war several thousand English and perhaps twice as many Indians lay dead, a casualty rate probably unequaled in any later American war. Of some ninety Puritan towns, fifty-two had been attacked and twelve destroyed by the "tawny serpents," as Cotton Mather called them. Not for forty years would the white frontier advance again to the point where it had been on the eve of the war. The Indian villages were devastated even more completely.

For the Indians of coastal New England it was nearly the last gasp. Had they been able to secure the aid of the Abenakis, a powerful tribe on the northern frontier that had strong connections with the French, or with the Mohawks, the easternmost Iroquois nation, the outcome might have been different. But the enemy that never let up on the native people was ancient intertribal hostility. Equally important, the stronger interior tribes cared more about their trading partnership with the English than the fate of the coastal Indians. For the survivors there remained only the bitter fact that the English had prevailed and must now be recognized as their "protectors." In the aftermath of the war the New England Confederation imposed harsher regulation even on the tribes that had remained neutral or rendered military assistance. By a law passed in 1677 most remaining Indians, regardless of their religious preferences, were confined in one of the four surviving

[5]Quoted in Alvin M. Josephy, Jr., *The Patriot Chiefs: A Chronicle of American Indian Resistance* (New York: The Viking Press, 1958), p. 35.
[6]Douglas Edward Leach, *Flintlock and Tomahawk: New England in King Philip's War* (New York: W. W. Norton & Company, Inc., 1966), p. 237.

praying villages controlled by English supervisors. Hundreds of others became tenant farmers and servants-for-hire in the English communities.

In spite of the finality of the English victory, accomplished as much by the exhaustion of the Indian effort as through English military superiority, Metacom's War demonstrated that some of the coastal tribes were prepared to risk extinction rather than become a colonized and culturally imperialized people. The Puritans never worked for a truly assimilationist policy because they were not prepared to accept the Indians except as unresisting subjects controlled by, but not included within, English society. The weakest of the coastal tribes succumbed to this policy, but the stronger chose to resist, even at the risk of annihilation.

BACON'S REBELLION

While New Englanders fought for their lives during 1675–76, the Chesapeake colonies were also locked in a struggle that involved not only conflict between native and settler communities but war within the white community. By the time Metacom's War was over in New England, several hundred whites and a larger number of Indians lay dead in Virginia and Maryland, the capital city of Jamestown was smoldering in ashes, and a thousand English troops were on their way across the Atlantic to suppress what the king took to be an outright rejection of his authority in Virginia. This deeply tangled conflict, called Bacon's Rebellion, took its name from the 29-year-old planter Nathaniel Bacon, who had come to the Chesapeake only two years before.

Bacon's Rebellion seemed to come almost without warning. Virginia had grown rapidly since mid-century, achieving a population of about 40,000 by 1670. Sir William Berkeley presided over the colony as royal governor, an office he had held intermittently for more than 20 years. Pitted against both the Indians and the royal governor was Bacon, a Cambridge-educated and scandal-ridden newcomer who enjoyed status as the governor's second cousin and a member of his council. Bacon had arrived in Virginia with sufficient wealth to purchase an already established tobacco plantation, complete with a number of slaves.

Bacon emerged as the spokesman of many who scrambled for economic gain in Virginia and were deeply troubled by declining opportunity, which they associated with Berkeley's Indian policy. In 1646, at the end of the second Indian uprising against the Virginians, the Powhatan tribes were guaranteed by treaty the territory north of the York River, which ran northwest from the Chesapeake Bay into the interior of Virginia. Red and white leaders had agreed that granting each society exclusive land rights in specified regions might keep the peace.

For almost three decades after 1646 conflict had been avoided. In fact a profitable trade for furs with several tribes developed, although some in Virginia grumbled that it was monopolized by the governor and his circle of favorites. This stabilization of Indian relations, however, became increasingly odious to the wave of new settlers who arrived in Virginia in the 1650s and 1660s, and especially to the hundreds of white indentured servants who had served their time only to find that in an era of depressed tobacco prices they could not compete with established planters. As their numbers grew, they put more and more pressure on the government to open up for settlement the lands north of the York River. Why should this area be reserved forever for a handful of Indians, they argued, when the Virginia charter ran all the way to the "South Sea," leaving plenty of room to the west for the local tribes? Governor Berkeley wrote home on several occasions that one of every three or four men was landless or impoverished and that all of them "we may reasonably expect, upon any Small advantage the Enemy may gaine upon us, would revolt . . . in hopes of bettering their Condicion by Shareing the Plunder of the Country with them."[7]

This land hunger and constriction of opportunity, mixed with Indian disgruntlement, turned into a classic case of how a small incident of frontier Indian–white tension turned into a galloping war. In July 1675 a group of Doegs, affronted by the failure of a planter to pay them for goods they had traded, attempted to steal his hogs. The planter's overseer killed one Doeg. The Doegs then took revenge, killing the overseer. Thirty of the neighboring planters launched a retaliatory assault. But they retaliated not only by killing ten Doegs but by slaughtering fourteen friendly Susquehannocks, who had been allied to the Virginians for many years. When the Virginia government did nothing to make reparations for the deaths of the friendly Susquehannocks, the Indians sought revenge through attacks on outlying settlements along the Maryland and Virginia frontier.

The spiraling violence, as white Virginians later admitted, stemmed from the land fever and hatred of Indians that led to "takeing up the very Townes or Lands they [the Indians] are seated upon, turning their Cattell and hoggs on them, and if by vermin or otherwise any be lost, then they exclaime against the Indians, beate & abuse them (notwithstanding the Governors endeavour to the contrary)."[8] Contributing to the frontiersmen's attacks was the fact that the Virginia Indians had been drastically reduced in number and power in the previous decades so as to offer only weak resistance to the "land lopers," as they were later dubbed. Fewer than one thousand Indian males remained in the Virginia region by this time, and

[7]Edmund S. Morgan, "Slavery and Freedom: The American Paradox," *Journal of American History*, 59 (1972–73): 21–22.

[8]"Virginia's Deploured Condition" (1676), Massachusetts Historical Society *Collections*, 4th Ser., 9 (Boston, 1869): 164.

these, as Berkeley had written in 1671, "are absolutely subjected, so that there is no fear of them."[9]

Such weakness proved an invitation to white violence. Marylanders and Virginians could easily put a thousand armed men in the field, and just this occurred in September 1675. One thousand Chesapeake planters and militia-men marched against an abandoned stockade on the Potomac River, which had been assigned to the Susquehannocks by the Maryland government. Surrounding a village containing about one hundred braves with their families, they demanded that the chiefs come out to parley. When the Susque-hannocks denied any responsibility for the frontier attacks, their chiefs were led away from the village and murdered.

Though the militia officers involved in this crime were tried, the local courts only fined them lightly or cleared them of the charges. Appalled by this English "savagery," Berkeley denounced the attack and the legal pro-ceedings. But he found scanty support in the colony. The Indians were heav-ily outmatched and served only as an obstacle to further expansion. Hence few Virginians would speak in their behalf or act against those who precip-itated hostilities with them. With the Susquehannocks now fully committed to war, despite overwhelming odds against them, Virginians prepared for their version of what they had already heard was happening to the north under the leadership of Metacom. Rumors swept through the colony that the Susquehannocks were offering vast sums to western Indian nations to join in attacking the Europeans, and even that a confederacy linking Metacom's followers and the southern Indians had been formed.

Bent on revenge, the Susquehannocks attacked during the winter of 1675–76. The assault took the lives of thirty-six colonists. Angered and apprehensive, the frontiersmen turned on the Indians closest at hand, the settled Appomattox and Pamunkeys, who lived within the white area of set-tlement on reservations which a postwar writer admitted "had long been coveted by neighboring Virginians."[10] In what has been labeled a "blood sac-rifice," Nathaniel Bacon assumed the leadership of a frontier movement and began annihilating friendly Indians in the region.[11] Arguing that the subject Indians "have been soe cunningly mixt among the severall Nations of fami-lyes of Indians that it hath been very difficult for us, to distinguish how, or from which of those said nations, the said wrongs did proceed," Bacon asked Governor Berkeley for a commission to lead his volunteers against any Indians he could find.[12] When Berkeley refused to sanction indiscriminate attacks, the fiery Bacon announced he would proceed with or without the governor's approval. Berkeley declared Bacon a rebel, stripped him of his

---

[9]Quoted in Wilcomb E. Washburn, *The Governor and the Rebel: A History of Bacon's Rebellion in Virginia* (Chapel Hill: University of North Carolina Press, 1957), p. 20.
[10]"Virginia's Deploured Condition," p. 166.
[11]Washburn, *The Governor and the Rebel*, p. 35.
[12]Quoted in *ibid.*, p. 37.

councilor's seat, and led an expedition of three hundred Virginia planters to capture the frontier leader. Bacon in turn gathered his forces around him and headed for the wilderness and "a more agreeable destiny then you are pleased to designe mee," as he defiantly informed the governor.[13]

Attempting to salvage the deteriorating situation, Berkeley dispatched punitive expeditions to chastise any Indians who had attacked the white settlers, while also pursuing peace negotiations. Meanwhile, he intended to build a string of forts along the frontier to keep peace between the two peoples. It was a defensive—and expensive—policy. The money to build and garrison the forts could come from only one place—the pocketbooks of the planters, who would have to pay increased taxes.

Berkeley misjudged both the white settlers and the Indians. The Susquehannock sachems could not control their own warriors, who were launching attacks even as their chiefs negotiated with the governor. As for the white Virginians, they wanted no part of the governor's expensive containment policy. The tobacco market had slipped badly in recent years, an epidemic had carried off half the colony's cattle the previous summer, a drought had cut deeply into the 1675 harvest, and now, they argued, the governor proposed a weak and expensive solution to the biggest Indian crisis in three decades. In their minds the problem could be more easily and less expensively solved.

By May 1676 Bacon had declared himself the leader of the rebellious frontiersmen, who were determined to pursue their own Indian policy. Their first objective was a fortified settlement of Occaneechee Indians, who had been regarded as friendly and had recently destroyed a band of Susquehannocks encamped near them as evidence of their fidelity to the Virginians. Attacking the unsuspecting Occaneechees at midnight, Bacon's men annihilated the band. Later critics claimed that £1000 in beaver skins inside the Occaneechee fort had whetted the appetites of Bacon's men.

With his supporters growing at every new attack on the Indians, Bacon marched to Jamestown to confront the governor, who had charged him with treason for defying royal government. Bacon demanded a commission to legitimize his attacks on the Indians; under great pressure the governor acceded. But when Bacon left with his Indian fighters, Berkeley again declared him in rebellion, gathered his own supporters, and pursued Bacon's force. For the rest of the summer Bacon's and Berkeley's forces maneuvered around each other, recruiting additional support, sniping at each other's heels in quasi-military forays, and puzzling over how to stop the chain of events that had started with a disagreement over Indian policy. Time was on the side of Berkeley because once the Indians had been crushed, the Virginia rebels were anxious to return to their homes. Moreover, Berkeley's reports of the rebellion in England had brought the dispatch of a thousand

---

[13]*Ibid.*, p. 41.

royal troops. By the time they arrived with a royal investigating commission in January 1677, Nathaniel Bacon was dead of swamp fever and his followers had melted back into the frontier region.

Although Bacon's followers were disaffected by high taxes, favoritism in government, and the tight grip on power and profit exercised by Berkeley and his friends, it was the governor's protective Indian policy before the first bloodshed and his unaggressive policy thereafter that provided the strongest impetus for insurrection. No longer fearing an Indian population shrunken by decades of disease and sporadic fighting, the Virginians demanded a war of extermination. Peace had been useful for many years because the Treaty of 1646 left plenty of room for expansion. But the population had quadrupled in the intervening thirty years while the Indians had grown only weaker. It was not peace that frontier Virginians now wanted but war.

The royal investigators perceived this genocidal mentality shortly after arriving in Virginia in 1677. In a message to the House of Burgesses, which was debating a peace treaty with the remaining Indians, the commissioners denounced the "inconsiderate sort of men who soe rashly and causelessly cry up a warr, and seem to wish and aime at an utter extirpation of the Indians." When a peace treaty was signed in May 1677, one of its articles referred specifically to the "violent intrusions of divers English into their [the Indians'] lands, forcing the Indians by way of Revenge, to kill the Cattle and hoggs of the English."[14] Thus Virginians recognized that settlers had purposely goaded Indians into retaliatory attacks, which were then used to justify a war of extermination.

Bacon's Rebellion proved that, even if dedicated to preserving peace between the two societies, the highest authorities in an English colony could not prevent genocidal attacks by white settlers. Though he represented the authority of the king in Virginia, Berkeley could not control those who saw the Indians as an impediment to acquiring new land on the frontier. After 1675 the House of Burgesses, reflecting the interests of local planters, withdrew the governor's power to disallow individual land grants, an authority that the governor had exercised since 1666 to prevent settlers from taking up land too close to Indian settlements. Thereafter, Virginians easily intimidated Indians into selling their land in areas adjacent to white settlement. As the Secretary of Virginia wrote in 1678, "the english would ordinaryly either frighten or delude them into a bargaine and for a trifle get away the grownd . . . , then he comes and settles himselfe there and with his cattle and hoggs destroyes all the corne of the other Indians of the towne. . . . This was a great cause of this last warr, and most of those who had thus intruded and were consequently the principall cause of it were notwithstanding amongst the forwardest in the rebellion and complained most of grievances."[15]

---

[14] *Ibid.,* p. 161.
[15] Quoted in *ibid.,* p. 161.

Power in the colonies tended to devolve to the local level, making it impossible for even the most fair-minded colonial governor to stabilize inter-cultural relations. Nobody vested with royal authority tried more consistently than William Berkeley to hold back the aggressive genocidal tendencies of the land-hungry Englishmen on the seventeenth-century Chesapeake frontier. For his troubles, Berkeley saw his colony plunge into civil war, the capital city burn to the ground, and a personal estate valued at £8,000 evaporate under the attacks of those who were prepared to fight against both their fellow Englishmen and the Indians.

For the Susquehannocks and other tribes of the coastal region the les-son must have been unmistakably clear. Even when they recognized the authority of the Europeans, declared themselves subject to English law, abided by that law, and even fought against the Indian enemies of the white government, they could not expect to live in peace. The same authority that bound them to treaties of amity and mutual defense with the colony of Virginia was the authority that was unable to control its own white subjects. They also learned that even when European society was divided against it-self, as in Virginia in 1676, they could be outmatched by the more populous and better-armed whites. Scattered in small towns, each representing a frag-ment of a tribe that had once been larger and more powerful, the coastal Indians were doomed whether they chose war or peace. The price of sur-vival in Virginia, as in New England, was the sacrifice of an independent tribal identity and submission to white civilization as tenant farmers, day laborers, and domestic servants.

THE COLONIZATION OF SOUTH CAROLINA

As some Englishmen spilled blood in Bacon's Rebellion, others mounted a colonizing effort to the south of the Chesapeake in what was to become South Carolina. This vast fertile region later became the center of the plan-tation slave system in North America; but in the 1660s, when English settle-ment began, it was in the eyes of the colonizers no more than another wilderness frontier.

South Carolina was one of the Restoration colonies, founded in the aftermath of a long period of English civil war and the reinstallation of the English monarchy in 1660. Strategic considerations dictated that England cement its claims on the North American coast by removing the Dutch in the Middle Atlantic area and establishing a presence between the Chesa-peake and Spanish Florida. With this in mind, Charles II issued charters for a cluster of colonies in the mid-Atlantic region—New York, New Jersey, Pennsylvania, and Delaware—and for the colony of Carolina on the lower Atlantic coast. All of these charters, specifying title to vast tracts of land and conferring rights of government, were granted to favorites and creditors of the king, men who had stood by Charles II when he was in exile during the republican regime of Oliver Cromwell in the 1650s. In the case of Carolina, the recipients of the king's favor were the Duke of Albemarle, who had been a leading officer in the royalist army; the Earl of Clarendon, the king's chief minister; the Earl of Craven, a prominent royalist during the years of the English civil war; Sir William Berkeley, the governor of Virginia; and Sir John Colleton, a prominent Barbados planter and supporter of the monarchy during its years of eclipse. All these men had claims on the king; all had political power the restored king was eager to keep on his side; and all saw the opportunity to extend their wealth and power by planting a colony in Carolina.

When Charles II granted a proprietary charter to these men in 1663, they set about devising a framework of government that would avoid the instability that had beset earlier English colonies and that would entice a large number of settlers to Carolina. The main work of devising a blueprint for the Carolinas fell to Anthony Ashley Cooper, an expert in colonial affairs who had served Cromwell while still maintaining friendly connections with the exiled king. In 1669 Cooper drafted a constitution for Carolina with the assistance of his friend and protégé John Locke, the tutor of Cooper's children and secretary to the Council for Trade and Plantations.

Cooper and Locke devised a bizarre combination of the modern and feudal. In order to attract colonists land was offered not at a bargain price but for nothing. At first each adult male immigrant could claim 80 acres; later the proprietors increased the ante to 150 acres. But this liberal land system was grafted onto a semi-medieval system of government, which provided the eight Carolina proprietors, their deputies, and a limited number of quasi-noblemen with a monopoly of legislative, administrative, and judicial power. They would hold undisputed reign through an elaborate system of courts, committees, and councils—all tied to the wisdom and authority of eight proprietors in London.

The reality of settlement in Carolina bore little correspondence to this plan. Nobody who came to the colony took the distant London proprietors very seriously, least of all the tough, unsentimental planters who streamed in from Barbados and Virginia where depressed economic conditions had made a new start in the Carolina wilderness seem attractive. They came to take up 150 acres of free land and quickly laid claim to the best land they could find without respect for proprietary plans for settling in compact, rectangular patterns. The land they occupied first lay along the rivers, the arteries of transportation by which they could transport their crops to market.

In government, as in land affairs, they did what they pleased. The London proprietors appointed a governor to take command, but he quickly found that without the cooperation of the local planters he could do nothing. Viewing the London proprietors as self-interested aristocrats who knew nothing about the rigors and problems of frontier life, the planters set about shaping their own institutions of government.

CAROLINA–INDIAN RELATIONS

For the scattered and politically separate tribes of the Carolina country—Guales, Yamasees, Apalachees, Tuskegees, Hitchitis, Westos, Creeks, Cusabos, Catawbas, and many others—the arrival of the English provided both opportunities and dangers, depending on their previous position. The missionized Indians of Spanish Florida probably feared the English, believing correctly that they would now be subject to English attacks and the onslaught of other tribes drawn into the English orbit. For the coastal Indians of the region around the mouth of the Ashley River, site of the maritime center of Charleston, the English may have appeared as saviors, for these tribes had been under heavy attack from their western neighbors for a number of years. "We have them in a pound," exclaimed one of the first English colonists in a letter to London, "for to the Southward they will not goe, fearing the Yamases . . . The Westoes are behind them a mortall enemie of theires, whom they say are ye man eaters. Of them they are more afraid then the little children are of the Bull beggers in England. To ye Northward they will not goe for their they cry that is Hiddeskeh, that is to say sickly, soe that they reckon themselves safe when they have us amongst them."[16] To the west of the Westos, the Creeks may also have looked favorably upon the English arrival because an alliance with the newcomers promised an opportunity to gain indisputable control of the Carolina interior.

Prior to English arrival the inland Westos had gained an edge in the regional internecine hostility largely because they had been able to build a trade connection with traders in Virginia, who provided them with guns. Now the Westos found they would have to use their English weapons against incoming Englishmen who had allied with their coastal enemies. Within months of their arrival the English had secured the friendship of the local tribes along the coast. Soon the Creeks, several hundred miles to the west, sent emissaries to the coast, professing their friendship and suggesting a military alliance.

For the English colonists, the intricacies of intertribal rivalry, once unraveled, offered unsuspected opportunities. The southeastern part of the continent, it was apparent, was more densely populated than the northeast. If the major tribes—Cherokees, Creeks, and Choctaws—could be drawn into trade, the settlers might reap vast wealth from contact with the native peoples. The Spanish had done little to exploit this potential, for their main goal had been to stake out a claim to the territory and protect it by establishing missions that gathered local Indians into a sedentary, agricultural, Christian life.

One of the first Englishmen in Carolina, Henry Woodward, quickly perceived the trade potential of the area. He had come to Carolina on a

[16]Quoted in *ibid.*, p. 67.

scouting expedition in 1666, remained for two years with the coastal Cusabos, and became the first Englishman to penetrate the Carolina interior—"a Country soe delirious, pleasant and fruitful," he reported, "that were it cultivated doubtless it would prove a second Paradize."[17] Woodward and the other leaders also knew that Virginians had already opened a profitable trade with the Catawbas and Westos to the west and northwest.

It was not beaver that beckoned in the Carolina Indian trade, for this valuable animal that had enriched so many traders to the north was available only in small numbers in the warmer climate of Carolina. Instead it was deerskin, also highly marketable in Europe and available in the Carolina country in great profusion. "There is such infinite Herds," wrote one of the Carolina leaders in 1682, "that the whole Country seems but one continued [deer] Park."[18] From 1699 to 1715 Carolina exported an average of 54,000 deerskins a year, and thereafter the trade increased, reaching more than 150,000 skins in some years.

But most of the original settlers came from the sugar island of Barbados. They had anticipated using African slave labor to carve out plantations, just as they had done in the Caribbean. But soon after arriving they saw that a faster way to wealth beckoned. The trade for deerskins almost immediately became a trade for Indians. This was not anticipated by the early Carolina settlers, and in fact the rapid growth of the Indian slave trade caused shock and consternation in London, where the proprietors had no desire to mimic Spanish enslavement of native peoples and also feared all-out war. African slavery was already a familiar part of New World colonizing, and Indians defeated in war had been enslaved in other colonies. Columbus had initiated this by sending about 1,400 Indians home to Spanish slave markets in the 1490s. Virginians were buying Indian slaves, usually children, by the 1670s. But nowhere in English North America had colonists instigated a systematic Indian slave trade based on predatory raids. Yet this quickly became the cornerstone of commerce for the Charleston merchants in the era before rice became the backbone of the economy. Inured to the use of slave labor from their experience in Barbados, the early Carolinians embraced Indian slavery without qualms.

In most respects the Indian slave trade resembled the African slave trade. The Carolinians did not penetrate the interior themselves but formed alliances with coastal native groups, whom they armed, rewarded with European trade goods, and encouraged to make war on weaker tribes, some of whom were ancient enemies. By the early 1670s slave coffles marched through the Carolina backcountry to the coast in much the same fashion as they filed through the African interior to the coastal trading forts. Once in

---

[17]Verner W. Crane, *The Southern Frontier, 1670–1732* (Ann Arbor: University of Michigan Press, 1956), p. 13.
[18]Quoted in *ibid.*, p. 111.

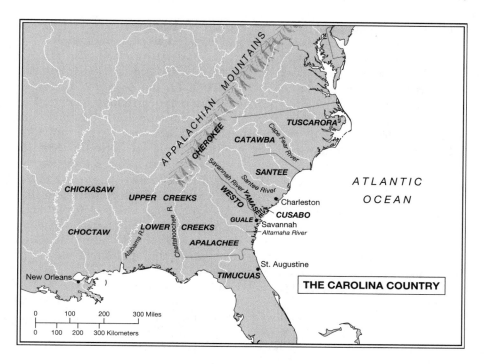

THE CAROLINA COUNTRY

Charleston, the captives were transferred by slave traders to ships for the "middle passage" to other colonies, much as Africans crossed the Atlantic during the process of forced relocation. Most of Carolina's Indian slaves were destined for the West Indies, although a sizable number remained in the colony and several thousand were shipped northward to New York and New England. In 1708 the population of the white settlements in Carolina included about 5,300 whites, 2,900 African slaves, and 1,400 Indian slaves.[19]

As the Carolina proprietors feared, the Indian slave trade plunged the colony into a series of Indian wars. Through their agents in the colony, the proprietors forged a trade agreement with the inland Westos. But independent planters, resentful of the Indian trade monopoly claimed by the proprietors in London, contrived to thwart this policy by eliminating the Westo tribe. The Carolina planters had no desire to risk their own lives against the Westos and in fact lacked sufficient strength to defeat the powerful tribe. But they solved their problem by arming a group of Shawnees, who had migrated across the Appalachian Mountains, and offering them lavish gifts to defeat and enslave the proprietary-linked Westos. In early 1680 the subcontracted war against the Westos began. Three years later the Carolina proprietors in London learned that not more than fifty of their former allies and

[19] *Ibid.*, p. 113.

trading partners were still alive. The rest had been killed or sold into slavery. Destroyed with the Westos was the proprietary Indian trade monopoly.

For the next few decades the private traders, who had now grasped control of the provincial government, armed the coastal Savannahs and engaged in "an orgy of slavedealing."[20] Typically, the price for an Indian slave was an English gun along with ammunition and perhaps a hatchet. The search for more and more slaves took the Savannahs farther and farther afield until by the end of the seventeenth century they were conducting slave operations deep into the interior and far down the coast into Spanish Florida. Indian slave trading reached its peak in the first decade of the eighteenth century. In 1704, a Carolina Indian trader, Thomas Moore, led about one thousand Creek warriors and fifty of his countrymen into Florida's Apalachee territory. Other raids in the next six years left the Spanish mission system in a shambles. Some ten to twelve thousand Timucuas, Guales, and Apalachees were caught in the net of English slavery. Marched to Charleston, they were sold to the slave dealers and shipped out to all points in England's growing colonial empire.

The London proprietors were helpless to stop these perversions of their Indian policy. When they denounced the Indian slave trade as immoral and reckless, the colonists replied that the public safety required the elimination of some of the lesser tribes and maintained that transporting them out of the colonies or using them as slaves kept them "from being put to Cruell deaths" by the Savannahs. The proprietors were not fooled by this twisted logic. They understood perfectly, as they informed the local government, that the colonists were exploiting the Savannahs'

> covetousness of your gunns, Powder, and Shott and other European Comodities . . . to ravish the wife from the Husband, Kill the father to get the Child and to burne and Destroy the habitations of these poore people into whose Country wee were Ch[e]arefully received by them, cherished and supplyed when wee are weake, or at least never have done us hurt.[21]

As some had predicted, abuses of the Indian trade and encroachments on their land finally led the Savannahs to end their alliance with the Carolinians. Understanding that war against those who exploited them might be too costly, most of the Savannahs decided in 1707 to migrate northward into the backcountry of Maryland and Pennsylvania. But rather than let the Savannahs extricate themselves from the trade dependency, the Carolinians offered huge bounties to a tribe of about 450 Catawba Indians to attack and extirpate them. Small numbers of Carolinians joined the Catawbas in attacking the Savannahs. Governor John Archdale justified the policy by writing that

[20]*Ibid.*, p. 139.
[21]Quoted in *ibid.*, pp. 139–140.

"thinning the barbarous Indian natives" had seemed necessary. The "thinning" was so thorough that by the end of the first decade of the eighteenth century the two principal tribes of the coastal plain, the Westos and the Savannahs, were virtually extinct.[22]

For the Indian tribes of the Carolina region the arrival of the English was disastrous. Many of the coastal tribes had been incorporated previously in the Spanish mission system. Though this had rendered them dependent and altered their way of life, it had not destroyed them. But the settlement of South Carolina had catastrophic effects, for it introduced a trade in European cloth, guns, and other goods that pitted one tribe against another and greatly intensified Indian warfare. Even the stronger tribes of the area with whom the English forged trade alliances found that after they had used English guns to enslave weaker tribes, they themselves were scheduled for elimination.

Yet, in spite of the attritional effects of trading with the English, the Indian desire for trade goods was so strong that nothing could deter new tribes from forging alliances with the colonizers while others were being destroyed. The Creeks, the strongest of the interior tribes, abandoned their ancient villages on the Chattahoochie River in the late seventeenth century and migrated eastward to the Altamaha in order to be closer to the English. Even a terrible smallpox epidemic that spread through their villages in 1697 did not convince the Creeks that the European connection might better be spurned. Vast quantities of deerskins, carried on the backs of native burdeners, moved eastward along the Indian trail that led from more than five hundred miles deep in the interior to the coastal trading center of Savannah. Supplied with English weapons, the Creeks also served the English by making war on the Spanish and their client tribes and on the Choctaws of the Alabama and Mississippi region. "Through the media of intensified warfare, hunting and trading," a historian of the Creeks has written, "the Creeks became, comparatively speaking, a fiercely acquisitive and affluent Indian society," and yet "abjectly dependent upon the English trading system."[23]

THE TUSCARORA AND YAMASEE WARS

In the early eighteenth century the depopulation of the region south of Virginia continued. Disease took a terrible toll in Indian villages, with major epidemics striking the region in 1698, 1718, and 1738. War added to the woes of southern tribes. The Tuscaroras were the first to be drawn into the ghastly

[22]John Archdale, "A New Description of Carolina" (1707), in Alexander A. Salley, *Narratives of Early Carolina, 1650–1708* (New York: Charles Scribner's Sons, 1911), p. 285.
[23]David H. Corkran, *The Creek Frontier, 1540–1783* (Norman: University of Oklahoma Press, 1967), p. 53.

cycle of trade, war, and elimination that the South Carolina colonizers coordinated from the small beachheads they had established along the coast.

The Tuscaroras were a numerous people living in North Carolina in large villages where they gathered hemp, grew crops, and tended orchards on tidewater plantations they had cultivated for generations. For years neighboring tribes, allied with Virginia and South Carolina traders, had raided their villages, stealing their children and selling them to the white slave traders. In 1709 they had watched a swarm of Germans and Swiss, led by a Baron de Graffenried, invade their lands with the tacit consent of the provincial government. In local trade they also found they could expect little from the Europeans' system of justice. They recognized, however, the difficulties of forging a pan-Indian alliance and were aware of what had happened to those who resorted to force against the colonial settlers. Better than this, they decided, they would migrate northward to Pennsylvania, where they might obtain refuge in the Quaker colony. In 1710 their leaders met with representatives of the Pennsylvania government and the Iroquois League under whose protection they wished to place themselves. Their hopes were shattered, however, for the Pennsylvania government backed away from promising refuge.

Finding withdrawal impossible, the Tuscaroras gathered as many local tribes with similar grievances as possible and fell on the European encroachers. They killed about 130 English and Germans in the initial attack. Boiling with internal dissension and as yet thinly populated, North Carolina turned to neighboring colonies for help since it had only a ragtag militia to send against the Indians. Virginia's government promised clothing and money but no men, for the Virginians were not ready to sacrifice their lives to defend the North Carolinians, with whom they were engaged in a bitter boundary dispute.

In South Carolina the embattled North Carolinians found the assistance they needed. Historians have sung the praises of the South Carolina government for altruistically coming to the rescue of its northern neighbors and for assuming "the financial and military burdens" of the war.[24] In truth the Indian slave traders of South Carolina gladly entered the fray because they sniffed profit in the breeze. Colonel John Barnwell, an important South Carolina Indian trader, led an army of 500 men into Tuscarora country. But the army included only 33 whites, for the South Carolinians intended their Indian allies, especially the Yamasees, to do most of the fighting for them. Behind the offer of assistance to the beleaguered North Carolinians stood the chance to defeat the Tuscaroras and enslave large numbers of them for sale on the West Indian market. Before Barnwell reached the Tuscarora forts in January 1712 many of the Indians in his army had deserted. But the

[24]For example, M. Eugene Sirmans, *Colonial South Carolina; A Political History* (Chapel Hill: University of North Carolina Press, 1966), p. 111.

remainder of the force defeated one group of Tuscaroras and took 30 slaves. To Barnwell's dismay, however, his Yamasee allies deserted with their prizes.

Barnwell moved on to destroy hundreds of Tuscarora houses and take several prisoners whom, as recorded in his journal, he "ordered immediately to be burned alive."[25] He then attempted to storm another Tuscarora fort; but finding his own forces weak and badly supplied, he arranged a truce. Faced with returning to South Carolina with only a handful of slaves, Barnwell broke the truce and scoured the countryside for additional prisoners on his way back to South Carolina. In response to this violation of the truce the Tuscaroras renewed their attacks and the South Carolinians were again invited to enrich themselves by helping their neighbors. A special representative of the North Carolina government, urging a second expedition, advertised the "great advantage [that] may be made of Slaves there," with three or four thousand Tuscaroras ready for plucking.[26]

The second expedition was led by another Indian slave merchant, James Moore, a veteran of slaving expeditions in Spanish Florida. Moore recruited an army composed of 30 white colonists and nearly 900 Cherokees, Yamasees, Creeks, and Catawbas. Storming the Tuscarora fort at Nooherooka in March 1713, they soundly defeated the North Carolina tribe. Moore's army burned alive several hundred of the enemy in the fort; slaughtered 166 male captives regarded as unsuitable for slavery; and led back to the Charleston slave market 392 Tuscaroras, mostly women and children The South Carolina attackers suffered 57 casualties—22 whites and 35 Indians. In the course of the war the loss of Tuscarora life reached nearly 1,000 and as many as 700 may have been enslaved.[27] The scattered remnants of the tribe drifted northward in the aftermath of the war, seeking shelter under the wing of the Iroquois and contributing to the Iroquois' distrust of English settlers.

In 1715, two years after the Yamasees had participated in the defeat and enslavement of the white man's enemies in North Carolina, they provided the leadership for the largest and most successful anti-European resistance movement in the eighteenth-century South. Spearheading a pan-Indian uprising that encompassed many of the fragmented remains of the coastal societies as well as the powerful and populous interior tribes—Creeks, Choctaws, and Cherokees—the Yamasees came as close to wiping out the European colonists as ever Native Americans came in the colonial period. Only the last-minute success of the Carolinians in winning the Cherokees to their side saved the colony from an Indian revolt that, according to the South Carolina Assembly, included fifteen Indian nations with a total population of more than thirty thousand.

[25]Quoted in Chapman J. Milling, *Red Carolinians* (Chapel Hill: University of North Carolina Press, 1940), p. 120.
[26]*Ibid.,* p. 128.
[27]Crane, *Southern Frontier,* p. 161.

The Yamasees, like almost every other southern tribe, had eagerly sought trade connections with the English and then lived to regret the dependency fostered by the trade. Even while the Yamasees were attacking weaker tribes in order to supply the Charleston slave traders and were helping the Carolinians subdue the Tuscaroras, they were reaching the desperation point in their relations with the English settlers. Cattle raisers in the coastal area south of Charleston expanded so rapidly in the first decade of the eighteenth century that the Carolina government was obliged to pass an act in 1707 "to Limit the Bounds of the Yamasee Settlement, to prevent Persons from Disturbing them with their Stocks." Despite the argument that the act was designed to help the Yamasees, the real intention, as its title indicated, was to restrict the Indians to reservations in order to open up the rest of the land to white settlers. Three years later the Carolina authorities were struggling with encroachers who were taking up land within the territory reserved for the Yamasees.

Even more oppressive were the Indian traders upon whom the Yamasee people had come to depend. The Indian commissioners listened to repeated reports "of the callous brutality of some of the traders, of petty thieving, of illegal enslavement of free Indians, of the abuse of rum to facilitate sharp dealing, of the use of cheating weights," and, as a Virginia Indian trader informed his London agent in 1715, of the debauching of Indian women when their men were on deer-hunting and slave-raiding expeditions.[28] Gradually the English reduced the Yamasees to peonage, as indicated by a report to the Indian commissioners in 1711 that they were in debt to the amount of 100,000 skins—the equivalent of 4 or 5 years of hunting. When Charleston traders began seizing Yamasee women and children to be sold as slaves in partial payment of these debts, the Yamasees revolted.

Attacking on Good Friday, April 15, 1715, the Yamasee carefully coordinated with the inland Creeks, who had been equally exploited in the trade. The powerful Creeks were spurred on by the French, who had been building forts and trading posts in the lower Mississippi valley since 1701 and trying to woo the Creeks away from the English. It may have been the emerging Creek leader, Brims of Coweta, who planned the attacks in a general strategy to drive the Europeans out of the Southeast. All along the border settlements and wherever traders resided, the Creeks and Yamasees struck, aided by lesser tribes of the coastal plain. Refugees poured into Charleston during the summer of 1715, as the Carolina government frantically patched together a military force of planters, indentured servants, slaves, and mercenaries from Virginia and North Carolina. Supplies arrived even from far-off New England, as the authorities in Charleston issued gloomy predictions that if the Carolinians succumbed, Indian tribes all over the continent would be inspired to hurl themselves at white settlements.

---

[28] *Ibid.*, pp. 165–66.

At first, the Yamasee guerilla tactics worked. Striking English settlements at will, the Yamasee had Carolinians despairing at Indians "skulking in the bushes and swamps that we know not where to find them nor could follow them if we did so that we may as well go to war with the wolfs and bears."[29] In the fall of 1715, the Carolinians mounted effective counterattacks on the Yamasee, but the more numerous Creeks were still carrying the torch to every settlement they could reach. More dangerous, they were negotiating with the Cherokees, the largest Indian nation neighboring the southern colonies. Residing in the mountainous southern Appalachia area, the Cherokees, according to an estimate in 1715, could muster nearly 4,000 warriors and boasted a total population four times as large. During the first half-year of the war the Cherokees had remained neutral, but the chances of the hard-pressed Carolinians seemed to rest on obtaining their support or at least preventing a Creek–Cherokee alliance. In an evenly matched struggle, where the Cherokees occupied a pivotal position, both sides made frantic attempts to secure their pledge of allegiance.

The Cherokees recognized the momentous importance of their decision and wavered back and forth, first agreeing to an alliance with the English in August 1715, but then failing to appear for a scheduled November offensive against the Creeks. Desperate for decisive action, the Carolina government sent a military expedition of three hundred men, including one company of black slaves, deep into the mountainous Cherokee country to galvanize the wavering Indian nation. While the expedition leaders promised a shower of trade goods and pressed the Cherokees for a commitment, a dozen Creek headmen were also haranguing the Cherokee chiefs and arguing for a joint attack on the white army encamped in the woods nearby. The Cherokees were split between a war party and a peace party. When the war party prevailed, they fell on the Creek emissaries and killed them. It was the Cherokees' dependence on the English trade goods that finally swung them against the Creeks. As they told the Carolinians, unless they were at war with the Creeks "they should have no way in getting of Slaves to buy ammunition and Clothing" from the white traders."[30]

With the Cherokees arrayed against them, the Creeks abandoned the towns they had settled in eastern Carolina in order to be nearer the source of English trade goods and migrated back to their old townsites on the Chattahoochee River. To replace their trading and military connections with the English they sought new links to the French on the Alabama River and the Spanish in Florida. The remaining Yamasees fled south to join the Spanish in Florida.

For white Carolinians, the flight of the Creeks and Yamasees left new lands open for the taking. But their thirst for revenge in a war that had cost

---

[29]Quoted in Colin Calloway, *New Worlds for All: Indians, Europeans and the Remaking of Early America* (Baltimore, Md.: Johns Hopkins University Press, 1997), p. 103.
[30]Crane, *Southern Frontier*, p. 182.

them more than 400 lives and £400,000 was nearly unquenchable. Many of the Yamasee and Creek Indians, wrote an Anglican clergyman in the colony, "were against the war all along; But our Military Men are so bent upon Revenge, and so desirous to enrich themselves, by making all the Indians Slaves that fall into their hands, but such as they kill (without making the least distinction between the guilty and the innocent, and without considering the Barbarous usage these poor Savages met with from our vilainous Traders) that it is in vain to represent to them the Cruelty and injustice of Such a procedure."[31]

The Yamasee War defined both the limits of white economic exploitation and the limitations of Indian resistance. Nowhere in colonial America was exploitation of the indigenous people less restrained by church, government, or the attitudes of the people than in South Carolina. By 1717 a white population of only about 1,500 males had succeeded in employing the larger tribes to enslave and shatter nearly a dozen coastal tribes and then had driven a wedge between the Creeks and Cherokees at the moment when an alliance between them might have ended English presence in the region. Throughout this process, covering almost a half century, the primary weapon of the English had been trade goods. Despite callow abuses in the Indian trade and the devastating toll that slave raiding took on tribes as far west as the Mississippi, it was only with great reluctance, usually accompanied by internal division, that tribes of the Carolina region turned on those who supplied them with European goods. As one Indian delegation put it during the Yamasee War, their people "cannot live without the assistance of the English."[32]

As in other parts of the continent, the key to English success in an area where they were greatly outnumbered was the promotion of intertribal hostility. This was not only instrumental in procuring slaves who could be profitably sold in New England and the West Indies, but also was a major factor in depopulating tribes whose land then became accessible to the settlers.

This doubly baneful effect of the English connection—always outweighed by the powerful Indian hunger for English trade goods—became the basis of French attempts to win the Creeks to their side. Since the closing years of the seventeenth century the French had been building forts and establishing contacts with the interior tribes. As early as 1702, Pierre Le Moyne Iberville, the architect of the French empire in Louisiana, parleyed with chiefs from the warring Choctaw and Chickasaw nations and attempted to convince them of the destructive nature of the English connection. For almost a decade, he pointed out, the Chickasaws had allied themselves with the Charleston traders, using English guns to raid the Choctaws and selling the captives they took

---

[31]*Ibid.,* p. 179n.
[32]Quoted in James H. Merrell, "The Indian's New World: The Catawba Experience," *William and Mary Quarterly,* 41 (1984): 553.

in order to procure still more guns and ammunition. In the course of taking about 500 slaves, the Chickasaws had killed more than 1,800 Choctaws and lost some 800 of their own warriors. Englishmen delighted in this arrangement, he explained, for they built their fortunes on the trade in slaves and guns while watching the Choctaws and Chickasaws decimate each other. When the two tribes had sufficiently weakened each other they would no longer be able to protect their land from the English settlers, whose strength grew with the death of every Indian, whether friend or enemy. Iberville offered peaceful trade with both nations, not for slaves but for deerskins.

For the land-hungry English cattle raisers and rice growers of eastern Carolina, who were importing slaves from Africa in ever-growing numbers by the early eighteenth century, the Indian slave trade had no direct benefits because the profits accumulated in the hands of the Charleston merchants. But the secondary advantages were invaluable, for the Indian population of the lower South followed a downward trajectory as a result of the slave trade and thus facilitated southward and westward expansion from the initial settlements around Charleston. The extent of the Indian slave trade has never been determined, but it is certain that the number enslaved reached the tens of thousands in the half century after Carolina was settled by Europeans. A conservative estimate might place the loss in the Indian population due to disease, war, and enslavement during the first half century of English settlement at about 60 percent.

QUAKER–INDIAN RELATIONS IN PENN'S "HOLY EXPERIMENT"

For several hundred years, historians have explained the history of Indian–white relations as an inevitable clash between "savage" and "civilized" people. Told from the victor's point of view, the outcome of the contest was predetermined. The irresistible rhythms of human life, we are told, the unswervable forces beyond control of puny individuals, the "laws of history" and "manifest destiny" determined the contest between two cultures. As one wise philosopher has explained, such arguments about inevitable historical outcomes shift the weight of responsibility from particular individuals and groups to "vast impersonal forces . . . better made to bear such burdens than a feeble thinking reed-like man."[33]

The notion that Indian–white relations were inevitably violent and inexorably resolved in the Europeans' favor is refuted by the arrival of a band of ideologically fired English settlers who reached North America only a few years after the Indian wars of the 1670s. William Penn and his Quaker

[33]Isaiah Berlin, *Historical Inevitability* (London: Oxford University Press, 1954), p. 20.

followers, who streamed into New Jersey and Pennsylvania in the 1680s, were entering a maelstrom of bloody racial conflict that had reached a peak in Metacom's War in New England, in the Indian war ignited by Nathaniel Bacon, and in the fierce Indian wars touched off by early colonizers in South Carolina. But unlike other colonists, Quakers came with peace on their minds. In fact, as pacifists, they categorically forswore violence. Along with Penn's pledge not to allow one acre of land to be settled until he had purchased it fairly from the local Lenni Lenape (later known as Delawares), pacifism made the crucial difference.

A mere handful of colonizers had settled in the fertile region between the Hudson River and the Chesapeake Bay before the 1660s, most of them Swedes, Dutch, and Finns under the control of the Dutch West India Company. Then, in the 1670s and 1680s, a wave of English settlers came to the Delaware River Valley, which comprised what would become the colonies of East and West Jersey, Pennsylvania, and Delaware. These were the tribal homelands of a loose collection of small tribes, of which the Lenni Lenape was the largest.

Among all the tribes of the coastal plain, the Lenni Lenape had retained their land and way of life the longest. This was primarily because only a small number of Europeans settled in their region during the half century when the populations of Massachusetts, Connecticut, Maryland, and Virginia were growing rapidly. When Europeans did arrive in large numbers, most of them came as devotees of the Society of Friends—a radical Protestant sect born in the heat of the English Civil War of the 1650s. Pledged to the principle of nonviolence and just relations among people of all religions and races, the Society of Friends, or Quakers, maintained peaceful interracial relations in the Delaware River Valley that stood in sharp contrast to other parts of North America.

The Quaker immigration focused first, in the 1670s, on East and West Jersey, formerly part of New Netherland. Then in the 1680s it shifted to Pennsylvania, which was to become the center of the Quaker's hopes for a utopia in the New World. Like the Puritans, Quakers burned with the bright heat of religious conviction. Like the Puritans, they regarded the English Protestant Church as corrupt and renounced its formalistic elements. But they carried the Puritan revolt against Anglicanism to its extreme, decrying all institutions standing between the individual believer and God. In this sense, the Quaker was essentially a mystic, persuaded that every believer might find God's grace within one's heart through one's own power, unaided by priests, ministers, liturgy, or other devices.

Quakers had suffered severe persecution in England after the rise of their movement in the 1650s and therefore began to formulate plans for founding overseas colonies of their own. They sent their advance agents, seen as God's shock troops, to many of England's colonies, where they were

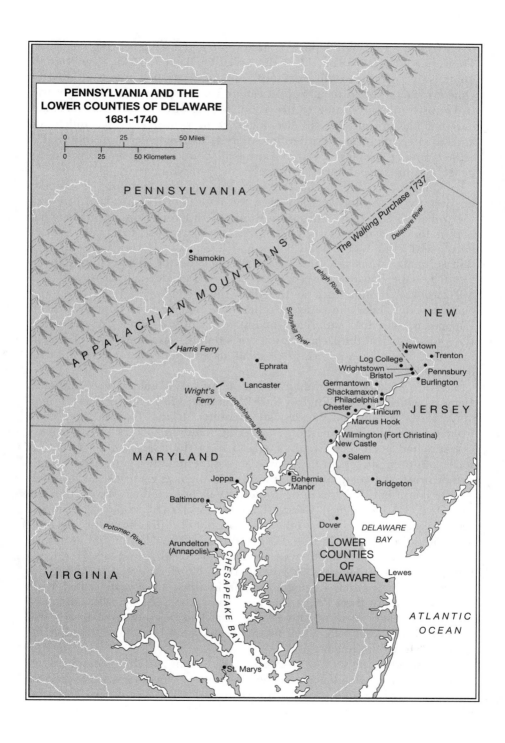

PENNSYLVANIA AND THE LOWER COUNTIES OF DELAWARE 1681-1740

| 0 | 25 | 50 Miles |
| 0 | 25 | 50 Kilometers |

PENNSYLVANIA

The Walking Purchase 1737

Delaware River

Shamokin

A P P A L A C H I A N   M O U N T A I N S

Lehigh River

Schuylkill River

Harris Ferry

NEW

Ephrata

Newtown
Trenton
Log College
Wrightstown
Pennsbury
Bristol
Germantown
Burlington
Shackamaxon
Philadelphia
Chester
Tinicum
Marcus Hook

Lancaster

Wright's Ferry

Susquehanna River

JERSEY

Wilmington (Fort Christina)
New Castle
Salem

MARYLAND

Joppa
Bohemia Manor
Bridgeton

Baltimore

Dover
DELAWARE BAY

Potomac River

Arundelton (Annapolis)
LOWER COUNTIES OF DELAWARE
Lewes

VIRGINIA

C H E S A P E A K E   B A Y

ATLANTIC OCEAN

St. Marys

often reviled, mutilated, deported, and even hanged for practicing their faith. Then in 1681, glad to be rid of the pesky Quakers, Charles II granted an immense territory to William Penn, one of the most important English Quakers. Penn vowed to make it a refuge for the persecuted of the world. In Pennsylvania, according to his vision, people of all colors, religions, and national backgrounds would live together in peace. However much war and violence might be regarded by others as unavoidable when the English settled among Indians or other European colonizers, Penn prepared for peace and interracial harmony to reign in Pennsylvania.

Quakers arriving in the Delaware River Valley, therefore, threatened no violence to the Indians. However, the natives of the area had little reason to believe that these Europeans would be different from others they had known for three-quarters of a century. From exposure to Dutch, Swedes, Finns, and English, the local tribes had learned of European technology, disease, material culture, and values. By the time the Quakers arrived, the Lenni Lenape had extensive experience with European firearms and alcohol, two key commodities in the trade they conducted in beaver, otter, and deerskins. Like almost every other tribe that came in contact with the Europeans, they had suffered a major population decline. On the eve of the Quaker arrival the Delaware warrior strength was about 1,000, less than half what it had been before three smallpox epidemics hammered the tribe between 1620 and 1670.

The Quakers who immigrated to Penn's new colony were primarily farmers, which meant that, like other colonists, they gave primary importance to the acquisition of adequate amounts of land. Nor did they differ from other English immigrants in seeking material success. Like Puritans, Quakers had been recruited in England from the rising middle groups of society; as their success in Pennsylvania over the next few generations would demonstrate, the economic urge pulsated in them as vigorously as in others on the continent. But offsetting these built-in potentialities for friction was the Quaker's ideological vision. They believed that despite a historical record that seemed to prove otherwise, people of different cultures and beliefs could live together in friendship and peace. Their optimism was not the product of ignorance, for they were fully aware of what had occurred when Europeans and Indians met in other parts of North America, including two bloody conflicts in New England and Virginia just a few years before Penn received his grant from Pennsylvania. Yet they were ideologically committed to pacifism, eager to avoid the conflict that had beset other colonies, and convinced that what others had not achieved could be accomplished in the Quaker "Holy Experiment."

Even before he set foot in Pennsylvania, Penn laid the groundwork for peaceful relations. In a letter transmitted by his commissioners who preceded him to Pennsylvania he wrote to the Delawares: "The king of the Countrey where I live, hath given unto me a great Province therein, but I desire to enjoy it with your Love and Consent, that we may always live together as Neighbors and friends . . ."[34] In this single statement Penn recognized the Indians as the rightful owners of the territory and gave notice that only with their consent would he allow settlers to establish their farms within the bounds of his charter. Colonists must purchase land from him. But he in turn sent advance notice that he would sell no land until he had first purchased it himself from the local chiefs. Penn strengthened his commitment by pledging that the injustices suffered previously by the Indians would no longer be tolerated. He promised strict regulation of the Indian trade and a ban on the sale of alcohol. Voltaire was later moved to write (though not with strict accuracy) that this was "the only league between those nations [Indian] and the Christians that was never sworn to, and never broken."[35]

When the first Quaker settlers arrived, they immediately began land negotiations with the Lenni Lenape. The Indians may have been suspicious of Penn's promises, which must have sounded like other European expressions of goodwill that had quickly evaporated. But the Lenni Lenape were no doubt impressed with the lavish supply of trade goods offered for the land along the Delaware River north of the site of what was to become the capital city of Philadelphia. Included were quantities of wampum, blankets, duffels, kettles, hoes, axes, knives, mirrors, saws, scissors, awls, and items of clothing. Also included were rum, powder, shot, and twenty guns, indicating that even those who professed nonviolence and wished to ban the sale of alcohol as a way of stabilizing relations could not afford to deny to Indians the trade goods they most desired.

Penn's arrival in 1682 brought him face to face with the Lenni Lenape. It was amity, not violence, that was on his mind, and the Indians may have detected this in his eagerness to learn about their language and culture. "I have made it my business to understand [their language], he wrote, "that I might not want an Interpreter on any occasion. And I must say, that I know not a language spoken in Europe that hath words of more sweetness in Accent and Emphasis, than theirs."[36]

Another factor conducive to peaceful relations was the absence of an extensive Indian trade. The fur trade flourished north of Pennsylvania, and though Penn made efforts to divert the interior trade so that it would pass through Philadelphia rather than Albany and New York, he was singularly unsuccessful. This was disappointing to Penn and his merchant friends, but in the long run it minimized the chances for misunderstanding and hostility between Pennsylvania and Indians. As for trade with more westerly Indians,

[34]C. A. Weslager, *The Delaware Indians: A History* (New Brunswick, N.J.: Rutgers University Press, 1972), p. 156.

[35]Quoted in Thomas E. Drake, "William Penn's Experiment in Race Relations," *Pennsylvania Magazine of History and Biography, 68* (1944): 372.

[36]Richard S. Dunn and Mary Maples Dunn, eds., *The Papers of William Penn,* vol. 2 (Philadelphia: University of Pennsylvania Press, 1981), p. 448.

the timing of the Quaker arrival made this impossible until well after the first generation of settlement. A thriving mid-Atlantic fur trade had existed between the Susquehannocks, who hunted in the regions inland from Delaware Bay, and the Dutch and Swedish traders, who had been established in the area since the 1620s. But the Susquehannocks had been weakened by competition and battle with the Iroquois to the north and then on the eve of the Quaker's arrival by hostilities with Marylanders and Virginians during Bacon's Rebellion. Thereafter the remnants of the tribe had migrated northward, where they placed themselves under the protection of their former enemies, the Iroquois. This had left eastern Pennsylvania inhabited only by small local tribes. Even as early as 1702 a prominent officeholder remarked that Penn's colony seemed "quite destitute of Indians"—a situation that made the Lenni Lenape more willing to sell land to Penn, knowing they had a land preserve to their west.[37]

So long as Penn's influence was as strong as his colony, Indian relations remained generally harmonious, aided by the absence of competition for land and the presence of only a meager fur trade. Penn resided only briefly in his colony and after 1712, when he suffered several disabling strokes, played almost no role in its affairs. Coinciding with the end of his influence was a development that sent Indian relations in Pennsylvania reeling in the direction that they had taken in other colonies: the arrival of waves of land-hungry and decidedly nonpacifist European settlers. When migrants who were not Quaker flooded the colony, the Friends commitment to pacifism wavered, and when Quakers lost political control of the area, the last chance of an autonomous Indian existence along the coastal plain of North American quietly disappeared. The limitations of the Quaker's Indian policies became clear. Penn's successors—first his wife and then his sons—never considered limiting the influx of non-Quaker settlers for the sake of the native peoples whom the massive immigration threatened.

Thus, the Quaker policy of toleration for all religious and ethnic groups attracted to Pennsylvania in the early eighteenth century the very European groups whose land hunger and disdain for the Indians undermined the Quaker attitude of trust and love. In 1710 and 1711 came the first of these, a group of Swiss Mennonites who settled sixty miles inland from Philadelphia. In 1717 a much larger group of German Protestants arrived, the vanguard of an influx of German immigrants who by mid-eighteenth century constituted about 40 percent of the colony's population. In the following year another wave of immigrants poured in—this time Scots-Irish, who began to locate near present-day Pittsburgh. None of these groups shared Quaker idealism about interracial harmony. They had been driven from their homelands by chronic economic depression and were

[37]Quoted in Francis Jennings, "The Indian Trade of the Susquehanna Valley," *Proceedings of the American Philosophical Society,* 110 (1966): 410.

concerned only about building a new life, centered around tilling the soil, in the remote regions of Penn's colony. To obtain land cheaply and live in a colony where they were free to practice their religion was all they asked. But they were not prepared in return to accommodate themselves to the local tribes, particularly if land speculators and government officials in Philadelphia cooperated with them in defrauding the Indians of their land.

Ironically, many of the Indians whom these refugees from European oppression confronted were also recent refugees. In the late seventeenth and early eighteenth centuries Pennsylvania's Susquehanna River valley became a sanctuary for a number of tribes that migrated from the south to west after hearing of the benevolent Quaker Indian policy. From Maryland came the Nanticokes and Conoys to escape war and enslavement that had decimated their tribes for several decades. "The People of Maryland," the Pennsylvania government was told by one Indian spokesman, "do not treat the Indians as you & others do, for they make slaves of them & sell their Children for Money."[38] From Virginia and North Carolina came the Tuscaroras and Tutelos for similar reasons. From the southwest came the Miamis and Shawnees, who had formerly lived in the Ohio River valley and traded with the French. Europeans who arrived later in the eighteenth century reaped benefits from these Indian refugees who cleared the land for crops, settled village sites near water transportation, and established trails for hunting. When Germans and Scots-Irish immigrants pushed into the interior, they used Indian routes to advance west, occupied Indian town sites, and took over the cleared fields.

The Lenni Lenape and other refugee tribes watched their situation deteriorate even as William Penn lay dying in England in 1718. They complained bitterly in Philadelphia that new settlers were building mill dams downstream from them, blocking the fish from coming upstream to spawn. Settlers poured in, squatting on land that had not been sold to Penn's government. But rather than fight, the tribes preferred to vacate their land, knowing what had happened in Virginia and New England when Indians resorted to violence. By 1724 the main branch of the Lenni Lenape, by now known as the Delaware, had migrated westward, part of them to an area not far beyond the limits of white settlement but others all the way to the Ohio River. They left heavy with resentment. A generation later, when they allied with the French and attacked their former English allies, the Pennsylvanians would reap the wind they had earlier sown. A leading Pennsylvanian wrote of their displacement: "These poor People were much disturbed . . . yet finding they could no longer raise Corn there for their Bread they quietly removed up the River Sasquehannah, though not without repining at their hard usage . . . Tis certain they have the same reason to resent this as all those other Indians on this Continent have had for the foundation of their

[38]Quoted in Weslager, *Delaware Indians*, p. 182.

Wars that in some places they have carried on so terribly to the destruction of the European Inhabitants."[39]

Eastern Pennsylvania was emptied of its Indian population in the second quarter of the eighteenth century. Pennsylvanians gained some Delaware land by assigning settler rights in the proximity of Indian villages—a tactic that usually drove Indians away. Settlers acquired other Delaware land by conniving with other Indians. Particularly, the Pennsylvanians turned to the Iroquois for help in expelling the last of the local tribes. The provincial government proposed an alliance with the Iroquois under which the powerful northern confederacy would assume suzerainty over all smaller tribes residing in Pennsylvania. The object of the alliance was to drive the Delawares from their homelands without having to resort to force. Thus in 1732 the Iroquois pressured one band of the Delawares to give up their lands at Tulepehocken, about sixty miles from Philadelphia, and migrate higher up the Susquehanna River to Shamokin where they were to live under the supervision of a minor Iroquois chief.

The Walking Purchase of 1737 fraudulently stripped the Delawares of their last land preserve, the area between the Lehigh and Delaware rivers known as the Forks of the Delaware, ended Penn's dream of harmony between Indian and European peoples, and initiated a turbulence that would

Lapowinsa, a Delaware chief, sat for this sympathetic portrait in 1735. Two years later he gave up a vast tract of land to William Penn's sons in the disreputable "Walking Purchase." (*Courtesy the Historical Society of Pennsylvania (HSP). Portrait by Gustavus Hesselius* [1834.3])

[39]Quoted in Francis Jennings, "The Delaware Interregnum," *Pennsylvania Magazine of History and Biography,* 89 (1965): 178.

soon end the "long peace." Two years before, James Logan, Pennsylvania's largest land speculator, produced what he alleged was a copy of an old deed signed in 1686 by which the forebears of the present Delaware leaders had ceded this land to William Penn. But the inability of Logan to produce an original copy, the lack of any reference to the transaction in the land records of Philadelphia, and the rarely mistaken oral tradition of the Indians, by which land transactions were scrupulously passed from generation to generation, all point to the conclusion that by now the Pennsylvanians were confident enough of their strength to force from the Delaware what they could not get by agreement.

Though the Delaware chiefs challenged the validity of the deed, they faced the combined opposition of the Pennsylvanians and the Iroquois. Finally they signed a confirmation of the alleged 1686 document, bowing to arguments that resistance would not halt incoming squatters from encroaching on their lands. In 1737, the Quaker government arranged to "walk off" the bounds of the Indian deed, which granted William Penn's heirs all the land from a specified point in Bucks County westward as far as a man could walk in a day and a half. Two of Penn's sons, who had recently arrived in Pennsylvania to bolster their sagging estates through the sale of land, personally participated in sending secret parties scouting through the woods to blaze a trail so that three specially trained walkers, operating as a relay team, could cover the ground as swiftly as possible. By this device the Penns extended their claim under the infamous "Walking Purchase" almost sixty miles into Delaware territory, far beyond the limits intended by the Delaware chiefs.

Nearly 1,200 square miles now became the property of the Penns. The 10 square miles they set aside as an Indian reservation did not diminish the bitterness of eastern Delaware leaders at this latest evidence of white dishonesty. While the Delawares refused to move off their land, white settlers poured in after purchasing small tracts of land from the Penns and James Logan, who had foresightedly made large purchases for himself in the area. With conflict impending, Pennsylvania authorities paid the Iroquois to remove the eastern Delawares. "We now expect from You," signaled Pennsylvania's governor to the Iroquois in 1741, "that you will cause these Indians to remove from the Lands in the forks of the Delaware and not give any further Disturbance to the Persons who are now in Possession."[40]

A year later Iroquois representatives gathered with the eastern Delaware chiefs in Philadelphia to fulfill their pledge. At a grand council the Iroquois flayed the Delawares:

> Let this Belt of Wampum serve to Chastize You; You ought to be taken by the Hair of the Head and shaked severely till you recover your

---

[40]Weslager, *Delaware Indians,* p. 190.

Senses and become Sober; you don't know what Ground you stand on, nor what you are doing ... We conquer'd You, we made Women of you, you know you are Women, and can no more sell Land than Women. Nor is it fitt you should have the Power of Selling Lands since you would abuse it. This land that you Claim is gone through Your Guts. You have been furnished with Cloaths and Meat and Drink by the Goods paid you for it, and now You want it again like Children as you are ... For all these reasons we charge You to remove instantly. We don't give you the liberty to think about it. You are Women; take the Advice of a Wise Man and remove immediately ... Depart the Council and consider what had been said to you.[41]

This withering blast stripped the eastern Delawares of their options. For several generations they had recognized themselves as subordinate to the Iroquois. But the tie had been reciprocal, for if the eastern Delawares recognized the authority of the Iroquois in matters of war and diplomacy, the Iroquois also counted on the Delawares as one of the southern "posts" of their league and respected Delaware management of their own land affairs. Now the eastern Delawares left Philadelphia humiliated by their former protectors. The Iroquois, lavishly entertained for their intercession, departed Philadelphia with a train of borrowed horses and wagons burdened down with shoes, stockings, hats, blankets, hatchets, hoes, and other goods. James Logan and the proprietors of Pennsylvania left with title to enough land to provide them with handsome income for years. The retreating Delawares would not forget, however. The taunts of the Iroquois that they were women and children still rang in their ears a dozen years later when they were among the first of the western tribes allied to the French to deliver a series of devastating strikes along the Pennsylvania frontier at the outset of the French and Indian War. The Indian friends of the Society of Friends had been turned into bitter enemies under the weight of population buildup, speculator greed, and the acquiescence of the second generation of Quakers.

The process of decimation, dispossession, and decline among the Indian societies of the coastal areas was thus accomplished in different ways during the first century of English colonization. In New England and on the Chesapeake, the demise was almost complete by the time English settlement was beginning in Pennsylvania and South Carolina. It had come in the north after steady resistance from the stronger tribes, who finally succumbed in pitched battle to an enemy that sought no genuine accommodation with them and was able to keep enough tribes out of the fray to prevail in a war of attrition. In Virginia and Maryland another course of events defeated the tidewater tribes. Here the Indians genuinely strove for accommodation

---

[41]*Minutes of the Provincial Council of Pennsylvania* (16 vols.; Philadelphia and Harrisburg, 1851–1853), 4: 578–80.

following the unsuccessful resistance movements of 1622 and 1644. As in New England, even as a friendly colonized people they were obstacles in the path of an acquisitive and expanding plantation society.

In South Carolina still another variation in the process of decline occurred. It was not dead Indians but Indians alive and in chains that benefited the white settlers. The buildup of the white population was slow enough and the desire among the Indians for trade goods intense enough that the white Carolinians could watch the coastal tribes obliterate each other in the wars for slaves, and then, when they were exhausted, employ the same strategy with the more powerful interior tribes.

The result was roughly the same in all the colonies along the seaboard. By the 1680s in the older colonies and by the 1720s in the newer ones, the coastal tribes were shattered. Devastated by disease and warfare, the surviving members of these tribes either incorporated themselves as subjects of stronger inland groups or entered the white man's world as detribalized servile dependents. The Indian's failure to survive cannot be attributed to an unwillingness or inability to intermix with the European newcomers—learning their languages, intermingling with them, adapting to their methods of trade and negotiation—as some historians have argued. The failure, rather, was to adapt too well to the material culture of the colonizers. The attachment to European trade goods and the persistence of ancient intertribal hostilities thwarted pan-tribal resistance, which alone could have ensured the survival of the coastal societies. "European trade had triumphed; European civilization had not."[42]

Too much can be made of the inability of the coastal tribes to unite in order to ensure their survival. Indian "factionalism" is the common explanation for their eventual defeat, and it carries with it the implication that Indians were incapable of political unification because of their backwardness. This is to forget, however, that "Indian" is a term invented by Europeans to describe a great variety of peoples who did not think of themselves as united in any racial, political, or even cultural sense. "European" is a similar term, used to embrace a number of people who would have shuddered at the idea that they were politically, culturally, or religiously the same. They had been fighting each other furiously in Europe for centuries. As colonizers in North America, they continued their antagonisms. Moreover, specific European groups, such as the English, were deeply factionalized. In Metacom's War these divisions among English colonizers were so great that they were only barely able to defeat an enemy whom they greatly outmatched in men and supplies. Metacom's difficulties in obtaining the aid of neighboring tribes was real; but this must be considered alongside the picture of

[42]James H. Merrell, *The Indians' New World: Catawbas and Their Neighbors from European Contact through the Era of Removal* (Chapel Hill: University of North Carolina Press, 1989), p. 91.

Governor Andros of New York invading Connecticut as the war was in progress, the sight of Bostonians expelling from their town the Massachusetts refugees who streamed in from burned-out frontier villages, and the fact of Rhode Island's neutrality during the war.

Although they were defeated, the coastal cultures performed a major service for tribes farther inland. Their prolonged resistance gave the interior societies time to adapt to the European presence and to devise strategies of survival as the westward-moving, swarming settlers approached them. "People like the Iroquois," it has been pointed out, "owed a great deal to the resistance of the coastal Algonkians, and both peoples were well aware of this."[43] The coastal tribes provided a buffer between the Indians of the interior and the Europeans, and when the coastal tribes lost their political autonomy, their remnants were often incorporated into the larger inland tribes. These were important factors in the far stronger opposition that the Iroquois, Cherokees, and Creeks offered to European encroachment—a resistance so effective that for the first century and a half of European colonization, the white newcomers were restricted to the coastal plain, unable to penetrate the Appalachians where the interior tribes, often allied with the French, held sway.

[43]T. J. C. Brasser, "The Coastal Algonkians: People of the First Frontiers," in Eleanor Burke Leacock and Nancy Oestreich Lurie, eds., *North American Indians in Historical Perspective* (New York: Random House, Inc., 1971), p. 73.

6

Europe, Africa, and the New World

The African slave trade, which began in the late fifteenth century and continued for the next 400 years, is one of the most important and tragic phenomena in the history of the modern world. Involving the largest forced migration in history, the slave trade and slavery were crucially important in building the trans-oceanic colonial empires of European nations and in generating the wealth that later produced the Industrial Revolution.

After 1492, Europe's orientation gradually shifted from the Mediterranean Sea to the Atlantic Ocean. The production locales of valuable and much desired commodities such as sugar, coffee, rice, and tobacco moved from the Old World to the Americas. In this radical reorientation, this creation of a dynamic system of trade and communication throughout the Atlantic basin, the continent of Africa became an essential factor. For Europeans, Africa became the indispensable source of human labor that enabled them to unlock the profits buried in the productive soils of America. One historian argues convincingly that European development of their colonies in the Americas "was strongly associated with slavery" and that African slaves, providing much of the colonial economies' labor, "accounted for most of the colonial export crops and . . . conferred wealth and income in greater measure on those places and times where slavery was established."[1]

The economic importance of the slave trade and slavery to Europeans who were connecting different zones of the Atlantic basin can hardly be overstated. But often overlooked in the story of post-1492 European settlement in the Americas is the cultural diffusion that took place when some twelve million Africans were brought to the western hemisphere. Six out of every seven persons who crossed the Atlantic to take up life in the Americas in the 300 years before the American Revolution were African slaves. As a result, in most parts of the colonized territories slavery "defined the context within which transferred European traditions would grow and change."[2] As slaves, Africans were Europeanized; but at the same time they Africanized the culture of Europeans in the Americas. In addition, the slave trade created the lines of communication for the movement of crops, agricultural techniques, diseases, and medical knowledge between Africa, Europe, and the Americas.

Just as they were late in colonizing the New World, the English lagged far behind their Spanish and Portuguese competitors in making contact with the west coast of Africa, in entering the Atlantic slave trade, and in establishing enslaved Africans as the backbone of the labor force in their overseas plantations. Moreover, among the English colonists in the New World, those on the mainland of North America were a half century or more behind those in the Caribbean in converting their plantation economies to slave labor. By 1670, for example, more than 100,000 slaves labored in Portuguese Brazil and about 30,000 cultivated sugar in English Barbados; but in Virginia only about 2,000 worked in the tobacco fields. Extensive cultural interaction of Europeans and Africans did not begin in North America until more than a century after it commenced in the southerly parts of the hemisphere. Much that occurred as the two cultures met in the Iberian colonies was later repeated in the Anglo–African interaction; yet the patterns of acculturation differed markedly in North and South America in the seventeenth and eighteenth centuries.

THE ATLANTIC SLAVE TRADE

A half century before Columbus crossed the Atlantic, a Portuguese sea captain, Antam Gonçalvez, made the first European landing on the west African coast south of the Sahara. What he might have seen, had he been able to travel the length and breadth of Africa, was a continent of extraordinary

---

[1]Barbara L. Solow, "Slavery and Colonization," in Solow, ed., *Slavery and the Rise of the Atlantic System* (Cambridge: Cambridge University Press, 1991), pp. 21–22.

[2]Sidney W. Mintz, "History and Anthropology," in *Race and Slavery in the Western Hemisphere,* Stanley L. Engerman and Eugene D. Genovese, eds. (Princeton, N.J.: Princeton University Press, 1975), p. 483.

variation in geography and culture. Little he might have seen would have caused him to believe that African peoples were naturally inferior or that they had failed to develop over time as had the peoples of Europe. Europeans invented the notion of African "backwardness" and cultural impoverishment after the slave trade had deposited millions of Africans in the Americas. This myth served to justify the cruelties of the slave trade and to assuage the guilt of Europeans involved in the largest forced dislocation of people in history.

The peoples of Africa may have numbered more than 50 million in the late fifteenth century when Europeans began making extensive contact with the continent. They lived in widely varied ecological zones—in vast deserts, in grasslands, and in great forests and woodlands. As in Europe, most people farmed the land and struggled to subdue the forces of nature in order to sustain life. That the African population had increased so rapidly in the 2,000 years before European arrival suggests the sophistication of the African agricultural methods. Part of this expertise in farming derived from skill in iron production, which had begun in present-day Nigeria about 450 B.C. This ability to fashion iron implements triggered the new farming techniques necessary to sustain larger populations. With large populations came greater specialization of tasks and thus additional technical improvements. Small groups of related families made contact with other kinship groups and over time evolved into larger and more complicated societies. The pattern was similar to what had occurred in other parts of the world—in the Americas, Europe, the Middle East, and elsewhere—when the "agricultural revolution" occurred.

Recent studies of "pre-contact" African history have shown that the "culture gap" between European and African societies when the two peoples met was not as large as previously imagined. By the time Europeans reached the coast of West Africa large trading empires had been in existence for centuries. The Kingdom of Ghana, for example, embraced the immense territory between the Sahara Desert and the Gulf of Guinea and from the Niger River to the Atlantic Ocean between the fifth and tenth centuries. Extensive urban settlement, advanced architecture, elaborate art, and a highly complex political organization evolved during this time. During Europe's Middle Ages two-thirds of all the gold circulating in the Mediterranean region came across the Sahara Desert from the gold-bearing regions of Ghana's Niger and Senegal rivers.

Invasion from the north by Muslim warriors weakened the Kingdom of Ghana, which in time gave way to the Kingdom of Mali. At the center of the Mali empire was the city of Timbuktu, noted for its extensive wealth and its Islamic university, where the faculty was as distinguished as any in Europe.

Lesser kingdoms such as those of Kongo, Zimbabwe, and Benin had also been in the process of growth and cultural change for centuries before Europeans reached Africa. Their inhabitants were skilled in metal working, weaving, ceramics, architecture, and aesthetic expression. Many of their towns rivaled European cities in size. Many communities of East and West Africa had complex religious rites, well-organized regional trade, codes of law, and elaborate political organization.

Of course, cultural development in Africa, as elsewhere in the world, proceeded at varying rates. Ecological conditions had a large effect on this. Regions blessed by good soil, adequate rainfall, and abundance of minerals, as in coastal West Africa, underwent rapid population growth and cultural elaboration after interregional trade began. Where inhospitable desert or nearly impenetrable forest held forth, social systems remained small and changed at a crawl. Contact with other cultures also brought rapid adaptations, whereas isolation impeded cultural change. The Kingdom of Ghana bloomed partly because of the trading contacts with Arabs, who had conquered the area by the eleventh century. Cultural change began to accelerate in East African Swahili societies after trading contacts began to flourish with the merchants from Arabia, India, and the East Indies in the tenth century.

The monstrous forced migration across the Atlantic began unofficially in the 1440s when Portuguese merchants began kidnapping and then trading slaves for horses on the West African Coast. In 1456, when Diego Gomes, representing the Portuguese crown, negotiated treaties of commerce and peace with several African coastal rulers, the slave trade received official sanction. So far as the Africans were concerned, the trade represented no striking new economic activity since they had long been involved in regional and long-distance trade across their continent. This was simply the opening of contacts with a new and more distant commercial partner. This is important to note because often it is maintained that European powers raided the African coasts for slaves, marching into the interior and kidnapping hundreds of thousands of helpless and hapless victims. In actuality, the early slave trade involved a reciprocal relationship between European purchasers and African sellers, with the Portuguese monopolizing trade along the coastlands of tropical Africa for the first century after making contact there. Trading itself was confined to coastal strongholds where slaves, most of them captured in the interior by other Africans, were sold on terms agreed to by the African sellers. In return for gold, ivory, and slaves, African slave merchants received European guns, horses, bars of iron and copper, brass pots and tankards, glass, beads, rum, and, especially, textiles. They occupied an economic role not unlike that of the Iroquois middlemen in the fur trade with Europeans.

Slavery was not a new social phenomenon for either Europeans or Africans. It flourished in ancient Greece and Rome, in early modern Russia and eastern Europe, in the Middle East, and in the Mediterranean world. Slavery had gradually died out in Western Europe by the fourteenth century, although the status of serf was not too different in social reality from that of the slave. But most important, in all these regions slavery and serfdom had nothing to do with skin color.

Within Africa itself, slavery had also existed for centuries. Africans, like other peoples, accepted it without question as a part of human organization and an important part of the accumulation of wealth. However, slavery involved personal service, often for a limited period of time, rather than life-long, degraded, agricultural labor. Slavery of a similar sort had also existed in Europe, mostly as the result of Christians enslaving Muslims and Muslims enslaving Christians during centuries of religious wars. One became a slave by being an "outsider" or an "infidel," by being captured in war, by volun-tarily selling oneself into slavery to obtain money for one's family, or by committing heinous crimes. Enslavement severely restricted an individual's rights and sharply limited opportunities for upward movement, but the en-slaved were regarded nevertheless as members of society, enjoyed protection under the law, and were entitled to certain rights, including education, mar-riage, and parenthood. Slaves in Africa often served as soldiers, adminis-trators, and even royal advisors. Most important, the status of slave was not irrevocable and did not automatically pass on to the slave's children.

For centuries African societies had been involved in an overland slave trade that transported black slaves from West Africa across the Sahara Desert to Roman Europe and the Middle East. But this was an occasional rather than a systematic trade, and it was designed to provide the trading nations of the Mediterranean with soldiers, household servants, and artisans rather than mass agricultural labor.

The African slave trade would never have become more than a minor commerce, as it was from the 1450s to the 1490s, without a growing labor shortage created by European overseas expansion. Between 1456 and 1505 Portugal brought about 40,000 enslaved Africans to Mediterranean Europe and the Atlantic islands—Madeira and the Canaries. But the need for slave labor lessened in Europe as European populations themselves began to grow beginning late in the fifteenth century. It is possible, therefore, that were it not for the colonization of the New World the early slave trade might have ceased after a century or more and be remembered simply as a short-lived incident stemming from early European contacts with Africa.

When Europeans reached the Americas, the course of history changed momentously. Once Europeans found the gold and silver mines of Mexico and Peru, and later, when they discovered a new form of gold in the pro-duction of sugar, coffee, and tobacco, their hunger for human labor grew astonishingly. At first Indians seemed to be the obvious source of labor, and in some areas, such as Mexico and Brazil, Spaniards and Portuguese were able to coerce native populations into agricultural and mining labor. But European diseases ravaged native populations, and the colonizers found that Indians, far more at home in their environment than white settlers, were difficult to subjugate. Indentured white labor from the mother country was another way of meeting the demand for labor, but this source was far too limited. It was to Africa that colonizing Europeans ultimately resorted.

Formerly a new source of trade, the continent now became transformed in the European view into the repository of vast supplies of human labor—"black gold."

From the early sixteenth to the late nineteenth centuries, almost four hundred years, Europeans transported Africans out of their ancestral homelands to fill the labor needs in their colonies of North and South America and the Caribbean. The most recent estimates, always slippery, place the number who reached the shores of the New World at about twelve million. Nearly as many, in the long period from 650 to 1900, were traded northward and eastward across the Sahara, the Red Sea, and the Indian Ocean. In addition, untold millions lost their lives while being marched from the interior to the coastal trading forts or during the "middle passage" across the Atlantic. Even before the English arrived in the Chesapeake Bay in 1607, the Spanish and Portuguese had carried several hundred thousand slaves to their Caribbean and South American colonies. Before European nations outlawed the slave trade in the nineteenth century, far more Africans than Europeans had crossed the Atlantic Ocean and taken up life in the New World. Black slaves, as one eighteenth-century Englishman put it, became "the strength and the sinews of this western world."[3]

Although the Spanish began to transport enslaved Africans across the Atlantic to work in the gold mines of Hispaniola in 1510, it was sugar that transformed the African slave trade. Produced in the Mediterranean world since the eighth century, sugar was for centuries a costly exotic item confined to sweetening the diet of the rich. By the mid-1400s, the liking for the taste of sweetness had spread rapidly, and the center of production had shifted to Madeira, the Portuguese island off the northwest coast of Africa. Here for the first time an expanding European nation established an overseas plantation society based on slave labor. From Madeira the cultivation of sugar spread to Portuguese Brazil in the late sixteenth century and then to the tiny specks of land dotting the Caribbean in the first half of the seventeenth century. By this time Europeans were developing an almost insatiable taste for sweetness. Sugar became one of the first luxuries that was transformed into a necessary item in the diets of the masses of Europe. The wife of the poorest English laborer took sugar in her tea by 1750 it was said. "Together with other plantation products such as coffee, rum, and tobacco," writes one anthropologist, "sugar formed part of a complex of 'proletarian hunger-killers,' and played a crucial role in the linked contribution that Caribbean slaves, Indian peasants, and European urban proletarians were able to make to the growth of western civilization."[4]

---

[3]Eric Williams, *Capitalism and Slavery* (Chapel Hill: University of North Carolina Press, 1966), p. 30.
[4]Sidney W. Mintz, "Time, Sugar, & Sweetness," *Marxist Perspectives*, No. 8 (1979), p. 60.

Once established on a large scale, the Atlantic slave trade dramatically altered the pattern of slave recruitment in Africa. At first, the slaves other Africans sold to Europeans were individuals captured in occasional wars or those whose criminal acts had cost them their rights of citizenship. But the vast new demand for a New World labor supply changed the process of obtaining slaves. Criminals and "outsiders" in sufficient number to satisfy the growing European demand in the seventeenth century could not be found. Therefore African kings resorted to warfare against their neighbors as a way of obtaining "black gold" with which to trade. European guns abetted the process. By 1730, Europeans were providing about 180,000 weapons a year to African slave-traders. The spread of kidnapping and organized violence in Africa soon became essential to maintaining commercial relations with European powers, while simultaneously muscling up the sway of the most militarily effective kingdoms.

In the forcible recruitment of slaves, young males—most of them 10 to 24 years old—were consistently preferred over women. Primarily this represented the preference of New World plantation owners for male field laborers. But it also reflected the decision of vanquished African villagers to yield up more men than women to raiding parties because women were the chief agriculturists in their society and, in matrilineal and matrilocal kinship systems, were too valuable to be sacrificed.

For the Europeans the slave trade itself became an immensely profitable enterprise. In the several centuries of intensive slave trading that followed the establishment of New World sugar plantations, European nations warred constantly for trading advantages on the West African coast. The coastal forts, the focal points of the trade, became key strategic targets in the wars of empire. The great Portuguese slaving fort at Elmina on the Gold Coast, begun in 1481, was captured a century and a half later by the Dutch. The primary fort on the Guinea coast, started by the Swedes, passed through the hands of the Danes, the English, and the Dutch between 1652 and 1664. As the demand for slaves in the Americas rose explosively after 1650, European competition for trading rights on the West African coast grew intense. By the end of the century monopolies for supplying European plantations in the New World with their annual quotas of slaves became a major issue of European diplomacy. The Dutch were the primary victors in the battle for the West African slave coast. Hence, for most of the century a majority of enslaved Africans who were fed into the expanding New World markets found themselves crossing the Atlantic in Dutch ships.

Not until the last third of the seventeenth century were the English of any importance in the slave trade. Major English attempts to break into the profitable trade began only in 1663, when Charles II, recently restored to the English throne, granted a charter to the Royal Adventurers to Africa, a joint-stock company headed by the king's brother, the Duke of York. Superseded by the Royal African Company in 1672, these companies enjoyed the exclusive right to carry slaves to England's overseas plantations. For thirty-four years after 1663 each slave they brought across the Atlantic bore the brand *"DY"* for the Duke of York, who himself became king in 1685. In 1698, individual merchants pressured Parliament to break the Royal African Company's monopoly. Thrown open to individual entrepreneurs, the English slave trade grew enormously. In the 1680s the Royal African Company had transported about 5,000 to 6,000 slaves annually (though interlopers brought in thousands more). In the first decade of free trade the annual average rose above 20,000. English involvement in the trade increased for the remainder of the eighteenth century until by the 1790s England had become the foremost slave-trading nation in Europe.

CAPTURE AND TRANSPORT OF SLAVES

No accounts of the initial enslavement of Africans, no matter how vivid, can quite convey the pain and demoralization that must have accompanied the forced march to the west coast of Africa and the subsequent loading aboard ships of those who had fallen captive to the African suppliers of the European slave traders. Without exaggeration, one historian has called it "the most traumatizing mass human migration in modern history."[5]

As the demand for African slaves doubled and redoubled in the eighteenth century, the hinterlands of western and central Sudan were invaded again and again by the armies and agents of both coastal and interior kings. Perhaps three-quarters of the slaves transported to English North America came from the part of western Africa that lies between the Senegal and Niger rivers and the Gulf of Biafra. Most of the others were enslaved in Angola on the west coast of Central Africa. Slaving activities in these areas were responsible for considerably depopulating the region in the eighteenth and nineteenth centuries.

Once captured, slaves were marched to the sea in "coffles," or trains. A Scotsman, Mungo Park, described the coffle he marched with for 550 miles through Gambia at the end of the eighteenth century. It consisted of 73 men, women, and children tied together by the neck with leather thongs. Several captives attempted to commit suicide by eating clay, another was abandoned after being badly stung by bees; still others died of exhaustion and hunger. After two months, with many of its members physically depleted by thirst, hunger, and exposure, the coffle reached the coast. There their captors herded them into fortified enclosures called barracoons.[6]

[5]Nathan I. Huggins, *Black Odyssey: The Afro-American Ordeal Under Slavery* (New York: Vintage Books, 1977), 25.

[6]Daniel P. Mannix and Malcolm Cowley, *Black Cargoes: A History of the Atlantic Slave Trade, 1518–1856* (New York: The Viking Press, Inc., 1962), pp. 101–02.

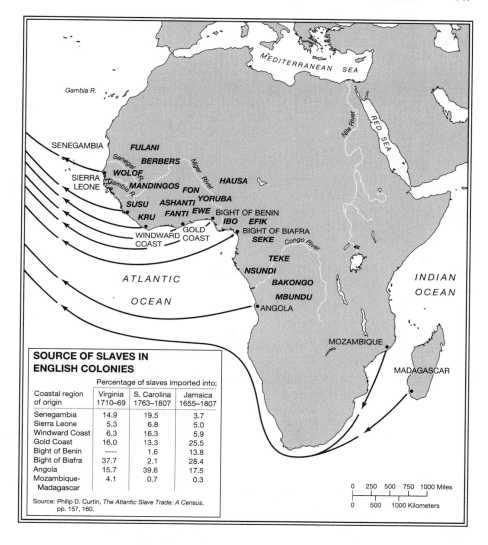

SOURCE OF SLAVES IN ENGLISH COLONIES

Coastal region of origin	Percentage of slaves imported into;		
	Virginia 1710–69	S. Carolina 1763–1807	Jamaica 1655–1807
Senegambia	14.9	19.5	3.7
Sierra Leone	5.3	6.8	5.0
Windward Coast	6.3	16.3	5.9
Gold Coast	16.0	13.3	25.5
Bight of Benin	----	1.6	13.8
Bight of Biafra	37.7	2.1	28.4
Angola	15.7	39.6	17.5
Mozambique-Madagascar	4.1	0.7	0.3

Source: Philip D. Curtin, *The Atlantic Slave Trade: A Census*, pp. 157, 160.

The anger, bewilderment, and desolation that accompanied the forced march, the first leg of the 5,000-mile journey to the New World, only increased with the actual transfer of slaves to European ship captains, who carried their human cargo in small wooden ships to the Americas. "As the slaves come down to Fida from the inland country," wrote one European trader in the late seventeenth century, "they are put into a booth or prison, built for that purpose, near the beach . . . and when the Europeans are to receive them, they are brought out into a large plain, where the [ships'] surgeons examine every part of every one of them, to the smallest member, men and women being all stark naked. Such as are allowed good and sound, are set on one side, and the others by themselves; which slaves so rejected are called Mackrons, being above 35 years of age, or defective in their lips, eyes, or teeth, or grown grey; or that have the venereal disease, or any other imperfection."[7] Such dehumanizing treatment was part of the commercial process by which slave traders selected and bargained for "merchandise." But it was also part of the psychological assault meant to strip away self-respect and self-identity from the Africans.

Cruelty followed cruelty. After purchase, many slaves were branded with a hot iron signifying the company, whether Spanish, Portuguese, English, French, or Dutch, that had purchased them. Thus were members of "pre-literate" societies first introduced to the alphabetic symbols of "advanced" cultures. "The branded slaves," one account related, "are returned to their former booths" where they were imprisoned until a full human cargo could be assembled.[8]

The next psychological wrench came with the ferrying of slaves, in large canoes, to the waiting ships at anchor in the harbor. An English captain described the desperation of slaves who were about to lose touch with their ancestral land and embark upon a vast ocean that many had never seen. "The Negroes are so wilful and loth to leave their own country, that they have often leap'd out of the canoes, boat and ship, into the sea, and kept under water till they were drowned, to avoid being taken up and saved by our boats, which pursued them; they having a more dreadful apprehension of Barbadoes than we can have of hell."[9] Part of this fear was the common belief that on the other side of the ocean Africans would be eaten by the white savages, "I was now persuaded that I had gotten into a world of bad spirits," wrote Orlando Equiano, one of the few slaves to publish a first-hand account of his enslavement, "and that they were going to kill me. Their complexions, too, differing so much from ours, their long hair, and the language they spoke . . . united to confirm me in this belief."[10]

The fear that inspired suicide while still on African soil intensified on the second leg of the voyage—the "middle passage" from the West African coast to the New World. Conditions aboard ship were horrendous, even though it was to the advantage of the ship captains to deliver as many slaves as possible on the other side of the Atlantic. Pitiful rations led to undernourishment, limited water produced dehydration, confinement below decks in leg irons for weeks spread diseases, the absence of basic hygiene ate at self-respect. Olaudah Equiano described how he was "put down under the decks,

---

[7]Quoted in Basil Davidson, *The African Slave Trade: Precolonial History, 1450–1850* (Boston: Little, Brown and Company, 1961), p. 92.

[8]*Ibid.*

[9]Quoted in Mannix and Cowley, *Black Cargoes*, p. 48.

[10]*The Interesting Narrative of the Life of Olaudah Equiano*, Written by Himself, edited by Robert J. Allison (Boston: Bedford Books, 1995), p. 53.

and there I received such a salutation in my nostrils as I had never experienced in my life: so that with the loathsomeness of the stench and crying together, I became so sick and low that I was not able to eat . . . I now wished for the last friend, death, to relieve me; but soon, . . . on my refusing to eat, one [sailor] held me fast . . . while the other flogged me severely."[11]

For ship captains good profits hinged on preserving rather than destroying life. Yet brutality was endemic, both in pitching overboard any slaves who fell sick on the voyage and in punishing offenders with almost sadistic intensity as a way of creating a climate of fear that would stifle insurrectionist tendencies. John Atkins, aboard an English slaver in 1721, described how the captain "whipped and scarified" several plotters of rebellion and sentenced others "to cruel deaths, making them first eat the Heart and Liver of one of them killed. The Woman he hoisted up by the thumbs, whipp'd and slashed her with Knives, before the other slaves, till she died."[12] Though the naval architects of Europe competed to produce the most efficient ships for carrying human cargoes to the New World, the mortality on board, for both black slaves below decks and white sailors above, was extremely high, averaging 10 to 20 percent on each voyage. The port physician of Charleston, South Carolina, opined "it is a wonder any escape with life" after inspecting many arriving in slave ships.[13]

That Africans sometimes attempted suicide and mutiny during the ocean crossing provides evidence that even the extraordinary force used in capturing, branding, selling, and transporting them from one continent to another was not enough to make the captives submit tamely to their fate. An eighteenth-century historian of slavery, attempting to justify the terroristic devices employed by slavers, argued that "the many acts of violence they [the slaves] have committed by murdering whole crews and destroying ships when they had it in their power to do so have made these rigors wholly chargeable on their own bloody and malicious disposition which calls for the same confinement as if they were wolves or wild boars."[14] The modern reader may suspect English self-justification in this characterization of enslaved Africans, but it also shows that submissiveness was often not a trait of those who were forcibly carried to the New World. So great was this resistance that special techniques of torture had to be devised to cope with the thousands of slaves who were determined to starve themselves to death on the middle passage rather than reach the New World in chains. Ship captains frequently ordered brutal whippings and hot coals applied to the lips to open the mouths of recalcitrant slaves. When this did not suffice, a special

[11]*Ibid.*, p. 54.
[12]Quoted in Davidson, *African Slave Trade*, pp. 94–95.
[13]Edmund Berkeley and Dorothy Smith Berkeley, *Dr. Alexander Garden of Charles Town* (Chapel Hill: University of North Carolina Press, 1969), p. 124.
[14]Edward Long, *The History of Jamaica* (London, 1774), quoted in Mannix and Cowley, *Black Cargoes*, p. 111.

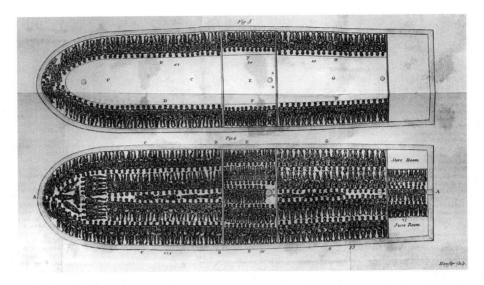

Pamphlets published in England in the late eighteenth century often used schematic drawings of slave ships to show the inhumanity of "tight packing." In this depiction of a 320-ton slave-trading vessel there appears to be a human cargo of 451 enslaved Africans. Because it was expected that numerous slaves would die in the "middle passage," ship captains often crowded more slaves into the hold than regulations allowed. (*Courtesy Library of Congress*)

instrument, the *speculum oris,* or mouth opener, was employed to wrench apart the jaws of a resistant slave.

Taking into consideration the mortality involved in the capture, the forced march to the coast, and the middle passage, probably not more than one in two captured Africans lived to see the New World or lasted there more than a year. Many of those who did must have been psychologically numbed as well as physically depleted by the experience. But one further step remained in the soul-testing process of enslavement—the auctioning to a New World master and transportation to his place of residence, where typically every fourth arriving African would die within the first four years on American soil. All in all, the relocation of any African brought westward across the Atlantic may have averaged about six months from the time of capture to the time of arrival at the plantation of a European slave master. During this protracted personal crisis, the slave was completely cut off from most that was familiar—family, wider kinship relationships, community life, and other forms of social and psychological security. Still facing these victims of the European demand for cheap labor was adaptation to a new physical environment, a new language, new work routines, and, most important, a life in which bondage for themselves and their offspring was unending.

THE DEVELOPMENT OF SLAVERY
IN THE NORTH AMERICAN COLONIES

Even though they were long familiar with Spanish, Dutch, and Portuguese use of African slave labor, English colonists did not turn immediately to Africa to solve the problem of cultivating labor-intensive crops. When they did, it could not have caused much surprise, for in enslaving Africans the English were merely copying their European rivals as they worked to fill the colonial labor gap. No doubt the stereotype of Africans as uncivilized made it easier for the English to fasten chains upon them. But the central fact remains that the English came to the New World, like the Spanish, Portuguese, Dutch, and French, to make a fortune as well as to build religious and political havens. Given the long hostility they had borne toward Indians and their experience in enslaving them, any scruples the English might have had about enslaving Africans quickly disappeared.

Making it all the more natural to employ Africans as a slave labor force in the mainland colonies was the precedent that English planters had set on their Caribbean sugar islands. In Barbados, Jamaica, and the Leeward Islands (Antigua, Monserrat, Nevis, and St. Christopher), Englishmen in the second and third quarters of the seventeenth century learned to copy their European rivals in employing Africans in the sugar fields and, through extraordinary repression, in molding them into a slave labor force. By 1680, when there were not more than 7,000 slaves in mainland North America and the institution of slavery was not yet unalterably fixed, upwards of 65,000 Africans toiled on sugar plantations in the English West Indies. Trade and communication were extensive between the Caribbean and mainland colonists, so settlers in North America had intimate knowledge concerning the potentiality of slave labor.

It is not surprising, then, that the North American colonists turned to the international slave trade to fill their labor needs. Africans were simply the most available people in the world for those seeking a bound labor force and possessed of the power to obtain it. What is surprising is that the North American colonists did not turn to slavery more quickly than they did. For more than a half century in Virginia and Maryland it was primarily the white indentured servant and not the African slave who labored in the tobacco fields. Moreover, those Africans who were imported before about 1660 were held in various degrees of servitude, most for limited periods and only a few for life.

The transformation of the labor force in the southern colonies, from one in which many white and a relatively small number of black indentured servants labored together to one in which black slaves served for a lifetime and composed the bulk of unfree labor, came only in the last third of the seventeenth century in Virginia and Maryland and in the first third of the eighteenth century in North and South Carolina. The reasons for this

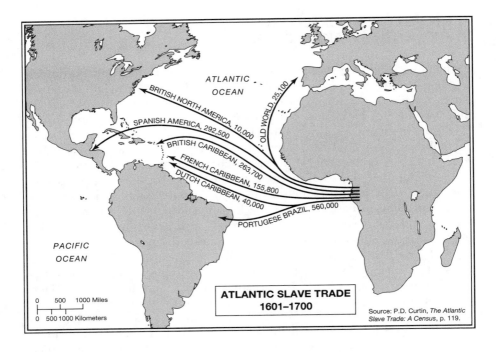

ATLANTIC
OCEAN

BRITISH NORTH AMERICA, 10,000

OLD WORLD, 25,100

SPANISH AMERICA, 292,500

BRITISH CARIBBEAN, 263,700

FRENCH CARIBBEAN, 155,800

DUTCH CARIBBEAN, 40,000

PORTUGESE BRAZIL, 560,000

PACIFIC
OCEAN

0   500   1000 Miles

0   500 1000 Kilometers

**ATLANTIC SLAVE TRADE
1601–1700**

Source: P.D. Curtin, *The Atlantic
Slave Trade: A Census*, p. 119.

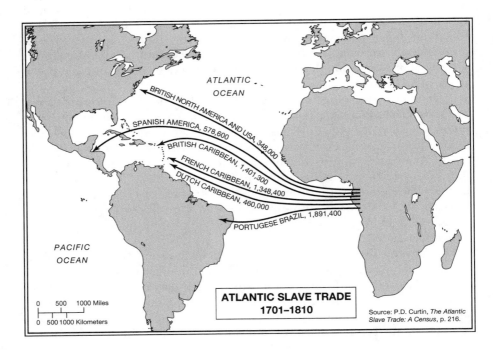

ATLANTIC
OCEAN

BRITISH NORTH AMERICA AND USA, 348,000

SPANISH AMERICA, 578,600

BRITISH CARIBBEAN, 1,401,300

FRENCH CARIBBEAN, 1,348,400

DUTCH CARIBBEAN, 460,000

PORTUGESE BRAZIL, 1,891,400

PACIFIC
OCEAN

0   500   1000 Miles

0   500 1000 Kilometers

**ATLANTIC SLAVE TRADE
1701–1810**

Source: P.D. Curtin, *The Atlantic
Slave Trade: A Census*, p. 216.

shift to a slave-based agricultural economy in the South are twofold. First, English entry into the African slave trade gave the southern planter an opportunity to purchase slaves more readily and more cheaply than before. Cheap labor was what every tobacco or rice planter sought, and when the price of slave labor dipped below that of indentured labor, the demand for black slaves increased. Second, the supply of white servants from England began to dry up in the late seventeenth century, and those who did cross the Atlantic were spread among a growing number of colonies. Thus, in the late seventeenth century the number of Africans imported into the Chesapeake colonies began to grow while the flow of white indentured servants diminished to a trickle. As late as 1671 slaves made up less than 5 percent of Virginia's population and were outnumbered at least three to one by white indentured servants. In Maryland the situation was much the same. But within a generation, by about 1700, Africans represented one-fifth of the population and probably a majority of the labor force. A Maryland census of 1707 tabulated 3,003 white bound laborers and 4,657 black slaves. Five years later the slave population had almost doubled. Within another generation white indentured servants were declining rapidly in number, and in all the southern colonies African slaves made up the backbone of the agricultural work force. "These two words, *Negro* and *slave*," wrote one Virginian, had "by custom grown Homogenous and Convertible."[15]

To the north, in Pennsylvania, New Jersey, and Delaware, where English colonists had settled only in the last third of the 1600s, slavery took root on a more limited basis because cold winters did not allow the labor-intensive year-round crops that made massive slave labor profitable. New York was an exception, and shows how a cultural preference could alter labor patterns usually determined by ecological factors. During the period before 1664, when the colony was Dutch, slaveholding had been practiced extensively, encouraged in part by the Dutch West India Company, one of the chief international suppliers of slaves. The population of New York remained largely Dutch for the remainder of the century, and the English who slowly filtered in saw no reason not to imitate Dutch slave owners. Thus New York became the largest importer of slaves north of Maryland. In the mid-eighteenth century, the areas of original settlement around New York and Albany remained slaveholding societies with about 20 percent of the population composed of slaves and 30 to 40 percent of the white householders owning human property.

As the number of Africans increased, lawmakers constructed legal codes for strictly controlling slave activities. These "black codes" were largely borrowed from the law books of the English West Indies. Bit by bit they deprived the African immigrant—and a small number of Indian slaves as

---

[15]Quoted in Winthrop D. Jordan, *White Over Black: American Attitudes Toward the Negro, 1550–1812* (Chapel Hill: University of North Carolina Press, 1968), p. 97.

well—of rights enjoyed by others in the society, including indentured servants. Gradually they reduced the slave, in the eyes of society and the law, from a human being to a piece of chattel property. In this process of dehumanization nothing was more important than the rule of hereditary lifetime service. Once servitude became perpetual, relieved only by death, the stripping away of all other rights followed as a matter of course. When the condition of the slave parent was passed on to the child, then slavery had been extended to the womb.

With the passage of time, Africans in North America had to adapt to a more and more restricted world. Earlier in the seventeenth century they had been treated much as indentured servants, bound to labor for a specified period of years but thereafter free to work for themselves, hire out their labor, buy land, move as they pleased, and, if they wished, hold slaves themselves. But, by the 1640s, Virginia was forbidding blacks the use of firearms. In the 1660s courts began describing marriages between white women and black slaves as "shameful Matches" and "the Disgrace of our Nation"; during the next few decades interracial fornication became subject to unusually severe punishment and interracial marriage was banned.

These discriminatory steps were slight, however, in comparison with the stripping away of rights that began toward the end of the century. In rapid succession slaves lost their right to testify before a court; to engage in any kind of commercial activity, either as buyer or seller; to hold property; to participate in the political process; to congregate in public places with more than two or three of their fellows; to travel without permission; and to engage in legal marriage or parenthood. In some colonies legislatures even prohibited the right to education and religion, for lawmakers thought these might plant the germ of freedom in slaves. Step by step, white masters hedged their slaves within a legal system that made no allowance for their education, welfare, or future advancement. Even the restraints on the slave owner's freedom to deal with slaves in any way he or she saw fit came under attack. Early in the eighteenth century many colonies passed laws forbidding the manumission of slaves by individual owners, a step designed to squelch the strivings of slaves for freedom and to discourage those who had been freed from helping fellow Africans to gain their liberty.

The movement to annul all the slave's rights had both pragmatic and psychological dimensions. The greater the proportion of slaves in the population, the greater the danger to white society, for every colonist knew that when he purchased a man or woman in chains he had bought a potential insurrectionist. The larger the specter of black revolt, the greater the effort of white society to neutralize it by further restricting the rights and activities of slaves. Following a black revolt in 1712 that took the lives of nine whites and wounded others, the New York legislature promptly passed a slave code that rivaled those of the southern colonies. Throughout the southern colonies the fear of slave insurrection ushered in routinized violence as the means of ensuring social stability. Allied to this need for greater and greater control was the psychological compulsion to dehumanize slaves by taking from them the rights that connoted their humanity. It was far easier to rationalize the merciless exploitation of those who had been defined by law as something less than human. "The planters," wrote an Englishman in eighteenth-century Jamaica, "do not want to be told that their Negroes are human creatures. If they believe them to be of human kind, they cannot regard them . . . as no better than dogs or horses."[16]

Thus occurred one of the great paradoxes in American history—the building of what many thought was to be a utopia in the wilderness upon the backs of black men and women wrenched from their African homeland and forced into a system of abject slavery. White colonists imagined America as a liberating and regenerating force, it has been pointed out, but it became instead the scene of a "grotesque inconsistency." In the land heralded for freedom and individual opportunity, the practice of slavery, unknown for centuries in the mother country, became as much a part of the landscape as trees and rivers. Following other parts of the New World, North America became the scene of "a disturbing retrogression from the course of historical progress."[17]

The mass enslavement of Africans profoundly affected white racial prejudice. Once inscribed in law, slavery cast Africans into such lowly roles that the initial bias against them was confirmed and vastly strengthened. Initially unfavorable impressions of Africans had coincided with labor needs to bring about their mass enslavement. But it required slavery itself to crystallize the negative racial feelings into a deep and almost unshakable prejudice that continued to grow for centuries. Irrevocably caught in the web of perpetual servitude, the slave had little opportunity to prove the white stereotype wrong. Socially and legally defined as less than human, African-Americans became a truly servile, ignoble, degraded people in the eyes of the Europeans. This was used as further reason to keep them in slavery, for it was argued that they were worth nothing better and were incapable of occupying any higher role. In the long evolution of racial attitudes in America, nothing was of greater importance than the enslavement of Africans.

SLAVERY IN NORTH AND SOUTH AMERICA

Because slavery existed in virtually every part of the New World, the best way to discover what was unique about the system of bondage that formed in the North American colonies is to compare it with slavery in other regions of

[16]Edward Long, *The History of Jamaica* . . . (London, 1774), II, Book 2, p. 270.
[17]David Brion Davis, *The Problem of Slavery in Western Culture* (Ithaca, N.Y.: Cornell University Press, 1966), p. 25.

the New World. Only about one in twenty slaves brought to the New World came to British North America. The 350,000 Africans who arrived there between 1619 and 1780 were dwarfed by the two million transported to Portuguese Brazil, the three million taken to British, French, and Dutch plantations in the West Indies, and the 700,000 imported into Spanish America. How did slaves fare in different parts of the New World, and how can we explain the differences in their treatment, their opportunities for emancipation, and their chances, once free, to carve out a worthwhile niche for themselves in society?

The first historians to study slavery comparatively in the Americas argued that crucial differences evolved between the status of slaves in the Spanish or Portuguese colonies and the English colonies. These differences, they maintained, largely account for the fact that racial mixture is much more extensive today in Latin America than in North America, that formal policies of segregation and discrimination were never embodied in Latin American law, and that the racial tension and conflict that has characterized twentieth-century American life has been largely absent in Latin American countries such as Brazil. Interracial marriage can be taken as one illuminating example of these differences. "Miscegenation," a word invented in New York City in 1864 to sneer at racial intermarriage, has never been prohibited in Brazil and such prohibition was thought a senseless and artificial separation of people. In the American colonies however, white cultural standard bearers thought otherwise. Legal prohibitions against interracial mixing began in the mid-seventeenth century, and virtually every American colony prohibited mixed marriages by the early eighteenth century. Modified from time to time, these laws remained in force throughout the period of slavery and in many states continued after the abolition of slavery. As late as 1948 mixed marriages were prohibited by law in twenty-nine states, including seventeen outside the South. Not until 1967 were state laws prohibiting interracial marriage struck down by the Supreme Court.

Such differences as these, it has been argued, indicate that slavery in Spanish and Portuguese America was never as harsh as in Anglo-America nor were the doors to eventual freedom so tightly closed. In Latin America, Africans mixed socially and sexually with the white population from the beginning; they were never completely stripped of political, economic, social, and religious rights; they were frequently encouraged to work for their freedom; and, when the gate to freedom was opened, they found it possible to carve a place of dignity for themselves in the community. In the North American colonies, by contrast, slaves lost all of their rights by the early eighteenth century and were thereafter treated as mere chattel property. Emancipation was rare, and several colonies prohibited it in the eighteenth century. Those African-Americans who did obtain their freedom, especially after the American Revolution, found themselves permanently consigned to the lowliest positions in society. Resenting the aspirations of free blacks, white lawmakers gradually rescinded the social and political rights initially granted them as citizens. In entitling his book *Slave and Citizen*, Frank Tannenbaum, a pioneer in the comparative study of slavery, summarized his view of the differing fates of the African migrant in the two continents of the Americas.[18]

By what series of events or historical accidents had the Africans in the Latin American colonies been placed on the road to freedom while in English North America the road traveled by blacks always led to a dead end, even after freedom was granted? Tannenbaum and those who followed him suggested that the answer lay in the different ideological and cultural climates in which the Africans struggled in the New World. Those who were enslaved in the Spanish and Portuguese colonies entered a culture that was Catholic in religion, semimedieval and authoritarian in its political institutions, conservative and paternalistic in its social relations, and Roman in its system of law. Africans brought to North America, by contrast, confronted a culture that was Protestant in religion, libertarian and "modern" in its political institutions, individualistic in its social relations, and Anglo-Saxon in its system of law. Ironically it was the "premodern" Spanish and Portuguese culture that protected slaves and eventually prepared them for something better than slavery. The Catholic church not only sent its clergy to the New World in far greater numbers than did the Protestant churches, but wholeheartedly devoted itself to preserving the human rights of Africans. Affirming that no individual, no matter how lowly his position or corrupt his behavior, was unworthy in the sight of God, the Catholic clergy toiled to convert people of every color and condition, wherever and whenever they found them. Indians and Africans in the Latin American colonies therefore became fit subjects for the zeal of the Jesuit, Dominican, and Franciscan priests. The church, in viewing masses of enslaved Indians and Africans as future Christians, had a tempering effect on what slave masters might do with their slaves or what legislators, reflecting planter opinion, might legislate into law.

In a similar way the application of Roman law in the Iberian colonies served to protect the slave from becoming mere chattel property, for Roman law recognized the rights of slaves and the obligations of masters to them. The slave undeniably occupied the lowest rung on the social ladder but he or she remained a member of the community, entitled to legal protection from a rapacious or sadistic master.

Still a third institution mediated between master and slave—the government itself. Highly centralized, the Spanish and Portuguese political systems revolved around the power of the monarch and the aristocracy, and this power was expected to radiate out from its metropolitan centers in Europe to the New World colonies. Colonies existed under strict royal

[18]Frank Tannenbaum, *Slave and Citizen: The Negro in the Americas* (New York: Alfred A. Knopf, 1946).

governance, and since the Crown, closely tied to the Catholic church, was dedicated to protecting the rights of slaves, slave owners in the colonies had to answer to a social policy formulated at home. In sum, a set of interconnecting institutions, derived from a conservative, paternalistic culture, worked to the advantage of African slaves by standing between them and their masters. Iberian institutions, transplanted to the New World, prohibited slave owners from exercising unbridled rein over their slaves and ensured that the slave, though exploited, was also protected and eventually prepared for full membership in the society.

In the English colonies of North America and the Caribbean, it is argued, these intermediating institutions were notably absent. Slave masters were far freer to follow their impulses in their treatment of slaves and in formulating laws that undergirded slavery. In North America, government was more localized and democratic, church and state more separate, and individuals less fettered by tradition and authority. Hence slaves were at the mercy of their masters to an unusual degree. The Protestant church had little interest in proselytizing slaves. When it did, its authority was far more locally based than in the Spanish and Portuguese colonies and therefore subject to the influence of the leading slave owners of the area.

Government too was less centralized; England allowed the colonists to formulate much of their own law and exercised only a weak regulatory power over the plantations. Anglo-Saxon law, transferred to the New World, was silent on the subject of slavery because slavery had not existed in England for centuries. This left colonists free to devise new law, as harsh and exploitative as they wished, to cope with the labor system they were erecting. In North America, it is maintained, slave owners molded a highly individualistic, libertarian, and acquisitive culture that brooked few checks on the right of slave owners to exploit their human property exactly as they saw fit. It was property rights that the Anglo-American culture regarded as transcendently important. With relatively few institutional restraints to inhibit slave owners, nothing stood between new African immigrants and a system of total subjugation. Consequently, Tannenbaum and others have argued, a far more closed and dehumanizing system of slavery evolved in the more "enlightened" and "modern" environment of the English colonies than in the more feudalistic and authoritarian milieu of the Spanish and Portuguese colonies.

In recent decades historians, sociologists, and anthropologists have challenged this analysis of slavery and race relations in the New World. By looking too intently at Spanish and Portuguese laws, traditions, and institutions in the mother countries, historians underestimated the gap that often separated legal pronouncements from social reality. Is it possible that in the Spanish and Portuguese law books slaves were carefully protected, but in actuality their lives were as bad as or worse than in the English plantations? Laws do not always reflect actual social conditions. If we had only the post-

Civil War legal statutes as a guide to the status of the African-Americans in the nineteenth and twentieth centuries, we might conclude that they enjoyed equality with white Americans in the modern era. The laws guarantee nothing less. But what the law specified and what actually occurred are two different things.

Looking more closely at local conditions in various New World colonies, historians have found that the alleged differences between North and South American slavery do not loom so large. Where the Catholic church and royal authority were well established, such as in urban areas, the treatment of slaves was indeed more humane than in areas of the American colonial South, such as South Carolina, where the Protestant churches took only shallow root. But in rural areas of the Spanish and Portuguese colonies, where slavery was most extensively practiced, the church's sway was not so strong and the authority of the Spanish colonial officials was more tenuous. In these areas individual slave masters were left to deal with their slaves as they saw fit, much as in the English colonies.

Moreover, recent studies show that wide variations in the treatment of slaves occurred within the colonies of each European nation. In Puritan New England and Quaker Pennsylvania conditions were never so inhumane as in the South, partly because the Puritan and Quaker churches acted as a restraint on the behavior of slave owners and partly because slaves, always a small percentage of the population, were more frequently employed as artisans and household servants than in the South, where mass agricultural labor was the primary concern of slave masters. Likewise, conditions were far better for slaves in the Brazilian urban center of Recife than on the frontier plantations of the remote southern province of Rio Grande do Sul.

Other factors, quite separate from the ideological or cultural climate of a given area, have claimed the attention of historians more forcefully in recent attempts to delineate differences in slave systems and to isolate the unique facets of English slavery in North America. The most important factor shaping a slave society was its economic base. Where blacks worked in the plantation system, producing cash crops such as sugar, coffee, tobacco, and rice, they suffered thralldom at its brutal worst. In these areas the conditions of human life could be appalling. These included English rice plantations in the eighteenth century, Portuguese coffee plantations in the nineteenth century, and sugar plantations of all European colonizers from the seventeenth to the nineteenth centuries. Maximizing profit was the overriding goal on such plantations, and it was best achieved by literally working slaves to death and then replacing them with newly imported Africans.

When agricultural areas were enjoying boom times and rapid expansion, as in the cases of eighteenth-century South Carolina and nineteenth-century Cuba, the exploitation of slaves was usually found at its extreme limits because special incentives existed for driving bondsmen and bondswomen to the limit of human endurance. Also of great significance in the lives of slaves was the kind of crop they were employed at growing. Sugar was particularly labor intensive, its cultivation requiring the most strenuous, debilitating labor, as opposed, for example, to wheat or corn. Perhaps nowhere was the treatment of slaves so callously regarded as on the sugar plantations of the Caribbean, where the combination of absentee owner-ship, the work regimen, and the highly capitalized nature of the economic system made life a living hell for slaves, regardless of whether they toiled on English Barbados, Dutch Surinam, French Saint Dominigue, or Spanish Cuba. Slaves were regarded "as so many cattle" who would "perform their dreadful tasks and then expire" after seven or eight years, as one English-man wrote in 1788.[19]

In fringe areas, by contrast, where slaves were used for occasional labor or as domestic servants and artisans, conditions were much better. In northerly areas only one crop a year was possible and winter brought slack times. In cities the work rhythms were not so intense and the social climate encouraged a religious and humanitarian ideology that tempered the bru-tality inherent in the master–slave relationship. In Anglo-Dutch New York City and Portuguese Recife, as well as in rural New England and New France, slaves were often badly used by their masters, but their chances for a semblance of a meaningful life were far greater than on the expanding cash crop plantations.

A second factor affecting the dynamics of particular slave societies was the simple ratio of blacks to whites. Where slaves represented a small frac-tion of the total population, such as in New England and the mid-Atlantic English colonies, slave codes did not strip African-Americans of all their rights. Religion and education were commonly believed to be beneficial to slaves, and no protests were heard when Quakers and Anglicans set up schools for Negroes in places such as Boston and Philadelphia. Marriage was customary and black parents often baptized their children in the Protestant churches, even though death brought burial in a separate "strangers" grave-yard. Slaves were freer to congregate in public places and were recognized before courts of law in these areas.

From Maryland to Georgia, however, conditions were markedly differ-ent. In the Chesapeake colonies, slaves represented about 40 percent of the population by the mid-eighteenth century, and in South Carolina they out-numbered whites at all times after 1710. In these areas lawmakers created far more repressive slave codes. The same was true in the English Caribbean islands, where whites were vastly outnumbered throughout the eighteenth century. Surrounded by those whom they had enslaved, control became a crucial factor for white slave owners, who lived in perpetual fear of black in-surrections. Numerically inferior, they took every precaution to ensure that

[19]Quoted in C. Vann Woodward, *American Counterpoint: Slavery and Racism in the North–South Dialogue* (Boston: Little, Brown and Company, 1971), p. 101.

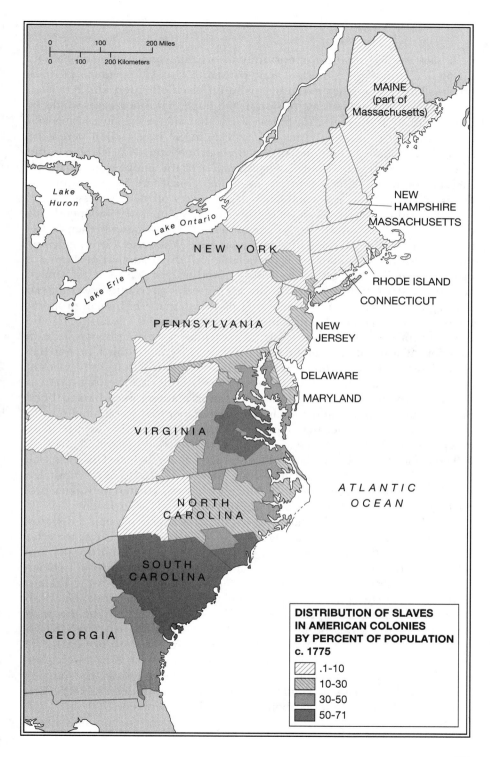

0 100 200 Miles
0 100 200 Kilometers

Lake Huron

Lake Ontario

Lake Erie

MAINE
(part of
Massachusetts)

NEW
HAMPSHIRE

MASSACHUSETTS

NEW YORK

RHODE ISLAND

CONNECTICUT

PENNSYLVANIA

NEW
JERSEY

DELAWARE

MARYLAND

VIRGINIA

*ATLANTIC
OCEAN*

NORTH
CAROLINA

SOUTH
CAROLINA

GEORGIA

**DISTRIBUTION OF SLAVES
IN AMERICAN COLONIES
BY PERCENT OF POPULATION
c. 1775**

.1-10

10-30

30-50

50-71

their slaves would have no opportunity to organize and plot against them. Living in a kind of garrison state amid constantly circulating rumors of black revolt, white planters heaped punishment on black offenders and retaliated with ferocity against black aggression in the hope that other slaves would be cowed into submissiveness. Castration for sexual offenses against whites and burning at the stake for plotting or participating in insurrection were common punishments in colonies with a high proportion of black slaves. But where slaves represented only a small fraction of the population usually no such elaborate attempts were made to define their inferior status in precise detail or to leave them so completely at the mercy of their owners.

Two other factors affecting the lives of slaves operated independently of the national backgrounds of their owners. The first was whether or not the slave trade was still open in a particular area. When this was so, new supplies of Africans were continuously available and the treatment of slaves was usually harsh. To work a slave to death created no problem of replacement. Where the slave trade was closed, however, greater precautions were taken to safeguard the capital investment that had been made in human property, for replacement could be obtained only through reproduction—a long and uncertain process. The sugar island of Barbados, for example, was a death trap for Africans in the eighteenth century. From one-third to one-half of all slaves died within three years of their arrival. But with fresh supplies of African slaves readily available and with virtually nothing to restrain them in the treatment of their human property, sugar planters were free to build their fortunes through an exploitation of slave labor that was limited only by calculations of cost efficiency. This, along with ravaging epidemics, resulted in a ghastly mortality. Between 1712 and 1762 deaths outnumbered births by 120,000 among a slave population that averaged about 50,000. This meant little to the English planters, for they could view this carnage as an inevitable if regrettable part of the process by which wealth was created and sugar produced for household consumption in every village in Great Britain.

A final factor affecting slave life was the prevalence of tropical diseases. In the temperate zones, including most of North America, slaves were far less subject to the ravaging fevers that swept away both Europeans and Africans in the tropical zone. This is of the utmost importance in explaining why mortality rates were lower and fertility rates higher in the English colonies of North America than in the Caribbean and South American colonies of various European powers. The startling fact is that less than 5 percent of the slaves brought to the New World came to British North America, and yet by 1825 African-Americans represented 36 percent of all peoples of African descent in the hemisphere. By contrast, Brazil, which imported about 38 percent of all slaves brought to the Americas, had only 31 percent of the African descendants alive in the hemisphere in 1825. The British West Indies imported about 850,000 slaves between 1700 and 1787, but the black population of the islands in the latter year was only about

350,000. In contrast, the American colonies imported less than 250,000 in the same period, but counted about 575,000 Negroes in the population in 1780. These starkly different demographic histories reflect several variables—differences in male–female ratios during the slave period, treatment of slaves, and fertility rates among free Negroes, for example. But however these factors may ultimately sort out, it is clear that Africans brought to the North American colonies, except those in South Carolina and Georgia, had a far better chance for survival than their counterparts in the tropical colonies.

Alongside the treatment of slaves on the plantations of the different European colonizers, we need to consider the access to freedom found by slaves in one colony as opposed to another. While historians are still arguing vigorously about the question of comparative treatment, they largely agree that slaves in the Spanish and Portuguese colonies had far greater opportunities to work themselves free of the shackles of bondage than did slaves in the English colonies. Census figures for the eighteenth century are fragmentary, but we know that by 1820 the ratio of free Negroes to slaves was about one to six in the United States, one to three in Brazil, one to four in Mexico, and one to two in Cuba. In Spanish Cuba alone, free blacks outnumbered by 30,000 the number of manumitted slaves in all the southern states in 1800, although the black population of the American South tripled that of Cuba.

Some historians have interpreted this greater opportunity for freedom in the Spanish and Portuguese colonies as evidence of the relatively flexible and humane nature of the system there and as proof of the Iberian commitment to preparing the enslaved African for citizenship. But others, who argue that demographic and economic factors were supremely important, are more persuasive. They point out that the white *need* for free blacks, not humanitarian concern for black freedom, motivated most Spanish and Portuguese slave owners to emancipate their human property. Because the English had immigrated to the American colonies in far larger numbers than the Spanish or Portuguese, they were numerous enough to fill most of the positions of artisan, overseer, cattle tender and militiaman—the "interstitial work of the economy."[20] But the relatively light European immigration to the Spanish and Portuguese colonies left them desperately short of people who could function above the level of manual labor. Therefore it became necessary to create a class of free blacks, working for whites as wage laborers; otherwise the economy would not have functioned smoothly for the benefit of white landowners, merchants, and investors. Where Africans were functional as freedmen in the white man's society, they were freed; where they were not, they remained slaves. To be sure, masters were seldom limited by law in manumitting their slaves in Spanish and Portuguese

[20]Carl N. Degler, *Neither Black Nor White: Slavery and Race Relations in Brazil and the United States* (New York: The Macmillan Company, 1971), p. 44.

colonies, as they were in English colonies; but this testifies more to the fact that the law followed the social and economic needs of society than to any benevolent concern for the slave derived from ancient precedent. If free blacks had not been needed in Latin American society or if it had been more profitable to close the door to freedom than to keep it ajar, it is unlikely that slaves would have been manumitted in such large numbers.

A second way in which free blacks were vital to the interests of white colonizers in Latin America and the Caribbean was as a part of the system of military defense and internal security. North American and Brazilian slave systems, for example, diverged strikingly in their attitudes toward arming slaves and in creating a community of free blacks. Brazilian colonists could not have repelled French attacks in the late sixteenth century, the Dutch invasion in the second quarter of the seventeenth century, and the French assaults in the early eighteenth century without arming their slaves. "Because the mother country . . . was too weak or unconcerned to offer much assistance," writes Carl Degler, "all the resources of the sparsely settled colony had to be mobilized for defense, which included every scrap of manpower, including black slaves."[21] In the American colonies, by contrast, the need to arm slaves was comparatively slight. Naval raiders of other European powers intermittently endangered colonial shipping, but the colonies were only rarely subjected to external attack. Where they were, principally in South Carolina, slave owners resorted to the Portuguese pattern. Threatened by the Spanish in Florida, the Carolinians passed a law in 1707 requiring every militia captain "to enlist, traine up and bring into the field for each white, one able Slave armed with a gun or lance."[22] In the Yamasee War of 1715, South Carolina gladly used slaves to stave off the attacks of their Indian enemies. But this was the exception rather than the rule.

For the internal security of plantation society, armed slaves would have been a contradiction, but free blacks were not. They could be used to suppress rebellion, to repel marauding escaped slaves living beyond the plantations, or to invade and defeat maroon communities. But rebellion and maroonage occurred primarily in plantation societies where blacks massively outnumbered whites and where the geography favored the establishment of communities of escaped slaves. Such was the situation in the English West Indies, where the mountainous island interiors provided ideal refuges for maroons. By freeing slaves, the Caribbean planters secured the loyalty and military service of a corps of islanders who kept the slave-based sugar economy going. In North America the security problem was less severe. The ratio of white to black was more even and geography did not favor maroonage because the interior was occupied by powerful Indian tribes who were only

[21] *Ibid.*, p. 79.
[22] Verner W. Crane, *The Southern Frontier, 1670–1732* (Ann Arbor: University of Michigan Press, 1956), p. 187n.

occasionally receptive to runaway slaves. Far from being regarded as loyal adjuncts of white society, the small number of free Negroes in the American colonies were usually seen as a threat to the security of the slave system and were therefore often compelled to leave the colony where they had been manumitted within a specific period of time.

A third, crucially important way in which the African was more valuable as a freed person than as a slave in the Caribbean and Latin American colonies was as a sexual partner. "No part of the world," writes one historian, "has ever witnessed such a gigantic mixing of races as the one that has been taking place in Latin America and the Caribbean since 1492."[23] In explaining this racial mixing, it is relevant that the Spanish and Portuguese had been interacting with people from Mediterranean, Middle Eastern, and North African cultures through centuries of war and economic relations. This developed in their societies a certain plasticity in race relations. The English, by comparison, had remained relatively isolated in their island fortress prior to the late sixteenth century, intermingling hardly at all with people of other cultures.

But the inherited Iberian attitudes, transported to the New World, would probably have faded had it not been for compelling circumstances that encouraged racial mingling in such places as Mexico, Peru, and Brazil. Spanish and Portuguese males emigrated without women to a greater extent than Englishmen, who came predominantly with their families. In the Spanish and Portuguese cases the colonizers carried with them a racial ideology that, while it favored white skin and European blood, was still malleable enough to justify mixing with Indian and African women. In the Latin American colonies interracial sexual relations were common, as the colonizers took Indian and African women as mistresses, concubines, and wives. Such partnerships were accepted with little embarrassment or social strain, for it was regarded as natural to have sexual relations with or even to marry a woman of dark skin.

Such was not the case in most of the English colonies. English women had come with English men to Puritan New England, establishing rough parity between the sexes from the beginning. This obviated the need for Indian and African women. In the southern colonies, where white women were in short supply for four or five generations, African women were also absent because the importation of slaves remained insignificant until the last decade of the seventeenth century. By the time black women were available in large numbers, the numerical disparity between white men and women had been redressed. It was not so much extreme ethnocentrism as it was the presence of white women that made racial crossings officially disreputable and often illegal, though practiced privately to a considerable extent. If white

---

[23]Magnus Mörner, *Race Mixture in the History of Latin America* (Boston: Little, Brown and Company, 1967) p. 1.

men had continued to lack English women at the time when African women began flooding into the southern colonies, then the alleged English distaste for dark-skinned partners would doubtlessly have broken down. Womanless men are not easily restrained by ethnocentrism in finding release for their sexual urges, as was demonstrated by the English experience in the West Indian sugar islands. In Barbados, Jamaica, and the Leeward Islands, English women were not as plentiful as in the mainland colonies. But surrounded by a sea of black women, Englishmen eagerly followed the practice of the Spanish and Portuguese, consorting with and occasionally marrying their slaves. "Not one in twenty can be persuaded that there is either sin or shame in cohabiting with his slave," wrote a Jamaica planter.[24] To outlaw sexual relations with African women, as was being done in the English mainland colonies in the eighteenth century, Winthrop Jordan has suggested, would have been more difficult than abolishing the sugar cane.[25] Where white women were absent, black women were needed; where they were needed, they were accepted and laws prohibiting interracial sex and marriage never entered the statute books.

Slavery in the Americas took many forms: in the treatment of slaves, the degree of openness in the system, and the willingness of the dominant society to mix intimately with the Africans in their midst. The cultural heritage brought to the New World by the various European settler groups played some role in the formation of attitudes, policies, and laws. But the exigencies of life in the New World, including economic, sexual, and military needs, did far more to shape racial attitudes and the system of slavery.

[24]Long, *History of Jamaica*, II, Book 2, p. 328.
[25]Jordan, *White Over Black*, p. 140.

7

The African Ordeal
Under Slavery

It is easy to assume that Africans, once sold into slavery and brought to the Americas, were simply fitted into a closed system of forced labor where they lived out their lives, abject and de-Africanized, as best they could. So much attention is lavished on the kind of slave system fashioned by slave owners—the black codes they legislated, their treatment of slaves, the economic development they directed—that the slaves themselves are often forgotten as active participants in a cultural process. How did they respond to the loss of their freedom and the separation from all that was familiar in their native culture? How did they live day by day in a vastly different culture? To what extent were they acculturated into white European society? To what degree did they mold a new Afro-American culture, distinct from the European culture surrounding them? Until we adopt the approach of studying the interior lives of slaves, replacing the question "What was done to the slaves?" with the question, "What did slaves do for themselves and how did they do it?", we will continue to view slaves only as the object, but not the subject, of our historical inquiries.[1]

[1]Eugene D. Genovese, *In Red and Black: Marxian Explorations in Southern and Afro–American History* (New York: Random House, Inc., 1971), p. 106.

COPING WITH ENSLAVEMENT

The central problem for Africans who found themselves in the possession of a European master 5,000 miles from their homeland was to create social spaces and lifeways that would allow them to live as satisfactorily as possible under an oppressive slave regimen. This problem was not one of merging a West African culture with a European culture, because the human cargoes disgorged from slave ships did not come from a single African society. Slaves arriving in North America were culturally diverse, coming from many different tribes with distinct characteristics. In the matter of language, for example, Africans had no common medium of communication, for they spoke a diversity of tongues. Similarly, they had been taken from regions in Africa where kinship systems, social organization, and political structures differed. Hence, arriving slaves did not form "communities" of people at the outset but could become communities only by forging a new culture out of the elements of many old cultures and shards of the dominant European culture that now bounded their existence. "What the slaves undeniably shared at the outset," it has been written, "was their enslavement; all—or nearly all—else had to be created by them."[2]

In the encounter between the diverse cultural heritages of the African slaves and the relatively homogeneous culture of the European slaveocracy, the preponderance of power exercised by the colonizers must always be kept in mind. Slaves, to be sure, drew upon their various African heritages to make life bearable in the New World. White slave owners were aware of these attempts of their slaves to maintain inherited cultural practices, and they undoubtedly allowed this insofar as it did not interfere with the "seasoning" of new slaves. When it impeded adaptation to the new system of life and work, slave masters tried to obliterate such Africanisms. But this involved a continuous struggle between slave and master. The master's ideal was to convert the slave into a mindless drudge who obeyed every command and worked efficiently for the master's profit. But never in the long history of slavery could the memory, habit, and belief of slaves be entirely wiped away. And never could slavery, however brutal and dehumanizing, completely overawe and cow its victims. Black men and women in the English colonies, as elsewhere, "were able to find the means to sustain a far greater degree of self-pride and group cohesion than the system they lived under ever intended for them to be able to do," not because "the system was more benign than it had been pictured, but rather that human beings are more resilient, less malleable, and less able to live without some

[2]Sidney W. Mintz and Richard Price, *An Anthropological Approach to the Afro–American Past: A Caribbean Perspective* (Philadelphia: Institute for the Study of Human Issues, 1976), p. 10.

sense of cultural cohesion, individual autonomy, and self-worth" than many historians have maintained.[3]

The status difference between slave and free, in other words, was immense, and power was very unequally divided. Yet Africans and Euro-Americans interacted continuously under slavery because both groups were tied together in a state of intimate interdependence. Masters could set the boundaries of the slave's existence, defining physical location, work roles, diet, and shelter; but the master had far less control over how slaves established friendships, fell in love, formed kin groups, raised their children, worshipped their gods, buried their dead, organized their leisure time, and so forth. At this "much deeper and more fundamental level of interpersonal relationships and expressive behavior" Africans in America exercised a considerable degree of autonomy and were thus able to draw on their cultural backgrounds in shaping an African-American character.[4]

In this process of adaptation there was a built-in premium on cultural innovation and creativity. This was both because slaves had to adjust rapidly to the power of the master class, which bore so heavily on them, and because of the initial cultural diversity of the Africans brought to the colonies. Thrown together with slaves from other tribes and thrust into a system of bondage, "all slaves must have found themselves accepting, albeit out of necessity, countless 'foreign' cultural practices."[5] Nostalgia for the homeland and for old ways no doubt endured, but the overriding instinct was to survive. This required rapid adaptation, learning new ways of doing things that ensured survival. It was imperative, therefore, that Africans adopt "a general openness to ideas and usages from other cultural traditions, a special tolerance (within the West African context) of cultural differences."[6] Yet in adopting new lifeways, Africans did not discard what was familiar and habitual. Rather, they adapted customary ways of living, working, worshipping, grieving, celebrating, and associating to the requirements of a brutal and foreign new environment. Of all the peoples converging in seventeenth- and eighteenth-century North America, the Africans, by the very conditions of their arrival, developed the greatest cultural dynamism and the greatest capacity for individual creativity and cultural change.

Masters, it can be readily imagined, were frequently insensitive to the cultural creativity of their slaves and to the local African-American lifeways that were being formed from the time Africans first landed. They preferred

[3]Lawrence W. Levine, *Black Culture and Black Consciousness: Afro–American Folk Thought From Slavery to Freedom* (New York: Oxford University Press, 1977), p. xi.

[4]David Dalby, "The African Element in American English," in *Rappin' and Stylin' Out: Communication in Urban Black America.* T. Kochman, ed. (Urbana: University of Illinois Press, 1972), p. 173.

[5]Mintz and Price, *Anthropological Approach to the Afro–American Past,* p. 24.

[6]*Ibid.,* p. 26.

to think of their slaves as animals or, in legal terms, as property. Property cannot think and create; animals cannot learn new languages, cultivate crops, create music and dance. This was the central contradiction in the New World system of chattel slavery—that while treating their human property inhumanely and defining their slaves as less than human, the master class implicitly had to recognize the humanity of their slaves, for the slaves' ability to work, think, and express emotion (and to revolt against, resist, and ridicule their oppressors) was in itself dramatic proof of this.

REGIONAL VARIATIONS
OF NORTH AMERICAN SLAVERY

"Saltwater" Africans, as colonists called slaves brought directly from Africa, and their creole offspring, slaves born in America, did not all face the same conditions in North America. African-American culture was shaped differently in distinct regions because slavery itself varied markedly. The complexity of black culture in North America cannot be understood without considering the shaping of these distinct, regional black societies over a period of more than a century.

Spanish and French Borderlands

Before a single enslaved African touched soil in the English colonies, slaves by the thousands were present in North America. They came first with fifteenth-century Spanish explorers. Juan Ponce de León's Florida expedition of 1513 included Africans, who served valuably as scouts and ship handlers. As many as one hundred Africans accompanied Lucas Vasquez de Ayllón's 1526 reconnaissance of the South Carolina coast. When a leadership crisis beset the 600-man expedition, some Africans fled to the Guale Indians and began the mixing of African and Indian blood that would continue in North America for centuries.

Another expedition, in 1528, produced the most colorful and talented African of sixteenth-century North America. Estevancio, born in Morocco, accompanied his Spanish master of the Narváez expedition through Florida and was one of four survivors of this ill-fated intrusion into Indian lands. During several years of enslavement in a Florida Indian tribe, Estevancio's talent blossomed as a healer, linguist, guide, and diplomat. When the four survivors fled Florida and made their way through hostile Indian land to Mexico, Estevancio was the indispensable man. In 1539, he was the trailblazer for Coronado's Spanish expedition into what would become Arizona and New Mexico.

The importance of Africans on these arduous expeditions through uncharted territory gave slavery a distinct character in the early Spanish settlements. The slaves did much of the difficult work as field laborers, on supply trains, and in fort and church construction; but they were equally important as soldiers, guides, and linguists. Moreover, they crossed their blood so frequently with the Indians, and sometimes with the Spanish, that slavery had little of the caste-like condition of English slaves. Two hundred years after Africans had accompanied the early Spanish expeditions through the southern parts of North America, African-Mexicans represented a significant fraction of settlers in Mexico's northern frontier, including what would become the American Southwest.

Similarly, in the Southeast, Africans carved out economic and social spaces for themselves that had little parallel in the later English colonies. For example, de Soto had dozens of slaves with him as he cut a terrifying swath through Florida in 1639–42, and some of the Africans escaped to live among the Indians. Africans also arrived with the Spanish in the 1560s and helped construct St. Augustine, the Spanish fortress in Florida erected in 1565. As its northern outpost, St. Augustine became critical to Spain's Caribbean defense. More than a century later, in 1686, St. Augustine's black militia regiments, both free and slave, fought lustily to dislodge the budding English settlements in South Carolina. For many decades after that, African-Spaniards on the Florida frontier demonstrated their military prowess as guerrilla fighters against the South Carolinians. For their bravery, dozens of them received freedom from Florida's Spanish governor in 1738, whereupon they promptly settled North America's first free black town, Pueblo de Gracia Reál de Santa Terese de Mose (known simply as Mose). Two miles north of St. Augustine, Mose was led by African-born Francisco Menendez. Though English attacks scattered the free blacks of Mose in 1740, the town regathered in 1752 and lasted until Spain ceded Florida to the British in 1763. A tiny outpost of free blacks in a region based on slave labor, Mose had a short and precarious existence but one that offered an important example of enslaved Africans wresting freedom on the frontiers of European settlement.

French slaves were as important to the development of Louisiana as they were to Spanish Florida. Arriving with skills as rice growers, indigo processors, metal workers, river navigators, herbalists, and cattle keepers, the West Africans became the backbone of the economy. Like the male slaves in Spanish Florida, they mingled extensively with Indian women, producing mixed-race children known locally as *grifs*. African women sometimes made interracial liaisons with French immigrants, often soldiers in search of partners.

Always precariously perched in Louisiana with limited numbers of French settlers, French governors used enslaved Africans extensively as militiamen and sometimes granted them freedom for military service. To secure freedom, Africans fought in the Chickasaw War of the 1730s and in the next decade against the Choctaws. For the French it was doubly advantageous to draw on black military skills because pitting them against hostile Indians reduced the chance of what might have been a disastrous Indian–African alliance. All in all, the chance of gaining freedom in extremely fluid French Louisiana exceeded that of any other colony in the southeastern part of the continent, and the absorption of free blacks into white society, particularly if they were of mixed race descent, was shockingly common from the English point of view. As in all places in the Americas where slavery ruled, violence and brutality were commonplace. But in French Louisiana the desperate need for African skills as well as African labor led to a porous line between white and black—a racial openness seldom found in the English colonies.

Representing the greater racial flexibility on the French frontiers in North America was the shrewd and ambitious Jean Baptiste Pointe Du Sable. Forging north from New Orleans in the 1770s, this mixed-blood immigrant from Saint Domingue, born of a French father and African mother, became a legendary trapper and hunter in the Illinois country controlled by the French. With his Potawatomi wife, he established himself at the mouth of the Chicago River near Lake Michigan, where he flourished as a trader, miller, and land speculator. From the village of Eschikagou arose the metropolis of Chicago.

The Chesapeake

Slavery in Virginia and Maryland evolved through three different periods. For nearly the first half century after Africans first arrived in Virginia, they were treated by the tobacco planters much as were white indentured servants. Life was brutal and often short, for the planters were intent on wringing every bit of profit they could from the tobacco frontier. The Africans were predominantly male, and many of those who did not succumb to disease and the work regimen gained their freedom and became landowners themselves. In this period before the 1660s, when slavery was legalized, they adapted rapidly to white society, for without many of their homelanders in the region—in 1675 there were only about 2,500 slaves in Virginia and half that number in Maryland—racial cohesiveness was difficult to maintain. Black and white bond laborers "ran away together, slept together, and, upon occasion, stood shoulder to shoulder against the weighty champions of authority."[7]

Beginning in the 1670s, Chesapeake planters began to import slaves in much larger numbers. By the early eighteenth century the agricultural labor force was overwhelmingly black. Probably 75,000 slaves, almost all of them coming directly from Africa, entered the Chesapeake colonies between 1700 and 1750. This had a profoundly Africanizing effect on black plantation society. In a period of rapid expansion, Virginia planters used many of these

[7]Ira Berlin, "Time, Space, and the Evolution of Afro–American Society in British Mainland North America," *American Historical Review*, 85 (1980): 69.

new immigrants to develop new upland plantations. There they worked in small groups to clear the land and plant tobacco, living on an unruly frontier remote from the older tidewater settlements. Planters used creole slaves far more frequently in the tidewater area, where sex ratios were becoming better balanced and black family life was developing.

The convergence of African and creole slave societies in Virginia and Maryland began in the 1740s. By this time natural reproduction was supplying most of the additional slaves that Chesapeake planters needed. By the eve of the American Revolution only 10 percent of the annual increase in Virginia's slave population could be attributed to imports from Africa. An increasingly creole black population was reproducing itself, and with this reproduction came a rapid balancing of the sex ratio, which in turn created greater possibilities for family life. Facilitating the growth of black kinship networks was the greater density of slave settlement, the growth of larger plantations where dozens of slaves labored together, and the development of a network of roads and market towns that allowed for greater mobility between plantations. In addition, as the Chesapeake economy began to shift in the 1740s from tobacco monoculture to a mixed economy of tobacco, wheat, and iron production, the nature of black labor began to change. More slaves learned artisan skills, required in a more diversified and urbanized economy. This expanded their universe, drawing many away from the dull, backbreaking labor of tending tobacco plants and giving them many points of contact with the larger society beyond the single plantation. Still, large numbers of slaves worked on small plantations, and none were ever free from the threat that the debts or death of their masters would put them on the auction block and shatter their family.

By the late colonial period Chesapeake Afro-Americans had achieved considerable "social space" in which to maneuver. They continued to live in close proximity to whites, for almost all Virginia and Maryland planters resided on their plantations and "prided themselves on regulating all aspects of their far-flung estates through a combination of direct personal supervision and plantation-based overseers."[8] But while slaves might work from sunup to sundown under the overseer's whip and the master's shadow, from sundown to sunup and during the Sabbath and holidays they were largely out of sight and sound of their owners. Black culture grew in the unintended interstices of an institution designed to extract labor from its victims. Because a growing proportion of them were American-born, had successfully established a family life, and labored within an increasingly diversified economy, they were becoming part of a unified Afro-American culture. At the same time, this culture was far more connected to Anglo-American culture and far more shaped by it than were the lowland colonies to the south.

---

[8]*Ibid.*, p. 76.

The Carolina and Georgia Low Country

Africans first came to the marshy waterways of the Carolina coast with their West Indian masters who settled the country, so they had already made an adjustment to life in the English-speaking parts of the New World. The Carolina frontier was a rugged, dangerous place in the late seventeenth century, as the colonizers engaged in Indian wars, Indian slave trading, and periodic skirmishes with the Spanish and French. This vulnerability to external enemies made slaves vital to colonial defense, and thus South Carolina became the one colony that offered freedom to any slave "who in Time of an Invasion kills an Enemey."[9] This relative flexibility in the slave system was magnified by the familiarity of West Africans with the semitropical environment of the lowlands. White settlers depended on their slaves to adapt African techniques of rice cultivation and cattle herding to a geography and climate foreign to their masters. "Transplanted Englishmen," it has been written, "learned as much or more from transplanted Africans as did the former Africans from them. . . . White domination made itself felt, but both whites and blacks incorporated much of West African culture into their new way of life."[10] Far more than on the Chesapeake, Africans defined the culture in which they labored in the early years of settlement.

In the early eighteenth century, after the agricultural skills of West Africans had made rice the keystone of the lowlands economy, slavery entered a new phase. Only about four thousand slaves toiled in South Carolina in 1708, but that number tripled in the next twelve years and then tripled again by 1740, when nearly forty thousand slaves inhabited the rice coast, outnumbering whites by two to one. This demographic revolution brought the end of the relatively open, flexible system of slavery known in the early years. Large rice and indigo plantations emerged. Slaves lived in larger units (much larger than the Chesapeake plantations) and worked under brutal conditions in field gangs. Increasingly, prosperous planters retreated to the coastal cities, especially Charleston, leaving field labor to the supervision of overseers and black drivers. By 1737 a Swiss newcomer opined that Carolina "looks more like a negro country than like a country settled by white people."[11]

A notable fracture appeared in the ranks of slaves as the coastal lowlands experienced the "rice and indigo revolution." In the capital city of Charleston, a creole population of African-Americans, representing more than half the city's population, lived in close proximity to white society. As house servants, boatmen, dockworkers, and artisans, they became relatively mobile, skilled, and privileged. Some mixed sexually with slave masters, producing a

---

[9][Thomas Nairne], *A Letter from South Carolina . . .* (London, 1710).
[10]Berlin, "Afro–American Society in British Mainland North America," p. 56.
[11]Quoted in Peter Wood, *Black Majority: Negroes in Colonial South Carolina from 1670 Through the Stono Rebellion* (New York: Alfred A. Knopf, 1974), p. 132.

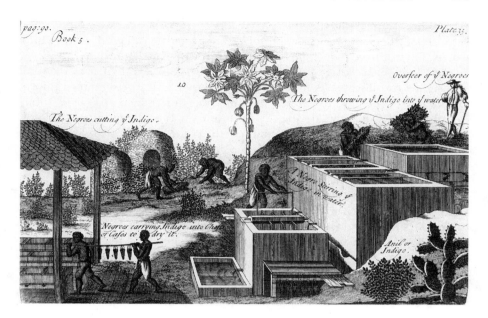

The work routines of cultivating, harvesting, and processing rice and indigo, pictured here, were carried out in an environment where heat, humidity, disease, brutality, and incessant labor took a terrible toll on slaves. Next to the sugar regimens in the Caribbean, rice and indigo production was the worst to be found in the Americas. *(By permission of the Folger Shakespeare Library)*

considerable mulatto population that formed the basis of a small free black population. Hewing close to white culture, these urban African-Americans mastered the English language and the intricate interracial personal relationships required in the cities to obtain privileges from the ruling whites.

But on the large plantations, black culture moved in the opposite direction. Slaves represented a large proportion of the population and lived in relative isolation from white culture. They had truck gardens to supply much of their own food needs and labored in the task system, where the daily work routine was defined by quotas—feet of irrigation ditch to be dug, rows of rice to be harvested, or mortars of rice to pound. Both of these developments gave them a degree of independence from close white management. Combined with the fact that so many of them were recently arrived from Africa, this led to the creation of a culture that more than anywhere else in British North America was West African in its characteristics. This was reflected in their distinctive language patterns, burial ceremonies, religion, and child-naming preferences. For example, Gullah became the primary tongue on the rice coast among slaves. A "pidgin," or mixture of several languages, it combined elements of English and a variety of West African dialects. Gullah emerged as the slaves' "central mode of communication and expression, linking together people of widely disparate backgrounds" who, because of their numerical superiority and relative isolation from white society, did not have to assimilate so thoroughly to white culture as did slaves in the Chesapeake colonies.[12] This greater degree of West African cultural persistence can also be seen in naming patterns. African day names (given for the day of the week on which the child was born) such as Quaco, Juba, Quashee, and Cuba can frequently be found in the plantation records of South Carolina but are far less common in plantation records of Virginia and Maryland. On the rice and indigo plantations of the Carolina lowlands African-Americans remained more culturally distant from the world of their captors than in other colonies, and thus culturally closer to Africa.

The same was true in Georgia, the last North American colony to be established by the British. For the first fifteen years after founding the colony in 1733, its proprietors worked wholeheartedly to prohibit slavery. But settlers became more and more vocal in demanding slaves—"the one thing needful," they claimed, for economic success. Once the threat of the Spanish in Florida was removed in the 1740s, the ban on slavery collapsed, and South Carolina planters flocked to Georgia to institute a slave economy that closely resembled what they had left behind in Carolina.

The North

Slaves in the North made up only 2–3 percent of the population in most of New England and Pennsylvania and up to 8–12 percent in Rhode Island, New Jersey, New York, and Delaware. Yet the northern colonies were more involved in slavery than these figures suggest. New England's shipowners and captains were deeply involved in slave trading, and the northern exports of wheat, fish, and wood products to the slave regimes of the West Indies proved central to economic growth. Representing a small minority in the population, enslaved Africans in the northern regions toiled differently than on southern plantations. Infrequently employed in field gangs, northern slaves typically worked as artisans, farmhands, or personal servants. Whereas a majority of southern slaves worked on plantations with many other slaves, the typical northern slave labored alone or with only a few of his or her countrymen. Moreover, the plantation slave quarters, where blacks could maintain a considerable degree of cultural autonomy and privacy away from the watchful eye of the owner, had no equivalent in northern slave life. Most northern slaves ate, slept, and lived in the house of the master. All of these factors—their low proportion of the population, wide dispersion, and unrelieved contact with whites—made attempts to retain a link to the African past very difficult, while ensuring that acculturation proceeded at a relatively rapid pace. A notable exception to this northern pattern was the Narragansett

[12]*Ibid.*, p. 191.

region of Rhode Island, where large landowners frequently owned 5 to 40 slaves and one merchant landowner in 1766 owned as many as 238.

In the northern cities slavery was far more deeply rooted than in the countryside. In New York City, where the Dutch had begun a tradition of relying on slave labor during the half century they controlled the town, almost 20 percent of the population was African-American in 1750 and two of every five householders owned at least one slave. In Philadelphia and Boston in the mid-eighteenth century, slaves made up about a tenth of the population and could be found in the homes of nearly every fifth family. In all three cities more than a thousand black slaves labored for their masters in the decade before the Revolution. These urban blacks were always rubbing elbows with lower-class whites—on the docks, at the markets, in the workplace of the master craftsman, in taverns, and at street entertainments such as cockfights. Slavery in the North was onerous to be sure, but its harshest features were mitigated by the absence of death-dealing gang labor in the fields, by the closer living relationship between masters and bond persons, and, in the cities, by the large degree of mobility and privileges that slaves gradually wrung from the master class.

The assimilationist tendency in the North was somewhat reoriented by the large influx of slaves directly from Africa beginning in the 1740s. As the northern colonies grew rapidly in the eighteenth century, the call for bond labor increased. More and more large shipments of slaves arrived, reaching a peak during the late 1750s when the Seven Years' War cut off the supply of white indentured servants from Ireland and Germany. Urban white officials noticed the introduction of African ways—burial ceremonies, dances, song, and other entertainments.

Perhaps the most vivid evidence of the infusion of an African strain in northern African-American culture was the mid-century introduction in many northern towns of "Negro Election Day," an annual festival that drew blacks from the surrounding countryside to the cities for feasting, parading, dancing, and the election of black kings, judges, and other officials. "All the various languages of Africa, mixed with broken and ludicrous English filled the air," reported a white observer in Newport, Rhode Island, "accompanied with the music of the fiddle, tambourine, the banjo [and] drum."[13] In a ritual of role reversal, blacks in the towns dressed in the clothes of their masters, rode their masters' horses, feasted and drank on tributes exacted from their owners, and symbolically ruled the town for a day. Negro Election Day imitated the masters' election-day festivities, but it was more. It gave northern slaves an opportunity to express the sorrows of thralldom and also provided a mechanism for blacks to choose and recognize their own leaders, who acted throughout the year in a semiofficial capacity as adjudicators of disputes and counselors to the black community. Through the " 'Lection

[13]Quoted in Berlin, "Afro–American Society in British Mainland North America," p. 54.

Day" festivals, black northerners remembered Africa while giving birth to a consciousness of African-American peoplehood.

Despite the infusion of African culture that accompanied the importation from Africa of thousands of slaves between 1740 and 1765, the overall tendency in the North, far more than in either area of the plantation South, was for a speedy merging with Anglo-American culture. Slavery was more benign in the North, slaves were more widely dispersed, and extensive black–white contact eroded African ways. Yet slaves in the North knew that bondage kept them distinct from white society, and no amount of assimilation would alter that intolerable fact.

SLAVE RESISTANCE AND REBELLION

While African-born and creole slaves struggled to adapt to bondage in various geographical and economic regions of North America, they also rankled, resisted, and rebelled in ways that kept their captors constantly aware of the costs of building and maintaining the edifice of slavery. The forms of resistance, like the forms of slavery itself, varied, depending on the circumstances of enslavement and the makeup of the slaves. For resisters, runaways, and rebels the goals varied: to extract better conditions from masters, to rejoin family members, to flee, to obtain a new master, or to avenge sadistic overseers.

The spirit of resistance among "saltwater" Africans fresh from their homelands was often immediate and open and was rarely easy to break. A North Carolinian was sure that newly imported slaves in his colony, most of them from Guinea, were far less industrious and more active in resisting slavery than "country-born" blacks.[14] "If he must be broke," warned another observer of the African newcomer, "either from Obstinacy, or, which I am more apt to suppose, from Greatness of Soul, [it] will require . . . hard Discipline. . . . You would really be surpriz'd at their Perseverance . . . they often die before they can be conquer'd."[15] A study of fugitive slaves in eighteenth-century Virginia and South Carolina makes clear that newly imported Africans often ran away and did so in ways that reflected the communal folk ethos which they had known on the other side of the ocean.

When they took flight, Africans did so in groups, particularly in company with slaves from their own country. In 1773, for example, fourteen freshly imported slaves fled as a group from a Virginia slave merchant, plunging into an unknown countryside in search of refuge.[16] Newspaper

---

[14]John Brickell, *The Natural History of North-Carolina* (Dublin, 1737; repub. Raleigh, N.C.:[n.p.] 1911), pp. 272–73.

[15]Quoted in Darold D. Wax, "Negro Resistance to the Early American Slave Trade," *Journal of Negro History,* 51 (1966): 11.

[16]Gerald W. Mullin, *Flight and Rebellion: Slave Resistance in Eighteenth-Century Virginia* (New York: Oxford University Press, 1972), pp. 39–47.

advertisements in South Carolina in the eighteenth century also reveal this kind of cooperative effort that brought slaves from the same region of Africa together in attempts at escape. The newspapers frequently advertised for groups of runaway "Gambia men" or slaves from the "Fullah Country." The Carolina backcountry as well as the Spanish–Indian Florida frontier acted as a magnet to those who were bent on escape, especially after 1733 when a Spanish decree promised escaped English slaves freedom in Florida. By 1738, enough Carolina slaves had escaped to Florida for the Spanish governor there to form a company of black militia.

This kind of overt rebelliousness often changed as Africans began absorbing the culture of the English-speaking plantation. Living on plantations with other slaves, many of them American-born, new arrivals learned the routine of planting, transplanting, weeding, worming, harvesting, and transporting crops. They also learned ways of reducing the tediousness of their tasks and minimizing the exertion that slave masters attempted to maximize. Dragging out the job, feigning illness, pretending ignorance, breaking tools, and other forms of "gold-bricking" were ways of avoiding physical depletion and also subtle forms of resistance against slavery itself. Planters like Landon Carter of Virginia complained endlessly that "my people seem to be quite dead hearted and either cannot or will not work."[17] An English observer of American slavery noted that the slave "does not appear to perform half as much, as a labourer in England" and added a comment about "the slovenly carelessness with which all business is performed by the slave."[18]

Enslaved Africans practiced many more direct forms of resistance: truancy, which usually took the form of hiding out in the woods; arson, by which the runaway slave struck against the white man's fields, barns, and houses; crop destruction; poisoning and murder; and organized pilfering, in which groups of slaves requisitioned chickens, livestock, crops, liquor, tools, and household items by moonlight and sold them in black-market systems that spread over considerable distances. In every case, they kept the slave system on edge.

When creole slaves moved from the field to the house and changed their role from gang laborers to household servants, they underwent further transformations that affected resistance. From the slaveholder's point of view, the slaves should congratulate themselves on this advance in position, for it brought them closer to "civilized" life, conferred status on them in the plantation hierarchy, and lightened the burden of their work. Although not many slaves resisted this chance for "advancement," accompanied by opportunities for better food, clothes, and shelter, many were aware that the role of domestic servant carried a heavy price, for it brought them into a far more intimate relationship with their captors and thus eroded their ability

[17]Quoted in Mullin, *Flight and Rebellion,* p. 53.
[18]Quoted in *ibid.,* p. 54.

to preserve some of the customary ways that could be practiced in the relative privacy of the slave quarters. The household slave lost full membership in the black community and the chance to be out of sight of the white people of the plantation. New demands to behave in less African ways were placed on these slaves, as every aspect of their behavior was now scrutinized by the master and mistress. Involved in a close, daily relationship with those who dominated their lives, many slaves developed speech problems such as stuttering—an outward sign of an inward difficulty in attempting to act in ways that satisfied the master and mistress but conflicted with inner impulses and feelings. Rebelliousness could not take the same forms as in the field; so in the "big house" drunkenness, malingering, and verbal and emotional contests of will with those whose authority hung over them became the slaves' means of resisting.

Because the plantation was a small world in itself, relatively self-sufficient and encompassing a wide variety of tasks, it required artisans skilled in carpentry, blacksmithing, milling, bricklaying, weaving, coopering, plastering, leatherworking, and butchering. As skilled workers, slaves became more fully assimilated into white society, moving more freely between house, field, and workshop, between the plantation and the town, and between the warehouse and the wharf. Other skilled labor, such as piloting tobacco- and rice-laden rafts and ferries through the mazelike inland waterways of the South, took the slave away from the plantation and out into a larger world. Slaves living in this wider world became skilled and imaginative in their manner of resistance. After running away, they often tried to pass for free Negroes in other colonies, hiring themselves out as sailors, trading from carts, and living in towns with other free blacks and poor whites. They learned to cope with the white world. When they ran away, it was not in groups but individually, and they used their new skills and their new resourcefulness—a measure of how fully they had become acculturated—to maneuver their way into situations that would improve their lot. Their status at the top of the slave hierarchy gave them skills and privileges they were often able to convert into attempts to subvert the slave system. A study of slavery in the eighteenth-century capital of Virginia notes the high incidence of runaways among slave artisans—the most fully acculturated African-Americans in the colony.[19]

Even in the North, where slavery was less harsh, few whites had illusions about the contentedness or submissiveness of slaves. Magistrates continually faced cases of black resistance to slavery from Maine to Delaware. The "fondness for freedom" that led slaves to defy their masters, run away, destroy property, and express their discontent in drunkenness and rowdyism repeatedly tried the patience of Bostonians. Puritan clergymen and magistrates

[19]Thad W. Tate, *The Negro in Eighteenth-Century Williamsburg* (Williamsburg: Colonial Williamsburg, 1965), pp. 198–99.

attempted to convince slaves that "Your Servitude is Gentle . . . you are treated, with more than meer Humanity, and fed and clothed and lodged, as well as you can wish for." They warned that "if you were Free, many of you would not Live near so well as you do." But still, wrote a Boston judge early in the eighteenth century, slaves engaged in "continual aspiring" after "forbidden Liberty."[20]

In Philadelphia, where the efforts of Quakers to abolish slavery may have produced the most humane type of slavery in North America, slaves also malingered, balked, and struggled for their freedom. Benjamin Franklin, himself a slave owner, wrote in 1770 to a European friend: "Perhaps you may imagine the Negroes to be a mild-tempered, tractable Kind of People. Some of them indeed are so. But the Majority are of a plotting Disposition, dark, sullen, malicious, revengeful and cruel in the highest Degree."[21]

Viewing the enslavement of Africans in America as an encounter between two cultures, we can see that slaves not only adapted to the death-dealing daily toil of the plantation but also educated themselves in strategies of survival, resistance, and rebellion. Slave owners wanted to socialize their slaves as quickly as possible, but ironically "assimilation into colonial society made a few Africans and many of their descendants outwardly rebellious and so, more difficult to control."[22] Slave masters extracted labor and obedience from their slaves in an overall sense—if they had not, slavery would have collapsed as an economic and social institution. However, they did so only with great difficulty, never with the degree of success they wished for, and often only after a price in destroyed property and even lives.

Revolt, of course, was the supreme expression of rebelliousness. Many historians have contrasted the relatively small number of American slave rebellions with the frequent revolts of Brazilian and West Indian slaves and have concluded that Africans in America were far less rebellious than slaves elsewhere in the hemisphere. Truly, no American parallel exists for the massive slave uprisings that occurred in Jamaica in the late seventeenth century or the wave of insurrections that kept the city of Bahia in northern Brazil in a state of disruption in the early nineteenth century. But almost nowhere was there slavery without violent resistance.

The largest uprising in colonial America took place in South Carolina in 1739, when about twenty slaves along the Stono River southwest of Charleston obtained a cache of arms, killed several whites, and fled toward the Florida frontier where they hoped to take refuge with the Spanish, as handfuls of slaves had done for years. Burning and plundering plantations

[20]Lawrence E. Towner, " 'Fondness for Freedom': Servant Protest in Puritan Society," *William and Mary Quarterly*, 3d Ser., 19 (1962): 202.
[21]"A Conversation between an Englishman, a Scotchman, and an American," in Verner W. Crane, "Benjamin Franklin on Slavery and American Liberties," *Pennsylvania Magazine of History and Biography*, 62 (1938): 8.
[22]Mullin, *Flight and Rebellion*, p. 38.

as they fled southward, the rebels recruited slaves who swelled the small army to about one hundred. The plan was squashed by the white militia, which quickly intercepted the slave band and, with Indian assistance, defeated the rebels in a pitched battle. Thirty slaves were killed in the white counter-attack or were executed after surrendering. South Carolina's frightened legislature stopped imports of new Africans for several years and tightened the screws on slaves' use of passes to move about on Sundays or holidays.

A few other revolts were nipped in the bud, such as the plot to capture Annapolis, Maryland, in 1740; but large-scale rebellions of this kind were rare in the history of American slavery. Nor is there an American parallel to the semi-states created by escaped slaves in Dutch Surinam, English Jamaica, French Guiana, Spanish Cuba, and Portuguese Brazil. In these hideaways thousands of runaway slaves built their own communities and held out for decades against periodic assaults of colonial troops. Only Spanish Florida, to which hundreds, but not thousands, of slaves fled in the eighteenth century, offers an American parallel.

However, examples such as these do not really prove the greater rebelliousness of Latin American slaves. Rather, they indicate that the chances for slaves to mount a successful rebellion increased in inverse proportion to the power of the white community. "The greater number of blacks, which a frontier has," warned one observer in 1741, "and the greater the disproportion is between them and her white people, the more danger she is liable to; for those [blacks] are all secret enemies, and ready to join with her open ones on the first occasion."[23] When slaves outnumbered whites six or eight to one, they could be counted on to rebel more frequently than when they were a minority or only a slight majority in the population.

By the same token, the incidence of flight from slavery correlated with the chances for successful escape. In Brazil, where Africans and Indians had mixed for generations, far more opportunities existed to hide out or join an Indian community beyond the frontier than in colonial America, where the slave plantations were rarely situated more than one hundred miles from the Atlantic coast and where African–Indian mixing was slight by comparison. Fewer open rebellions in the English mainland colonies do not prove the greater servility of the American slave but only indicate the greater problems faced by potential insurrectionists in rising against their oppressors. Under different conditions, rebelliousness became channeled into other forms—more subtle, less dangerous, and more effective.

Almost all the colonies passed special laws against arson and poisoning in the eighteenth century and then reorganized these laws a generation later, increasing the severity of punishment. This is only one indication of

---

[23] [Benjamin Martyn], *An Impartial Inquiry into the State and Utility of the Colony of Georgia* (London, 1741), quoted in Peter Wood, *Black Majority*, p. 166.

the persistent resistance to enslavement and the enduring hostility of slaves against their masters. In fact, "the sharpest evidence of slave resistance," it has been observed, "is not the historical record of armed revolts . . . so much as the codes that legalized branding, flogging, burning, the amputation of limbs, hamstringing and murder to keep the slaves 'non-violent'."[24]

A similar kind of evidence that blacks did not lapse into passive dependency and abject obedience is found in the fear of black rebellion that coursed through white communities. A vivid example can be found in the reaction of the southern colonies to the onset of the Seven Years' War in 1755. William Shirley, commander of the British forces in North America, complained that nothing could be expected of the southern militias because if they left their local communities the slaves would flee en masse to the French, who were promising "liberty & Lands to settle upon." Lewis Evans, a Pennsylvania strategist, also conceded that the southern militia could not make a move: "The Thing is impossible," he wrote, "they have . . . scarce Whites enough to prevent the Defection of their Slaves; and if any considerable Party should happen to be defeated, when abroad, it could be scarce possible to prevent their total Revolt."[25] The governor of Virginia hoped to spare a few militia units for the intercolonial war effort but greatly feared "the Combinations of the Negro Slaves, who have been very audacious on the Defeat on the Ohio [of Braddock's army]." He prayed that "we shall be able to defeat the Designs of our Enemies and keep these Slaves in proper Subjection."[26]

Even in the North it proved impossible to shape slaves into mild-tempered, compliant workers. In New York City in 1712, a group of more than twenty slaves, determined to overthrow their oppressors, set fire to a building and then lay in wait for the white men who came to extinguish the flames. Wielding knives, axes, and guns, they killed nine whites and injured many others before making their escape. It was later reported that "had it not been for the Garrison [of English soldiers] there, that city would have been reduced to ashes, and the greatest part of the inhabitants murdered."[27] After the rebels were suppressed, officials investigated the plot and took about seventy slaves into custody. Forty-three were brought to trial, and twenty-five, including several women and Indian slaves, were convicted. The white terror of black insurrection was evident in the sentences imposed: Thirteen slaves died on the gallows, one was starved to death in chains, three were burned at the stake, and one was broken on the wheel. Six

[24]Sidney Mintz, "Toward an Afro–American History," *Journal of World History* (published in Switzerland), 13 (1971): 321.
[25]Quoted in Lawrence H. Gipson, *The Great War for Empire: The Years of Defeat, 1754–1757* (New York: Alfred A. Knopf, Inc., 1946), pp. 14–15.
[26]*Ibid.*, p. 15.
[27]Quoted in Kenneth Scott, "The Slave Insurrection in New York in 1712," *New York Historical Society Quarterly*, 45 (1961): 51.

others killed themselves rather than endure retribution at the hands of the white community.

After white New Yorkers had suppressed the 1712 revolt, their legislature quickly passed a new slave code, which strictly regulated the slaves' freedom of movement and stripped away most of the rights that until this time distinguished their lot from that of their southern counterparts. In neighboring colonies, legislators scurried to impose new restrictions on blacks or, as in Pennsylvania, to pass import duties so high as to make further importations of Africans unprofitable.

Even the medieval torture imposed on the black conspirators of 1712 did not achieve the desired results of cowing northern slaves into submissiveness. A generation later, a wave of slave unrest swept the eastern seaboard. It began in New Jersey in 1740 with a few incidents of barn burning. Two slaves paid with their lives for this act of rebellion. A few months later a rash of thefts and fires struck New York City, the largest urban center of slavery in the colonies next to Charleston, South Carolina. Among the buildings ignited was Fort George, which housed the English garrison. Indicted in these incidents were a white tavern keeper, his wife, and an indentured servant girl who served as a prostitute in the tavern. Helped along by some low-grade torture and a promise of immunity, the servant girl confessed that her master was involved with several slaves in a conspiracy to burn the town to the ground and kill all its white inhabitants. The authorities brought two slaves to trial for theft and possible conspiracy. When the conspiracy charge against them could not be substantiated, they were hanged for theft, dying "very stubbornly" on the gallows without confessing to anything more.

A month later the tavern keeper and his wife were hanged for treason, though they too went to their deaths with closed lips concerning a slave plot. When the servant-prostitute went to the gallows for conspiracy, she died renouncing the statements she had made concerning black insurrectionists. But fear of black revolt and a desire to cow the city's blacks had overtaken the town, and the dragnet began pulling in slaves, who were threatened with torture and execution if they did not reveal the identity of the slave conspirators. In the following months white authorities extracted 67 confessions from terrified slaves. Before the trial was over, 150 slaves and 25 whites had been imprisoned, 17 slaves and 4 whites had been tortured and hanged, 13 slaves had been burned at the stake, and 72 others transported to the West Indies, Newfoundland, and Madeira.

Many of those arrested, tortured, deported, or killed may have been innocent victims of the fear and anger that overtook New York in 1740 and 1741, but revolt was certainly in the minds of many of the city's slaves. White New Yorkers knew that slaves, at their core, were indeed insurrectionists and would repeat acts of aggression and rebellion against the white community unless the most draconic measures were taken. Had New Yorkers regarded their slaves as docile and childish "Sambos," no such conspiracy would have been believable and no such brutal punishment would have been meted out. New Yorkers were not eager to destroy human property in which they had invested. But they lived with a gnawing fear that their slaves would revolt, for they knew from everyday slave behavior that the African captive was a truculent, resistant worker whose desire for freedom seldom flagged. Incidents such as the one in New York show that even in the northern colonies slaves awaited opportunities to cast off their chains or inflict on white society some of the pain that had been apportioned to them.

BLACK CULTURE IN COLONIAL AMERICA

Resistance and rebellion were forms of attacking the system of slavery, of attempting in piecemeal fashion to bring the institution to an end. With power massively stacked against the slave in this quest, it is not surprising that the incidence of organized group resistance was low. More important than counting slave rebellions is understanding how slaves, living within the confining limits of a degrading, brutal system, struggled to carve out areas of cultural and personal autonomy in order to make life bearable. Viewing the plantation or the city as "a battlefield where slaves fought masters for physical and psychological survival"[28] enables us to turn our gaze to the private side of black life and culture in colonial North America.

In this quest for the essence of slave culture several things must be kept in mind about the acculturation process. First, slaves came from a diversity of cultures in West Africa and therefore did not bring to the New World a single collective culture. Beneath this tribal diversity flowed a number of important shared characteristics; but upon arriving in North America slaves could only forge communities and fashion a culture by blending their various cultural heritages within the limiting framework imposed by the slave system itself. This process of amalgamating specific cultural backgrounds within the context of the European slave masters' culture began with language aboard the slave ships, where on the long middle passage enslaved Africans devised a variety of pidgins to allow communication.

Second, in drawing on their various cultural backgrounds while adapting to slavery in the Americas, slaves found it far easier to perpetuate or adapt religious values, expressive forms, craft skills, and modes of socializing and forming male–female bonds than to recreate formal institutions. A Dahomean priesthood could not survive the transition to the slave South, but voudou and burial rituals could. Yoruban regal ceremonies had no opportunity to transit the Atlantic, but the ceremonial use of the drum did.

---

[28]John W. Blassingame, *The Slave Community: Plantation Life in the Antebellum South* (New York: Oxford University Press, 1972), p. 184.

With these two strictures in mind, it is possible to examine how slaves created a new culture in colonial America, focusing particularly on religion, work, the family, and aesthetics. In these areas African slaves struggled to fashion their lives in ways that skirted or challenged white control. The unending struggle of enslaved Africans was to preserve their humanity within the boundaries of a soul-wracking system of compelled labor.

Religion

Slaves brought with them to the New World a complex religious heritage, and no amount of desolation or physical abuse could wipe out these deeply rooted beliefs. In fact, people enduring the kind of daily stress inherent in the master–slave relationship typically turned for relief to their deepest emotive sources. Coming from cultures where the division between sacred and secular activities was much narrower than in European society, where life and afterlife were not regarded as so separate and the present united with the past and the future, African slaves made religious activities "areas of considerable potential creativity and social strength."[29] Religion was at the heart of African-American slave culture, and the development of African Christianity in the eighteenth century reflected both the proximity of slaves to the religion of their masters and the endurance of the religion they carried from their homelands.

Most of the slaves coming to the North American colonies, though they were born in a variety of societies with many religious differences, shared certain religious principles and ritual patterns. Widespread among the societies from Senegambia to Angola on the west coast of Africa was belief in a Supreme Creator of the cosmos and a pantheon of lesser gods who were associated with forces in nature such as rain, animals, and the fertility of the earth. These gods had the power to intervene in the affairs of humankind and therefore had to be propitiated. Ancestors, in the West African belief system, also had the power to affect the welfare of village life, for they mediated between the living and the lesser gods. It was therefore important to ensure the entrance of deceased family members into the spiritual world with elaborate funeral rites that honored them properly for the role they would play after death. Finally, West Africans believed in spirit possession, where the gods spoke to men and women through priests and other religious "experts."

While differing from the religious beliefs of their slave owners, Africans stood on some common ground with them. Africans and Europeans shared beliefs about a physical world where everyone lived and an "other world" inhabited by the souls of the dead. Both cultures believed the

[29]George Rawick, *From Sundown to Sunup: The Making of the Black Community* (Westport, Conn.: Greenwood Publishing Co., 1972), p. 32.

"other world" could not be seen but could be known through revelations that spiritually gifted persons could interpret. These roughly shared foundations of religious feeling made it possible for a hybrid African Christianity to develop. African religious customs, funeral rites, sacred images, and charms for protection against evil spirits were no doubt attenuated on New World plantations or melded with elements of Christianity. How fast this happened is murky, but clearly it varied from place to place. In New England, slaves were few in number and the attempts to indoctrinate them in Christian belief were relatively strenuous. Both private religious instruction and public churchgoing were common among slaves, and by the mid-eighteenth century many black children were attending schools opened by Anglicans and Quakers. In the northern towns Protestant ministers performed slave marriages and baptized their children. Also because slaves usually lived within white households in small numbers rather than in slave quarters amid a black community, African ways eroded more rapidly than in the South.

On southern plantations, slave masters were not so eager to see their slaves instructed in Christianity. But the missionary wing of the Anglican church sent its agents into many areas in the eighteenth century, and other churches also began to instruct slaves. Moreover, African beliefs and rituals persisted longer than in the North because on the plantation the slave could maintain a greater sense of a collective experience and was constantly in touch with Mother Africa through freshly arriving slaves. Realizing this, slave masters were caught in a dilemma. If the perpetuation of African religion fostered a collective identity and fed the spirit of resistance, then it was imperative to replace it with Christian belief. But at the same time the owner was not eager to have his human property subjected to a new religion that would make an enslaved African a less willing worker. So, when masters permitted their slaves to attend church, it was with the hope that they would learn the Christian ideals of meekness, humility, and obedience, as the missionaries promised, and not the ideals of the brotherhood of man or the story of the Hebrew flight from oppression.

The dispensers of Christian instruction always struggled with the problem of exposing slaves to the elements of religious thought that would make them submissive while quarantining them from the elements that fed the desire for freedom. Protestant clergymen impressed upon slaves that acceptance of Christ was not to be confused with obtaining freedom, and most colonies passed laws to make crystal clear that baptism did not place the master under the slightest obligation to manumit his slaves. But try as they might to suppress it, the idea spread among slaves in the eighteenth-century South that baptism was a first step in this direction. Whether this reflected slave familiarity with the Western tradition that no Christian could enslave another Christian or sprang from another source is uncertain. But the equation of baptism and eventual freedom spread. In 1730, following a period of unusual missionary activity in Virginia, a number of baptized slaves began circulating the word that their acceptance of Christ entitled them to freedom. Several hundred slaves gathered in Norfolk and Princess Anne counties in Virginia to foment a rebellion, but white planters discovered the plan and hanged four black leaders. Thereafter the resistance to catechizing slaves grew.

Another obstacle to Christianization was the opinion of many slave owners that exposure to the tenets of the carpenter of Nazareth made slaves "proud and saucy." As Thomas Bacon, a Chesapeake clergyman, told slaves, "You must not be eye servants, that is such as will be very busy [only] in your master's presence."[30] But it was widely believed, as a Swedish traveler in America noted, that if slaves were Christianized, their masters "would not be able to keep their Negroes so subjected afterwards" because of the pride which Africans would develop "on seeing themselves upon a level with their masters in religious matters."[31]

The Great Awakening in the 1740s ushered in a new era of activity among those eager to Christianize slaves and a new era of receptivity among slaves to the precepts of Christianity. In the Anglican parish of Williamsburg, the capital of Virginia, white ministers baptized nearly a thousand slaves in a single generation from 1746 to 1768. Presbyterians were also active in the southern colonies beginning about 1740. Samuel Davies, a leading Presbyterian, boasted that he had one hundred slaves in his congregation in Hanover County, Virginia, in 1750 and a few years later claimed that some three hundred blacks received instruction from him. The Anglican Jonathan Boucher recorded that he baptized 315 slaves on a single day in 1767. By this time many Virginia slaves, especially those living in the vicinity of small towns such as Williamsburg and Norfolk, had been indoctrinated in Christian religion by Anglicans, Presbyterians, and Methodists.

What gave these efforts special force was the appeal that the revivalists' style and message had to slaves. For a people whose ancestral religion was grounded primarily in an understanding of nature as in-dwelling and whose eschatological vision allowed for no sharp differences between the secular and the sacred, religion and daily life being conjoined, Protestantism always had a limited appeal. Highly literate and rational, sanitized of its mystical elements, guarded over by professional clergymen who stressed passivity among worshipers, the Protestant service had little power to render intelligible or tolerable the strange and repressive world in which slaves found themselves. But the revivalists of the 1740s and 1750s, preaching a personal rebirth, using music and body motion, and asking for the dynamic participation

---

[30]Bacon, *Sermons Addressed to Masters and Servants* . . . in *Bases of the Plantation Society,* ed., Aubrey C. Land (New York: Harper & Row, Publishers, 1969), p. 232.
[31]*Peter Kalm's Travels in North America,* ed., Adolph B. Benson (New York: Dover Publications, Inc., 1966), I: 209.

of each individual in an intense emotional experience, had a tremendous appeal to Africans. Here was a religious outlook that had meaning for the daily experience of slave life and shared enough with ancestral styles and beliefs such as spirit possession to allow for the creation of a unique Black Christianity. Especially in the ecstatic expression associated with evangelical religion, in the dancing, shouting, rhythmic clapping, and singing, the merging of West African spirit possession and European Christianity took place. Indeed, to some degree African culture influenced white awakeners, especially in a more ecstatic spirituality and in new ideas of heaven as a place to be reunified with ancestors.

Slave masters hoped that Christian doctrine, whether of the ascetic, rational variety or the emotional, revivalistic type, would be the opiate of their slaves. Even if their chattels shared nothing of what their labor produced, even if they lost all their rights in a life of perpetual servitude, they could at least comfort themselves with the knowledge that Christianity sanctified the weak, the poor, and the humble. With this formulation in mind, those who have studied black religion have traditionally explained that the most important effect of Protestantism on the slave community was to deflect the minds of slaves "from sufferings and privations of this world to a world after death where the weary would find rest and the victims of injustice would be compensated."[32] But slaves did not passively accept what the Anglican or Presbyterian minister chose to inculcate. They drew selectively from white Christianity and shaped their own religious experience in a fashion that not only gave them an area of life that was semi-independent from the control of the master but also provided an important psychological mechanism for channeling anger and projecting aggression in ways that would not bring physical retribution from the white community.

Black spirituals reveal a great deal about this two-edged nature of religion. Many of the slave spirituals were adaptations of white spirituals or a unique blend of African rhythm patterns, Anglo-American melodies, and adapted words, which reflected the pain of the slave experience. Some of the spirituals were called "sorrow songs" and the musical expression of this pain was no doubt cathartic for those who sang them communally. Another theme of the spirituals, however, was that of worth and strength. We cannot know whether such songs as "We Are the People of God," or "I Really Do Believe I'm a Child of God," or "I'm Born of God, I Know I Am" were sung by slaves in the eighteenth century because it is extremely difficult to date their origins. But there is little reason to believe that if slaves found them sustaining in the nineteenth century, they would not have created songs and spirituals with similar themes in the pre-Revolutionary period. What is impressive about these songs is that they portray feelings of worthiness and

---

[32]E. Franklin Frazier, *The Negro Church in America* (New York: Schocken Books, 1964), p. 45.

even a belief that slaves will ultimately prevail because they are superior to the masters. In the midst of a society that worked to convince slaves of their lack of worth, the poverty of their African culture, and their barbarism, the songs show a strong black self-esteem, an abiding feeling of communal fellowship, and a sense of purpose to life. Black religious music demonstrates how difficult it was for white society to remake the black consciousness and to coerce the black slave into internalizing white values.[33]

The theme of resistance and rebellion was also woven into many of the slave songs. The spiritual celebrating Samson, who sang, "If I had my way, I'd tear this building down," may have had only Biblical meaning for the whites who sang it on Sunday mornings in the parish churches of the South. But for black workers in the field the building was the edifice of slavery and tearing it down meant nothing less than the destruction of the slave system. Similarly, the spiritual "Didn't My Lord Deliver Daniel," which referred to the deliverance of the Hebrews from their enemies, had a more modern meaning for the black slaves who adopted the song as one of their own.

Almost all the symbolic figures of the black spirituals—Daniel, David, Joshua, Jonah, Moses, and Noah—were children of the Hebrews, figures from the Old Testament who struggled against their persecutors in this world and not in the afterlife. Some of them were delivered from oppression in ways that had special meaning for slaves. The Red Sea opened to allow the Hebrew slaves to pass through and then closed to engulf Pharaoh's armies; the blind and vulnerable Samson brought the mansion of his conquerors crashing down. In these spirituals slaves sang about far more than deliverance in the next world. As Lawrence Levine has pointed out, their religious music was not sacred in the narrow sense of being strictly attached to religious ceremony and the Sunday service. It was sacred in a distinctly African way, in the larger context of uniting one's present condition with the ritual and mythical past and linking it also to the possibility of rebirth in the future. Slaves trapped in the grasp of lifelong servitude created a measure of cultural autonomy "by transcending the narrow confines of the world in which they were forced to live. They extended the boundaries of their restrictive universe backward until it fused with the world of the Old Testament, and upward until it became one with the world beyond. The spirituals are the record of a people who found the status, the harmony, the values, the order they needed to survive by internally creating an expanded universe. . . ."[34] Through religious music and through plantation conjurers, voudou men, and witch doctors, African-Americans struggled to

---

[33]Lawrence W. Levine, "Slave Songs and Slave Consciousness: An Exploration in Neglected Sources," in *Anonymous Americans: Explorations in Nineteenth-Century Social History*, ed. Tamara K. Hareven (Englewood Cliffs, N.J.: Prentice-Hall, Inc., 1971), pp. 99–130.
[34]*Ibid.*, p. 115.

adjust to white culture while still maintaining a separateness from the world of their masters.

Work

Throughout most of the Atlantic world, from southern New England to the southernmost reaches of Latin America, African labor was vital in the development of agricultural economies. One southern planter put it succinctly: "The planters in general have throve and grown rich . . . by the help and labour of their slaves for their Lands tho' ever so fertile are of no use or profit without them."[35]

African-American slaves in the English colonies turned daily labor—the very core of their existence and the entire reason for the investment of capital in chattel property—into a contested area and adapted African work habits to New World conditions in a way that made life more bearable. Slaves were only too well aware that the labor they did benefited only the master. But in their daily work they behaved in a number of ways—shamming sickness, breaking hoes, uprooting freshly planted seedlings, and harvesting carelessly—that signaled their defiance of the exhortations and floggings of the masters, overseers, and drivers. From these responses masters learned that there were limits beyond which they could not go, for to push too hard was only to prove the law of diminishing returns. To deny the slaves the traditional Sunday holiday or the usual Christmas respite, for example, could result in less rather than more work being done in the future. Similarly, to set work standards too high only encouraged slaves to accomplish less or to retaliate against their masters. The lesson was clearly stated in 1732 by the South Carolina *Gazette,* which reported that a master who had driven his slaves late into the night, cleaning and barreling a rice crop, found his barn "and all that was in it" burned to ashes by morning.[36]

Masters, of course, wanted to wring from their slaves the maximum amount of work. To do this they employed a gamut of devices, running from the whip at one end of the spectrum to positive incentives at the other. Many of them concluded that nothing could turn the slave into a willing worker. "I find it almost impossible," complained Landon Carter, one of Virginia's largest slave owners, "to make a negro do his work well. No orders can engage it, no encouragement persuade it, nor no Punishment oblige it."[37] In the end, southern planters learned that, though the white work ethic could never be instilled in those who labored only to produce profits

[35]Quoted in Philip D. Morgan, *Slave Counterpoint: Black Culture in the Eighteenth-Century Chesapeake and Low Country* (Chapel Hill: University of North Carolina Press, 1998), p. 146.

[36]South Carolina *Gazette,* Oct. 14, 1732, quoted in Wood, *Black Majority,* p. 293.

[37]Jack P. Greene, ed., *The Diary of Colonel Landon Carter of Sabine Hall, 1752–1776* (2 vols.; Charlottesville: University of Virginia Press, 1965), II, 733.

for others, they could get the most from their slaves by delegating authority and creating a hierarchy of black workers. The tasking system, used especially along the rice coast of South Carolina and Georgia, was another method of obtaining satisfactory output and, from the slaves' point of view, ensuring work boundaries that left them relatively free of direct supervision and time to cultivate their own plots or take their ease. On nearly every rice plantation the slaves' work rhythm had to be negotiated between African workers and European masters. "Should any owner increase the work beyond what is customary," wrote one South Carolina planter, "he subjects himself to the reproach of his neighbors, and to such discontent amongst his slaves as to make them of little use to him."[38]

Slaves also reacted in positive ways to work, developing a "black work ethic." Because most slaves had been seized from agrarian societies, they were already partially prepared for agricultural field work. This part of the adjustment to slavery was probably easier than most others, the more so for women because they had been primarily responsible for crop cultivation in their homelands. In the colonial South, masters kept most slave women at work in the fields. Reflecting work patterns that were traditional, slaves proved that they would work harder and longer at tasks that required collective labor, but offered resistance to working by themselves. In this preference for collective labor they demonstrated an attitude toward work that was in sharp contrast with the European norm of the individual following his "calling" and laboring independently. Their African background had inured them to collective agricultural labor, and they strove to maintain this pattern of work in their lives as slaves.

The lives of most slaves were measured out by the requirements of the particular crop they worked: rice, indigo, tobacco, or wheat. But gradually in the eighteenth century, as staple economies matured and plantation size increased, a growing percentage of slaves escaped field labor. Overseeing other slaves, working in crafts, serving multiple roles in plantation houses, and transporting goods, enslaved Africans found new occupational opportunities that at least partially improved their lives. In the South Carolina low country, about one in four males worked outside the fields by the 1780s and in the Chesapeake region perhaps one in three. In the North, at least half of all slaves worked outside agricultural regimens. Notably, women had much less chance of escaping grueling field labor because slave men dominated the crafts and transportation services, leaving domestic work in the planter's house as the only opportunity for women to get out from under crop labor.

If enslaved craftsmen became common in northern towns by the mid-eighteenth century, they dominated the work of carpentry, blacksmithing,

---

[38]Quoted in Morgan, *Slave Counterpoint,* p. 184.

coopering, shoemaking, and tailoring on large southern plantations. One northern visitor in the Chesapeake observed that "The principal planters . . . have nearly everything they can want on their own estates. Amongst their slaves are found taylors, shoemakers, carpenters, smiths, turners, wheelwrights, weavers, tanners, etc."[39] He might have added potters, basketmakers, iron-makers, boatbuilders, bricklayers, and stonemasons. As wagoneers, boatmen, and fishermen, slaves also came to dominate the waterways of the South.

Household slaves, coming to enfold the lives of perhaps one of every ten slaves in the most established parts of the South, also found at least some respite from punishing field labor. Men served as gardeners, stable-men, coachmen, grooms, butchers, cooks, and waiting men while women performed as housemaids, nurses and midwives, dairymaids, cooks, poultry-women, bakers, spinners, and weavers.

Family

At the level of the family—the close intimate connections between man and woman, parent and child, and brother and sister—slaves developed the most important bastion of defense against the hardships of slavery. In West Africa all social relations were centered in kinship, and kinship lines, stretching backward to include the dead, were vitally important to the individual in locating himself or herself in the local society. Hence, in developing new lifeways under the ordeal of slavery, Africans had to surmount the horror of being torn from their kinship networks and deprived of their prior status in ancestral societies. For this reason the task of rebuilding kin groups, within which the most intimate aspects of life were carried out—love, sexu-ality, birth, child rearing, and death—must have been regarded as of the utmost importance.

From the master's point of view slave family life was theoretically im-possible. Allegiance and the flow of authority was to run in only one direc-tion—from bond servant to owner and never between slaves themselves. In most English colonies, unlike Spanish and Portuguese America, law prohib-ited contractual marriage, for chattel could not make contracts. But in reality, domestic life was another area in which slaves and masters struck a bargain. For their part, slave owners found that it was hardly conducive to the profitable management of the plantation or farm to prohibit family life. For the slaves, defining their own social and interpersonal relations within the confines of slave quarters became so important that they were willing to risk the master's ultimate power of life and death over them to secure the right to play an active role in shaping familial relationships.

To be sure, slave masters placed obstacles in the way of slaves as they attempted to reconstruct African kinship ties in the New World. Once

---

[39]Quoted in *ibid.*, pp. 225–26.

formed, a marriage-like relationship was rarely secure because it could be precipitously ended by the sale of either party. This happened repeatedly. Likewise, children were often torn from the family through sale or dealt to the master's children when they married. Also, many masters hired out their slaves, adding to the difficulties of maintaining a stable relationship.

Family life was also stunted by the general shortage of women, although the excess of males was never so pronounced in the mainland colonies as in the Caribbean islands and many parts of Spanish and Portuguese America. Throughout the seventeenth and eighteenth centuries, slaves were imported in a ratio of about three men to two women. This excess of males, especially in the South, meant that permanent or semipermanent relationships were possible for perhaps half to two-thirds of male slaves. As natural increase swelled the slave population after 1730, this disparity between the sexes gradually disappeared, but it was not until a generation or so after the closing of the slave trade in 1808 that parity was finally reached. In the North, where slaves were sparsely held, this problem was intensified because, although the sex ratio was more even than in the South, most slave owners held only one or two slaves, which meant that male and female slaves only occasionally lived together under the same roof. They had to seek partners on neighboring farms or even distant ones.

Still another barrier to satisfactory family life was the role that white males played as sexual aggressors against black women. How many black women were assaulted or lured with favors into sexual relations with white masters cannot be known, although judging from the sizable mulatto population by 1800, the number cannot have been small. Interracial sex was particularly widespread in the South, where white women were less available to white men and black women more so than in the North. The South Carolina *Gazette* in 1732 called miscegenation an *"Epidemical Disease,"*[40] and 35 years later a visiting New Englander noted that "the enjoyment of a negro or mulatto woman is spoken of as quite a common thing: no reluctance, delicacy, or shame is made about the matter."[41]

For a black husband to know of or witness the assault of a white slave owner upon his wife was probably the most psychologically destructive and socially disruptive weapon in the white man's arsenal. "In its political contours," it has been pointed out, "the rape of the black woman was not exclusively an attack upon her. Indirectly, its target was also the slave community as a whole. In launching the sexual war on the woman, the master not only asserted his sovereignty over a critically important figure of the slave community, he would also be aiming a blow against the black man."[42] Sexual exploitation of black women often had traumatic effects on slave attempts

[40]Quoted in Wood, *Black Majority,* p. 235.
[41]Quoted in Morgan, *Slave Counterpoint,* p. 406.
[42]Angela Davis, "Reflections on the Black Woman's Role in the Community of Slaves," *Black Scholar,* 3 (1971–72): 13.

to build stable relationships because the male head of the family was usually powerless to defend those closest to him from the most intimate and painful form of attack. Many black novelists and writers in the decades following the end of slavery harked back to this theme, indicating how strongly the pain continued to reverberate in the black consciousness. W.E.B. DuBois, writing three-quarters of a century after emancipation, wrote:

> I shall forgive the white South much in its final judgment day: I shall forgive its slavery, for slavery is a world-old habit; I shall forgive its fighting for a well-lost cause, and for remembering that struggle with tender tears; I shall forgive its so-called "pride of race," the passion of its hot blood, and even its dear, old, laughable strutting and posing; but one thing I shall never forgive, neither in this world nor the world to come: its wanton and continued and persistent insulting of the black womanhood which it sought and seeks to prostitute to its lust.[43]

Not all interracial liaisons were cruel and coercive, however. Many amounted to common-law marriages between slave masters and their slaves. Most affectionate interracial unions, it appears, began with a white master who came to love a black mistress. Such was the case of Thomas Wright, a Virginian who fathered six children with Sylvia, his slave. This couple openly lived together in the 1780s and 1790s, and Wright's attachment to Sylvia led to freeing her, providing for her after his death, and openly recognizing his children, one of whom inherited his father's plantation and married a white woman.

Such relationships, which sometimes endured for the lifetimes of the partners, were nonetheless threatening, both to the slave community and to the white plantation ideal. They spanned the theoretically unbridgeable gap between the slave and free sectors of society, and they often produced children who lived in a twilight zone, even though they were legally slaves. White paternity and affection for mulatto offspring often led to favored treatment and sometimes to manumission, but for the black male the advantages of this crack in the wall of slavery had to be weighed against the pain that attended the sight of a sister, daughter, or former mate entering the slave master's private world.

Even in the face of these formidable obstacles, slaves were able to fashion intimate ties between man and woman, parent and child. Slaves frequently formed monogamous relationships, and if these did not last as long as in white society, a large part of the explanation lies in aspects of the system that were beyond the slave's control—the shorter lifespan of African-Americans, the breakup of marriage through the sale of one or both partners, and the call of freedom that impelled many slaves to run away. Many planters encouraged their slaves to live together and to take up the role of

---

[43]W. E. B. DuBois, *Darkwater: Voices from Within the Veil* (New York: AMS Press, 1969), p. 172.

parents, for they found that slaves were more dutiful and less likely to flee when they were tied to a spouse and offspring. It was not so much a concern for the morality of their slaves as an interest in maximizing the output of labor and minimizing insubordination that led owners to promote slave marriage and family life.

Within the black family what were the roles of the man and the woman? This vexed question has assumed new importance because the idea is currently prevalent that the welfare family, headed by a woman, is a replication of a slave matriarchate. In this view the slave mother, as the noted sociologist E. Franklin Frazier has written, "was generally the recognized head of the family group. She was the mistress of the cabin to which the 'husband' or father often made only weekly visits. Under such circumstances a maternal group took form and the tradition of the Negro woman's responsibility for her family took root."[44] Following this formulation, it is assumed that the slave emerged after emancipation with only a faint tradition of normal family life. Buffeted by the problems of trying to adapt as a freeman to an increasingly urban and industrial world, ex-slaves were never able to knit together the same nuclear, two-parent family that served as the norm in the white community.

Although the black matriarchal family structure no doubt existed to some extent in the eighteenth-century southern colonies, it was probably not the characteristic slave family. Slave men were undoubtedly emasculated in important ways because they could not occupy the dominant role in family and community relationships as they had in the villages of Africa. But the black male did assert his authority by supplementing the food supply through trapping and fishing; by organizing the garden plot behind the slave cabin; by disciplining his children; and most of all by being the principal figure in the active resistance to slavery. Slave men did marry slave women and together they established a relatively stable family life, considering the deterrents inherent in the situation. In some cases slaves were able to preserve these relationships by threatening rebellion. For example, the government of South Carolina, reeling under the blows of the Yamasees in 1715, negotiated a promise of 130 militiamen from Virginia in exchange for an equal number of slave women. But threats of a full-scale insurrection if the women were sent northward forced the Carolinians to renege on their part of the bargain.[45]

While slave men struggled to preserve their familial role, black women came to occupy a position in the family and in the black community that was strikingly different from that of white women. By custom and law in the Anglo-American world, women were regarded as inferior to men and

[44] *The Negro Family in America,* quoted in *Black Matriarchy: Myth or Reality?,* ed. John H. Bracey, August Meier, and Elliott Rudwick (Belmont, Cal.: Wadsworth Publishing Co., 1971), p. 8.

[45] David D. Wallace, *South Carolina: A Short History, 1520–1948* (Chapel Hill: University of North Carolina Press, 1951), p. 91.

subservient to them in almost all matters. Moreover, on southern plantations, the ideology of domesticity kept white women confined in the home
where they were expected to be the guardians of white virtue and culture.
Black women, by contrast, remained indispensably important to both the
work of the plantation and the stability of the slave community. They worked
in the fields and they worked in the slave cabin. It was ironic, Angela Davis
has written, that the slave woman "had to be released from the chains of the
myth of femininity. . . . In order to function as slave, the black woman had
to be annulled as woman—that is, as woman in her historical stance of ward-
ship under the entire male hierarchy. The sheer force of things rendered
her equal to her man. . . . Male supremacist structures could not become
deeply embedded in the internal workings of the slave system."[46]

Caught in the net of slavery, the black woman, paradoxically, maintained
a position of strength and autonomy within the black community that made
her far more equal to the male than was the case of women in white society.
The black family was a partnership of equals in the tasks performed and responsibilities shouldered. In this respect it bore closer resemblance to Algonquian and Siouian family structure than to European family organization, for
in Indian cultures women were also vitally important in agricultural work,
child-rearing responsibilities were shared, and the woman in general maintained a degree of power and autonomy not allowed in Euro-American society.

Because slavery was above all else a system for extracting the maximum
amount of labor from its victims, it chronically involved cruelties that often
made family life almost impossible to maintain. But, in general, North American slaves were better clothed, fed, and treated than those in the West Indies,
Brazil, or other parts of the New World where settled white society took only
shallow root and plantation owners found it more profitable literally to work
their slaves to death and then purchase fresh replacements from Africa.
When conditions were at least conducive to sustaining life, slaves were effective in defining a culture of their own. As one black scholar has written:
"Slaves were able to fashion a life style and a set of values—an ethos—which
prevented them from being imprisoned altogether by the definitions which the
larger society sought to impose. This ethos was an amalgam of Africanisms
and New World elements which helped slaves . . . 'feel their way along the
course of American slavery, enabling them to endure.' . . ."[47]

Aesthetics

What a society values for its beauty and the pleasure it gives can loosely be
called *aesthetics*. This is the part of African culture that was most resistant to
the brutality of slavery. How to form a pot from clay, style one's hair, arrange

[46]Davis, "The Black Woman's Role," p. 7.
[47]Sterling Stuckey, "Through the Prism of Folklore: The Black Ethos in Slavery," *The
Massachusetts Review,* 9 (1968): 418.

fabric over the body, play an instrument, play on words, or use one's voice became parts of the culture enslaved Africans developed in the American colonies.

Music and dance were central to everyday life in the field where slaves toiled, in the quarters where they lived, and in woods and along river banks where they gathered in off-hours. "We are almost a nation of dancers, musicians, and poets," Olaudah Equiano wrote in his autobiography of eighteenth-century enslavement.[48] Jefferson (who viewed African culture negatively in most respects) admitted that Africans "are more generally gifted than the whites with accurate ears for tune and time."[49] Dancing was rarely absent when slaves gathered, usually to the accompaniment of drums, rattles, sometimes banjoes, and clapping. In all of this the African musical and dance heritage remained vibrant. Surviving the middle passage, they melded with

Africans attached great value to music and dance in their homelands, and enslavement in the Americas probably heightened this attachment. This watercolor, painted in about 1800, shows South Carolina slaves dancing the "juba"—a West African dance. The gourdlike banjo and the twisted leather drumsticks are of African design, and the headdress of the dancers is typical of the Carolina Low-country. *(Abby Aldrich Rockefeller Folk Art Center, Williamsburg, VA)*

[48]Robert J. Allison, ed., *The Interesting Life of Olaudah Equiano* (Boston: Bedford Books, 1995), p. 36.
[49]William Peden, ed., *Notes on the State of Virginia by Thomas Jefferson* (Chapel Hill: University of North Carolina Press, 1954), p. 140.

European musical traditions, particularly in the African appropriation of the violin or fiddle. But always, complex rhythms sounded out with rattles, drums, and gongs were distinctively African.

Aesthetic adornment also exhibited African cultural retention while simultaneously showing cultural borrowing. The designing and shaping of hair, using braiding and plaiting with beads, shells, and strips of material, drew upon homeland fashions and patterns. So did adorning the body with brass wire earrings, beaded armbands and necklaces, and cloth bands draped over or wrapped around the body. Headgear, prized in Africa, made its way across the Atlantic; but in this sartorial area rapid innovation with beaver and raccoon skins, as well as Scotch bonnets, created African-European effects. More important than the exact blending of cultures from two continents was the role of personal adornment in refusing to succumb to the dehumanization that slavery visited on every African forced across the Atlantic.

How much of African culture survived under eighteenth-century slavery can never be determined quantitatively. Nor is it especially important to do so. It is enough to understand that Africans in the English plantations adapted elements of African culture to the demands of a new life and a new environment. There can be little doubt that slave masters were intent on obliterating all Africanisms that reduced the effectiveness of slaves as laborers and that they had some success in this. It is also true that slavery eliminated many of the cultural differences among slaves, who came from a wide variety of African cultural groups—Fulanis, Ibos, Yorubas, Malagasies, Ashantis, Mandingos, and others. At the same time, it must be remembered that throughout the eighteenth century, unlike in the nineteenth, large numbers of new Africans were arriving each year. Slave importations grew rapidly in the eighteenth century so that probably never more than half the adult slaves were American-born. This continuous infusion of African culture kept alive many of the elements that would later be transmuted almost beyond recognition. By fashioning their own distinct culture, within the limits established by the rigors of the slave system, blacks were able to forge their own religious forms, their own music and dance, their own family life, and their own beliefs and values. All of these proved indispensable to survival in a system of forced labor. Though slaves might have feigned deference or submissiveness and were severely constrained in many respects, they drew upon important elements of traditional culture and learned to carve out important areas of activity that gave meaning and importance to life.

8

The Transformation
of European Society

In 1650 the European population of the colonies clinging to the eastern edge of the continent was about the same as the daytime population of a large university campus today—roughly 50,000. Fifty years later this number had increased fivefold to a quarter million. By 1750 the number had again increased fivefold, including about 240,000 Africans. Such a rate of population growth was unknown in other parts of the world. By the middle of the eighteenth century the inhabitants of the English colonies in North America were one-third as numerous as the English themselves, and the rate at which the gap between the two populations was closing led early demographers such as Benjamin Franklin to estimate that before another four generations passed the colonizers would outnumber the population of England itself.

EIGHTEENTH-CENTURY EUROPEAN IMMIGRANTS

These rapidly multiplying proto-Americans were not only English. The seventeenth-century immigrants had come primarily from England, mixing with a small number of Dutch, Swedes, and Finns already settled along the seaboard and with a relatively insignificant number of Germans, Scots-Irish, French, and Africans who arrived late in the seventeenth century. But the eighteenth century belonged to the non-English so far as immigration was concerned. Beginning in the second decade of the century thousands of Germans, Swiss, Ulster Scots-Irish, and Africans began pouring into the colonies. Some came voluntarily and some involuntarily. But whether they arrived as slaves, indentured servants, or free persons, they drastically altered the gene pool of the existing population. By the end of the colonial period, as the Revolution loomed on the horizon, roughly half the inhabitants of the thirteen colonies had no English blood in their veins. This proportion of non-English was greater than at any time in American history, even after the tremendous influx of Europeans in the late nineteenth and early twentieth centuries.

Historians have told us primarily about the lives of only a tiny fraction of this population. We know a great deal about the political and military leaders, the men who amassed fortunes, and those who because of their high positions in society left their names and opinions in the official and private records of the time. But the cultural change occurring in the century prior to the Revolution bore far more relation to the roughly congruent behavior of thousands of "historically voiceless" individuals than to the actions of leaders whose words and deeds form the basis of most of our written history. After the Revolution John Adams would write that "the poor man's conscience is clear; yet he is ashamed . . . he feels himself out of the sight of others groping in the dark. Mankind takes no notice of him. He rambles and wanders unheeded. In the midst of a crowd, at church, in the market . . . he is in as much obscurity as he would be in a garret or a cellar. He is not disapproved, censured, or reproached; he is only not seen."[1] Similarly, historians have "not seen" the largest part of colonial society whose footprints are only now being discerned in the sands of time.

Yet the work, the wanderings, the attitudes, and the hopes and fears of the masses of inconspicuous individuals led to cultural change so distinct in North America in the eighteenth century that Europeans never tired of touring the colonies and setting down the characteristics of the people they saw—so different from what they knew in Europe. What they described, though they did it in an entirely untheoretical way, was a set of economic activities, forms of social and political organization, and a constellation of values and beliefs that were fused together in what we call a culture. During the first three-quarters of the eighteenth century this culture was transformed so extensively that a John Smith or a John Winthrop, had he still lived, would have been amazed at what he saw.

The social origins of those who flocked to the colonies in the eighteenth century played a part in the social transformation. From the top layers of European society came almost nobody. In the seventeenth century a small

---

[1]Quoted in James A. Henretta, *The Evolution of American Society, 1700–1815* (Lexington, Mass.: D.C. Heath and Company, 1973), pp. 3–4.

number of Englishmen at the apex of the social pyramid had taken an active role in colonizing the New World—men such as Walter Raleigh and Richard Grenville in Virginia; the Calverts, who founded Maryland; the insiders at the court of Charles II who became the proprietors of Carolina and New Jersey; and a handful of others. But for the most part they contributed money and organizational ability rather than their lives. Only a few tore free of their moorings in England and immigrated permanently to North America. In the eighteenth century upper-class immigrants were even rarer. Only an occasional Baron de Graffenried or Count von Zinzendorf, usually leaders of groups of Germans, Swiss, or Scots-Irish immigrants, represented the upper stratum of European society.

Below the nobility were the country gentry, and grouped with them on the social scale were officeholders, members of the professions, and the wealthier merchants. These men ran the joint-stock companies which had been so important in launching the early seventeenth-century settlements, and they continued to provide a major portion of the investment capital necessary for the economic development of overseas territories. In the seventeenth century they contributed substantially to the Atlantic migration, either by coming themselves or by sending their younger sons. The Oxford- and Cambridge-trained Puritan ministers, many of the early merchants of Boston and Philadelphia, and some of the large planters of Virginia, Maryland, and the Carolinas were included in this category. But in the eighteenth century they came in smaller numbers.

A rung below the gentry were the yeoman farmers of the countryside and the artisan-shopkeepers of the cities. In Europe's social hierarchy these were respected men who bulked large in the membership of the church and were entitled to participate in the political life of the community. Through hard work, good fortune, or a judicious marriage they often hauled themselves upward a rung on the social ladder or at least lived to see a son enter one of the professions or embark on a career as a merchant. They may have composed as much as one-third of the immigrants to the colonies. Once there, they provided the backbone of the middle class and often moved rapidly upward in a society that had plenty of room at the top. As a group, they were skilled, industrious, and ambitious; their fortunes advanced much faster than if they had remained at home.

Taken together, these recruits from the nobility, gentry, and middle class of European society accounted for roughly one-half of all those Europeans who traveled the water highway to the west side of the Atlantic in the seventeenth century and probably less than a third of the eighteenth-century immigrants. The remaining colonizers consisted mostly of indentured servants—men, women, and children who lacked sufficient resources to pay their way to the New World and therefore contracted out their labor for a number of years in return for passage. Their backgrounds were mixed. Some were obscure shopkeepers, artisans, schoolteachers, and farmers who were down on their luck or sorely pressed by a downturn in economic conditions. Many more had never risen above the subsistence level and could not expect to do so. These were the sturdiest of them. The lowliest were paupers and petty criminals—people who sometimes left England, Scotland, Ireland, and Germany voluntarily and sometimes at the request of the authorities. Local officials could rid themselves of the community's undesirables and reduce the poor taxes by banishing the disinherited to what they promised would be a new life—or a quick death—in the New World. The Scottish Privy Council, for example, in attempting to organize a colonizing expedition to New York in 1669, sent out warrants to local authorities to recruit "strong and idle beggars, vagabonds, egyptians, comon and notorious whoores, theeves and other dissolute and lousy persons banished or stigmatized for gross crymes."[2] Between 1718 and 1775 British authorities transported 50,000 convicts—mostly young males convicted of petty crimes, especially theft—to the American colonies.

Indentured Servants

Since the indentured servant came to represent a high proportion of the eighteenth-century immigrants, it is important to understand the mechanics of the profitable business of transporting bound laborers to the colonies. Like African and Indian slaves, white indentured servants were invaluable in a society that was rich in land but poor in labor. Labor in the colonies, Benjamin Franklin wrote in 1759, "is performed chiefly by indentured servants brought from Great Britain, Ireland, and Germany, because the high price it bears cannot be performed in any other way."[3] Franklin was forgetting that enslaved Africans were as numerous as white servants in 1759, even in his hometown of Philadelphia, and that in the southern colonies they comprised the bulk of the labor force. But his general point is valid: Colonial North America was being developed by unfree laborers. No matter whether he was a small tobacco planter in Virginia, a shopkeeper in New York, a farmer in Connecticut, or a shipwright in Boston, nearly every free member of colonial society wanted a bound laborer by his side as soon as he had accumulated the £20 to £40 required to purchase one. Additional labor meant the ability to produce more goods or services, which in turn meant greater profits. In an age before machines, commanding the labor of others became crucially important.

The terms of indentured servitude were simple. A servant bound himself or herself by contract to a ship captain for a specified length of time, usually four to seven years. In return the captain agreed to transport the servant

---

[2]Quoted in Peter Gouldesbrough, "An Attempted Scottish Voyage to New York in 1669," *Scottish Historical Review*, 40 (1961): 56.
[3]Quoted in Marcus W. Jernegen, *Laboring and Dependent Classes in Colonial America, 1607–1783* (New York: Frederick Ungar Publishing Co., 1965), p. 55.

across the Atlantic and place him or her on the auction block in one of the colonial seaports. The ship captain signed the work contract over to the highest bidder at the time of the auction. By the terms of the indenture the servant agreed to serve faithfully in return for food, clothes, shelter, and, at the end of the contract, a small sum of money, occasionally some tools, and sometimes the right to a few acres of land.

The traffic in bound labor became a regular part of the commerce linking Europe and North America. A combination of merchants, ship captains, immigrant brokers, and recruiting agents kept thousands of Europeans on the road to the colonies throughout the pre-Revolutionary period. Like any other cargo, servants were loaded onto boats, carried across the ocean, and sold on the other side. The system provided labor for the established members of colonial society, eventual freedom and the chance for a better life for those caught in the net of European poverty, and profits for the middlemen involved. To be sure, the system was full of abuses. Just as the trade in Indian and African slaves was ridden with callous disregard for human life, so also the trade in contract white labor was often a dirty business. Kidnapping and shanghaiing of drifters and drunks was endemic. Many unfortunate seaport dwellers woke one morning with a head-splitting hangover to find themselves in the hold of a ship headed westward across the Atlantic. Once on the ship, they found appalling conditions. The description of Gottlieb Mittelberger, who accompanied a boatload of German servants sailing from Rotterdam to Philadelphia in 1750, conveys some feeling for what those seeking a better life in the American colonies endured after they sold their labor for some of the prime years of their life:

> During the journey the ship is full of pitiful signs of distress—smells, fumes, horrors, vomiting, various kinds of sea sickness, fever, dysentery, headaches, heat, constipation, boils, scurvy, cancer, mouth-rot, and similar afflictions, all of them caused by the age and the highly-salted state of the food, especially the meat, as well as by the very bad and filthy water, which brings about the miserable destruction and death of many. Add to all that shortage of food, hunger, thirst, frost, heat, dampness, fear, misery, vexation, and lamentation, as well as other troubles. Thus, for example, there are so many lice, especially on the sick people, that they have to be scraped off the bodies. All this misery reaches its climax when in addition to everything else one must suffer through two or three days and nights of storm, with everyone convinced that the ship will go to the bottom with all human beings on board. . . . Children between the ages of one and seven seldom survive the sea voyage; and parents must often watch their offspring suffer miserably, die, and be thrown into the ocean, from want, hunger, thirst, and the like. I myself, alas, saw such a pitiful fate overtake thirty-two children on board our vessel, all of whom were finally thrown into the sea.[4]

[4]Gottlieb Mittelberger, *Journey to Pennsylvania,* ed. and trans. Oscar Handlin and John Clive (Cambridge, Mass.: Harvard University Press, 1960), pp. 12–15.

Mittelberger described how shipmates turned on each other after reaching the limits of endurance. But mostly they recalled the villages from which they had come: "Oh! If only I were back at home, even lying in my pig-sty!" Probably one-quarter of those embarking from European ports never lived to see the forests of the New World or, in their weakened condition, died shortly after arrival—a mortality rate approximating that of the Atlantic slave trade. For those who did survive the ordeal, the dangers of "seasoning" in North America—the acclimatization to new conditions—lay ahead. In addition they faced a physical and psychological adjustment to an environment and a master that were completely unknown. Especially in the southern colonies, agricultural labor took a deadly toll among those whose masters were determined to extract as much labor as possible during the years of the work contract. Adding to the difficulty of the servant's life was the right of the master to forbid marriage. Because it invariably led to pregnancy among female servants, and thus a loss of time, most masters denied their servants a family life.

Given the harshness of the indentured labor system, it is not surprising that colonial newspapers were filled with advertisements for runaway servants, interspersed with notices for runaway slaves. Servants knew the penalties for this: whipping and additional service, usually reckoned at twice the time lost to the master, but sometimes, as in Pennsylvania, calculated at a five-to-one ratio and in Maryland at ten-to-one. Even so, servants fled their masters by the hundreds and occasionally staged minor insurrections. When war came, they flocked to enlist in the British army. Many masters were willing to take the compensation paid by the army and let a balky servant go.

The great goal of every servant was to obtain a place on the ladder of opportunity—or what *seemed* to be such a ladder from a vantage point in the villages of Scotland, Ireland, and Germany. But as one historian has reminded us, "it will not do simply to assume that freed servants, especially those from the tobacco fields, were in any mental or physical condition to start vigorous new lives, or that long and ripe years of productivity lay ahead of them."[5] Although it is extremely difficult to follow the lives of freed servants, the most informed study of white servitude indicates that out of every ten indentured servants only one attained a position as a farmer in comfortable circumstances and one more achieved the status of artisan. The other eight died before they obtained their freedom or became propertyless day laborers, vagrants, or denizens of the local almshouse after completing their indentures.[6] The life chances of a servant were better than this in the seventeenth century but worsened thereafter, as some of the early fluidity of society disappeared. Though our attention has been claimed by the handful of servants who prospered or achieved fame—revolutionary leaders such as

[5]Richard Hofstadter, *America at 1750: A Social Portrait* (New York: Alfred A. Knopf, 1972), p. 61.
[6]Abbot E. Smith, *Colonists in Bondage: White Servitude and Convict Labor in America, 1607–1776* (Chapel Hill: University of North Carolina Press, 1946), pp. 297–300.

Daniel Dulany, Charles Thomson, and John Lamb—the statistical probability for rising even to the middle class was slight. Among the mass of those who sought opportunity in the British American colonies, it is the story of relentless labor and ultimate failure that stands out. The chief beneficiaries of the system of bound white labor were not the laborers themselves but those for whom they labored.

LAND, GROWTH, AND CHANGING VALUES

Out of the combination of fertile land, a pool of bound laborers, and the ambition of thousands of small farmers and artisans who labored independently, two variants of agricultural society emerged in eighteenth-century North America. In the North, small communities made up of farmers and artisans dotted the landscape. New Englanders engaged in mixed farming, which included farming the forests for timber used in barrels and ships, and farming the offshore waters for fish that provided one of the staples in the diet of the fast-growing slave population of the West Indies. The Middle Colonies specialized in producing corn, wheat, beef, and pork. By mid-eighteenth century they were provisioning not only the West Indies but also parts of Spain, Portugal, and England. Slaves were few in number in most of the northern communities, rarely representing more than 5 percent of the population. A large percentage of free men owned land; and, though differences in ability and circumstances led gradually to greater social and economic stratification, the truly rich and abjectly poor were few in number and the gap between them was small in comparison to European society. Most men lived to acquire a farm of at least fifty acres. They extracted from the soil a modest income that allowed for security from want and provided a small inheritance for their children.

In the southern colonies, where tobacco, rice, indigo, and timber products predominated, many yeomen farmers also struggled independently, although they were more frequently dispersed across the land than clustered in villages. These men have been far less noticed by historians than the plantation owners with slaves and indentured servants. But the usual picture of a southern plantation society made up of immensely wealthy men exploiting the labor of huge gangs of black slaves is badly overdrawn. Perhaps as many as 40 percent of the southern white males worked as tenant farmers or agricultural laborers, and of the remaining men who owned land, about two out of every three in the Chesapeake region worked farms of two hundred acres or less. In North Carolina farms were even smaller and men of real wealth rarer. In South Carolina the opposite was true; slaveholding was more widespread, plantations tended to be larger, and planters of substantial wealth represented a larger proportion of the population. As early as 1726 in St. George's Parish, 87 of 108 families held slaves. A generation later in St. Bartholomew Parish about 250 white families owned more than 5,000 slaves.[7] On the eve of the American Revolution the governor of South Carolina assured a prospective rice planter that "You'll never make yourself whole with less than Thirty Negroes."[8]

On the whole, probably not more than 5 percent of the white landowners were wealthy enough by mid-eighteenth century to possess a plantation worth £1,000—not too different from the North. Similarly, those owning large numbers of slaves were not as numerous as we commonly think. The number of southern slaves increased rapidly in the eighteenth century, rising from about 20,000 in 1700 to 240,000 in 1750. But a majority of white adult males held no slaves at all at mid-century, and those who operated plantations with more than 20 slaves probably did not exceed 10 percent of the white taxables. South Carolina excepted, the South throughout the pre-Revolutionary period was dominated numerically by small landowners whose holdings, if perhaps twice the size of the average New England farm, were not more than half again as large as the typical farm in Pennsylvania, New Jersey, or New York.

Nonetheless, the ideal in the South was the large plantation where black slaves would make the earth yield up profits sufficient to support the leisured life. Statistically speaking, not many white colonists in the South achieved the dream. But that is what people worked for, and they came to identify the quest for material comfort with the exploitation of African slave labor in an era when the northern colonists were beginning to phase out white bound labor and turning to a market economy where both goods and labor were freely exchanged.

The Protestant work ethic, which purportedly propelled people upward by inculcating a life of frugality, industriousness, and highly rationalized economic activity, perhaps operated less compellingly in the psyches of southern colonists than in their northern counterparts. But the abundant, fertile land of the South and the wider availability of slaves after 1690 provided all the incentive necessary for an aggressive, competitive society to develop. Much folklore about southern cavaliers reposing under magnolia trees has been handed down in the history books, but in the eighteenth century European colonizers in the South as avidly pursued wealth and material comfort as European colonizers in the North. If the warm climate of the South bred languor, it was also true that farmers in the South had no long frozen winters when there was little to do but mend harness and chop wood. The typical New England farm produced just one crop each year; but a

[7]Frank J. Klinberg, *An Appraisal of the Negro in Colonial South Carolina: A Study in Americanization* (Washington, D.C.: The Associated Publishers, 1941), pp. 58–60; William Langhorne, "An Account of the Spiritual State of State of St. Bartholomew's Parish" (1752), *South Carolina Magazine of History,* 50 (1949): 200.

[8]Quoted in Philip D. Morgan, *Slave Counterpoint: Black Culture in the Eighteenth-Century Chesapeake and Low Country* (Chapel Hill: University of North Carolina Press, 1998), p. 35.

South Carolina rice or indigo plantation produced two. Moreover, the restraints of a New England community orientation and the Puritan bias against the accumulation of wealth which was not disposed of in socially useful ways never hindered entrepreneurial activity in the South. Organized religion was only shallowly rooted in most of the southern colonies and the community orientation never took hold because communities themselves were few and far between.

Paradoxically, one of the effects of the growth and success of the colonies in eighteenth-century British America was to shatter the utopian dream of the first generation that communities could be built where men and women worked for the commonweal, not only for themselves. The Puritan work ethic and an atmosphere of seemingly limitless opportunity encouraged men to work arduously at their callings. That was to the good. And their labors had generally been rewarded with success. So was that. But living where the ratio of people to land was so favorable compared to the societies from which they came, many colonists developed an aggressive outlook that patterned their behavior. What was to hold a man back in these uncharted expanses of land and unclaimed river valleys, as soon as the Indians were gone? In Europe, the absence of uncultivated lands ripe for exploitation and the grinding poverty that enshrouded the lives of the great mass of people produced in the peasant consciousness a very low level of expectations. "The frontier zone between possibility and impossibility barely moved in any significant direction, from the fifteenth to the eighteenth century," writes Fernand Braudel.[9] But it moved in North America. The new concept was of a society where anything was possible. A competitive, entrepreneurial spirit began to take hold.

Religion and commitment to community, which acted as brakes on competitive, individualistic behavior, were by no means dead in the eighteenth century. But in general, defining one's life as a preparation for the afterlife declined greatly. Even in the seventeenth century Roger Williams had deplored the "depraved appetite after the great vanities, dreams, and shadows of this vanishing life, great portions of land, land in this wilderness, as if men were in as great necessity and danger for want of great portions of land, as poor, hungry seamen have, after a sick and stormy, a long and starving passage."[10] In the eighteenth century land became ever more regarded not simply as a source of livelihood but a commodity to be bought and sold speculatively as a means of building a fortune. Franklin's little how-to-do-it best-seller, *The Way to Wealth,* caught the spirit of the aggressive entrepreneurial eighteenth century. The brakes on economic ambition had been suddenly

[9]Fernand Braudel, *Capitalism and Material Life, 1400–1800,* George Weidenfeld, trans. (New York: Harper Torchbooks, 1973), p. ix.
[10]Quoted in Francis Jennings, *The Invasion of America: Indians, Colonialism, and the Cant of Conquest* (Chapel Hill: University of North Carolina Press, 1975), p. 181.

removed and with the decline of fervid Puritanism in the eighteenth century there was little left to restrain predatory instincts in those who were eager to pit themselves against their fellows in the pursuit of material gain. "Every man is for himself," lamented a prominent Philadelphian in 1706, only a generation after Penn had planted the seed of his "holy experiment."[11] Two generations later the lieutenant-governor of New York, who had grown up in the colony, put it more explicitly: "The only principle of life propagated among the young people," wrote Cadwallader Colden, "is to get money and men are only esteemed according to what they are worth—that is the money they are possessed of."[12] A contemporary in Rhode Island echoed the thought when he wrote "A Man who has Money here, no matter how he came by it, he is Everything, and wanting [lacking] that he's a meer Nothing, let his Conduct be ever so ereproachable."[13]

As these acquisitive values took hold, the individual replaced the community as the conceptual unit of thought. The advice of the ancestors, such as the Puritan minister John Cotton, to "goe forth, every man that goeth, with a public spirit, looking not on your owne things only," or Winthrop's maxim that "the care of the publick must oversway all private respects," carried less and less weight in eighteenth-century society. A French visitor, who took up residence in New York, described this psychological reorientation:

> An European, when he first arrives, seems limited in his intentions, as well as in his views; but he very suddenly alters his scale.... He no sooner breathes our air than he forms schemes, and embarks in designs he never would have thought of in his own country.... He begins to feel the effects of a sort of resurrection; hitherto he had not lived, but simply vegetated; he now feels himself a man, because he is treated as such; ... he begins to forget his former servitude and dependence....[14]

This transformation of attitudes, while it helped promote phenomenal growth and unleashed economic energies, paradoxically led toward material success that contained within it the seeds of social strain. The demand for land east of the Appalachian Mountain barrier grew rapidly after 1740, as the population rose through immigration and natural increase. Especially in New England, ungranted land in the coastal region was a thing of the past, and the division and redivision of original land grants among sons and grandsons progressed as far as it could go without splitting farms into unviably

[11]Quoted in Gary B. Nash, *Quakers and Politics; Pennsylvania, 1681–1726* (Princeton, N.J.: Princeton University Press, 1968), p. 303.

[12]Quoted in Henretta, *Evolution of American Society*, p. 99.

[13]Quoted in Carl Bridenbaugh, *Cities in Revolt; Urban Life in America, 1743–1776* (New York: Capricorn Books, 1964), p. 140.

[14]J. Hector St. John Crèvecoeur, *Letters from an American Farmer* (New York: E.P. Dutton & Co., 1957), pp. 54–56.

small economic units. New land—on the Maine frontier, in western Massachusetts and Connecticut, across the Appalachians in Pennsylvania, Virginia, Maryland, and the Carolinas—was the obvious solution to the problem of overcrowding. Land companies emerged in the mid-eighteenth century to claim the valuable western lands. Their investors understood the enormous appreciation in value that would occur as the next generation came of age and sought *lebensraum* to the west. But before a westward movement could begin, interior Indian peoples, as well as the French and Spanish, had to be overcome.

THE CITIES

Even though only about 5 percent of the eighteenth-century colonists lived in cities (and none of these cities exceeded 16,000 in 1750), the commercial capitals of coastal North America were the cutting edge of economic, social, and political change. Almost all the alterations that we associate with the advent of capitalist society occurred first in the seaport towns and then radiated outward to the villages and farms of the hinterland. In the maritime centers of colonial life the transition first occurred from a barter to a commercial economy; where a competitive social order replaced one based on ascribed status; where a hierarchical and deferential polity gave way to participatory and contentious civic life; where factory production began to replace small-scale artisan-style production.

In the seaport towns of Boston, Newport, New York, Philadelphia, and Charleston the competitive and acquisitive ethos took hold more rapidly than in the rural areas. This did not mean that artisans and laborers always worked feverishly to ascend the ladder of success. Craftsmen who commanded five shillings a day knew that weather, sickness, and the inconstancy of supplies made it difficult to work more than 250 days a year, which brought an income of £35 to £60. Hence, laboring people were far from the day when the failure to acquire property or accumulate a minor fortune produced guilt or aroused their anger against those above them. Their desire was not to reach the top but to get off the bottom. Yet they came to expect a "decent competency," as it was called, and did not anticipate the miserable hand-to-mouth existence of the laboring poor everywhere in Europe. Many of those who started as blacksmiths, carpenters, coopers, and shipwrights rose to the level of shopkeeper or even merchant. A handful did even better, such as William Phips, a sheep farmer and ship's carpenter from Maine who rose to the governorship of Massachusetts, or Benjamin Franklin, a poor printer who came to stand for the opportunities for upward mobility that many thought differentiated the American colonies from Europe.

In the half century between 1690 and 1740, Boston, New York, and Philadelphia blossomed into commercial centers that rivaled such British provincial ports as Hull, Bristol, and Glasgow. This urban growth reflected the development of the hinterlands to which they were commercially linked. More and more, these seaports were drawn into the international market-place of the Atlantic basin. More and more, economic decisions were dictated by an emerging commercial ethic that rubbed abrasively against traditional restraints on entrepreneurial activity. The older economic ethic, medieval in origins, rested on the assumption of a world made up of many semiclosed economies, each operating in a nearly self-sufficient way. A city, according to this model, was connected to the immediately surrounding area, but the area itself remained self-contained.

By the early eighteenth century, the North American seaports had become a part of a far wider Atlantic basin network that linked them not only to their hinterlands but also to Newfoundland, the West Indies, Portugal and Spain, England and Ireland, and West Africa. Economic decisions were made under the new order of things not with reference to local and public needs but according to laws of supply and demand that operated internationally. This wider market was indifferent to individuals and local communities; the flow and price of commodities, as well as labor and land, were dictated by the invisible laws of the international marketplace. If grain fetched eight shillings a bushel in the West Indies, for example, and only five in Boston, then a New England merchant was entitled to send all the wheat he could purchase from local farmers to the more distant buyer.

Not until war in Europe created a genuine crisis did the full extent of the tension between the new entrepreneurial freedom and the older concern for the public weal become manifest. Such a moment occurred in Boston during Queen Anne's War (1702–13) when Andrew Belcher, one of the town's largest grain merchants, decided to ship large quantities of wheat to the West Indies, where prices were far higher than in Massachusetts. Threatened with a bread shortage and appalled that a leading townsman would put profits ahead of the welfare of the community, ordinary Bostonians descended on one of Belcher's ships, which was about to sail with 6,000 bushels of grain, and sawed through the rudder. They then tried to run the disabled ship aground in order to liberate the grain from its holds. Such food shortages rarely occurred in the American colonies, usually only during wartime when unusual amounts of grain were needed for military provisioning. But when they did, urban people demanded to be fed at prices they could afford, regardless of the modern economic notions invoked by merchants that the laws of supply and demand must rule.

The urban social strain that grew with the spread of the individualistic and entrepreneurial ethic became more evident in the European wars of 1739 to 1747 into which the colonies were drawn. New England was drained of manpower and resources in King George's War (1744–48), as its inhabitants engaged in costly attempts to overcome the French enemy to the north. But the war also offered opportunities for merchants and others to run up profits through war contracts and privateering. "A covetous selfish Spirit" ran through the people, lamented one Massachusetts spokesman, and "every Man looks at his own Things, and not at the Things of others." Gone was a "publick Spirit" and in its place stood a "Greedy desire of Gain."[15] Another commentator noted that food prices had escalated sharply during the war and that all around Boston men were turning from their professions to become buyers and butchers of livestock. They understood that by intercepting Boston's meat supplies and holding them for a time, they could drive up prices and take over the function of the town's butchers and hucksters. Known as "forestalling," this amounted to a sort of economic warfare between rural and urban society. The war against the French had not unified Massachusetts but instead had set one element against another in the pursuit of private gain.

The fissuring of an interdependent economic community was equally visible in the action of merchants in other colonies during King George's War. Foodstuffs exporters in New York and Philadelphia piled up profits by trading illegally with the French and Spanish enemy in the West Indies. Diverting food supplies from New England to the Caribbean, where the enemy paid high prices in order to feed their slave populations, they smuggled their way to fortune. "How surprizing it is that for the Sake of Private Gain, his Majesty's declared Enemies should be thus openly assisted to destroy his Subjects," cried the *Boston Evening Post*.[16] This betrayal of the public good by private economic interest padded the food bill of every Bostonian. War had fueled the free market, with everyone from the lowliest tar aboard a privateer to the largest war contractor and merchant smuggler seeking to capitalize on new opportunities for gain.

The throwing off of governmental and ideological restraints, and the enthronement of the concept of self-interest, provided the perfect rationale for rapidly developing a vast area of land blessed with abundant natural resources and peopled by ambitious, tough-minded, innovating Europeans. The new system of values legitimated private profit-seeking, promoted the abandonment of economic regulation, and projected a future in which men's energies were cut loose from age-old mercantilist controls instituted to promote the good of all. This, it was argued, would produce a far better common good. Thus two conceptions of economic life and social relations jostled for ascendancy in the Euro-American mind.

Such thinking paralleled emerging values in England and Europe. There too a new model of economic and social life had emerged, predicated on the notion that the market mentality was preferable to the older corporate ideal of persons finely attuned to the public good because that idealistic model refused to take men as they really were. Self-denial, moral

[15]Nathaniel Appleton, *The Cry of Oppression* (Boston, 1748), pp. 36–37.
[16]*Boston Evening Post*, Feb. 1, 1748.

rectitude, and the subordination of private to public interests lay as dead weights on the economic order. National prosperity required something different—acceptance of the notion that "the self-seeking drive appeared more powerful than institutional efforts to mold people's actions."[17] If each individual sought his or her own improvement, all these separate efforts would produce, through a mysterious process later described by Adam Smith as the "invisible hand," a natural harmony and a prosperous, free society. Men could not be compelled to work for the good of the whole. But left to sort out their wants and to pursue their own material desires in open competition, they would collectively form an impersonal market that would regulate human affairs to everyone's advantage.

CHANGING SOCIAL STRUCTURE

Population growth and economic development, carried on for a century and a half by opportunistic individuals, changed both the structure of colonial society and the attitudes of the people toward social structure—but changed them in opposite directions. Seventeenth-century Europeans on both sides of the Atlantic accepted the naturalness of hierarchy in human affairs, the inevitability of poverty, and the right of those in the upper stratum of society to rule those below them. The belief was general that social gradations and internal subordination were not only sanctioned by God but were essential to the maintenance of social cohesion. Therefore care was taken to differentiate individuals by dress, by titles, in social etiquette, and even in penalties imposed in criminal proceedings. Puritans, for example, did not simply file into church on Sunday mornings and occupy the pews in random fashion. Instead, each seat was assigned according to the social rank of the person in the community. "Dooming the seats," as the assignment process was aptly called, was the responsibility of a church committee, which used every available yardstick of social respectability—age, parentage, social position, service to the community, and wealth—in drawing up a seating plan for the congregation. Puritans never entered their church without being reminded where they stood in the ranks of the community.

The philosophical commitment to hierarchy was strongest among the elite, but most of immigrant society was lower-middle class in its composition. With land widely available, the spectrum of wealth remained relatively narrow throughout most of the seventeenth century. Even in the cities, where the redistribution of wealth proceeded the fastest, the dawn of the eighteenth century witnessed a colonial society that was mostly middle class in character. In the Hudson River Valley and in the southern colonies a handful of

[17]Joyce Appleby, "The Social Origins of American Revolutionary Ideology," *Journal of American History,* 64 (1978): 944.

large plantation owners had made their mark, but the largest slave owners in Virginia at the beginning of the eighteenth century still owned fewer than one hundred slaves and not more than a handful of men had as much as £2,000 to leave to their heirs. As late as 1722 one of Philadelphia's richest merchants died with personal possessions worth just over £1,000—a sizable estate but unimpressive by European standards.

In the eighteenth century, and especially in the half century before the Revolution, the customary commitment to hierarchy and deference waned at the same time that stratification in society was increased. Social attitudes and social structure were moving in opposite directions. Below the elite free whites developed the ideal of egalitarianism. The middling sort of people, wrote a Philadelphian in 1756, "enjoy and are fond of freedom, and the meanest among them thinks he has a right to civility from the greatest."[18] Such comments were common. The Frenchman, Crèvecoeur, was surprised to see hired workers who "must be at your table and feed . . . on the best you have," and the schoolteacher Philip Fithian wrote of "labourers at the tables and in the parlours of their betters enjoying the advantage, and honour of their society and conversation."[19]

For most American colonists, then, the ideal was a society where a wealthy aristocracy did not dominate and no masses of poor whites were ground into the dust. When Benjamin Franklin toured the English countryside in 1772 he was appalled at what he saw and raised thanks that America was different. He described "landlords, great noblemen, and gentlemen, extremely opulent, living in the highest affluence and magnificence" alongside "the bulk of the people, tenants, extremely poor, living in the most sordid wretchedness, in dirty hovels of mud and straw, and clothed only in rags." Shaking his head, Franklin took solace in the knowledge that North America was different. Ignoring Indians and Africans, he wrote: "I thought often of the Happiness of New England, where every Man is a Freeholder, has a Vote in publick Affairs, lives in a tidy, warm House, has plenty of good Food and fewel, with whole cloaths from Head to Foot, the Manufacture perhaps of his own Family."[20] The German Mittelberger summed up the twin ideals of economic equality and democratic scorn for authorities and authoritarian institutions. Pennsylvania, he said, was "heaven for farmers, paradise for artisans, and hell for officials and preachers."[21]

If Franklin and Mittelberger reflected the growing celebration of America's egalitarian society, they also had reason to know that eighteenth-century society, even for white colonists, was moving away from this New World ideal. As the old deferential attitudes gave way to brash, assertive, individualistic

[18]Quoted in Hofstadter, *America at 1750,* p. 131.
[19]*Ibid.,* p. 141.
[20]*The Writings of Benjamin Franklin,* 10 vols., ed. Albert H. Smyth (New York: The Macmillan Co., 1907),V: 362–63.
[21]Mittelberger, *Journey to Pennsylvania,* p. 48.

modes of thought and behavior—what would become known as "the democratic personality"—society became more stratified and wealth became less evenly distributed. Population growth and economic development in the eighteenth century made rich men of those with capital to speculate in land, buy slaves and servants, or participate in trade. The aggrandizement of wealth became apparent in all sections of the country—North and South, rural and urban. In Boston, Newport, New York, Philadelphia, and Charleston stately townhouses rose as testimony to the fortunes being acquired in trade, shipbuilding, and land speculation. Probably the last of these was the most profitable of all. "It is almost a proverb," wrote a Philadelphian in 1767, "that Every great fortune made here within these 50 years has been by land."[22] By the late colonial period it was not unusual to find merchant land speculators with estates valued at £10,000–£20,000. Even in the rural areas of the North wealthy farmers amassed estates worth £4,000–£5,000. In the South, plantation magnates built even larger fortunes, for the rapid importation of African slaves after 1720 accelerated the rate at which profits could be extracted from the cultivation of tobacco or rice. By the eve of the Revolution the great planters of the Chesapeake region, men such as Charles Carroll, Robert "King" Carter, and William Byrd, had achieved spectacular affluence. Their estates, valued at £100,000 or more, were equivalent in purchasing power to a fortune of about six million dollars in 1990. It was not unusual to see 300 to 400 slaves toiling on such plantations, whereas in the late seventeenth century the largest slaveholder on the continent had no more than 50 bound laborers.

While the rapid increase in population and large-scale capital investment in land and slaves enabled a small number of men to accumulate fortunes that would have been noteworthy even in English society, the development of colonial society also created conditions in which a growing number of persons were finding it difficult to keep bread on the table and wood in the fireplace. This was especially true in the cities, where the social stratification proceeded most rapidly. All the major cities built almshouses and workhouses in the second quarter of the century to provide for those who could not care for themselves—the aged, indigent, sick, insane, and orphaned. Between 1725 and 1760, the poor in the cities increased more rapidly than the urban population as a whole, and after about 1750 poverty was no longer confined to the old or physically depleted.

Boston, the first utopian settlement in British North America, was the first to feel the pinch of economic hardship. The city had grown to about 12,000 in 1720 and increased to some 16,000 in the next two decades. But from 1740 until after the Revolution the city's population stagnated while New England's economy languished. Expenditures for poor relief edged upward in the 1730s and grew faster than the population in the 1740s. In 1753

---

[22] *Pennsylvania Magazine of History and Biography,* 1 (1877): 277.

the Overseers of the Poor reported to the Massachusetts legislature that poor relief expenditures in Boston were double that of any town of comparable size "upon the face of the whole Earth" by the reckoning of those acquainted with such matters. Though this may or may not have been true, it was certain that a large number of people in the town were in real distress. In 1757 the Overseers reported that "the Poor supported either wholly or in part by the Town in the Alms-house and out of it will amount to the Number of about 1000," and those receiving private charity from churches and philanthropic organizations swelled the total.[23]

The differing abilities of men to manipulate their economic environment, capitalize on the freedom to exploit white and black labor, and obtain title to Indian land were eventually recorded on the tax lists of the community, where each man's wealth was set alongside that of his neighbors. Colonial historians have scrutinized these tax lists and found that population growth and economic development led toward a less even distribution of wealth and an increase in the proportion of those without property in virtually every community. The change occurred slowly in rural areas and proceeded more rapidly in the seaboard centers of commercial activity.

In the rural town of Northampton, Massachusetts, for example, the upper 10 percent of property owners controlled 25 percent of the taxable wealth in 1676 and slowly increased their control of the community's assets to 34 percent in 1759. At the same time the proportion of the community's taxable property owned by the bottom third of the society remained steady at about 10 percent. In Chester County, Pennsylvania, a fertile wheat-growing region southwest of Philadelphia, the wealthiest tenth of the farmers commanded about 24 percent of the wealth in 1693 and almost 30 percent by 1760. During the same period the lowest 30 percent of the landowners saw their economic leverage decline from 17.4 to 6.3 percent of the taxable assets of the county. In three counties of Maryland the percentage of white freemen who owned land dropped from 44 to 37 between 1756 and 1771.

In the cities the rate of change was far greater. Boston's upper tenth in 1687 held 46 percent of the taxable property while the lowest 30 percent had a meager 2.6 percent of the wealth. Four generations later, in 1771, the top tenth had 63 percent of the wealth; the lowest three-tenths had virtually nothing—a mere .10 percent of the community's taxable resources. Economic polarization in Boston, where the population was static after 1735 and economic recession hit hard at many elements of the community, was duplicated in vigorously expanding Philadelphia. In 1693, little more than a decade after settlement, the wealthiest tenth laid claim to 46 percent of the city's wealth. Three-quarters of a century later, in 1772, they possessed 71 percent of the taxable wealth. As in Boston, these gains were not made at

[23]*Records Relating to the Early History of Boston,* 39 vols. (Boston: Rockwell and Churchill, 1881–1909), 14: 240, 302.

the expense of those in the bottom third of society, who possessed only a meager 2.2 percent of the wealth in 1693, but were accomplished at the expense of those in the middling elements of society.

If poverty touched the lives of a growing part of the urban laboring class, it was the usual condition on the frontier. Here the gap between rich and poor hardly existed because the rich were nowhere to be found. The social order of the mid-eighteenth century frontier was even cruder than rural society on the edge of the continent a century before. Whether in the towns of western Massachusetts and Connecticut, founded in the second and third quarters of the eighteenth century by the sons of Yankee farmers; or the lands along the Mohawk River in New York and the Susquehanna River in Pennsylvania, which represented the hopes of the German and Scots-Irish immigrants; or the backcountry of Maryland, Virginia, and the Carolinas, which sponged up some 250,000 souls in the late colonial period, frontier society was composed of small farmers and rural artisans who all stood roughly on the same plane. They purchased land cheaply, often for as little as four shillings an acre, and struggled to carve farms from the wilderness. Many hoped to get enough land under cultivation within a few years to produce surplus crops for market. But with only the help of one's sons and a few farm animals this often took most of a man's life. Others struggled only to make enough improvements on a piece of land so that other settlers pushing westward on the next wave of settlement would find it attractive enough to pay a price that rewarded their labor.

On the New England frontier, where people pushed westward in groups, they founded new towns and churches as they went, quickly reproducing the institutions of eastern society. While poor, these simple villagers and farmers lived a life where institutional ligaments had not been altogether severed. But southward from New York on the east side of the Appalachian slopes frontier society existed in what many observers took to be a semi-barbarous state. William Byrd described one of the largest plantations on the Virginia frontier in 1733 as "a poor dirty hovel, with hardly anything in it but children that wallowed about like so many pigs."[24] Charles Woodmason, an Anglican minister who spent three years tramping from settlement to settlement in the Carolina backcountry in the 1760s, was appalled at what he found. "For thro' want of Ministers to marry and thro' the licentiousness of the People, many hundreds live in Concubinage—swapping their Wives as Cattel, and living in a State of Nature, more irregularly and unchastely than the Indians."[25] Woodmason carried with him all the English prejudices usually harbored against the Presbyterian Scots-Irish, the main

[24]Quoted in Richard R. Beeman, "Social Change and Cultural Conflict in Virginia: Lunenburg County, 1746 to 1774," *William and Mary Quarterly*, 35 (1978): 445.
[25]Charles Woodmason, *The Carolina Backcountry on the Eve of the Revolution*, ed. Richard J. Hooker (Chapel Hill: University of North Carolina Press, 1953), pp. 15, 33.

inhabitants of the region. But there is little reason to doubt that the crudeness of life he described actually existed. After preaching at Flat Creek to "a vast Body of people . . . Such a Medley! such a mixed Multitude of all Classes and Complexions," he paled at their after-service "Revelling Drinking Singing Dancing and Whoring" and threw up his hands that "most of the Company were drunk before I quitted the Spot—They were as rude in their Manners as the Common Savages, and hardly a degree removed from them." Some of what he saw made him close his eyes in horror, but he kept them open long enough to observe the young women who "have a most uncommon Practise. . . . They draw their Shift as tight as possible to the Body, and pin it close, to shew the roundness of their Breasts, and . . . their Petticoat close to their Hips to shew the fineness of their Limbs—so that they might as well be in Puri Naturalibus—Indeed Nakedness is not censurable or indecent here, and they expose themselves often quite Naked, without Ceremony—Rubbing themselves and their Hair with Bears Oil and tying it up behind in a Bunch like the Indians—being hardly one degree removed from them."[26]

THE GREAT AWAKENING

Nowhere did the line between social and economic change on the one hand and religion on the other crumble more swiftly than in the experiential and ideological upheaval called the Great Awakening. More than a solely religious movement, this period of sustained religious enthusiasm reflected a profound cultural transformation that had been building for several generations.

At its core the Great Awakening was "a search for new sources of authority, new principles of action, new foundations of hope" among people who had come to believe that the colonial churches "no longer met the spiritual needs of the people."[27] The Awakeners preached that the old sources of authority were too effete to solve the problems of the day, too encrusted with tradition, hypocrisy, and intellectualism to bring hope and faith to a generation that was witnessing the remaking of the world of their fathers. A new wellspring of authority was needed, and that source, the evangelists preached, was the individual himself. Like the Quaker "inner light," which dwelled in every man and woman, the "new light" within the awakened would enable them to achieve grace through the conversion experience. When enough people were "born again," as the evangelists of the Great Awakening phrased it, they would forge a new sense of community, achieve a new brotherhood of man, and restore the city on the hill. The Awakening,

---

[26]*Ibid.*, pp. 56, 61.
[27]William G. McLoughlin, *New England Dissent, 1630–1833: The Baptists and the Separation of Church and State* (Cambridge, Mass.: Harvard University Press, 1971), p. 335.

in its way, was a "revitalization movement," similar to those that occurred periodically in Indian societies when new leaders rejected corrosive changes and urged their followers to return to the traditions of the past.

The Awakening's first stirrings in the colonies occurred in the 1720s in New Jersey and Pennsylvania and then in the 1730s in Jonathan Edward's church in Northampton, Massachusetts. But not until 1739, with the arrival of George Whitefield from England, did it strike with full force. Whitefield was a master of open-air preaching and had trekked across the English countryside for several years preaching the word of God. A diminutive man with a magnificent voice, he began a barnstorming trip along the coast of North America in 1739 that evoked a mass response of a sort never witnessed before in the colonies. Thousands turned out to see him, and with each success his fame grew. Especially in the cities, which were the crucibles of social change, his effect was extraordinary. People fought for places in the churches to hear him or congregated by the thousands in open fields to receive the "divine fire" he kindled.

Some of Whitefield's appeal can be attributed to his genius for dramatic performances, his perfection of the art of advanced publicity, and his ability to simplify theological doctrine and focus the attention of masses of people on one facet of religious life—the conversion experience. In his electrifying performances, where he cast away written sermons, where his spastic body movements and magnificent voice control replaced dry, logical, rigidly structured sermons, thousands experienced the desire to "fly to Christ." But it was the message as well as the medium that explains why people flocked to hear Whitefield. He assaulted traditional sources of authority, called upon people to become the instruments of their own salvation, and implicitly attacked the upper-class notion that the simple folk had no minds of their own.

When Whitefield began his American tour in 1739, upper-class leaders did not perceive the social dynamite buried deep in his message. After all, his preaching produced thousands of conversions and filled the churches that had been languishing for more than a generation. Whitefield magnified the importance of religion in almost everyone who heard him, so it is no wonder that he was welcomed as "an angel of God, or as Elias, or John the Baptist risen from the dead."[28] But Whitefield's popularity soon waned among the gentry because he was followed by itinerant Awakeners whose social radicalism was far less muted, and because of the effects the evangelists' message had on the lower orders. Roaming preachers like Gilbert Tennant infused evangelical preaching with a radical egalitarianism that left many former supporters of Whitefield sputtering. Tennant attacked the established clergy as unregenerate and encouraged people to forsake their ministers. "The sapless Discourses of such dead Drones" were worthless, he

---

[28]Perry Miller, *Jonathan Edwards* (New York: World Publishing Co., 1949), pp. 166–67.

proclaimed.[29] James Davenport, another itinerant preacher, told huge crowds that they should drink rat poison rather than listen to the corrupt clergy. Even more dangerous, Davenport indicted the rich and powerful, criticized the growing gap between rich and poor, and exhorted ordinary people to resist those who exploited and deceived them. Only then, he cried, would the Lamb Jesus return to earth.

Crowds followed Davenport through the towns, singing and clapping so that "they look'd more like a Company of *Bacchanalians* after a mad Frolick, than sober Christians who had been worshipping God," as one distressed Boston newspaper complained.[30] Respectable people became convinced that revivalism had gotten out of hand. Revivalism had started out as a return to religion among backsliding Christians but now was turning into a social experience that profoundly threatened the established culture, which stressed order, discipline, and submissiveness from laboring people. The fear of the Awakeners' attacks on genteel literate culture, on wealth and ostentatious living, was epitomized in New London, Connecticut, in 1743 when Davenport scandalized the gentry by inducing a huge crowd

> to burn "sundry good and useful treatises, books of practical godliness, the works of able divines," as well as "hoop petticoats, silk gowns, short cloaks, cambrick caps, red heeled shoes, fans, necklaces, gloves, and other such apparell." While psalms and hymns were sung over the pile, the preacher added his own pants, "a pair of old, wore out, plush breaches." This, commented one critic, would have obliged him "to strutt about bare-arsed" had not the fire been extinguished.[31]

By 1742 New England and the middle colonies were being crisscrossed by itinerant gospelers and haranguers, all of them labeled social incendiaries by the established clergy. Of all the signs of social leveling that conservatives saw springing from evangelicalism, the one they feared the most was the practice of public lay exhorting. Within the established churches there was no place for laypersons to compete with the qualified ministry in preaching the word of God. Nor was there room for "self-initiated associations of the people meeting outside of regularly constituted religious or political meetings." To do so was to relocate authority collectively in the mass of common people.[32]

Almost as dangerous, lay preachers ruptured the idea of sacred space by going outside the church to unconsecrated profane space—streets, fields, and barns, where they kindled spiritual renewal. This attack on "the notion of

[29]*Ibid.*, p. 166.
[30]*Boston Evening Post*, Aug. 2, 1742.
[31]J. M. Bumstead and John E. Van de Wetering, *What Must I Do to Be Saved? The Great Awakening in Colonial America* (Hinsdale, Ill.: The Dryden Press, 1976), p. 90.
[32]Harry S. Stout, "Religion, Communications, and the Ideological Origins of the American Revolution," *William and Mary Quarterly*, 34 (1977): 527.

sacred space was also an attack on the entire social and political order, a bold attempt to introduce what contemporaries saw as 'Anarchy and Confusion' into the peaceable kingdoms of New England."[33] Lay exhorters shattered the monopoly of the educated clergy on religious discourse. They put all people on a plane in matters of religion, gave new importance to the oral culture of common people, and established among them the notion that their destinies and their souls were in their own hands instead of the hands of the elite clergy. They turned the world upside down by allowing those who had traditionally been consigned to the bottom of society to assume roles customarily reserved for educated, adult men. Lay exhorters, preaching the Lord's truth extemporaneously, crossed class lines and defied assigned sexual and racial roles. Especially infuriating to established clergymen was the evangelicals' willingness that lay women might speak publicly if spiritually moved. "The encouraging WOMEN, yea GIRLS to speak in the assemblies for worship," declaimed the shocked Charles Chauncy, "is a plain breach of that *commandment of the LORD,* where it is said, *Let your WOMEN keep silence in the churches.*"[34]

The Great Awakening thus represented far more than a religious earthquake. Through it, ordinary people haltingly enunciated a distinctive popular ideology that challenged inherited cultural norms. As many historians have noted, the Awakening represented a groundswell of individualism, a kind of protodemocratic spirit that anticipated the Revolution. Especially among the middling people of colonial society, who partook of spontaneous meetings, assumed new power in ecclesiastical affairs, and were encouraged by the evangelists to adopt a skeptical attitude toward dogma and authority, the revival years involved an expansion of political consciousness and a new feeling of self-importance. But among the lowliest members of society, including impoverished city dwellers, servants, slaves, and those who struggled to gain a foothold on the treacherous slopes of economic security, the Awakening experience did not propel them forward toward democratic bourgeois revolution but backward to an earlier age when it was conceived that individuals acted not for themselves, always striving to get ahead at the expense of their neighbors, but pulled together as a community. Hence the dispossessed harked to the anti-entrepreneurial, communalistic tone permeating the exhortations of the radical evangelists such as Tennant, who preached that in any truly Christian community "mutual *Love* is the *Band* and *Cement.* . . . For men, by the Neglect of its Exercise, and much more by its Contrary, will be tempted, against the *Law of Nature,* to seek a *single* and independent State, in order to secure their Ease and Safety."[35]

Radical Awakeners were not preaching class revolt or the end to wealth-producing commerce. What they urged was "a thorough reconsideration of

---

[33]Susan Juster, *Disorderly Women: Sexual Politics and Evangelicalism in Revolutionary New England* (Ithaca: Cornell University Press, 1994), 22.
[34]Quoted in *ibid.,* 31.
[35]Gilbert Tennant, *Brotherly Love Recommended* (Philadelphia, 1748).

the Christian ethic as it had come to be understood in the America of the 1730s."[36] Nor were those who harked to the Awakeners inspired to foment social revolution, for in fact the seeds of overt political radicalism were still in the germinative stage. But the multitudes who were moved by the spiritual intensity and emotional warmth of the revivalists, in the North in the 1740s and in the South during the next decade, began to believe that it was justifiable in some circumstances to take matters into their own hands. This is why Jonathan Edwards, a highly intellectual, latter-day Puritan minister, was seen by the commercial elite and their clerical allies as "the grand leveler of Christian history," even though sedition and leveling were not what he had in mind.

Producing the greatest flow of religious energy since the Puritan movement a century before, the Great Awakening also supplied "the most pertinent and usable model for radical activists in the years that lay ahead."[37] Originating as an outpouring of the heart, the Awakening built on the tensions and contentions in colonial society that had grown from generations of social and economic change. Church by church Awakeners learned that to advance their minority rebellious ideology they must persuade the majority or, if necessary, withdraw to establish new churches. In the process, they assaulted "the institutional structures that sheltered orthodoxy and fortified its authority."[38] Finding their allies among the common people, the Awakeners challenged traditional customs of social deference and developed new arguments justifying the rights of minorities. Thus the Great Awakening became a "practice model" that would have an immense importance in the political crisis leading toward the American Revolution.

[36]Alan Heimert, *Religion and the American Mind from the Great Awakening to the Revolution* (Cambridge, Mass.: Harvard University Press, 1966), p. 32.
[37]Patricia V. Bonomi, *Under the Cope of Heaven: Religion, Society, and Politics in Colonial America* (New York: Oxford University Press, 1986), p. 152.
[38]*Ibid.*

9

Wars for Empire and Indian Strategies for Survival

Between 1675 and 1763 three European powers—France, Spain, and England—employed diplomacy and war in a struggle for trade and territory in the vast area between the Mississippi River and the Atlantic Ocean, and in the waters of the Caribbean. Both the trade and the territory they coveted in North America required them to be in close and continual touch with the powerful tribes of interior North America. Our history books have largely forgotten what was patently obvious throughout this period—that European governments, whether in New Spain, New France, New England, or elsewhere in the European colonies, were continually negotiating, trading, and fighting with and against various Indian societies, and filing reports, requests, and complaints to the home governments concerning the state of Indian affairs. Those in charge of colonial affairs in Madrid, Paris, and London knew almost as much about the Indian inhabitants of the territories they claimed as they did of their own colonists.

In this three-cornered fight for a continent, Indians are often imagined as merely the objects of European power, manipulated like pawns on a continental chessboard before finally being swept from the board altogether. This view is part of the myth of the overwhelming cultural superiority and military force of the European colonizers and the Indians' acquiescence when confronted with it. But the power of the Europeans has been greatly exaggerated and that of native societies greatly underestimated, though certainly the power equation was tilting toward the English and French by the 1720s. It is more accurate to say that Indian societies of the interior were not only reciprocally involved in the complicated maneuvers between contending European powers but played a dynamic role in the unfolding of events. They could not turn back the clock or drive the Europeans back into the sea. But the interior tribes were far stronger than the less populous coastal tribes that had succumbed to the invaders in the seventeenth century. They were therefore able to interact with the Europeans in a much different way.

Throughout the eighteenth century Indians helped to shape their own history. Pitted against each other and sometimes divided among themselves, the European powers had too few resources to overpower the inland tribes. They had to rely on Indian allies to maintain themselves even in the limited areas they occupied. Understanding the Europeans' weaknesses gave Indian nations an opportunity to exercise initiative and to gain much in exchange for their support. That they were eventually the losers does not obscure the fact that the interaction was truly a two-way process. Europeans used Indians to enhance their own power, and Indians used Europeans in precisely the same way.

IROQUOIS DIPLOMACY

Only by also looking at European imperial rivalry from the Indian point of view can the real nature of intercultural contact in North America be understood. For example, while European governors and colonial bureaucrats put millions of words on paper, moved armies and navies across an ocean, and engaged thousands of people in the manufacture and shipment of Indian trade goods, all as a part of empire-building, the pre-literate woodlands Iroquois, never numbering more than 2,000 warriors and 10,000 people after devastating epidemics had halved their population by the 1640s, were adroitly pursuing their own self-interest and shaping events in North America. The French historian La Potherie wrote in 1722: "It is a strange thing that three or four thousand souls can make tremble a whole new world. New England is very fortunate in being able to stay in their good graces. New France is often desolated by their wars, and they are feared through a space of more than fifteen hundred leagues of the country of our allies."[1] A generation later an Indian "expert" in New York warned the governor that "on whose ever side the [Iroquois] Indians fall, they will cast the balance."[2]

For the first two-thirds of the seventeenth century, the Iroquois involvement in trade with Europeans focused on their connection to the Dutch.

---

[1]Quoted in Anthony F. C. Wallace, "The Origins of Iroquois Neutrality: The Grand Settlement of 1701," *Pennsylvania History*, 24 (1957): 235.

[2]Archibald Kennedy to George Clinton, 1746, Clinton Papers, vol.3, Clements Library, University of Michigan.

Superior Dutch woolens, guns, and other metal goods made the connection valuable to the Iroquois, though their militant quest for beaver, with which to conduct trade, cost them heavily.

By the mid-1660s, however, sharp challenges to the Dutch by English and French rivals obliged the Iroquois to find new trading partners. Almost simultaneously, the French and English eagerly became their suitors. In New France in 1661, royal government supplanted the joint-stock company that had colonized north of the Iroquois since early in the century. With royal government came one thousand soldiers to pursue an aggressive policy of French territorial expansion. By the early 1680s, France had not only consolidated its hold in the St. Lawrence River valley but had established a string of trading posts and forts along an arc that swung north and west of the English settlements like a long encircling arm. Into Iroquoia, along with the French fur traders, came black-gowned Jesuits.

While the Iroquois reckoned with this new French intrusiveness, they also had to adjust to the English conquest of New Netherland in 1664. For the remainder of the century, the Iroquois would split between pro-English and pro-French groups, sometimes with tragic results. Making the Iroquois situation all the more fragile was the fact that the French and English, busily trying to remove each other from the map of North America in two wars that were local versions of major Anglo–French conflicts in Europe, leaned hard on their Iroquois allies to help defeat their enemies.

In replacing the ruptured Dutch lifeline, the Iroquois at first gravitated toward the French, who were as eager as the Dutch to supply the Indians with guns, cloth, metal implements, and strong liquor. In this context, Jesuit priests found a welcome in many Iroquois villages, though the desire of the "Black Robes" for a thoroughgoing change of behavior as well as belief caused tension. Slowly, as the English traders presented superior woolen cloth and offered high prices for beaver skins, the French connection began to wear thin. By the 1680s, with the balance beginning to tip toward the English, the Iroquois expelled Jesuit priests from their villages.

If the English reminded the Iroquois of the Dutch in their disinterest in converting Indians to Christianity, they also seemed alike in their avidity for the skins of fur-bearing animals. For the Iroquois this was not unwelcome, at least not at first. But as in the earlier beaver wars against the Huron, the Iroquois now turned aggressively toward their western neighbors. Needing captives to replace their disease-ridden ranks as well as pelts to fuel the trade for English goods, the Iroquois battled Miamis, Illinois, Ojibwas, Foxes, Shawnees, and Ottawas in the 1670s and 1680s. From the north, in the closing decades of the seventeenth century, came stinging raids from the French. Whether aligning with the French or the English, the Iroquois found themselves seeking cross-cultural alliances to achieve the dominance in the West that was indispensable in keeping the fur trade healthy.

King William's War from 1689 to 1697—for Europeans a battle for economic and territorial ascendancy in North America—was so traumatic for the Iroquois that they came to understand that their survival depended on extricating themselves from the imperial wars of their European trading partners. "You are pleased to Recommend us to Pursue our Enemies the French Vigorously which wee will endeavor to the Uttmost for they are your Enemies also," a Mohawk chief promised the English in 1689. "Yea if all our People should be Ruined and Cutt in Peeces, wee will never make peace with them."[3] And so it was that the Mohawks and other Iroquois tribes spilled their blood in a series of bungled assaults on Quebec in 1690 and 1691. In these poorly supplied joint expeditions of Indian and English warriors, the Iroquois often destroyed pro-French Iroquois who still remained in villages near Montreal or along Lake Ontario. But they paid dearly for these fratricidal attacks and were humbled by a French–Indian attack on the Mohawks in 1693, a heavy blow that evoked a caustic Mohawk comment: "You tell us we are one heart one flesh and one blood. Pray let us know the reason why you do not come to Our assistance according to your former promise that We may live and dy together."[4] The Iroquois sustained further poundings from western and northern enemies and a formidable invasion of Iroquoia in 1696 by two thousand French soldiers marching with their Indian allies.

By the end of the seventeenth century, after years of exhausting warfare, it became apparent to all parties involved that though the English vastly outnumbered the French, they could not defeat the Canadians because of disunity among the English colonies and the unwillingness of the government at home to supply military forces. Nor could the French either destroy an Anglo–Iroquois alliance or forge a Franco–Iroquois alliance because they lacked sufficient military strength for the former and suffered a competitive disadvantage in the fur trade that prohibited the latter. The Iroquois retained the strategic geographical position in the northern part of the continent. But in spite of their successes and the expansion of their influence over tribes to the south and west of them, they paid dearly in maintaining a pivotal role in the fur trade. By the end of the seventeenth century, hard hit by French attacks, war weary, and suffering disastrous population losses, they sought a formula for maintaining their security while withdrawing from the attritional warfare that had weakened them so seriously.

The solution to their problem was sudden and bold. In the summer of 1700 the Iroquois entered negotiations with both the English and the French, signing treaties almost simultaneously at Montreal and Albany a year later. To the French they promised neutrality in any future war between England

[3]Quoted in Daniel K. Richter, *The Ordeal of the Longhouse: The People of the Iroquois League in the Era of European Colonization* (Chapel Hill: The University of North Carolina Press, 1992), p. 162.
[4]Quoted in *ibid.*, p. 175.

and France—a great gain for the French, who had often been stung by the Iroquois military forays. To the English, who now lost a military ally, the Iroquois ceded their western hunting lands, conquered a half century before from the Hurons. By this clever piece of diplomacy, the Iroquois implied that their primary allegiance was still to the English. But it was only a symbolic land cession, for the English had no ability to occupy or control this territory; in fact the lands in question had recently been reconquered by the French and their allies, the Wyandots. To complete their compromise negotiations the Iroquois made peace with the tribes to the west of them, while urging the English and French "to put a stop" to their destructive animosities so "that wee may have the benefit of the peace concluded between the two Kings in Europe."[5]

For almost half a century after the 1701 treaties the Iroquois policy of balancing one European power with another worked well. The Five Nations (which became the Six Nations after the addition of the Tuscaroras) disengaged from the costly beaver wars, pursued their role as fur suppliers, and increased their population by absorbing remnants of coastal tribes decimated by Europeans and elements of western tribes they had themselves conquered. At first a fragile new framework for less violent intercultural relationships, the "Grand Settlement of 1701" gradually took hold. Less than a year after the Iroquois had concluded their treaties at Albany and Montreal in 1701, another Anglo–French war broke out. But while the French and their local Indian allies put the torch to towns along the New England frontier, the Iroquois remained on the sidelines, exhorting "you both to make peace together," as one Iroquois spokesman told the French governor of Canada.[6] Though they were sometimes tempted to strike at the French, whose Indian allies still harassed them, the Iroquois were confirmed in their opinion that the English were unreliable military allies by New York's refusal to come to New England's aid. Afraid of jeopardizing their profitable fur trade and the black-market traffic they were conducting with the French Canadian enemy, the New Yorkers kept their minds to commerce and, according to some Massachusetts authorities, even marketed in Albany plunder from devastated New England frontier towns. The Iroquois' one act of assistance was to send three Mohawks and one Mahican to London with two prominent New Yorkers to argue for English assistance in the war against Canada. Arriving in London in 1710, they paid their respects to Queen Anne, stopped the show when they attended the theater, ran down a stag in the royal park, and were followed by throngs everywhere they went. But this was only a diversion. For more than a generation the Iroquois pursued the rebuilding of their torn society through diplomacy rather than war.

[5]Quoted in *ibid.*, p. 206.
[6]Quoted in *ibid.*, p. 219.

This Mohawk chief, Sa Ga Yeath Qua Taw No Tow in his language and called Brant by the English, arrived in London in 1710 to parley with Queen Anne. His grandson, Joseph Brant, made the same trip 65 years later and joined the British to thwart American independence. The Dutch painter Verelst captured Brant with his spectacular tattooing, which the London press said won "not . . . so much terror as regard." *(Courtesy Library of Congress)*

At the conclusion of Queen Anne's War in 1713, the English made substantial gains in North America. France ceded Nova Scotia, Newfoundland, and Hudson's Bay to England; recognized the sovereignty of the British over the Iroquois (the Iroquois made no such concession); and permitted English traders to open commerce with the western tribes that had previously been linked to the French. But these concessions on paper meant little, for the English could not implement them by occupying the areas they had gained or by establishing trading posts deep in the interior. Not for another generation would the English find the strength to concern themselves with these distant regions. For now they fixed their attention on the buildup of population between the coast and the Appalachian Mountains. Only in constructing a fort and trading post at Oswego on Lake Ontario did England take advantage of the French concessions. The final act of the imperial drama, and the fate of the Iroquois and more western tribes, was postponed for forty years.

CREEK DIPLOMACY

Just as a time of trouble impelled the Iroquois to disengage from attritional warfare by substituting council fire diplomacy for the battlefield, the Creek confederation of the Southeast mastered the principles of *realpolitik* following the Yamasee War of 1715–17. Like the Iroquois, the Creeks had been a defensive and loosely integrated confederacy before European settlement began. They too capitalized on European trade to become the most formidable society in a vast region coveted by England, France, and Spain. And like the Iroquois, they initially enhanced their strength but then suffered through the intensification of warfare brought about by the introduction of the European trade. Less than two decades after the Iroquois cemented their "playoff system" between the English and French, the Creeks had made themselves "the custodians of the wilderness balance of power in the South."[7] Through a quarter-century of adroit maneuvering they extended and withdrew promises to the English, French, and Spanish in order to extract trade and military concessions. At the same time they maintained their autonomy. Just as the English attempted to play Creeks and Cherokees against each other—"how to hold both as our friends, for some time, and assist them in Cutting one another's throats without offending either," as one Carolinian put it—the Creeks worked to keep French, English, and Spanish pitted against each other, with no one of the European powers gaining dominance over the other two. So skillful was the Creek leader Brims in this that one Englishman opined that he was "as great a Politician as any Governor in America."[8]

The new policy of aggressive neutrality was a logical course for the Creeks to follow after flagrant abuses by the Carolina traders infected the trading alliance with the English earlier in the century. Greatly aroused, the Creeks had declared war against their exploiters, but their inability to persuade the Cherokees to join them in an all-out offensive against the English thwarted their efforts in the Yamasee War. Thereafter, they pursued a policy of limited cooperation. Despite their defeat in war and heavy population losses from smallpox, it was far from a passive strategy. Instead it was the active response of Indian leaders who were attempting to regather their people's strength while recognizing the advantages of interacting with the foreigners in their country.

The Creek politics of survival had to be devised within the context both of intra-Indian rivalries and of Anglo–French–Spanish rivalry. Ever since the English had arrived in Carolina and harassed the northern frontier of Spanish Florida, Spain had dreamed of mounting an expedition by land and sea that would wipe out English pretensions in the region. The Spanish made such an attempt in 1702, but it was an abysmal failure, producing only an English counterattack two years later that laid waste to most of the Spanish missionary frontier in Florida. The English planned attacks on French trading posts on the lower Mississippi and along the Gulf of

---

[7]Verner W. Crane, *The Southern Frontier, 1670–1732* (Ann Arbor: University of Michigan Press, 1956), p. 260.
[8]*Ibid.*, pp. 263, 260–61.

Mexico in 1708. But a more profitable way of striking at nascent French power was found in 1711. Coordinating a military expedition primarily composed of Indian allies, the English attacked the Choctaws, the principal Indian allies of the French. Yet none of these assaults on the frontier outposts of rival European nations succeeded in establishing English control in the lower South. It was this design of English hegemony that the Creeks hoped to prevent while still maintaining trade connections with them.

In the aftermath of the Yamasee War the Creeks took measures to restore the balance of power by making overtures to the Spanish, against whom they had fought at English instigation for many years. First, Chief Brims sent his son to St. Augustine in 1716 with instructions to allow the Spanish to build a fort at Coweta, the principal town of the Lower Creeks. Then he sent other Creek emissaries to Mexico City to seal an alliance. A year later Creek leaders conferred with the Senecas, more than a thousand miles to the north, and with the English in Charleston. By 1717, they had fashioned a complicated arrangement by which some of their villages would remain within the Spanish orbit and some within the English. They signed a treaty with South Carolina that left them free to trade with whomever they pleased but set fixed rates in their trade with the English, guaranteed ammunition and arms for use against tribes not friendly to the English, and established a policy of mutual accountability for Creeks and Carolinians who committed crimes or injuries against each other.

Brims symbolized his strategy of dynamic equilibrium by commissioning one son as his principal emissary to the English and another son as main emissary to the Spanish. English Carolinians and Spanish Floridians, both struggling for the upper hand with the Creeks, attempted to persuade Brims to name "their" son his successor. The English tried to gain a controlling hand among the Creeks in 1722 by commissioning Ouletta, the son whom Brims sent to the English as an emissary of the Creek nation. Two years later the Yamasees, inveterate enemies of the English and still allied with the Spanish, shattered this attempt to force a recognition of English sovereignty by murdering Ouletta. Seepeycoffey, the Spanish client son of Brims, was now the only candidate as Brims's successor. When Seepeycoffey died in 1726, Brims's brother inherited the primary claim to headship of the Creeks.

Until he died in the early 1730s Brims maintained the policy of playing Spanish and English against each other. The Creeks continued to aid the Yamasees, with whom the English were intermittently at war, and they continued to attack the Cherokees, with whom the English were closely allied. The English attempted various strategies to coerce the Creeks into an unqualified English connection—interference in Creek political affairs, trade embargoes, and the threat of a joint Cherokee-English war against them. These tactics succeeded in bringing the Creeks closer to the English and in convincing them to break off their traditional support of the Yamasees; but the Creeks still preserved their autonomous position and remained the pivotal

Tomochichi, who was born before the first Englishman set foot in the Carolinas, sat for his portrait with his nephew in 1734. Ear piercing and body painting (or tattooing) were common among Native Americans. Tomochichi's nephew holds an eagle, signifying his clan membership. *(Courtesy Smithsonian Institution, National Anthropological Archives, Bureau of American Ethnology Collection)*

force in the region. The Creeks, wrote the Assembly of South Carolina in 1737, "have been treated with as Allies but not as Subjects of the Crown. . . . They have maintained their own Possessions, and preserved their Independency."[9] Numerically strong and diplomatically skilled, the Creeks preserved their central position for many years after the Yamasee War. Their emissaries ranged for thousands of miles, parleying with the Spanish in St. Augustine, Vera Cruz, and Mexico City; with the English in Charleston and London; with the French at Fort Toulouse on the Alabama River; and with headmen of other Indian nations from the Florida border to the Great Lakes. At times they carried out simultaneous negotiations with two warring European powers, just as the Iroquois had conducted dual negotiations at Montreal and Albany in 1701.

In the decades after Brims's death, the Creeks preserved their policy of neutrality at critical junctures. In 1739, when England declared war on Spain, the Carolina government pressured the Creeks to join General James Oglethorpe, who had founded the colony of Georgia between South Carolina and Florida only seven years before, in an assault on St. Augustine. Although warriors from a few villages joined the English expedition, which ended in disaster, most of the Creeks remained out of the fray, convinced that the key to Creek survival was trading with whomever offered the best prices but allying militarily with no single European power. The Creeks might

[9] *The Colonial Records of South Carolina, Journal of the Commons House of Assembly, Nov. 10, 1736–June 7, 1739,* ed. J.H. Easterby (Columbia: Historical Commission of South Carolina, 1951), p. 75.

well have congratulated themselves for adhering to their policy, for the Cherokees who joined the English brought back smallpox that spread disastrously in the Cherokee towns in 1740–41. In the next year, a Creek headman gave new expression to the old strategy: "The [Creek] land belonged to the English as well as the French and indeed to neither of them. But both had liberty to Come there to Trade."[10]

In the 1740s, when France joined Spain in war against England, the Creek policy of neutrality was again put to the test. Summoning headmen from the Upper Creek towns to Charleston in 1746, the governor of South Carolina promised bountiful rewards if the Creeks would join an English military assault on Fort Toulouse, the main French bastion on the Alabama River. Back in their own country, however, Creek headmen vetoed the project, again thwarting the English in their efforts to obtain the Indian support they needed to drive the French from the lower South. South Carolina attempted again to mobilize the Creeks and Cherokees for attacks on the French in 1747. Failure was again the result when Malatchi, the youngest son of Brims and a pro-French chief, gained recognition as emperor of the Lower Creeks. Malatchi had been at the Charleston conference in 1746 and had refused to let the Carolina governor browbeat him with threats of withdrawing the English trade. He had returned to the Lower Creek villages, spoken against the English plan, and then personally visited St. Augustine and Fort Toulouse to inform the Spanish and French of the English proposals. Creek leaders summarily told the English that they were welcome to trade in Creek country but could not build forts and should expect no Creek support for military expeditions against the Spanish or French.

CHEROKEE DIPLOMACY

The Cherokees, numbering about 12,000 in 1750, were numerically stronger than the Iroquois and Creeks, and the English regarded their allegiance, or at least their neutrality, as indispensable to security in the region from Virginia to Georgia. Settled in the Appalachian Mountains to the west of the Carolina and Georgia settlers, and known for the valor of their warriors, they had been allied to the English in trade and war since the late seventeenth century. Faced with other Indian enemies, the Carolinians came to regard Cherokee support as a cornerstone of their Indian policy. The Cherokees were aware of this. They understood that they had played the decisive role in the Yamasee War of 1715, maneuvering, as the Carolinians admitted, in the best tradition of European power politics. "The last time they were here

[10]Quoted in M. Eugene Sirmans, *Colonial South Carolina; A Political History* (Chapel Hill: University of North Carolina Press, 1966), p. 198.

[in Charleston] they insulted us to the last degree," complained Carolina leaders in 1717, "and indeed by their demands (with which we were forced to comply) made us their tributaries."[11]

The support of the Cherokees wavered after the Yamasee War, especially in the 1730s. The abuses of English traders during that decade aroused their ire, and when an immigrant German mystic, Gottlieb Priber, reached them in 1736, he found them ripe for his peculiar message. Priber's genuine respect for Indian culture and his disaffection from European society, which he regarded as hopelessly corrupt, made him welcome in the Cherokee towns. Priber preached about the need to establish communal states in the English colonies, based on Plato's Republic. Wherever he went he was regarded as a dangerous radical, for very few colonizers wanted to abandon the concept of private property and return to an Arcadian past. But the Cherokees' values were much closer to Priber's, and they esteemed him for teaching them the use of weights and measures so they could protect themselves against dishonest traders. Priber also cautioned them to maintain their freedom by trusting no Europeans and encouraged them to cultivate trade connections with the French at New Orleans as a way of diminishing the English influence. His plan for Indian survival in the South depended on a confederacy of all the region's major tribes and an iron resolve among the Indians to surrender no territory, make no concessions to any European power, and continue the balance-of-power strategy in relations with the French, English, and Spanish. He also planned a city of refuge within Cherokee territory for criminals, debtors, and escaped slaves, who would live interracially and communally without regard to marriage. That the Cherokees regarded him as "a great beloved man" indicates how his radical ideas about race and gender politics resonated in the Cherokee mind, even while they maintained close relations with the Carolinians.

A sign that Cherokee strength endured long after the Iroquois grasp on the northern region faded appeared when South Carolina authorities ordered Priber's arrest in 1739. The Cherokees refused to surrender him. But in 1743, while making his way to the French in New Orleans, the Creeks captured him and turned him over to the English. He died in prison in Frederica, Georgia, much to the regret of his Cherokee friends.

In 1748 the South Carolina government further antagonized the Cherokees by refusing to honor a treaty of mutual support when the Upper Creeks attacked the Cherokees. In response the Cherokees fell upon abusive white Carolina traders, demonstrating that they did not regard themselves as English dependents and possessed enough power to control their own destiny. Making periodic overtures to the French, the Cherokees kept the English off balance.

---

[11]Quoted in David D. Wallace, *South Carolina: A Short History, 1520–1948* (Chapel Hill: University of North Carolina Press, 1951), p. 90.

That the dependency of the English upon the Cherokee was at least as great as Cherokee dependence upon the English was plainly admitted in 1750 when the governor of South Carolina reminded the assembly that "it is absolutely necessary for us to be in friendship with the Cherokees, for all they are reckoned to be about three thousand gunmen, the greatest nation we know of in America except the Choctaws. . . . "[12] Because the Choctaws had long been tied to the French in the lower Mississippi area, the Cherokees provided an indispensable buffer between the English and their French enemies. Recognizing this, the Crown committed £6,000 for presents to the Creeks and Cherokees in 1749 and 1750, sterling testimony to the English regard for maintaining the alliance. South Carolina expenditures for Indian presents doubled between 1750 and 1758, reaching £14,837 in the latter year—further proof of the English dependence on them.[13]

TRANSFORMATIONS IN INDIAN SOCIETY

During the first half of the eighteenth century, the interior Indian nations of North America demonstrated their capacity for adapting to the presence of Europeans and for turning their economic and political interaction with them to their own advantage. For a century and a half the Indians had observed the culture of the Europeans. From it they drew selectively, adopting through the medium of the fur, skin, and slave trade European articles of clothing, weapons, metal implements, and a variety of ornamental objects. To this degree their material culture changed. Incorporating of material objects such as the iron hatchet and copper kettle weakened native skills. But agriculture, fishing, and hunting, the mainstays of Indian subsistence before the Europeans came, remained so thereafter. European implements such as the hoe only made Indian agriculture more efficient. The knife and fishhook enabled the natives to fish and trap with greater intensity in order to obtain the commodities needed in the barter system. Scissors, needles, and thimbles made it easier for Indian women to stitch and decorate clothing. However, pottery making declined and the hunter became more dependent on the gun. Very slowly, skill in fashioning beautiful clay pots or arrowheads ebbed.

Still, interaction with European societies over many generations transformed Indian culture in important ways that boded ill for the future. By looking at several aspects of life among the interior tribes—trade, warfare, political organization, and the use of distilled spirits—we can sort

---

[12]David H. Corkran, *The Cherokee Frontier: Conflict and Survival, 1740–1762* (Norman: University of Oklahoma Press, 1962), p. 15.

[13]Sirmans, *Colonial South Carolina*, p. 275; Wilbur R. Jacobs, ed., *Indians of the Southern Colonial Frontier: The Edmond Atkin Report and Plan of 1755* (Columbia: University of South Carolina Press, 1954), pp. 27n, 31n.

out the overall effects of Indian contact with Europeans while at the same time exploding some of the myths that have clouded Native American history for years.

The Fur Trade

The fur trade is the proper place to begin a consideration of the transformation of Indian societies because from almost the first moment of contact it brought and kept Native Americans and Euro-Americans together. For a long time historians of the fur trade focused on the rugged trappers and colorful fur company entrepreneurs, making folk heroes of them while all but ignoring the Indians' role or the effects of the fur trade on native societies. Studies in recent years, however, have restored Native Americans to the central role they played in the fur trade.

Indian tribes had traded extensively with each other over long distances for centuries before Europeans arrived, and the exchange of goods was fundamental to most aboriginal economies. Some tribes, such as the Jumanos in the Southwest and the Great Lake Ottawas, were long-distance traders, moving the goods of one tribe to another across vast distances. The simple commodity exchange of the pre-contact period also served the purpose of maintaining social and territorial relations among neighboring tribes. Profit was not involved, so the trade tended to reinforce peaceful relations rather than inciting competition and conflict. The arrival of Europeans eager to trade ushered in a new epoch for native peoples. Each side—European and Indian—had something to gain. However, the success of these new trade encounters depended on meshing native ideas about reciprocity with European goals of making profits and establishing footholds in new territories. From the Indian point of view trade was carried on within the context of a political and social alliance and, accordingly, surrounded by ceremonial gift-giving. Haggling over prices appalled them at first, for, according to their values, trade was an aspect of friendship.

It is not necessary to turn Indians into acquisitive capitalists to explain their desire for trade goods. They did not seek the trade goods because they wished to become part of a bourgeois culture, accumulating material wealth from the fur trade, but because they recognized the advantages, within the matrix of their own culture, of goods fashioned by societies with a more complex technology. It was the utility of the Europeans' trade goods, not the opportunities for profit provided by the fur trade, that drew Native Americans into it. "The beaver does everything perfectly well," one Indian fur trapper asserted; "it makes kettles, hatchets, swords, knifes, bread . . . in short, it makes everything."[14] From the Indian point of view, beaver skins were easy

---

[14]Quoted in James Axtell, *After Columbus: Essays in the Ethnohistory of Colonial North America* (New York: Oxford University Press, 1988), p. 167.

to obtain and the trade goods reasonable. "The English have no sense," said one Indian. "They give us twenty knives . . . for one beaver skin."[15]

Whatever the tensions created by the encounter of tribal and bourgeois values in the fur trade, supplying pelts to the Europeans on a large scale required a reallocation of human resources and a reorganization of the tribes' internal economies. Subsistence hunting, limited by the food requirements of a tribe, turned into commercial hunting, limited only by the quantity of trade goods desired. Indian males spent far more time away from the villages trapping and hunting, and the importance of their activity to the life of the tribe, which soon became dependent on trade goods, undermined the relatively egalitarian matrilineal base of society. Women were also drawn into the new economic organization of villages, for the beaver, marten, or fox, once killed, had to be skinned and the skins scraped, dressed, trimmed, and sewn into robes. Among some tribes the trapping, preparation, and transporting of skins became such a time-consuming industry that food resources had to be procured in trade from other tribes. Ironically, the reorientation of tribal economies toward the fur trade dispersed villages and weakened the localized basis of clans and lineage. Breaking up in order to be nearer the widely spread trapping grounds, Indian villagers moved closer to the nomadic woodland existence that Europeans had charged them with at the beginning of contact.

Involvement in the fur trade also drastically altered the relationship of Native Americans to their ecosystem. In their pre-contact cosmology many Indian cultures regarded the destinies of man and animal as linked, for both inhabited a spiritual world governed by a Great Creator. This spiritual symbiosis between human and animal life imposed obligations on hunters and animals alike. "Man and Nature both had to adhere to a prescribed behavior toward one another."[16] The Indian hunter knew that he must never take more animals than he needed and must treat their bodies with respect; the animals in return must not resist capture but must "consciously surrender themselves to the needy hunter." In this sense, killing was ordained and the hunter was engaged in a "holy occupation."[17]

The tremendous destruction of animal life triggered by the advent of trade with Europeans altered the spiritual framework within which hunting had traditionally been carried out. Trappers declared all-out war on the beaver and other fur-bearing animals, which was, in effect, a repudiation of man's traditional role within the cosmos. The spiritual relationship between man and animal had not been broken, but it was severely tested.

---

[15]Quoted in Colin G. Calloway, *New Worlds for All: Indians, Europeans, and the Remaking of Early America* (Baltimore: Johns Hopkins University Press, 1997), p. 45.
[16]Calvin Martin, *Keepers of the Game: Indian–Animal Relationships and the Fur Trade* (Berkeley and Los Angeles: University of California Press, 1978) p. 73.
[17]*Ibid.*, p, 115.

A final effect of the trade was to broaden the scale of intertribal tensions, which often led to war. Pre-contact trade had been based on intertribal cooperation. But Europeans of different nationalities competed for client tribes in the fur trade, and the tribes were therefore sucked into the rivalry of their patrons. In addition, as furs became depleted in the hunting grounds of one tribe, they could maintain their trade connection with the Europeans only by conquering more remote tribes whose hunting grounds had not yet been exhausted or by using armed force to intercept the furs of other tribes as they were being brought to trading posts near the coast. The Mohawks of the Hudson River valley drove the Mahicans away from Dutch traders in 1624–28 in order to ensure their preeminent position in the fur trade. Likewise, the Iroquois decimated and dispersed the Hurons of the eastern Great Lakes region in the mid-seventeenth century as a part of their drive for "beaver hegemony." By the end of the century the Iroquois themselves were exhausted and their population depleted by the incessant warfare they had engaged in while attempting to maintain the role of fur trade broker for the entire Northeast.

Warfare

"Myth contrasts civilized war and savage war," writes Francis Jennings, "by accepting the former as a rational, honorable, and often progressive activity while attributing to the latter the qualities of irrationality, ferocity, and unredeemed retrogression."[18] The point is important because a particularly emotional component of the stereotype of the American Indian has always been the blood lust that supposedly inspired "warfare that was insane, unending, continuously attritional from our point of view [and] . . . so integrated into the whole fabric of Eastern [Indian] culture, so dominantly emphasized within it, that escape from it was well-nigh impossible."[19] In point of fact, Indian societies in North America were relatively free of warfare, especially if compared with European societies of this era.

Before the arrival of Europeans, intermittent violence between tribes did occur. Indian warriors fought to gain status, to arrange the killing of a tribe member, to use a captive to fill one's thinning ranks, or to expand a tribe's territorial claims. Europeans, in fact, were adept at playing on these intertribal hostilities as they sought Indian allies after planting their first settlements.

But the nature of pre-contact Indian war was far different than the wars known in Europe, both in duration and in scale of operations. In the Thirty

---

[18]Francis Jennings, *The Invasion of America: Indians, Colonialism, and the Cant of Conquest* (Chapel Hill: University of North Carolina Press, 1975), p. 146.
[19]*Ibid.*, p. 149, quoting Alfred L. Kroeber, *Cultural and Natural Areas of Native North America* (Berkeley and Los Angeles: University of California Press, 1939), p. 148.

Years' War (1618–48), rival armies employed terror tactics that wasted entire towns and killed women and children as well as men indiscriminately. Unlike the Europeans, Native Americans could not conceive of total war that was fought for months or even years, that did not spare noncombatants, and that involved the systematic destruction of towns and food supplies. Indians conducted wars more in the manner of short forays, with small numbers of warriors engaging the enemy and one or the other side withdrawing after a few casualties had been inflicted. Roger Williams wrote that in New England the Indian wars "are farre lesse bloody and devouring than the cruell Warres of Europe" and related that "when they fight in a plaine, they fight with leaping and dancing, that seldom an Arrow hits, and when a man is wounded, unless he that shot follows upon the wounded, they soon retire and save the wounded."[20] John Underhill, hero of the Pequot War, thought that the intertribal hostilities were "more for pastime than to conquer and subdue enemies." Even in hand-to-hand combat, the Indians "fell on pell mell after their feeble Manner: Indeed it hardly deserves the name of Fighting."[21] Warfare was a ritualistic encounter with the object not of shedding as much of the enemy's blood as possible or devastating his villages and crops but making a show of force that would convince him of one's strength.

Willingly drawn into the fur trade and eventually dependent on it, Indian societies embarked on intensified intertribal conflict. Added to the level of killing was the effect of European weaponry, which Indians mastered quickly. Adding flintlock muskets to their traditional tomahawk and bow and arrow, the tribes inflicted far greater casualties in their conflicts than in the pre-contact period. Yet war never became what it was for Europeans. An Iroquois war party that "seemed on the brink of triumph could be expected to retreat sorrowfully homeward if it suffered a few fatalities . . . [because] casualties would subvert the purpose of warfare as a means of restocking the population." In fact, replacement of population was itself a motive in the Iroquois wars against the Hurons and other tribes in the seventeenth century. The "mourning war"—an attempt to replace people lost to disease with captives, and thus to ensure social continuity—was closely connected with the war to control fur sources. "Vacant positions in Iroquois families and villages were both literally and symbolically filled [by war captives]" writes one historian, "while [Iroquois] survivors were assured that the social role and spiritual strength embodied in the departed's name had not been lost."[22]

---

[20]Quoted in Jennings, *The Invasion of America*, p. 150.

[21]John Underhill, *News from America; or, A New and Experimentall Discoverie of New England* (London, 1638).

[22]Daniel K. Richter, "War and Culture: The Iroquois Experience," *William and Mary Quarterly*, 40 (1983): 535–36.

Political Organization

Another cultural change resulting from contact with European societies was in political organization. This varied from society to society, but the examples of the Creeks and Cherokees are instructive. Though they belonged to different linguistic groups and frequently warred against each other, their pre-contact political structures were similar, and they encountered the same historical forces in the seventeenth and eighteenth centuries—trade, war, and land encroachment. A fundamental feature of their pre-contact political structures was the local autonomy of towns and clans. It was to the town, not to the "confederacy," that the Creeks and Cherokees gave their primary loyalty. Town and clan headmen sometimes tried to coordinate the policy of various towns, but no party in disagreement with a majority decision was compelled to act against its wishes. Thus, in the early years of contact, towns or groups of towns often parleyed separately with Europeans, made particular agreements with traders, and acted semi-independently in military affairs.

Important changes in political structure occurred as the result of trade, war, and diplomatic contact with Europeans in the eighteenth century. Towns began to align depending on their proximity to French or English traders. A split between the Upper Creek and Lower Creek towns, for example, developed because the former lived within the French trading orbit, while the latter had easier access to the English. Similarly, the towns of the Overhill Cherokees gravitated toward the French and the Middle and Lower Cherokees traded with the English. The need to deal with English, French, and Spanish traders and governments also obliged the towns to move toward firmer confederacies where coordinated action would give them greater strength in their dealings with outsiders.

Another political change involved a gradual move toward centralized tribal leadership and the establishment of patrilineal dynasties among the headmen or "micos." This altered the traditional structure and criterion of leadership. Before contact with Europeans, leadership was local and descended in the dominant matrilineal clan of the village. But in the eighteenth century the tendency was to create supra-town chiefs and to allow their power to pass on to their sons rather than to their sisters' sons. One cause of these shifts was that English, Spanish, and French authorities wanted to deal with one chief rather than many and tended to promote and support the candidacy of the chief's son, consistent with the European view of male-dominated social and political organization. This European attempt to influence the internal politics of Indian societies was meant to further the colonizers' control in their dealings with Indian military allies and trading partners. Also favoring the development of patrilineal institutions was the intensified hunting, trading, and warring of the eighteenth century, which generally elevated the importance of male roles in Indian society.

Another way to control the political dynamics of Creek and Cherokee societies was to support the candidacy of a particular headman's son or even to commission certain individuals in order to facilitate communication and cooperation. The English tried to establish Ouletta, the son of the Creek headman Brims, as their client. When he died, they transferred their recognition to the Spanish candidate, his brother Seepeycoffee. Annual gifts, essential for good relations, were distributed through commissioned headmen, thus enhancing their prestige within their own society. The English practice of picking particular headmen with whom to negotiate conferred power on those who often had not earned their authority in the traditional way, according to matrilineage and honor, but simply through the intervention of an external authority. In time, a commission from colonial officials became important in the degree of influence wielded by a particular chief.

Intermarriage with an Indian woman was another way of gaining influence in a tribe, particularly if the woman was from an influential clan. Mary Musgrove Bosomworth, a niece of Brims, married three Englishmen in succession; and, though she was fiercely anti-English on occasion, her husbands attained positions of great importance within the Creek confederation. Thus, through commissioning client headmen and marrying Indian women, the Carolinians worked to strengthen the pro-English faction in the Creek confederacy and to wield influence in their political decisions.

Although recruiting headmen in a way that benefited the English upset traditional lines of political authority, it can also be regarded as a purposeful adjustment of traditional political practices by Indian peoples who faced new and powerful invaders bearing highly desirable trade goods. By modifying the customary criteria of kinship, the Creeks selected leaders better equipped to act in their interest. Greater access to the English or Spanish came by marrying one's sister to a European, by accepting a commission, or by having a European father. In none of these cases were the Creeks simply passive objects responding to white initiative. In a period of shifting power among the European groups present in the region, they were "coping creatively in a variety of ways with the different situations in which they found themselves."[23]

Like the Creeks, the Cherokees changed their political practices in the eighteenth century in response to new needs related to war and trade with Europeans. Before about 1730 the nearly autonomous village was the locus of Cherokee political authority. Little need existed for the political unification of towns. But tension with their Creek neighbors, encouraged by the English, and intermittent hostilities with the English themselves created a need for political centralization. By mid-century the Cherokees had formed a supravillage political organization. Civil chiefs or "priests," under the lead-

[23]Robert F. Berkhofer, Jr., "The Political Context of a New Indian History," *Pacific Historical Review*, 40 (1971): 364.

ership of Old Hop, gathered together the fragmented authority of the earlier period and formed a tribal "priest state" in which the Cherokee towns coordinated decision making.

When this proved inadequate in the difficult, strife-filled years after mid-century, warriors began to assume the dominant role in tribal councils. The warrior commanded great respect before this but was outranked by the civil chiefs. By the 1760s, adapting to a new era of strife, the Cherokees made "warring and warriors an unambiguous part of the good life" and gave the war chiefs new and coercive political authority over the nation.[24] By this process the Cherokees made political changes that enabled dozens of villages to unify and amalgamate their strength.

Alcohol

A final aspect of culture change, which was both cause and effect, was the use of distilled spirits. Rum became an important item in the Indian trade because traders pushed it hard and because Indians acquired a taste for it. Increasing the volume of the trade was almost always foremost in the minds of traders and coastal merchants; hence the economic benefits of the Indians' desire for rum mattered most to them. From the Indian point of view, alcohol became an important element in internal and intertribal relations. The quality of English as opposed to French rum became a major consideration in diverting the northern fur trade from Montreal to Albany. The decision of the Georgia government to allow no traffic in alcohol—a part of their attempt to reform the Indian trade in the 1730s—brought only protests from the Creek headmen, who understood the debilitating effects of rum on Creek society but were unwilling to give up the power they enjoyed as distributors of it.

How were Indian societies affected by the use of alcohol? The modern tendency has been to see alcohol as a painkilling device used by a people caught between two cultures. Unable to maintain their traditional ways of life after becoming dependent on European material goods, but equally unable to gain acceptance into white society, Indians, it is argued, turned in despair to rum. Historians, anthropologists, and psychologists have viewed drunkenness as a way of escaping internalized feelings of unworthiness that came from prolonged contact with a white society that called them "savages" and "barbarians." Drunkenness provided at least temporary flight back to a romanticized past and gave momentary salve in resolving a painful crisis of identity. The difficulty with this explanation is that whatever its value in revealing the causes of alcoholism in modern society, it does not satisfactorily explain drunkenness among either Indians or Europeans in the eighteenth

[24]Fred Gearing, "Priests and Warriors; Social Structures for Cherokee Politics in the 18th Century," American Anthropological Association Memoir, 93 (1962): 102.

century. Europeans were not known for identity crises in pre-Revolutionary society; yet their alcoholic consumption was staggering even by modern American standards and was far greater than among Indians in this period. If nothing else, mere availability assured this. The spigots in thousands of colonial taverns rarely ran dry, but distilled spirits were available only intermittently to Indians spread over thousands of square miles of the interior.

When it is understood that the consumption of alcohol has different meanings in different cultures and that drunken behavior takes many forms according to varying cultural norms, the role of alcohol in Indian societies can be better understood. Anthropologists and historians have recently argued that for Indians in the early period of European contact, drinking was primarily "an institutionalized 'time-out' period from ordinary canons of etiquette." Only later, in the nineteenth and twentieth centuries, did it become a form of social protest and a means of release from despair. In the seventeenth and eighteenth centuries Indians imbibed rum for cultural reasons that made sense within the context of their own culture— "expansive conviviality, the letting down of customary decorum, and in some cases, serious dignified drinking into a comatose state."[25] Indians incorporated the consumption of alcohol into a value system that earlier had adopted the smoking of tobacco as a way not only to nurse sociability and generosity—"passing the pipe"—but also as a custom invested with religious functions and meanings. When one trader observed that Carolina Indians went about drinking solemnly "as if it were part of their Religion," he was unconsciously noting "a virtual means of achieving an altered state and communing with spiritual powers."[26]

Alcohol became important in Euro-Indian relations in another way. Colonial leaders and traders commonly distributed it as a prelude to negotiations for land or trade goods. If many eighteenth-century commentators are to be believed, this was all to the advantage of the colonizers because Indians became befuddled and were then easily swindled. This, however, was probably the exception rather than the rule. Indians did not relish being cheated any more than Europeans, and according to the testimony of many traders they were as skillful at driving a bargain as their white trading partners. The distribution of alcohol at the beginning of negotiations was, in their terms, a ritual for ensuring a mutually beneficial contract. So long as Indians had more than one place to trade, it was hardly good business practice for traders to drive them into the arms of competitors by getting them drunk and stealing their furs.

[25]Nancy Oestreich Lurie, "The World's Oldest On-Going Protest Demonstration: North American Indian Drinking Patterns," *Pacific Historical Review*, 40 (1971): 321; Craig MacAndrew and Robert B. Edgerton, *Drunken Comportment, A Social Explanation* (Chicago: Aldine Publishing Co., 1969).

[26]James Merrell, *The Indians' New World: Catawbas and their Neighbors from European Contact through the Era of Removal* (Chapel Hill: University of North Carolina Press, 1989), p. 39.

This is not to deny that sharp practices occurred. On occasion unauthorized traders brought casks of rum to an Indian village, watched it eagerly consumed, and left with a winter's catch of furs and skins. But Europeans complained about being "held up" by Indians as often as Indians complained about European trickery. And when the trading was done at frontier posts or in Indian villages, which was the practice throughout the Carolina region and in the hinterlands of Virginia and Pennsylvania in the eighteenth century, it was not to the trader's advantage, or even good for his health, to cheat Indians who had been robbed of their senses by the demon rum. Indians took their furs where they could obtain the best prices and the amplest supply of trade goods. Their extraordinary mobility over land and inland waterways, combined with the availability of more than one European supplier, made it imperative for colonial traders to maintain a relationship that was to the Indians' satisfaction. When they did not, as in the case of the Carolina traders, the Indians took their trade to the French, the Spanish, or to rival traders in Georgia and Virginia.

When Indian societies lost their land, their autonomy, and their confidence in their traditional belief system, drinking could change from a form of social relaxation to a solvent for internalized aggressive impulses against whites. This seems to have been the case among some of the remnants of coastal tribes, which by the eighteenth century had lost their land and their power. They existed only as clients of white society, and the chronic and debauched drinking that many observers described may indicate their precarious inner state. Almost powerless and unable to express their hostility toward whites, their frustrations accumulated and were turned inward. Only drinking, and in extreme cases suicide, provided release from this situation.

The costs of alcohol abuse mounted rapidly by the 1720s when the flow of rum and brandy into Indian villages grew from a trickle to a torrent. As one historian of the Iroquois has put it "No less than modern drug lords, the traders at Oswego [the English trading post on Lake Ontario] dispensed death, and Iroquois leaders were powerless to stop them."[27] One Iroquois leader protested bitterly to Albany officials in 1730: "You may find graves upon graves along the Lake, all which misfortunes are occasioned by Selling Rum to Our Brethren."[28] In South Carolina, where the rum trade began early but did not dominate the Indian desire for European items, alcohol represented four-fifths of the trade goods purchased by the Indians in 1770 according to the British agent to the Choctaws. Two years later, traveling through Choctaw towns, the agent "saw nothing but Rum Drinking and Women Crying over the Dead bodies of their relations who have died by Rum."[29]

---

[27]Richter, *The Ordeal of the Longhouse*, p. 266.
[28]Quoted in *ibid.*
[29]Quoted in Peter C. Mancall, *Deadly Medicine: Indians and Alcohol in Early America* (Ithaca, N.Y.: Cornell University Press, 1995), p. 94.

All over North America, whether in the region colonized by the French, Spanish, or English, by the early eighteenth century Indians were paying a terrible price to quench their thirst for liquor. Indian women may have suffered the most. Drinking binges produced unspeakable domestic violence, created animosity in Indian villages, weakened the constitution of bodies already under assault from European diseases, endangered yet-unborn children of pregnant Indian women, impoverished tribes that drank away the profits from trading animal pelts, sharpened the white image of the violent "savage" Indians, and ate away at the individual self-respect and communal pride that pre-contact Indian values inculcated. Indian trader John Lawson described the tragic abuses of Indian women. He saw Indian men who "when they have a design to lie with a woman . . . strive to make her drunk" and then "take the advantage to do with them what they please, and sometimes in their drunkenness, cut off their hair and sell it to the English, which is the greatest affront can be offer'd them."[30] Englishmen seized the same advantage. Virginia's William Byrd enjoyed "Jenny, an Indian girl, [who] had got drunk and made us good sport."[31] "In alcohol's empire," writes one historian, "Indians suffered."[32]

CULTURAL PERSISTENCE

While the interior tribes blended a wide variety of European trade goods into their material culture and adapted their internal economies and political structures to meet new situations, they held fast to their traditional culture in other ways. Iroquois, Creeks, Cherokees, and other tribes were singularly unimpressed with most of the institutions of European life and saw no reason to replace what they valued in their own culture with what they disdained in the culture of others. This applied to the newcomers' political institutions and practices, their systems of law and justice, religion, education, family organization, and their child-rearing practices. In all these areas Native Americans carefully observed European customs but saw little worthy of emulation. Indeed, so far as they could ascertain, these institutions often failed to work successfully in the Europeans' own societies.

The Anglican missionaries of the Society for the Propagation of the Gospel were plagued by this paradox in their efforts to convert Indians to Christianity. Why, asked Indians, should they convert to a system that, despite its claims of superiority, was ridden with crime, social disorder, and political factionalism? "[The Indians] are for the most part great lovers of

---

[30]Lawson, *A New Voyage to Carolina*, . . . ed. Hugh T. Lefler (Chapel Hill: University of North Carolina Press, 1967), pp. 211–12.

[31]William Byrd, *The Secret Diary of William Byrd of Westover, 1709–1712*, ed. Louis B. Wright and Marion Tinling (Richmond: The Dietz Press, 1941), p. 245.

[32]Mancall, *Deadly Medicine*, p. 85.

Justice & Equity in their dealings," wrote Robert Maule, an Anglican missionary in South Carolina in 1709, "and I have asked some of them whether they would learn to be or had any desire to become of the white men's religion. They have plainly told me no; what's the matter sayd I, why so? Because, replys they, Backarara [the white man] no good; Backarara Cheat; Backarara Lye, Backarara Drink Brandy, me no Love that."[33] Itinerant clergymen in the Carolinas repeated the same message over and over in their reports to superiors in London. Most of the settlers, wrote a plaintive Charles Woodmason at the end of the colonial period, lived "after a loose and lascivious manner. . . . The Manners of the North Carolinians in General, are Vile and Corrupt—the whole Country is a Stage of Debauchery Dissoluteness and Corruption. . . . Polygamy is very Common, . . . bastardy, no Disrepute—Concubinage General."[34] Could it be any wonder, then, that he was unable to convince the Indians of the superiority of the white way of life?

John Lawson, an official in the Carolinas in the early eighteenth century, captured the essence of the reason for the lack of cultural borrowing outside the realm of material objects. "They are really better to us," he wrote in 1708, "than we are to them; they always give us Victuals at their Quarters, and take care we are arm'd against Hunger and Thirst: We do not do so by them (generally speaking) but let them walk by our Doors Hungry, and do not often relieve them. We look upon them with Scorn and Disdain, and think them little better than Beasts in Humane Shape, though if well examined, we shall find that, for all our Religion and Education, we possess more Moral Deformities, and Evils than these Savages do, or are acquainted withal."[35] Indians were not secretive in their disdain of white culture. When it was suggested to the Iroquois in 1744 that they send some of their young men to Virginia for a white education, they counterproposed that "if the English Gentlemen would send a Dozen or two of their children to Onondaga, the great Council would take care of their Education, bring them up in really what was the best Manner and make men of them."[36]

In marriage and social relations it was much the same. Although Europeans often disparaged Indian customs of companionate marriage or serial monogamy and accused them of "licentiousness," "debauchery," and "faithlessness" in their sexual practices, domestic relations among the Indians,

---

[33]Robert Maule to Society for the Propagation of the Gospel [June 3, 1710], SPG Mss, A5, No. 133 (microfilm of Library of Congress transcripts), UCLA Research Library.

[34]Charles Woodmason, *Carolina Backcountry on the Eve of the Revolution: The Journal and Other Writings of Charles Woodmason, Anglican Itinerant*, ed. Richard J. Hooker (Chapel Hill: University of North Carolina Press, 1969), pp. 80–81.

[35]Lawson, *A New Voyage to Carolina*, pp. 243.

[36]Quoted in A. Irving Hallowell, "The Backwash of the Frontier: The Impact of the Indian in American Culture," in Paul Bohannan and Fred Plog, eds., *Beyond the Frontier: Social Process and Cultural Change* (Garden City, N.Y.: The Natural History Press, 1967), p. 325.

as a few European observers admitted, were entirely satisfactory to them and seemed infinitely better than those of their European critics. Shortly after his arrival in the colonies, Thomas Paine reported the opinion of an "American savage" concerning Christian marriages. "Either the Christian's God was not so good and wise as he was represented," the Indian reportedly avowed,

> or he never meddled with the marriages of his people; since not one in a hundred of them had anything to do either with happiness or common sense. Hence as soon as ever you meet, you long to part; and not having this relief in your power, by way of revenge, double each other's misery. Whereas in ours [Indian marriages] which have no other ceremony than mutual affection, and last no longer than they bestow mutual pleasures, we make it our business to oblige the heart we are afraid to lose; and being at liberty to separate, seldom or never feel the inclination. But if any should be found so wretched among us, as to hate where the only commerce ought to be love, we instantly dissolve the band. God made us all in pairs; each has his mate somewhere or other; and it is our duty to find each other out, since no creature was ever intended to be miserable.[37]

In sum, though Indian societies embraced a vast array of material goods and modified their political structures, many aspects of Indian life endured in the long period of interaction with Europeans. Indian societies were as selective as European societies in borrowing from the cultures they encountered. They incorporated what served them well and rejected what made no sense within the framework of their own values and modes of existence.

Despite many areas of cultural persistence, the involvement of Indian societies in the European trade network brought many changes that worked to the Native Americans' disadvantage. Trade hastened the spread of epidemic diseases, raised the level of warfare, depleted ecozones of animal life, and drew Indians into a market economy in which "they eventually destroyed the basis for the very economy they were trying to practice."[38] Over a long period of time, the fur trade constricted the economic freedom of Indian societies, for they reorganized productive relations within their own communities to serve a trading partner who, through the side effects of the trade, became a trading master.

---

[37]Philip S. Foner, ed., *The Complete Writings of Thomas Paine*, 2 vols., (New York: Citadel Press, 1945) 2:119–20.
[38]Jennings, *The Invasion of America*, p. 87.

10

The Seven Years War and Its Aftermath

For the first third of the eighteenth century interior tribes such as the Creeks, Cherokees, and Iroquois maintained a state of equipoise with European colonial societies by artfully playing one colonizing power against another and serving periodic reminders to the Europeans that Indian trade and military assistance were as valuable to them as the European trade goods were to Native American societies. "To preserve the Ballance between us & the French," wrote New York's Indian secretary, "is the great ruling Principle of Modern Indian Politics."[1] Indians were useful to Europeans, Europeans were useful to Indians, and power, though tipping toward the Europeans, was roughly divided between them. But in the second third of the eighteenth century historical forces were at work, both in the sphere of international politics and in the more limited sphere of the colonizers' communities, that would end the equilibrium between Indian and European peoples while deeply dividing colonial society itself.

---

[1]Peter Wraxall, *An Abridgment of the Indian Affairs* . . . , Charles H. McIlwain, ed. (Cambridge, Mass.: Harvard University Press, 1915), p. 219.

POPULATION INCREASE

In North America, a tremendous population buildup, especially in the English colonies, created a shortage of land on the coastal plain and by the 1750s was propelling thousands of land-hungry settlers toward the mountain gaps in the Appalachians in search of new territory. From a population of a quarter million in 1700, the English colonies grew to 1.2 million in 1750 and increased another 400,000 in the next decade. Three quarters of this increase came in the colonies south of New York. The advance agents of this enormous westward rush were eastern land speculators. They had only to watch the German and Scots–Irish immigrants disembarking daily at Baltimore, Philadelphia, and New York to understand that fortunes were to be made by those who could lay claim to land west of the existing settlements.

With capital provided by London investors, Virginia tobacco planters, and northern merchants formed land companies in the 1740s and 1750s to capitalize on this demographic explosion. The Ohio Land Company, organized in 1747, laid claim to half a million acres in the Ohio Valley. The Susquehannah Land Company, organized five years later, declared rights to hundreds of thousands of acres in Pennsylvania. In the next decade the Delaware Company, Miami Company, Indiana Company, and other private syndicates all raced to establish claims. Though some, like the Susquehannah Company, advertised that their purpose was to "open the most effectual Door for carrying the Light of the glorious Gospel of Christ among the numerous tribes of Indians that inhabit those inland Parts," nobody was confused about the principal object in mind.[2] Inexorably, the agents of English society exerted pressure on Indian leaders to cede and sell their lands in order to pave the way for new white settlements. The farther west settlement moved, the closer it came to the western trading empire of the French and the Indian nations allied to them.

THE SEVEN YEARS WAR

On the other side of the Atlantic the revival of international rivalries hastened this showdown west of the Appalachian Mountains. In 1748 France and England had seemingly resolved the differences that had led them to war in 1744, but even as the ink was drying on the articles of conciliation, they prepared for a renewal of hostilities. The powerful merchant element in England, supported by American clients, called for a destruction of French overseas trade. Even before events in Europe brought formal declarations of war,

[2]Petition of Subscribers to the Susquehannah Company, 1755, in Julian P. Boyd, ed., *The Susquehannah Company Papers* (Wilkes-Barre, Pa.: Wyoming Historical & Genealogical Society, 1930), 1: 255.

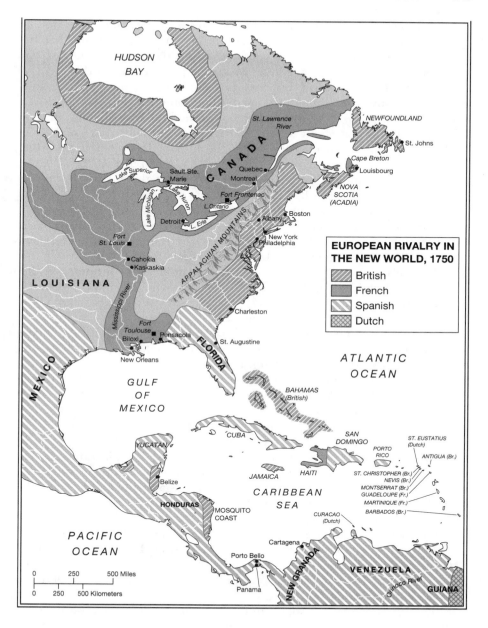

EUROPEAN RIVALRY IN THE NEW WORLD, 1750

- British
- French
- Spanish
- Dutch

HUDSON BAY

NEWFOUNDLAND

St. Johns

St. Lawrence River

Cape Breton

CANADA

Louisbourg

Lake Superior

Sault Ste. Marie

Quebec

Montreal

NOVA SCOTIA (ACADIA)

Lake Michigan

Lake Huron

Fort Frontenac

L. Ontario

Detroit

L. Erie

Albany

Boston

APPALACHIAN MOUNTAINS

New York

Philadelphia

Fort St. Louis

Cahokia

Kaskaskia

LOUISIANA

Mississippi River

Charleston

Fort Toulouse

Biloxi

Pensacola

St. Augustine

FLORIDA

New Orleans

ATLANTIC OCEAN

GULF OF MEXICO

BAHAMAS (British)

MEXICO

CUBA

SAN DOMINGO

ST. EUSTATIUS (Dutch)

PORTO RICO

ANTIGUA (Br.)

YUCATAN

JAMAICA

HAITI

ST. CHRISTOPHER (Br.)

NEVIS (Br.)

MONTSERRAT (Br.)

GUADELOUPE (Fr.)

MARTINIQUE (Fr.)

BARBADOS (Br.)

Belize

CARIBBEAN SEA

HONDURAS

MOSQUITO COAST

CURACAO (Dutch)

PACIFIC OCEAN

Cartagena

Porto Bello

NEW GRANADA

VENEZUELA

Orinoco River

GUIANA

Panama

0   250   500 Miles

0   250   500 Kilometers

fighting began in the North American wilderness. By the time it was over, in the early 1760s, France had surrendered its North Atlantic claims. For Indians, this shattered the precious system of balancing European powers, the key to maintaining their power in a fast-changing precarious world.

In the 1740s, English fur traders from Virginia and Pennsylvania pushed deep into the Ohio Valley, establishing outposts on the Ohio River and its tributaries. By 1749 the French commander at Fort Miami, south of Detroit, reported that about three hundred English traders were operating in the Ohio country, successfully luring the Indians into their trade orbit. For decades, men with a sense of geopolitics had realized that the struggle for the continent hinged on control of the trans-Allegheny West. For more than a century the English had been content to populate the narrow coastal plain, leaving the continental heartland to their rivals and obtaining their share of the Indian trade through connections centered at Albany and Charleston. Now they challenged the French where the French interest was vital. The British were now poised to sever Canada from Louisiana.

France's choices were to resist or surrender the continent to the English and Spanish. The French chose the former. Determined to block further English expansion, they established forts throughout the Ohio Valley and tried to pry various Indian tribes loose from their English connections. The Iroquois, Shawnees, and Delawares of the Ohio region listened to French overtures that only an alliance with the French would guarantee their survival. "The English," warned one French emissary in the early 1750s, "are much less anxious to take away your peltries than to become masters of your lands . . . and your blindness is so great, that you do not perceive that the very hand that caresses you, will scourge you, like negroes and slaves, so soon as it will have got possession of those lands."[3]

Though the tribes were aware of the westward surging white population, they were unwilling to break the connections with English traders that brought them commodities the French could not match in price and quality. Moreover, English strength in their region was a reality and French talk of trade south of the Great Lakes only a promise. In 1752 France began a campaign to alter this situation, attacking English trading posts and building forts of their own. By 1754, they had driven the English traders out of the Ohio Valley, established themselves as far east as the forks of the Ohio River, near the present Pittsburgh, Pennsylvania, and smartly rebuffed the ambitious young Colonel George Washington, who attempted to expel them from Fort Duquesne.

English attempts to respond to this bold French campaign were fatally crippled by internal division. This was starkly revealed at the Albany Congress of 1754, an attempt of the colonies to unify for military purposes and

---

[3]Quoted in William J. Eccles, *The Canadian Frontier, 1534–1760* (New York: Holt, Rinehart and Winston, Inc., 1969), p. 158.

through united action to woo the all-important Iroquois out of their position of neutrality. One of the main purposes of the Congress was to demonstrate to the Iroquois that fighting resolve and cohesion prevailed in the English colonies. But while representatives of the colonies attempted to work out a plan of confederation, land agents from Connecticut and Pennsylvania were deep in intrigue concerning the purchase of Iroquois lands west of the Susquehanna River—an intrigue in which lesser Indian chiefs participated by signing away land when they knew that the councils of the Iroquois nations would not sanction such transactions. The attempt at intercolonial cooperation fell to pieces, and the Iroquois left the conference convinced that the English were "like women: bare and open and without fortifications."[4]

It was decided in the capitals of Europe, not North America, to force a showdown. What ensued is known as the Seven Years War or the French and Indian War. London dispatched two regiments under the command of General James Braddock. In Paris, orders sent three thousand regulars to the French strongholds at Louisbourg on Cape Breton Island, guarding the St. Lawrence River, and at Quebec. The year it took Braddock to make his way across the Atlantic and then lead his army, reinforced by American enlistees, across Virginia and into the western wilderness was the last of his life. Less than twenty miles from Fort Duquesne the French and their Indian allies ambushed the British-Americans in 1755 and routed Braddock's reputedly invincible army of 2,200 with an attacking force one-third as large. Two-thirds of the English force were killed and wounded; the survivors fled, leaving artillery, horses, cattle, and supplies behind.

For the rest of the summer and autumn in 1755, Indian raiders terrorized the Virginia and Pennsylvania backcountry. For years they had nursed grudges against white land encroachers and ungenerous traders. Now was their opportunity to align themselves with the French and to even scores that went back decades. Among the first to strike at the English, Scots-Irish, and German communities were the Delawares, who a generation before had been cheated out of their tribal lands in eastern Pennsylvania. Just as they had streamed westward as refugees from colonial oppression, now they sent thousands of European refugees fleeing eastward as they burned, killed, and pillaged along the Pennsylvania frontier. "Almost all the women & children over Susquehanna have left their habitations, & the roads are full of starved, naked, indigent multitudes," cried one colonist.[5]

In 1756 and 1757 one French victory after another threw the English colonies into panic. The English post at Oswego, at the eastern end of Lake

[4]E.B. O'Callaghan, ed., *Documents Relative to the Colonial History of the State of New York* (Albany: Weed, Parsons & Co., 1855), 6: 870.

[5]Quoted in Douglas E. Leach, *The Northern Colonial Frontier, 1607–1763* (New York: Holt, Rinehart and Winston, Inc., 1966), p. 200.

Ontario, fell in August 1756. Two thousand troops at Fort William Henry, at the foot of Lake George, surrendered in August 1757. So desperate was the English situation that the governor of Pennsylvania, terrified at Indian attacks that had carried within thirty miles of Philadelphia, considered allowing hostile Indians free passage through his colony if they promised to concentrate their attacks on the Virginia frontier. Other raids on the New England border, in the Mohawk Valley of New York, and along the entire frontier from New York to Georgia, led to gloomy speculations in the English settlements that the continent would fall to the French and their Indian allies. Never was disunity within the English colonies so painfully felt. Seventy thousand French Canadians and their Indian allies had taken on a million and a half English colonists, supported by the British army, and whipped them hollow.

In these circumstances, English hopes rested on obtaining the support of (or, at the very least, pledges of neutrality from) the five main Indian confederacies of the interior—the Iroquois, western Delawares and Shawnees, Cherokees, Creeks, and Choctaws. If the French drew them into their camp, even the massive reinforcements of British troops and supplies being mobilized under the direction of William Pitt might not be able to stem the Gallic tide. Perhaps at no time since the initial settlers had been obliged to rely upon the coastal Indians for food to see them through the "starving time" were the English colonists so dependent on Indian support.

It was not clear how Indian support or neutrality could be secured. A century of intermittent hostility and the frantic hungering after the Indians' western lands during the previous decade suggested that the allegiance of the populous interior tribes would be difficult to obtain. Edmond Atkin, Charleston Indian trader and soon to become English Superintendent of the Southern Indians, sounded a prophetic note: "The Importance of Indians is now generally known and understood. A Doubt remains not, that the prosperity of our Colonies on the Continent, will stand or fall with our Interest and favour among them. While they are our Friends, they are the Cheapest and Strongest Barrier for the Protection of our Settlements; when Enemies, they are capable by ravaging in their method of War, in spite of all we can do, to render those Possessions almost useless."[6]

INDIAN STRATEGY IN THE SEVEN YEARS WAR

The case of the Iroquois is illustrative of the English vulnerability to which Atkin pointed. In negotiations with the French, the English pretended that Iroquois support was a certainty and bluntly informed the governor of

[6]Wilbur R. Jacobs, ed., *Indians of the Southern Colonial Frontier: The Edmond Atkin Report and Plan of 1755* (Columbia: University of South Carolina Press, 1954), pp. 3–4.

Canada that all members of the Iroquois tribes were indisputably subjects of the King of England.[7] But the English knew that the allegiance of the Iroquois and their dependents, the eastern Delawares, could be secured in only two ways: through purchase or through a demonstration of power so great that the Iroquois would be convinced that the English would prevail with or without their support and would accordingly find it politic to choose the winning side at the outset. The first stratagem failed in 1754 when representatives of the Six Nations left the Albany Congress with thirty wagonloads of gifts but gave in return only tantalizing half-promises of support against the French, who continued to score major victories in the next three years. Only when paid as mercenaries, such as in 1757 when about five hundred Mohawks collected £33,602 for services rendered to the English forces in New York, would the Iroquois support the Anglo-Americans.[8]

Colonial leaders made further attempts during the next two years to get the Iroquois to subdue the attacking Delawares, who had driven the Pennsylvania settlers out of the ancient Delaware homeland. Pennsylvania itself was deeply divided between pacifistic Quakers, who believed that Scots-Irish frontiersmen were only reaping what they had sown through years of abusing and defrauding Indians, and militant Anglicans and Presbyterians, who wanted taxes passed for a stern counteroffensive against the attackers. "The Indians learned our Weakness, by being informed of our Divisions," wrote the colony's official interpreter in 1757 after a conference convened for the purpose of buying off the Delawares' wrath.[9]

Not until October 1758 could the English get a promise from the Iroquois to halt the Delaware attacks on the Pennsylvania settlements. Agreement was reached at Easton, Pennsylvania, where the Indians left the conference with a wagon train of "gifts." It is easy to suppose that these Indian concessions were simply a response to white stimuli. From the Indian point of view, however, the Easton Treaty had a different meaning. The Iroquois made no military commitment to the English. And in exchange for their pledge of neutrality and their promises that the hostile Delawares would be quieted, they resecured a vast tract of land west of the Susquehanna River that they had ceded to Pennsylvania four years before at the Albany Congress. This restored their territorial security west of the Alleghenies.

Except for the halfhearted support of the Mohawks, the easternmost of the Six Nations, the Iroquois either maintained their neutrality or, as in the case of the Senecas, fought with the French in the campaigns of 1757 and

---

[7]Governor Clinton to Governor of Canada, Oct. 10, 1748, in O'Callaghan, ed., *Documents Relating to History of New York*, 6: 492.

[8]Wilbur R. Jacobs, *Diplomacy and Indian Gifts: Anglo–French Rivalry Along the Ohio and Northwest Frontiers, 1748–1763* (Stanford: Stanford University Press, 1950), p. 178.

[9]Lawrence H. Gipson, *The British Empire Before the American Revolution*, 14 vols. (New York: Alfred A. Knopf, 1936–69), 7: 58.

In his left hand, an Indian orator, either a Shawnee or Delaware chief, holds a wampum belt over the obligatory council fire, to initiate a diplomatic negotiation with Colonel Henry Bouquet who had led an expedition against the Ohio River valley Indian tribes at the end of the French and Indian War in 1763. In the following year, Bouquet pressed the defeated Indians, pictured here, to hand over all English captives taken by the tribes during the long war. This lithograph appeared in a contemporary book by William Smith, *An Historical Account of the Expedition against the Ohio Indians in the year 1764* (Philadelphia, 1766). *(Courtesy The Library Company of Philadelphia)*

1758. The Mohawks' allegiance to the English can be explained by their proximity to the English trading center at Albany, by the huge amounts they were paid for their services, and by the fact that William Johnson, appointed British Superintendent of the Northern Indians, had married a Mohawk woman and lived among them for years. Colonial leaders who had attempted to woo the Iroquois in the dark years from 1754 to 1758 found that the Six Nations steadfastly pursued their traditional policy of disengagement from European wars.

In 1759, however, the Iroquois reversed their position. Feelers by Johnson in February led him to report optimistically that if the English mounted an expedition against the French stronghold at Fort Niagara "or elsewhere, thro' the Country of the Six Nations, I shou'd be able to prevail upon the greater Part if not the whole of them, to join His Majesty's Arms."[10] Assessing the Anglo-French military situation, the Iroquois reformulated their policy. After four years of French victories the tide had turned in the British favor in July 1758 when Louisbourg and Fort Frontenac, the strategic centers of French power at opposite ends of the St. Lawrence, fell before Anglo-American assaults. In November 1758 the French abandoned Fort Duquesne at the forks of the Ohio River. By the end of the year the upper Ohio Valley was in English hands for the first time in four years. William Pitt had mobilized the fighting power of the English nation, putting more men in the field than existed in all of New France, and the colonists had put aside their intramural squabbling long enough to stem the French tide.

These English victories helped to move the Iroquois away from their long-held position of neutrality. Another incentive to join cause with the English was the capture of French ships bringing trade goods to Montreal, a turn of fortune that vastly improved the English position in wooing the Six Nations. In April 1759, the Iroquois chiefs came to the Mohawk town of Canajoharie and promised eight hundred warriors for an attack on Fort Niagara, the strategic French fur trading depot on Lake Ontario. The Iroquois had calculated correctly: The French were going down to defeat in North America and were an unreliable trading partner.

Throughout the war the Six Nations accurately assessed the shifting military balance between the rival European powers and formulated their own policy accordingly. Though they wrote no field memoranda and moved no troops or supplies through the terrain, their communication network extended across the entire region in which the French and English were fighting. In their councils they demonstrated a keen understanding of when the strategic balance was tipping in the British direction. Most histories of the Seven Years War applaud William Johnson's skill in "winning over" the Iroquois and "persuading" them to join the English side. But the evidence indicates that the Iroquois shrewdly reassessed their own position and calculated how their self-interest could best be served. Despite English blandishments, presents, and even the return of previously acquired territory, the Iroquois refused to join the English through the first four years of war or even to allow Anglo-American passage through their territory. But when the military superiority of the English began to show itself in 1759, the Iroquois quickly adjusted their policy of neutrality and joined in reaping the benefits of victory. If their policy of *realpolitik* failed at all, it was in not perceiving that the maintenance of French power in North America was essential to their long-range interests.

[10]*Ibid.*, p. 342.

The Cherokees also played power politics during the Seven Years War but less successfully than the Iroquois. In 1753–54 the governor of Virginia worked hard to gain Cherokee support for Washington's attempt to dislodge the French at the forks of the Ohio, believing that only with Indian support could the English overcome the larger French forces. The Cherokee chiefs responded by promising the Virginians a thousand warriors; but at the same time they pressed South Carolina for better trading prices and consulted with the French at Fort Toulouse on the Alabama River. They expressed interest in a revival of the old Virginia-Cherokee trade, which in the past had been employed by the Cherokees to remind the Carolinians that their trade was desirable but not irreplaceable. In the end their promise to send warriors to join Washington on his foray into the wilderness disappeared like smoke.

In 1755, when the Virginians came again to seek support for Braddock's campaign, the Cherokees used promises of hundreds of warriors to gain a trade with Virginia on more favorable terms than the Carolinians offered. Well aware that South Carolina and Virginia were close to blows in their struggle for control of the Cherokee trade, the Cherokees withheld the warriors when trade negotiations failed. When Braddock suffered his disastrous defeat a few months later, he had only eight Indians with his army.

In May 1755 South Carolina agents met the Cherokee headmen deep in the backcountry for treaty making. When the Cherokees agreed to recognize the English king as their sovereign and to cede some of their lands to the Crown, the Carolinians believed they had accomplished a major breakthrough in luring the Indians out of their neutrality. In exchange they pledged to supply more trade goods at lower prices and to build a fort in Cherokee country that would offer protection against French and Creek enemies.

How badly the English could misapprehend Indian uses of diplomacy became clear in the next five years. Although the governor of South Carolina boasted that the treaty of 1755 added "near 10,000 people to his Majesty's subjects and above 40,000,000 acres to his territories," the Cherokees regarded themselves as subject to British authority only so long as it served mutually satisfactory goals.[11] About 250 Cherokees fought with the Virginia militia on the western frontier in 1757, but they agreed to serve not as allies but as mercenaries. When they were not paid according to agreement, they promptly plundered Virginia frontier settlements in order to collect by force what the white government failed to give them. The process was repeated in the next year, but this time Virginia frontiersmen began ambushing hundreds of Cherokees who were returning from battle and living off the land as they made their way home. Thirty Cherokees lost their lives at the hands of their allies in 1758. Spurring the Indian-hating Virginians

[11]Quoted in David H. Corkran, *The Cherokee Frontier: Conflict and Survival, 1740–1762* (Norman: University of Oklahoma Press, 1962), p. 61.

was the colony's £50 scalp bounty, meant to apply to enemy Indians such as the Shawnees. To avaricious Virginians scalps were scalps, whether Cherokee or Shawnee. Each earned its bearer the equivalent of a year's income as a frontier farmer.

Nothing more than a few such incidents were required to fan into a roaring blaze the anti-English embers that had been kept alive in the Cherokee towns by the pro-French factions. Messengers went out to the Creeks and Chickasaws, and by the winter of 1758–59 talk of an Indian uprising had spread across the southern frontier. English agents countered with the warning that an English blockade of French shipping in North America would make it impossible for the Indians to obtain guns, ammunition, and even normal trade goods from the French.

Nonetheless, backcountry skirmishing from Virginia to South Carolina continued, soon turning the southern sector of the Seven Years War into a war with the Cherokees. With 1,500 men Governor Lyttelton of South Carolina invaded Cherokee territory. The peace treaty that he extracted from the Cherokees blamed the Indians for all that had happened. The Cherokee chiefs signed it under duress, but it served only to inflame them more.

The war erupted again in 1760. This time the Cherokees were far more united in opposition to the English. The new governor of South Carolina, William Bull, soon recognized that the united Cherokees were more than a match for the largest force of militiamen he could put in the field. Bowing to circumstances, he agreed to a treaty that made concessions to the Cherokees on "terms that perhaps may not be thought suitable, according to the Rules of Honour, observed among Europeans," as he delicately put it.[12] The arrival of 1,300 crack Scottish troops under Sir Jeffrey Amherst and the subsequent expedition against the Cherokees proved again the difficulties of fighting Indians in their own territory. Bogging down in the hilly terrain, ambushed at every turn, the expedition "accomplished little, except possibly to boost Cherokee morale."[13] Badly stung, the British force returned to Charleston. Shortly thereafter, Fort Loudoun, the main English garrison in Cherokee country, surrendered to a Cherokee siege. But 1,800 British regulars, joined by 700 provincial militiamen, tried again in the summer of 1761, and this time, by burning Cherokee villages and crops, they succeeded. With supplies from the French virtually cut off, the Cherokees submitted to a peace treaty that acknowledged English sovereignty and established the eastern boundary of the Cherokee territory.

Throughout the Rebellion of 1759–61, the Cherokees made attempts to enlist the support of the Creeks. Two generations before, the refusal of the Cherokees to join the Creeks in the Yamasee War against the Carolinians

---

[12]Quoted in M. Eugene Sirmans, *Colonial South Carolina; A Political History* (Chapel Hill: University of North Carolina Press, 1966), p. 335.

[13]*Ibid.*, p. 336.

had deprived the Creeks of their victory. Now the Creek decision to remain neutral cost the Cherokees decisively. Left to fight the English themselves, the Cherokees struggled against food shortages, lack of gunpowder, and a smallpox epidemic. The only trade goods reaching them from the French, ironically, were provided by New England ship captains, who brought contraband supplies to the French forts on the Gulf of Mexico. The desperate shortage of trade goods forced the Cherokees back to ancient customs—fashioning clothes from deer and bear skins and tipping their arrows with bone points instead of trader's brass. Cut off from an alternate supply of trade goods and unable to organize a pan-Indian offensive, they joined the French as losers in the Seven Years War.

Whereas the Iroquois made common cause with the English once French weaknesses were evident, and whereas the Cherokees alternately allied with and fought against the English during the Seven Years War, the Creeks held fast to the policy of neutrality that had been the hallmark of their diplomacy since the Yamasee War. Their major concerns were trade and the maintenance of political sovereignty. Through the 1750s and early 1760s the Creeks ranged from the Cherokee country to the French trading posts at Fort Toulouse and Mobile, accepting presents from both English and French and driving hard bargains for more favorable terms in the deerskin trade. Pro-French, pro-English, and neutralist factions argued bitterly in the Creek towns. But by 1757, British naval superiority had strangled French shipping. This undermined the arguments of the Creek headmen who were advocating a pan-Indian, anti-English rebellion of Shawnees, Cherokees, Creeks, Chickasaws, and Catawbas. The English solidified their position with the Creeks in 1758 and 1759 by showering them with presents. Sensitive to the possibility that the Cherokee insurgency might spread, Governor Ellis of Georgia spent the spring of 1760 trying to "set every Person of Influence upon endeavoring to create a Rupture between those two Nations—the Creeks and Cherokees."[14]

While refusing to join the Cherokees, the Creeks used their neighbor's rebellion for their own benefit. When English trade goods became scarce or when prices rose, they dropped the word to English traders that the arguments of the Cherokees and French had taken on a new persuasiveness. Actually the outbreak of the Cherokee rebellion had badly divided the Creeks. The pro-French faction continued to urge the Cherokees on to greater efforts against the English and even murdered eleven English settlers in an attempt to precipitate an English attack that would galvanize the Creek nation behind the Cherokees. The Carolina and Georgia governments failed to rise to the bait, however. The decision not to respond to the murder of the traders or even to demand that the Creeks put the murderers to death

[14]Quoted in W.W. Abbot, *The Royal Governors of Georgia, 1754–1775* (Chapel Hill: University of North Carolina Press, 1959), p. 80.

was dramatic evidence of the precarious position of the southern colonists and their vital need to keep the Creeks neutral. Had the balance of power lain with the English, they would have taken strenuous measures to make the Creeks accountable for such killings.

In spite of Cherokee victories in 1760 and in spite of their desire to check English expansionism, the Creek strategic options were crucially limited by the inability of the French to supply an alternate flow of vital weapons and trade goods. At a grand meeting of the French, Cherokees, and Creeks at Fort Toulouse in March 1761, it became clear that the French had no munitions, presents, or trade goods to back up their talk of expelling the English from the continent. English victories in the North had nearly sealed the fate of the French on the continent. For a half century the Creeks had maintained their neutrality and kept open a profitable trade with both the French and English. But in the process they had become dependent on the European trade connection, which was shortly to be monopolized by the English.

Anglo-American victories in the North began in 1759 with the capture of Fort Niagara, continued with Wolfe's dramatic victory at Quebec, and culminated in the following year with the fall of Montreal. This marked the end of hostilities in North America. Almost two centuries of French presence on the continent was coming to an end.

For the Indian nations that had demonstrated such independence of action and impressive power during the Seven Years War, the Peace of Paris came as a hammer blow. Unlike the coastal tribes, whose numbers and autonomy had ebbed through contact with European colonizers, the interior tribes had grown stronger, more militarily awesome, and more technologically developed as a result of their political and economic connections with the English, French, and Spanish. Although they had become dependent on the European trade, they had been able to turn this dependency to their own advantage so long as more than one source of trade goods existed. They had mastered the European style of diplomatic intrigue, used it to serve their own self-interests, and proved their ability to evade or defeat numerically superior European forces.

But while they played a powerful role on land, the Indian nations possessed not a shred of power to control the ocean separating Europe and North America or the trade goods that flowed across it. In the end it was this factor that undermined their strength. Control of the Atlantic by the British navy dealt a near-fatal blow to the playoff system, for the French in North America without trade goods were hardly better than no French at all. The inability to obtain French trade goods diminished Native Americans' room for maneuver and rendered futile the nascent pan-Indian movements against the English. Had the interior tribes been unified under French arms and supplies, the designs of the French imperialists to rule the continent might have materialized.

By the terms of the Peace of Paris, signed by England, France, and Spain in 1763, Canada and all of North America east of the Mississippi River became English territory. France ceded the lands west of the Mississippi to Spain. Spain ceded Florida to England. From that year onward English sway in the eastern half of North America was unchallenged in the courts of Europe. No longer could the Creeks, Cherokees, or Iroquois employ the playoff system to gain advantages in trade, since only one source of trade goods remained. Also, hostilities between the colonies, which Indian groups had often exploited, subsided, for the wartime effort had unified the thirteen English provinces to an unprecedented degree. Two centuries of European rivalry for possession and control of eastern North America had come to a dramatically swift end. Iroquois, Cherokees, Creeks, and other interior tribes were now forced to adjust to this reality.

INDIAN–WHITE RELATIONS AFTER 1763

At the conclusion of a long international war the English government planned a continental Indian policy in North America where for a century and a half each colony had been left to conduct its own Indian affairs. Stung by the fact that most of the North American tribes had given their allegiance to the French in the Seven Years War, the English government launched a new policy intended to separate Native Americans and colonizers, while guaranteeing the integrity of Indian territory. "It is just and reasonable, and essential to our Interest, and the Security of our Colonies," stated the King's proclamation in 1763, "that the several Nations or Tribes of Indians with whom We are connected, and who live under our Protection, should not be molested or disturbed in the Possession of such Parts of our Dominions and Territories as, not having been ceded to or purchased by Us, are reserved to them, or any of them, as their Hunting Grounds."[15]

By the terms of the Proclamation of 1763, British policymakers created a racial boundary from Maine to Georgia, roughly following the crestline of the Appalachian Mountains. Colonial governors were ordered to forbid "for the present and until our further Pleasure be known" any surveys or land grants beyond the Appalachian watershed. "All the Lands and Territories lying to the Westward of the Sources of the Rivers which fall into the Sea from the West and North West" were specifically reserved for Indian nations. All white settlers already beyond the Appalachian divide were charged to withdraw east of the line.

[15]Quoted in Francis Paul Prucha, *American Indian Policy in the Formative Years; The Indian Trade and Intercourse Acts, 1790–1834* (Lincoln: University of Nebraska Press, 1970 rpr.), p. 5.

The Proclamation of 1763 is one of the most poignant documents in American history. Historians who subscribe to the "frontier thesis" of Frederick Jackson Turner have argued that this attempt to dam up the energy of restless westward-looking Americans alienated the colonists and provided a major impetus for throwing off the restraining yoke of the mother country. Other historians, while agreeing that the proclamation was an irritant contributing to revolutionary sentiment, point out that those most alienated by it were the large land speculators of the eastern seaboard, who boiled at seeing such a fabulous source of profit put beyond their grasp. What has rarely been noted is that for several years before the bureaucrats in London drew the 1763 boundary the Indian tribes of the interior—from the Senecas, Ottawas, Illinois, Miamis, and Sioux of the North to the Cherokees, Creeks, and Choctaws of the South—had themselves been attempting to fix a territorial line that would limit white expansion. Their attempts were inspired by their certainty that, contrary to the language of the Proclamation of 1763, they did *not* live under English "protection" but in fact could protect their own interests and ensure their survival only by throwing off English "protection" and fighting to preserve their land.

Though the interior Indian tribes had no way of counting the population increase in the Thirteen Colonies, they were keenly aware that waves of settlers were moving into their tribal hunting grounds almost on the heels of the Anglo-American armies that had pushed the French out of the Ohio Valley beginning in 1759. More than half of the population increase occurred in New York, Pennsylvania, and Virginia. Through the western parts of these colonies land-hungry speculators and immigrants began pouring as soon as the French were expelled. Both before and after the Proclamation Line of 1763 had been set, land poachers were staking out claims to lands to which the English, by the terms of their own treaties with Indian tribes, had no claim. Creek lands, for example, were guaranteed by a treaty signed in 1733, and the limits of white settlement in Cherokee territory had been set at the end of the Cherokee War in 1761 in a treaty with the government of Virginia. But neither of these treaties stopped white land speculators and settlers, who swarmed into Indian territory, secure in knowing that their provincial governments had neither the desire nor the power to do much about it.

Even without the possibility of French aid, the Indian response was to meet force with force. Bloody clashes pockmarked the southern frontier in the early 1760s, as Indians and settlers fought over Indian lands the provincial governments had guaranteed to the tribes. Some Indian leaders attempted to form another pan-Indian defensive league, even at the risk that the English would cut off their supply of trade goods. Meanwhile, the colonists did their best at a series of conferences to wheedle land cessions from the Creeks and Cherokees, while privately they fanned enmity between the major tribes.

The determination of the southern tribes to resist English encroachments, even with the French removed from the continent, was vividly displayed
in 1763 by the refusal of the Creeks to surrender their tribesmen who had murdered fourteen white land poachers. The Creeks, on the other hand, were unable to forge a southern Indian alliance in 1763 when such a unified Indian
movement might have joined a major Indian uprising in the Northwest to give
the native peoples their best advantage of the eighteenth century.

If the Indian reaction to the Anglo-American victory over France was
not one of cowed submission in the South, it was even more aggressive in the
North. In June 1761 the Senecas, always the most pro-French of the Six
Nations, carried a red wampum belt (signifying an intention to go to war) to
Detroit where the British army was garrisoned among the various tribes that
had formally fought with the French—the Delawares, Shawnees, Ottawas,
Hurons, Chippewas, Wyandots, and Potawatomies. The Senecas were taking
the lead in resisting the new English Indian policy, which curtailed trade, increased British garrisons, required the Indians to bring their furs to the
British forts, ended the system of annual "presents" that Indian leaders regarded as a kind of rent for land occupied by British forts, prohibited trade
in rum, and in general instituted trading terms far less satisfactory to the
Indians than those existing before the war. The Senecas had an additional
incentive for taking to the warpath. General Amherst, the commander-in-
chief of the Anglo-American forces during the Seven Years War, had rewarded
some of his officers with Seneca lands near Niagara in violation of a treaty
between the Iroquois and the New York government. Such generosity at the
expense of the Senecas was not lightly regarded in the Indian towns.

The Senecas proposed a coordinated attack by the northern tribes on
all the English outposts that ranged along the Great Lakes and as far south
as Pittsburgh. Acting together, the tribes would drive the English out of the
Ohio Valley, out of Iroquois country, and back across the mountains to
the Piedmont. Whether this "nativistic" plan included a resolve to give up the
English trade altogether is not certain, although it is possible that after
many years of trade difficulties they considered no trade at all preferable to
a restricted trade at pinched prices. Although the western tribes rejected the
Seneca plan after long discussion, they were far from pleased by what they
heard from Sir William Johnson, the Northern Indian superintendent, when
he arrived at Detroit. Johnson claimed he came to brighten "the chain of
friendship" and spoke glowingly of the King's concern for the welfare "of all
his subjects." But he promised nothing in regard to the high price of trade
goods, the unavailability of rum, the stoppage of annual presents, and the inadequate supplies of ammunition now allotted to the tribes. These, he said,
were matters of official policy beyond his control.

Although Johnson reported optimistically to General Amherst at the
conclusion of the conference, averring that he left Detroit with matters
"settled on so stable a foundation there that unless greatly irritated thereto,

they will never break the peace," the fact was that the Indians, for all their show of amity, were deeply embittered.[16] The most experienced English trader in the Ohio Valley, George Croghan, accurately perceived the situation. The Indians "had great expectations of being very generally supplied by us, and from their poverty and mercenary disposition they can't bear such a disappointment. Undoubtedly the general [Amherst] has his own reason for not allowing any present or ammunition to be given them, and I wish it may have its desired effect, but I take this opportunity to acquaint you that I dread the event as I know Indians can't long persevere. . . . Their success at the beginning of this war on our frontiers is too recent in their memory to suffer them to consider their present inability to make war with us, and if the Senecas, Delawares and Shawnees should break with us, it will end in a general war with all western nations. . . ."[17]

Adding to the inflammatory state of affairs were the preachings of Neolin, a charismatic Delaware prophet. Just when the English were cutting off guns and gunpowder to which the Indians had become accustomed and threatening their land base, Neolin began a journey through the Delaware territories, preaching that Native Americans must return to "their original state that they were in before the white people found out their country." The alternative, he argued, was slow extinction at the hands of the settlers swarming across the mountains. Several traders described the renaissance of traditional Indian culture reached by the Delaware prophet. Neolin's vision, conveyed to him in dreams by the Master of Life, was that the Indians' salvation lay not in adopting Christianity and European culture but in returning to ancient customs. Rum must be forsworn. The material objects of white culture must be abandoned. Population increase must be curbed through abstinence so that the difficult return to the old ways could be accomplished. Indians could only escape the desperate trap they were in by regaining sacred power.

Neolin's message resonated with tremendous force not only in Delaware country but also among other western Indian nations. It called not only for cultural renaissance but also for revolutionary resistance. "Wherefore do you suffer the whites to dwell upon your lands?" he asked. "Drive them away; wage war against them. I love them not. They know me not. They are my enemies, they are your brothers' enemies. Send them back to the lands I have made for them. Let them remain there."[18] Throughout 1762 Neolin's admonitions were passed by word of mouth and on inscribed deerskin parchment from one Indian settlement to another.

[16]Quoted in Howard H. Peckham, *Pontiac and the Indian Uprising* (Chicago: University of Chicago Press, 1961), p. 86.
[17]*Ibid.*, pp. 97–98.
[18]Anthony F.C. Wallace, *The Death and Rebirth of the Seneca* (New York: Alfred A. Knopf, 1970), p. 118.

Neolin's plan for propitiating the Master of Life's anger with the Indians' dependence on European guns and alcohol did not prescribe a complete return to the traditional elements of Delaware culture. Instead, it proposed a blend of native and European elements. Some of the old customs, such as war rituals and polygamy, were not to be revived and some Christian concepts, such as written prayers and a written "Bible" or "Great Book," were to be retained. But Neolin's appeal for the de-Europeanization of Delaware culture amounted to an independent, creative, and sacred response to the bleak situation that confronted interior tribes after the defeat of the French. After his disciples carried his message throughout the western territories, large numbers of Indians, acting on his advice to boycott European trade goods, hunted only to supply their own needs. Most spectacularly, an Ottawa leader named Pontiac became a convert to Neolin's doctrine and made it the spiritual underpinning of the uprising he led against the English beginning in May 1763.[19]

According to a French account, Pontiac inspired his warriors with a speech that reflected Neolin's nativism. "It is important for us, my brothers," he exhorted, "that we exterminate from our lands this nation which seeks only to destroy us."[20] Under this banner Pontiac led an assault on Fort Detroit, the strongest of the British garrisons in the Great Lakes region. While the Ottawas lay siege to the fort, other tribes rubbed out the British outposts in the western Great Lakes region and as far east as Pittsburgh. But the Indians were unable to overwhelm the three major British forts at Detroit, Niagara, and Pittsburgh. The war dragged on through the summer with several thousand traders and settlers falling to Indian ambushes and assaults. When news of it reached London, the government hurriedly issued the Proclamation Act. Military reinforcements arrived from the East, creating a standoff by summer's end. Pontiac fought sporadically for another two years, and the English colonies hummed with rumors that he was conspiring with Creek and Choctaw chiefs to organize a grand alliance of eighteen Indian nations. But lacking vital supplies of powder, shot, and guns, the tribes were forced to sue for peace. Without the presence in North America of another European power they could not overcome their supply problems.

In one tragic incident stemming from Pontiac's uprising, frontiersmen showed that neither Crown nor colonial government meant much to them in their hatred of Indians. Stung by Pontiac's marauders, who had set upon Pennsylvania's western settlements, Scots-Irish farmers avenged themselves on a small band of peaceful, Christianized Conestoga Indians who farmed a few acres and peddled their wares among the whites who surrounded them. After butchering six defenseless Conestogas, the "Paxton Boys," as they called themselves, invaded the workhouse in Lancaster, where magistrates

---

[19]*Ibid.*, pp. 120–21.
[20]Quoted in Peckham, *Pontiac and the Indian Uprising,* p. 119.

sheltered fourteen other Conestogas to protect them from the enraged frontiersmen. The Paxton Boys slaughtered them as the Indians sat in a circle with hands joined and prayers on their lips. One Conestoga held a copy of the friendship treaty signed by William Penn in 1701 where Indians and Quakers pledged "that they shall forever hereafter be as one Head & One Heart, & live in true Friendship & Amity as one People."[21]

A month later, the Paxton Boys organized a march on Philadelphia to convince the legislature that it was far too timid in raising troops to defend the frontier. With clubs and pitchforks, they threatened to make as much blood run in Philadelphia as it had in Lancaster. Benjamin Franklin, now famous for his experiments with electricity, sprang into action. After helping to organize the militia in Philadelphia to repulse the marching frontiersmen, Franklin took up his pen to write *A Narrative of the Late Massacres . . . of a Number of Indians*, a scorching condemnation of the "Christian white savages" who massacred the friendly, acculturated Indians. Although the perpetrators of lynch law were never tried or punished, Franklin's impassioned attack on them aroused the conscience of many Pennsylvanians. "The only Crime of these poor Wretches," he wrote, "seems to have been, that they had a reddish brown Skin, and black Hair; and some People of that Sort, it seems, had murdered some of our Relations. If it be right to kill Men for such a Reason, then, should any Man with a freckled Face and red Hair, kill a Wife or Child of mine, it would be right for me to revenge it, by killing all the freckled red-haired Men, Women, and Children, I could afterwards anywhere meet with."[22]

Though Pontiac's resistance movement collapsed, the major interior tribes continued to preserve their political autonomy in the decade prior to the outbreak of the American Revolution. "The Six Nations, Western Indians, etc.," wrote William Johnson to London in 1764, "having never been conquered, either by the English or French, nor subject to the[ir] Laws, consider themselves as a free people."[23] Yet preserving political independence could not stem the tide of frontier land speculators and farmers. By itself this demographic pressure was enough to overcome all the efforts of the English government to fashion an Indian policy based on fair trade relations and respect for land boundaries.

Two factors determined the fate of the trans-Appalachian Indian territories after 1763. First, the English government, staggering under an immense debt accumulated in fighting the Seven Years War, was unwilling to commit resources for maintaining garrisons in the interior to enforce the

[21] *Minutes of the Provincial Council of Pennsylvania*, 10 vols. (Harrisburg, 1851–52), II, 15–17.

[22] Franklin, *A Narrative of the Late Massacres*, in Leonard Labaree, et al., eds., *The Papers of Benjamin Franklin* (New Haven: Yale University Press, 1959), XI, 142–69, quoted sentences on p. 55.

[23] Quoted in Prucha, *American Indian Policy*, p. 19.

provisions of the Proclamation Act of 1763. Consequently, the British abandoned their interior garrisons after Pontiac's Revolt and scrapped their plan to coordinate and control the Indian trade and Indian affairs of the various colonies. Reliance was placed on drawing lines on maps—lines that theoretically separated Indians and colonizers.

Second, English officials had hardly a shred of power to enforce regulations in the interior, particularly after 1764 when a whole cluster of issues concerned with imperial authority in the colonies threw the colonists into a quasi-revolutionary state. The Proclamation Line of 1763 existed only on paper, and neither colonists nor Indians took it seriously. Colonial governors, often closely connected with land speculators, bombarded colonial administrators in London with reasons why exceptions should be made to the Proclamation Act. These included scores of false assertions that interior tribes had abandoned their claims to various parcels of land west of the Appalachians. When such requests were denied, the governors turned their heads and permitted land grants, surveys, and private purchases of land from Indian tribes such as the Creeks and Cherokees, who did not recognize the right of the English government to demarcate boundaries. When settlers moved onto land still claimed by the Indians, they were usually left to fight it out among themselves.

Colonial governors and officials spent most of their energy not in enforcing the Proclamation Act but assisting expansionist-minded speculators and settlers by promoting intertribal Indian hostility. The main points of English Indian policy—prevention of encroachment on Indian lands and equity in the Indian trade—were reduced to a shambles in the decade before the Revolution. Few colonists on the frontier held back their land hunger when they saw that Indians were bereft of a European ally and an alternate supply of trade goods. Nor could anybody in England discover a means of compelling the Americans in the West to obey Crown commands at a time when even along the Atlantic seaboard the King's authority was under challenge.

For the interior tribes, the alternatives were limited after Pontiac's Revolt. They could seek other Indian allies to forge another pan-Indian uprising, as did one faction of the Creeks led by The Mortar, who had been staunchly anti-English for decades. They could seek private revenge for white depredations and land grabbing, as did Logan, a displaced Cayuga living on the Virginia frontier, whose family had been wiped out by outlaw frontiersmen and who led a party of warriors in retaliatory raids that set off the brief but bloody Lord Dunmore's War in 1774. They could continue to seek French support in New Orleans while hoping for a renewed French presence on the continent, as did the Choctaws. Or they could bow to the white tidal wave and sell off their land, piece by piece at the best price possible, to private individuals and land companies who knew they could safely ignore both the Proclamation of 1763 and colonial statutes forbidding such purchases.

THE COLONIZERS' SOCIETY AFTER 1763

Although the Seven Years War is primarily remembered as the climactic military struggle in which Anglo-American arms finally overcame the hated French in North America, it was also a war that deeply affected white communities. It was a war that convinced the American colonies of their growing strength and maturity, yet ironically left them weakened in manpower and debt-ridden at its end. It brought the greatest infusion of English capital in their history, yet rendered them unusually sensitive to the disadvantages of the British mercantile connection. It drove forward the commercialization of life, especially in the seaport towns, yet exposed in stark detail the social costs of the transition to the market economy.

War contracts and the general quickening of the economy brought prosperity to most of colonial America during the war years. But after the series of triumphant victories over the French in 1759 and 1760, the war theatre moved to the Caribbean, and a commercial downturn struck hard. Especially along the seaboard, unemployment, high prices, and a great rise in war-widowed families caused a crumbling of economic security. The greatest hardships fell upon the laboring classes, which included many artisans who occupied positions on the middle rungs of the social ladder. It was they who had the smallest savings and the thinnest margin between profit and loss and who devoted the largest proportion of their budgets to food, rent, clothing, and fuel—expenses that could be little trimmed when times worsened. The war had created a class of wealthy merchants, but it had also left many communities strewn with crippled, widowed, and destitute persons. Pauperism spread in all the colonial cities and authorities struggled for ways of providing for the poor.

If all colonists had suffered equally in the aftermath of the Seven Years War, the depression of the early 1760s might have unified colonial society. It might have served to warn Americans that while growing more powerful in numbers, they were becoming less powerful in their ability to control the violent fluctuations in the Atlantic economy. This perception of the problem as externally caused did dominate thinking among merchants, large landowners, lawyers, and government officials. The drastic overhaul of imperial policy which Parliament instituted at the end of the war gave much credence to this point of view. It was apparent that an invigorated customs service, cracking down on colonial smugglers, dried up profits on the illegal importing of French tea and sugar. Clearly, the establishment of vice-admiralty courts placed violators of the Navigation Acts beyond the forgiving attitudes of local juries. It was plain that the Currency Act of 1764, restricting issuance of paper money in New York and Pennsylvania, put a further damp on trade already depressed. And the Stamp Act of 1765 obviously laid additional levies on communities still trying to pay off a heavy war debt. For many Americans the post-1763 parliamentary legislation and the contractionary actions of their British creditors were signals that a maturing American people might now have their necks pinned to the ground by the paw of an insensitive British lion.

This feeling of alienation from the mother country was shared by many in the lower levels of the white communities. But interwoven with this perception was another strand of thought. War, it was understood, had required financial sacrifice from everyone in the form of higher taxes. Furthermore, war had spilled much blood, primarily the blood of the lower classes. That too was the usual way of things. But many were disturbed that eight years of conflict had left many communities with swarms of the poor and a few men standing high above their neighbors. This social transformation, occurring most dramatically in the cities, was apparent to all who witnessed the urban mansions of the merchants rise in the 1760s at the same time that large almshouses were under construction to house the multiplying destitute. "Some individuals," charged a New Yorker in 1765, "by the Smiles of Providence, or some other Means, are enabled to roll in their four wheel'd Carriages, and can support the expense of good Houses, rich Furniture, and Luxurious Living. But is it equitable that 99, rather 999, should suffer for the Extravagance or Grandeur of one? Especially when it is considered that Men frequently owe their Wealth to the impoverishment of their Neighbors?"[24] This was the language of emerging class tension, bred out of ancient feelings of self-worth by those who labored with their hands, nurtured by periodic adversity, and extended and clarified by the depressing aftermath of the Seven Years War.

For many colonists who struggled for security in the aftermath of the Seven Years War, a move to new lands on the frontier seemed a solution to their problems. By itself, the population buildup was a powerful incentive for such a move, and the attraction of the frontier was increased by depressed conditions in many coastal communities. For those who exercised this western option the overall result was an increase in tension between themselves and the Native Americans into whose lands they pushed. For those who remained behind, economic problems had to be worked out within the boundaries of their own community or within communities to which they migrated in search of opportunity. Thus it was that the depression that enveloped coastal communities beginning in 1760 was accompanied by political turmoil.

It was not political power itself that those at the lower levels of these communities groped for after the Seven Years War but an equitable system in which they could pursue their modest goals. When their economic security was threatened, they responded by attempting to influence, not dominate, politics and to redress grievances rather than dismantle the system of

---

[24]*New-York Gazette*, July 11, 1765.

upper-class domination of politics inherited from their fathers. Yet they began to make excursions into "radical" politics in order either to conserve the corporate community of the past or to pry open the doors of opportunity in the new entrepreneurial age. Such forays into political activism, first nurtured during the Great Awakening, had a cumulative effect. A sense of their own power grew as their trust in those above them diminished and as their own experience expanded in making decisions, exercising leadership roles, and refuting those who were supposed to be wiser because they were wealthier. Hence factional politics intensified in the late colonial period. As never before, members of the lower ranks began to act for and of themselves, propelling forward their own leaders, making their muscle felt, and wreaking bitter violence—as in the Stamp Act riots of 1765—against those they construed as their enemies. In this sense the Seven Years War that gave the Anglo-Americans supremacy in North America, the Seven Years War that placed the interior Indian tribes in an increasingly untenable position, was also the Seven Years War that initiated the rupture between colonists and mother country and led to political divisiveness within the colonizers' communities.

11

The Tri-colored American Revolution

Every textbook properly lavishes attention on the American Revolution because it brought independence from Great Britain and created the United States of America. But until recently textbooks have largely ignored the Indian and African-American peoples of North America who fought in the Revolution or were deeply affected by its outcomes. This chapter makes no attempt to recount the complicated events that led to the Revolution, nor to detail the military struggle that ended with the British capitulation at Yorktown in 1781, nor to analyze the breathtaking attempts of state and local governments to fashion constitutions and new rulebooks by which white Americans might live as a free and independent people. Rather, this chapter focuses on the connections among red, white, and black peoples of the Revolutionary era and how the Revolution altered these relationships.

THE ABOLITIONIST IMPULSE

For African-Americans the period following the Seven Years War was one of both hope and despair. In the northern colonies a handful of reformers raised the banner of abolitionism sufficiently high to make the question of slavery a public issue for the first time since Africans had arrived in

Jamestown in 1619. Quaker humanitarians such as John Woolman and Anthony Benezet led the way and were joined by a score of New England ministers, black spokesmen, and emerging revolutionary radicals. All of them argued that slavery was immoral and contradicted the principles of liberty and opportunity that demarcated the American experience from that of post-feudal Europe.

In developing a rationale for revolution in the decade after the Seven Years War and in mounting propaganda attacks on England, colonial leaders found themselves asking questions not only about the nature of English authority and its legitimate limits in the colonies, but also about the nature of the colonial society they had built. The revolutionary arguments about "the natural rights of man," the "consent of the governed," the nature of "freedom" and "tyranny," and the naturalness of equality contained intellectual dynamite. These stirring words and phrases led toward regions where even the most radical patriot leaders had not intended to go. They were primarily concerned with the threatening actions of Parliament and the King's ministers. But when they spoke of inalienable rights of the dignity of all men or abuses of power, they unconsciously pointed a finger at themselves. The more they used catchwords such as "slavery" and "tyranny" to describe British imperial reforms, the more difficult it became to ignore domestic slavery, which by the 1760s embraced about 20 percent of the population in the colonies.

Men on both sides of the Atlantic and on both sides of the Anglo–American argument pointed out the contradiction. How could Americas treat Africans "as a better kind of Cattle . . . while they are bawling about the Rights of human Nature?" asked one English official.[1] An American patriot chided his countrymen: "Blush ye pretended votaries for freedom! ye trifling patriots! who are making a vain parade of being advocated for the liberties of mankind, who are thus making a mockery of your profession by trampling on the sacred natural rights and privileges of Africans; for while you are fasting, praying, nonimporting, nonexporting, remonstrating, resolving, and pleading for a restoration of your charter rights, you at the same time are continuing this lawless, cruel, inhuman, and abominable practice of enslaving your fellow creatures."[2]

The values invoked in defense of colonial freedom were thus used to indict the system of labor that undergirded the colonial economy of the South and supported economic enterprise in the North. Slavery insulted the principles for which revolutionaries were preparing to fight. "Oh the shocking, the intolerable inconsistence! . . . This gross, barefaced, practiced

---

[1]Quoted in Winthrop Jordan, *White Over Black: American Attitudes Toward the Negro, 1550–1812* (Chapel Hill: University of North Carolina Press, 1968), p. 291.

[2][John Allen], *The Watchmen's Alarm to Lord N__h* (1774), in Bernard Bailyn, *The Ideological Origins of the American Revolution* (Cambridge, Mass.: Harvard University Press, 1967), p. 240.

inconsistence!" cried Samuel Hopkins, a Congregationalist minister of Rhode Island on the eve of war.[3]

Not only the dehumanization of blacks under slavery but also the accompanying degradation of whites concerned many of those who declared their opposition to slavery in the pre-Revolutionary decade. John Woolman, whose abolitionist efforts of the 1750s were widely ignored, was convinced that slaveholding, even by the kindliest of masters, "depraved the mind in like manner and with as great certainty as prevailing cold congeals water." The absolute authority exercised by the master over the slave established "ideas of things and modes of conduct" that inexorably molded the attitudes of children, neighbors, and friends of slaveholders.[4] As Woolman traveled through the colonies he became convinced that slavery was indelibly fixing the notion of white superiority in the white mind. Such an idea was incompatible with both the Christian concept of the brotherhood of all humans and rationalist thought of the eighteenth century that stressed natural equality. Because slaves were always employed in servile labor and lived in abject conditions, most people grew to look upon them "as a contemptible, ignorant Part of Mankind."[5] The outward condition of the slave, the result of white desire for material gain, was taken to correspond with the inward condition of the displaced African. But for Woolman, the slave's outer degradation was a function of the white man's "inner corruption." White men, in the process of enslaving the African, had enslaved themselves. The imprisonment of blacks was external and physical, while for the white it was internal and spiritual. In either case the implications for the health of American society were fearful to contemplate.

From this increasing awareness of white racial prejudice and its effects came a movement to end slavery. For the first time the incompatibility of enslaving Africans with the same principles that white colonial society claimed as the foundation of its uniqueness gained wide recognition. In response, a number of northern colonies abolished the slave trade or taxed it out of existence before the Declaration of Independence was signed. Slavery, however, was not abolished, so while a small number of merchants were forced to reroute their ships, it cost other colonial whites little or nothing.

In the South the ideological war against slavery got nowhere. The 1760s, in fact, saw the largest slave importations of any decade in the colonial period. In South Carolina slaves imported between 1760 and 1770 exceeded those brought in during the previous quarter century, and in the early 1770s the influx increased again. After the Seven Years War more than 85 percent of all American slaves toiled in the plantation colonies of Maryland, Virginia,

---

[3]Quoted in *ibid.*, p. 244.
[4]Quoted in Gary B. Nash, "Slaves and Slaveholders in Colonial Philadelphia," *William and Mary Quarterly*, 3d Ser., 29 (1973): 243.
[5]Quoted in Jordan, *White Over Black*, p. 273.

North Carolina, and South Carolina, with the number in Virginia almost equaling those of the other southern provinces. Virginians had never owned more than half as many slaves as the sugar plantations of Jamaica between 1670 and 1730. But they overtook the Jamaicans by 1760 and a decade later counted almost 200,000 slaves in the colony.

The massive capital investment in black labor made the question of abolishing slavery almost academic in the parts of the country where it counted most. In Virginia, which had a white population equivalent to that of Sacramento, California, or Jersey City, New Jersey, today, the capital investment in slaves was about £5.5 million, or in terms of today's money, about one billion dollars. Who would compensate slaveholders for this property? Thus, while African-Americans heard of pamphlets advocating abolition and even pondered reports that the legislatures of Virginia and other colonies were debating the issue, slaveholders with large sums invested in the situation were organizing to turn back the campaign that sought to eliminate what had become their primary source of wealth, power, and prestige. The abolitionist critique of American society resounded loudly where only one of every ten American slaves lived; it was rarely heard, or listened to, where the other nine toiled.

STRUGGLING FOR LIBERTY

We can only imagine how the spirits of enslaved Africans must have been lifted by eavesdropping on their master's dinner-table conversations, working in taverns and coffeehouses where Revolutionary politics were hatched, and reading or hearing about pamphlets pronouncing the necessity of ending slavery. What is certain is that many slaves acted on their hatred of their clanking chains to petition for their freedom in ways calculated to prick further the conscience of the master class. Couched cautiously at first, their petitions became bolder as the war approached. "We expect your house [the legislature] will . . . take our deplorable case into serious consideration, and give us that simple relief which, as men, we have a natural right to," remonstrated four slaves in rural Massachusetts in 1773. Six years later in Connecticut, blacks echoed these claims to freedom: "We do not ask for nothing but what we are fully persuaded is ours to claim," for "we are the Creatures of that God, who made of one Blood, and Kindred, all the Nations of the Earth." Therefore, "there is nothing that leads us to a belief, or suspicion, that we are any more obliged to serve them [our masters] than they us, and . . . can never be convinced that we are made to be slaves."[6]

---

[6]Quoted in Benjamin Quarles, "The Revolutionary War as a Black Declaration of Independence," in Ira Berlin and Ronald Hoffman (eds.), *Slavery and Freedom in the Age of the American Revolution* (Charlottesville: University of Virginia Press, 1983), p. 290.

By its very nature, the Revolutionary War created unprecedented situations and opportunities for slaves. A wave of black insurrectionary activity coursed through South Carolina in the 1760s. In 1765, more than one hundred slaves made a concerted attempt to establish a refugee colony in the interior. White Charlestonians took alarm the next year when black men took literally the white rhetoric concerning liberty and equality by parading through the streets chanting "Liberty, Liberty!" White authorities put the city under arms for a week as rumors of insurrection spread through the colony. A nervous legislature quickly passed a three-year prohibitive tariff on imported slaves, which had the desired effect of choking off the flood of nearly 7,000 slaves who had arrived from Africa in 1765.

With the huge movement of both civilian and military populations in and out of nearly every major seaport from Savannah to Boston between 1775 and 1781, urban slaves had unprecedented chances for making their personal declarations of independence and for destabilizing the institution of slavery. Similarly, in the countryside, as Tory and Whig militia units crisscrossed the terrain, plundering the farms and plantations of their enemies, slaves found ways of tearing holes in the fabric of slavery.

A turning point in the calculation of enslaved Africans came in November 1775 when the royal governor of Virginia, Lord Dunmore, issued a dramatic proclamation that guaranteed freedom to slaves and indentured servants who could escape their masters and reach the King's forces. Against this concrete offer of unconditional freedom, slaves had only the chance that the American patriots would respond to calls for abolition and follow the urgings of the first abolition society established in Pennsylvania just a few months before. Waiting for possible freedom as a white gift at some indeterminate point turned out to be a poor substitute for immediate freedom. When word of Dunmore's Proclamation spread quickly through the South, slaves by the thousands fled their masters to British troops, where officers formed them into the Black Regiment of Guides and Pioneers. Some marched in uniforms with the chilling inscription on their breasts, "Liberty to Slaves."

Dunmore's Proclamation galvanized the South against England, for it conjured up the vision of a large body of free Negroes, armed by the British, abroad in the land. The proclamation, wrote one prominent Southerner, tended "more effectually to work an eternal separation between Great Britain and the Colonies—than any other expedient, which could possibly have been thought of." Another put it more graphically: "Hell itself could not have vomited anything more black than this design of emancipating our slaves."[7]

Thousands of black Virginians made an attempt to reach the British garrisons in 1775 and in the war years that followed. Making personal declarations

---

[7]Quoted in Benjamin Quarles, *The Negro in the American Revolution* (Chapel Hill: University of North Carolina Press, 1961), p. 20n.

of independence, they achieved liberty by joining those whom white American patriots called enemies of freedom. In general, the appraisal of Joseph Galloway, a Philadelphia loyalist, would seem to characterize the African-American population as the Revolution began. "The Negroes," wrote Galloway, "may all be deemed so many Intestine [internal] Enemies, being all slaves and desirous of Freedom, and would, was an opportunity offered them, Take up Arms against their masters."[8] This black war for independence in North America occurred in every part of the country and was especially intense whenever slaves were within running distance of the British army or navy.

In the South, the pursuit of freedom through flight to the British, while it can never be exactly calculated, was so large that the British army was often hard pressed to provision them. Thomas Jefferson, Virginia's wartime governor, reported that 30,000 slaves fled their masters during the British invasion of Virginia in 1781. Probably two-thirds of Virginia's slaves were young children, women with infants, physically depleted men and women over 45, and men whose flight would have left their families at the mercy of revengeful masters. After accounting for those in situations that made flight nearly impossible, it can be estimated that nearly half the slaves who may be considered eligible escapees, predominantly male, sought their freedom behind British lines. In South Carolina and Georgia, a similar proportion of adult males fled to the British during the southern campaigns between 1779 and 1781.

In the North, where hardly more than one-tenth of the half-million enslaved Africans lived, the hungering for freedom was no less intense, even though slavery was milder than in the plantation South. Even in the budding capital of American abolitionism, where many believed that the city's slaves were docile and contented, white Philadelphians were shocked when a "gentlewoman," walking near Christ Church, was insulted by a black man only a few weeks after Dunmore's Proclamation. When the white woman reprimanded him, he shot back "Stay you d[amne]d white bitch 'till Lord Dunmore and his black regiment come, and then we will see who is to take the wall."[9] When the British occupied Philadelphia in September 1777 for nine months, hundreds of Philadelphia slaves fled to the British, confirming one Lutheran leader's belief that it "is almost universal among the Negroes in America" that they secretly hoped for the British to whip the Americans "for then all Negro slaves will gain their freedom."[10] In New York City and its surrounding hinterland, slave flight seems to have been even greater. The slave of Quaker John Corlies is illustrative. Named Titus by his

[8]Benjamin F. Stevens, ed., *Facsimiles of Manuscripts in European Archives Relating to America, 1773–1783* (London, 1889–1895), 24, No. 2097.

[9]*Pennsylvania Evening Post*, 14 December 1775.

[10]*The Journals of Henry Melchior Muhlenberg*, 3 vols (Philadelphia: Evangelical Lutheran Ministerium of Pennsylvania and Adjacent States, 1942–58), III: 78.

master, this 21-year-old fled his owner in 1775 and headed south to join the black regiment being formed by Lord Dunmore. Renaming himself Colonel Tye, he was soon back in northern New Jersey organizing other slaves and free blacks to fight against the Americans. For five years, he served as the leader of a local guerrilla band that terrorized the patriot farmers of northern New Jersey. Known as "one of Lord Dunmore's Crew," Tye fought for five years before dying from battle wounds and lockjaw.[11] Known all over New Jersey, he stood as a symbol of black rebellion, a testimony to the fact that the American Revolution was the greatest slave rebellion in the long history of North American slavery.

Tye and thousands of other enslaved blacks show that the high-toned rhetoric of natural rights and moral rectitude that accompanied the onset of the Revolution had only a limited power to soften the hearts of American slave masters. To be sure, several thousand masters manumitted their slaves; but as a proportion of all slave owners, these manumitters were insignificant compared to those who finally could not give up their investment in human property. The American Revolution brought to the fore a sharp collision between human rights and property rights; the latter becoming ascendant among the majority of slave owners confirmed Adam Smith's hard-nosed proposition that morality could rarely, if ever, transcend economic interest.

While the Colonel Tyes were numerically dominant among the half-million black Americans in choosing the British side, many free blacks and a small number of slaves fought for the American cause. These were the minority celebrated by William C. Nell, the first black American historian, who in the 1850s held high the abolitionist banner by pointing to the blood shed for the "glorious cause" by black Americans in the time of the nation's birth. Among those whom Nell celebrated in his *Colored Patriots of the American Revolution* was Prince, the slave of a New Hampshire soldier, who had pulled one of the oars carrying George Washington across the Delaware River in a piercing snow and sleet storm on Christmas night, 1776. Another was James Armistead, a Virginia slave whose master gave him permission to enlist under Lafayette, the French general who came to fight with the Americans. Armistead played a dramatic role as a double-spy, infiltrating the British lines at Yorktown while posing as a runaway Virginia slave and bringing back to the American forces crucial information that gave the Americans the upper hand in the climactic battle of the war. In 1786, the General Assembly of Virginia emancipated Armistead (who would call himself James Lafayette thereafter).

Another who fought with the Americans was a man who became the new nation's wealthiest free black, a considerable essayist, an eloquent abolitionist, and the progenitor of a talented family of children and grandchildren.

---

[11]Graham R. Hodges, *African-Americans in Monmouth County During the Age of the American Revolution* (Madison, Wisc.: Madison House, 1997), pp. 13–23.

When Lafayette returned to America in 1824 for a triumphal tour, he visited Richmond, Virginia, where he met James Armistead Lafayette, his servant and aide during the Revolution. John B. Martin, an important painter of white politicians, captured the dignity of the old soldier dressed in his military coat, now living on a pension awarded for his revolutionary service. *(Courtesy Valentine Museum, Richmond, Virginia)*

James Forten's great-grandfather had been brought in chains from Africa to the Delaware River and had been one of the first slaves in Pennsylvania to buy his freedom. Forten's father, born free, was a sailmaker, and he sent his son James to Anthony Benezet's school, where he learned to read and write and imbibed many of the kindly Quaker's principles about the universality of humankind. In 1781 at age 15, Forten signed onto Stephen Decatur's 22-gun privateer as a powderboy and began a career of heroic acts that would gain him fame in Philadelphia. "Scarce wafted from his native shore, and perilled upon the dark blue sea," wrote Nell, "than he found himself amid the roar of cannon, the smoke of blood, the dying and the dead."[12] This purplish passage referred to the bloody engagement of Decatur's *Royal Louis* with the British ship *Lawrence*, in which Forten was the only survivor at his gun station. But Forten's colors showed even truer on the next voyage, when the British captured his ship after a battle at sea. The British captain's son befriended Forten, who was offered free passage to England and the patronage of the captain's family. "NO, NO!" replied Forten, "I am here a prisoner for the liberties of my country; I never, NEVER, shall prove a traitor to her interests."[13] His offer spurned, the British captain consigned

[12]William C. Nell, *Colored Patriots of the American Revolution* (repub. New York: Arno Press, 1968), p. 167.
[13]*Ibid.*, p. 170.

Forten to the *Old Jersey*, the rotting deathtrap prison ship anchored in New York, where thousands of Americans died. Released seven months later as the war was drawing to a close, the 16-year-old Forten made his way shoeless from New York to Philadelphia. At the time, however, his exploits were notable primarily for their atypicality, for few American blacks had reason to be infected by patriotic fever.

EXODUS OF PRO-BRITISH SLAVES

For thousands of American slaves who fought for "life, liberty, and the pursuit of happiness" on the British side, the end of the war in 1783 ushered in a new perilous chapter. There could be no staying in the land of the victorious American revolutionaries, for the new United States was still slave country from North to South, and the blacks who had fought with the British were particularly hated and subject to re-enslavement. But where would England send the American black loyalists? The West Indian sugar islands were built on slave labor and had no place for a large number of free blacks. England itself wished no influx of ex-slaves because London and other major cities already felt themselves burdened by growing numbers of impoverished blacks demanding public support. The answer to the problem was Nova Scotia, the easternmost part of the Canadian wilderness that England had acquired at the end of the Seven Years War. Here, amidst the sparsely scattered old French settlers, the British could relocate the American blacks who had been their military supporters.

Thomas Peters came to symbolize the exodus of the pro-British American blacks in 1783. Kidnapped from the Yoruba tribe in what is now Nigeria and brought to North America by a French slave trader, Peters had been purchased in Louisiana about 1760. He resisted enslavement so fiercely that his master sold him into the English colonies. By 1770, Peters belonged to an immigrant Scots planter on North Carolina's Cape Fear River. Here he toiled while the storm brewed between England and the colonies.

Peters' plans for his own declaration of independence may have ripened as a result of the rhetoric of liberty he heard around his master's house, for William Campbell had become a leading member of the Sons of Liberty in Wilmington, North Carolina. When 20 British ships entered the Cape Fear River in March 1776 and disembarked royal troops, Peters seized the moment. Redefining himself as a man, instead of William Campbell's property, Peters escaped. After fighting with the British-officered Black Pioneers, he was evacuated from New York City by the British, with several thousand others, to disembark in Nova Scotia. The whims of international war and politics had destined him to pursue the struggle for survival and the quest for freedom in this unlikely corner of the earth.

The reception by the white Nova Scotians, including several thousand disbanded British soldier-settlers looking for a new lease on life, was decidedly frigid. White Nova Scotians were no more willing than the Americans had been to accept free blacks as fellow citizens and equals. Attacks on free black citizens convinced Peters and other black leaders after six years of travail in Nova Scotia that they must pursue their dream of freedom and equality elsewhere. Carrying a petition from several hundred black families, Peters made his way to London in 1790. There he was able to work out details of a plan to transport the Nova Scotian blacks to the west coast of Africa, where English abolitionists were planning a refuge for England's poor free blacks.

This extraordinary mission to England—undertaken by an uneducated ex-slave who dared to proceed to the seat of British government without any knowledge whether he would find friends or supporters there—proved a turning point in black history. Peters returned to Nova Scotia in the fall of 1791 with a promise that a fleet of ships would arrive the next spring to carry the ransomed sons and daughters of Africa back to their homelands. Peters traveled on foot from village to village, spreading the word that the Sierra Leone Company had been chartered to launch a new society of those wishing to return to Africa from scattered parts of the British empire. On January 15, 1792, under sunny skies and fair wind, a fleet of British ships stood out from Halifax harbor, laden with several thousand Africans who fervently desired to "kiss their dear Malagueta," the Malagueta pepper or "grains of paradise" which grew prolifically in the region for which they were heading. After a difficult voyage, Thomas Peters, according to legend, led his shipmates ashore in Sierra Leone singing "The day of jubilee is come, return ye ransomed sinners home."[14] In less than four months he died of fever and was buried in Freetown, the aptly named capital of the new African nation. Although the British compatriots led by Peters were only a fragment of the black Americans of the Revolutionary era, they were the advance guard of the emigrationists who sporadically in the first half of the century would give up hope for freedom and equality in the United States and return to Africa in one small wave after another.

THE WAR COMES TO AN END

At the end of the Revolutionary War, a small percentage of black Americans had gained their freedom from conscience-stricken masters or had escaped from bondage. Some superannuated slaves had masters who chose to free

---

[14]Quoted in Gary B. Nash, "Thomas Peters: Millwright and Deliverer, " in David G. Sweet and Gary B. Nash (eds.), *Struggle and Survival in Colonial America* (Berkeley and Los Angeles: University of California Press, 1981), p. 83.

them rather than support them in their unproductive, declining years. Most who had been manumitted were in the North or in the Chesapeake region of the upper South. In the North, they could look to certain states for hope that the end of slavery might soon come. Pennsylvania passed a gradual abolition law in 1780; in Massachusetts, slavery was abolished by judicial decision in 1783; in Vermont, the constitution of 1777 declared slavery illegal. All states except South Carolina and Georgia halted the importation of slaves. Yet in New York and New Jersey, where thousands of slaves were still trapped in slavery at the end of the war, gradual abolition laws would not be passed for another generation.

Most of the Revolutionary generation, even in the North, drank very cautiously from the wells of republicanism while keeping track of their economic interests. By the end of the war in 1783, it was becoming clear to vast numbers of black Americans that much of the early Revolutionary rhetoric about natural rights had been exhausted. Reform-minded white Americans confronted two main problems. The first was economic: How would slave owners be compensated? The second was social: How would freed slaves fit into the social fabric of the new nation? Solutions to these two thorny problems hinged, in turn, first on a willingness to make economic sacrifices, and second on an ability to envision a biracial republican society. Northerners as well as southerners lost the abolitionist fire and would never rekindle it in their own generation. By the time they were in their graves the best opportunity for abolishing slavery had been lost.

For some half-million black Americans who saw the flame of freedom flickering out at the end of the war, the road ahead was confused and discouraging. Slavery was ebbing in the North, but it was surging in the South—the result of a rising birthrate that made further importation of African slaves almost unnecessary. Moreover, those who remained enslaved had to struggle ahead after suffering the exodus of many of the most physically vigorous, psychologically aggressive, and politically able. Emerging from the war, the African-American population included a disproportionate number of older slaves, women with small children, and those physically broken or emotionally paralyzed by the slave experience. Gradually the slave population regained gender balance. By 1790, nearly 660,000 slaves faced a bleak future with only a southern free black population of 32,000 offering some hope.

LEADERS OF THE FREE BLACKS

Yet in spite of the heavy losses of black males in the prime of life, vigorous and visionary free black communities began to form throughout the North. The largest were in the maritime towns because that was where work and companionship were most available. But hardly any sizable town between Maine and Maryland failed to develop a subcommunity of free blacks, each with men and women who emerged as leaders. By looking at several of these leaders we can see some of the pathways that led from the denial of autonomy under slavery to creative, though often obstructed, roles under freedom.

Jupiter Hammon of Long Island exemplifies the cautious, tentative yearning for freedom among slaves who could not make a clean break from their masters—and from the detested institution of slavery. Born in 1711 into the possession of the prominent Lloyd family of merchants and manorial landlords, Hammon served as a valued house servant. Early converted to Christianity, Hammon wrote poetry filled with ecstatic yearnings for salvation in the afterlife. When the Lloyds fled Long Island after the British occupied New York City in 1776, Hammon, already 65 years old, willingly stayed at their side. He continued to preach the gospel of the redeeming salvation that would come to those, black and white alike, who accepted Christ. "If we are slaves it is by the permission of God; if we are free it must be by the power of the most high God. . ." .[15]

Even in this quiescent house servant, sparks of the freedom fighter smoldered. His *A Winter Piece* in 1782 urged the moral reformation of African-Americans and exhorted them to retain their African identity while remaining within the white-dominated young American nation. After the war, Hammon adopted a gradualist approach to the abolition of slavery. In his last written piece, *An Address to the Negroes in the State of New York*, published as the Constitutional Convention was gathering in Pennsylvania, Hammon "hoped that God would open their eyes [i.e., those of white Americans], when they were so much engaged for liberty, to think of the state of the poor blacks, and pity them."[16] Hammon had imbibed much of the conservative message in Christianity that urged the dispossessed to look for release in the afterlife; but even this black minister had edged his way toward using his literary gifts for the cause of black independence.

In the new nation, the human material out of which postwar black society would have to be constructed included thousands who were less cautious than Hammon. Yet some of them had played their hands carefully during the war because they had already secured a small stake in American society. Such a man was Prince Hall of Boston. The slave of a Boston merchant and worshiper at School Street Church shepherded by the New Light revivalist Andrew Crosswell, Hall was about 40 when the war broke out. He received his freedom in 1770 and very quickly played a role in the five

---

[15]Quoted in Phillip M. Richards, "Nationalist Themes in the Preaching of Jupiter Hammon," *Early American Literature*, 25 (1990): 123–38.
[16]Quoted in Gary B. Nash, *Race and Revolution* (Madison, Wisc.: Madison House, 1990), p. 63.

petitions that Boston's blacks placed before the legislature just before the war. Several of these remonstrances against slavery came from a group of 14 black Masons, Hall among them, who had joined a Masonic lodge formed by one of the British regiments that was occupying the Massachusetts capital. "We expect great things from men who have made such a noble stand against the designs of their *fellow-men* to enslave them," read one petition. Another petition declared that "we have in common with all other men a natural right to our freedoms . . . as we are a freeborn people and have never forfeited this blessing by any compact or agreement whatever."[17]

Hall might have joined the British forces before they retreated from Boston in March 1776. But instead, he cast his lot with the land of his birth. After the war, the fires that burned in Hall never subsided. But Boston's small black community of several hundred had much to suffer. While a judicial decree abolished slavery in 1783, black freedmen and freedwomen soon learned that freedom came only by degrees. Black Bostonians found only ill-paid work and deep prejudice against them. In 1786, when Shays's Rebellion swept Massachusetts, Hall tried to offset white hostility by offering what he called the Commonwealth's "meanest members in this time of trouble and confusion" to fight against the agrarian insurgents.[18]

Spurned by the governor and discouraged at their plight, Hall led Boston's free black community in an entirely different direction. Hardly six weeks after offering to march against the Shaysites, Hall petitioned the legislature on behalf of the city's African-Americans to support a plan for returning to Africa. Believing that they would never escape the racism that hobbled them, they wished "earnestly . . . to return to Africa, our native country . . . where we shall live among our equals and be more comfortable and happy, than we can be in our present situation."[19] This was probably the first colonization impulse—an early form of black nationalism—to emerge in the new American republic, an indication that the republic was seen by black citizens as a flawed, racially divided society.

When Hall's colonization plan failed, he continued to organize, protesting the exclusion of black children from tax-supported free schools, protesting against the kidnapping of free blacks into slavery, and calling for the end of the slave trade. Death silenced his voice in June 1807, just six months before the slave trade legally ended.

We can see a different postwar strategy at work in the grappling for identity and the future of black Americans of another African-American,

---

[17]Quoted in Sidney Kaplan, *The Black Presence in the Era of the American Revolution, 1770–1800* (Greenwich, Conn.: New York Graphic Society, 1973), p. 12.
[18]*Ibid.*, p. 184.
[19]*Ibid.*, p. 186.

Richard Allen. Allen, 24 years younger than Prince Hall, had grown up as a slave to the family of Benjamin Chew, a wealthy, conservative lawyer and proprietary officeholder in Pennsylvania. Chew sold Allen's family to a Delaware farmer in the early 1770s, and it was here in about 1777 that Allen experienced a religious conversion at the hands of itinerant Methodists. Allen's master also fell to the power of the Methodist message, and, nudged along by economic necessity, became enough convinced of the sin of slaveholding to allow Allen and his brother to purchase their freedom. In 1780, with the war still raging, Allen, age 20, began a six-year religious sojourn, interspersing work as a sawyer, wagon driver, and shoemaker. Stints of itinerant preaching carried him by foot over hundreds of miles to black and white audiences in dozens of villages, crossroads, and farms. In the mid-1780s, Allen received the call to preach in Philadelphia to a small group of free blacks who were worshipping at St. George's Methodist Church, a rude, dirt-floored building in the German part of the city.

Allen soon increased the black Methodist flock with his oratory skills and steady demeanor. He joined another recently released slave, Absalom Jones, in launching the Free African Society of Philadelphia, the first black mutual aid association in the new nation. This led to a desire for an independent black church. Allen's fervent Methodism brought him into conflict with other emerging black leaders, who wished for a nondenominational or "union" church. Thus, within a few years, two black churches took form. In both cases the guiding idea was that black Americans emerging from slavery required independent black churches because, as the Philadelphia black leaders phrased it, "men are more influenced by their moral equals than by their superiors" and "are more easily governed by persons chosen by themselves for that purpose than by persons who are placed over them by accidental circumstances."[20] In this quietly radical message, the seed of black autonomy was planted in the capital city of American abolitionism.

The autonomous black churches founded in Philadelphia only a decade after the war ended were critically important in furthering the social and psychological rehabilitation of recently freed slaves. Both as places of refuge and citadels of strength, the emerging independent black churches gave free blacks, and slaves within reach of their influence, a sense of peoplehood within a white republic that was increasingly hostile to the free black presence. The "coming out" from white churches, as it was expressed, involved a painful and sometimes dangerous process of rebirthing. The desire "to worship God under our own vine and fig tree," as Allen put it, was in essence a desire to stand apart from white society, avoiding both the

[20]"Address of the Representatives of the African Church [of Philadelphia]," quoted in Gary B. Nash, *Forging Freedom: The Formation of Philadelphia's Free Black Community, 1720–1840* (Cambridge, Mass.: Harvard University Press, 1988), p. 113.

paternalistic benevolence of its racially liberal members and the animosity of its racially intolerant members.[21]

It was this distancing from whites that allowed former slaves to strike out on independent courses in other areas of concern. From Allen's church, Mother Bethel, flowed petitions and sermons against slavery and the slave trade, plans for black schools and mutual aid societies, protests against race discrimination in the city of brotherly love, and, on occasion, emigrationist schemes.

Hammon, Hall, and Allen represent the different forms taken by the quest for place and self-definition as African-Americans emerged from the Revolution. Between the 1780s and the 1820s, during the life-span of the Revolutionary generation, black Americans by the thousands wrestled to find an identity, trying to reconcile their consciousness of being African with that of being American. For the most part, they had to solve this problem by living a double existence, maintaining a dialectical relationship between the two parts of their identity. This is what W.E.B. DuBois called "two unreconciled strivings; two warring ideals in one dark body, whose dogged strength alone keeps it from being torn asunder."[22]

THE RED REVOLUTION

For some 200,000 Native Americans living between the Atlantic Ocean and the Mississippi River, the American Revolution was also a time to "try men's souls." Thayendanegea, or Joseph Brant, stands as an illuminating example. Thayendanegea was born about the same time as Thomas Peters but in an Iroquois village on the other side of the world. At age 13, Thayendanegea served the Anglo-American cause in the Seven Years War by fighting with William Johnson against the French at Crown Point in 1755. Eight years later he aided the colonists again by battling against Pontiac's Indian insurgents, who tried to expel the British soldiers and their encroaching American cousins from the Ohio country.

As he matured in the 1760s, Thayendanegea grew to understand that despite the trading alliance the Iroquois had maintained with the northern colonies for generations and despite the close ties that the Mohawks (the easternmost of the six Iroquois nations) maintained with William Johnson, his people were now seriously threatened by the rapidly growing white

[21] *The Life Experience and Gospel Labors of the Rt. Rev. Richard Allen, to Which is Annexed the Rise and Progress of the African Methodist Episcopal Church in the United States of America* (Nashville: Abingdon Press, 1983), p. 26.

[22] W. E. Burghart DuBois, *The Souls of Black Folk* (New York: New American Library, 1970), p. 3.

population. Barely 20,000 white colonists inhabited New York in 1700, but by 1740 their number had increased to 65,000 and by 1770 to 160,000. Many times in the twilight of the colonial period, the Mohawks had been swindled out of land by rapacious New York land speculators and frontiersmen. So as the war clouds gathered in 1775, Thayendanegea, 33 years old, took ship to London to see what the English King would offer the Iroquois for their support in a war that, while still not formally declared, had been in the shooting stage since early in the year. Like his grandfather, Chief Hendrick, who had been among the Iroquois chiefs who traveled to London to consult with Queen Anne 65 years before, Thayendanegea was greeted as royalty in England. He was feted by the King, written about in the *London Universal Magazine,* and had his portrait painted. But his mission was to determine how life, liberty, and the protection of property might best be preserved by his people. His decision, made before leaving London, augured the reckoning of a vast majority of Indian tribes in the next few years—that only by fighting against the independence-seeking Americans could Indian tribes

Thayendanegea, known to the English as Joseph Brant, sat for his portrait on both sides of the Atlantic. This portrait was painted by George Romney, one of London's best known portrait painters. It may have been painted when Brant was in London in 1775, parleying with King George III and his ministers about Iroquois allegiance to England in the war brewing in the colonies. *(William Leete Stone,* Life of Joseph Brant-Thayendanegea. *Published by A. V. Blacke, New York, 1838)*

themselves remain independent. He returned to New York a few weeks after the Declaration of Independence had been signed at Philadelphia, served with the British General, George Howe, at Long Island in the first major defeat of Washington's army, and then in November 1776 began a long trek through the lands of the Iroquois and their confederates in the Ohio country to spread the message, as he wrote, that "their own Country Liberty" were "in danger from the Rebels."[23] Thayendanegea's diplomatic mission was crucial in bringing most of the Iroquois into the war on the British side in the summer of 1777.

During the war Thayendanegea seemed to be everywhere—at Oriskany in August 1777 when the British and their Indian allies, in one of the bloodiest battles of the Revolution, defeated the Americans who were trying to reach the besieged Fort Stanwix, which controlled access to the western Mohawk Valley and the Great Lakes; at Cherry Valley in the summer of 1778 when the Iroquois drove thousands of American farmers from their fields in southern New York and northern Pennsylvania; and a dozen battles in the campaign of 1779 when the American general, John Sullivan, invaded the Iroquois country, burning towns, scorching the earth, and pursuing his blunt motto: "civilization or death to all American savages." For the entire war, Thayendanegea played a leading role in virtually eliminating the New York and Pennsylvania backcountry (a major grain and cattle-growing area on which the Continental army had depended for supplies) from contributing much to the war effort. "A thousand Iroquois and five hundred Tory rangers," writes one historian, "were able to lay in waste nearly 50,000 square miles of colonial territory."[24]

Though never militarily defeated during the war, the Iroquois lost about one-third of their people and were abandoned by their British allies at the peace talks in Paris. When peace came in 1783, they were left to cope with an aggressive, combat-experienced, and land-hungry American people. Confronting insurmountable odds and thunderstruck that British diplomats sold them out to their American enemies, the Iroquois signed dictated treaties that dispossessed them of most of their land and consigned them to reservations that within a generation became "slums in the wilderness." Thayendanegea spent the last twenty years of his life trying to lead the Iroquois in adjusting to the harsh new realities by which a proud and independent people found that the pursuit of happiness by white Americans required red Americans to surrender life, liberty, and property.

[23]Barbara Graymont, *The Iroquois in the American Revolution* (Syracuse, N.Y.: Syracuse University Press, 1972), p. 109.
[24]Anthony F .C. Wallace, *The Death and Rebirth of the Seneca* (New York: Alfred A. Knopf, 1972), p. 146.

The story of Thayendanegea and the Iroquois encapsulates important facets of the Indians' American Revolution. At the heart of this red struggle were the twin goals of political independence and territorial defense. Black Americans, who had neither liberty nor land, fought for the former in order someday to gain the latter. Red Americans, who had both, struggled to preserve both. Like most black Americans, most Indian tribes concluded that their revolutionary goals could best be achieved through fighting *against* the side that proclaimed the equality of all men and with the side that the Americans accused of trampling on their natural, irreducible rights. The logic of nearly two hundred years of abrasive contact with colonizing Europeans compelled the choice, for it was the settler-subjects of the English king who most threatened Indian autonomy, just as it was the royal power that, before the Revolution, had attempted to protect Indian land from white encroachment by means of the Proclamation Line of 1763 and the regulation of trade. American Indians fought an anticolonial war against those attempting to slip their colonial yoke.

In pursuing their revolutionary goals, Indian tribes shared with the American enemy the problem of how to overcome a long tradition of local identity and intertribal factionalism—how, in other words, to forge a confederated resistance movement. Just as the white "tribes" of Connecticut and New York had to put aside localist attachments and long-standing disagreements, just as Virginians and North Carolinians had to bury animosities that went back several generations, just as northern and southern colonies had to compose their differences, so the Iroquois, Shawnee, Cherokee, Delaware, Creek, Miami, and other tribes searched for ways to forge a pan-Indian movement out of generations of intertribal conflict. For the white revolutionists, as John Adams said, the issue was to make thirteen clocks strike as one. For the red revolutionists east of the Mississippi, the problem was identical. In both societies new leaders emerged in the process of wrestling with this central question, and usually they were men whose military abilities or political persuasiveness gained them attention, suggesting that the fate of their people lay in their hands. Our history books rarely record the names of Red Jacket or Cornplanter of the Seneca, Attakullakulla and his son Dragging Canoe of the Cherokees, Red Shoes of the Creek, White Eyes of the Delaware, or Little Turtle of the Miami. But they were as much the dominant new figures of the revolutionary era in Indian society as were Washington, Hamilton, Nathanael Greene, Richard Henry Lee, and John Paul Jones in white society. Moreover, they were well known to the revolutionary leaders, for Indian tribes of the interior were formidable adversaries who could never be ignored.

In the interior of eastern North America, almost all Indian nations followed the Iroquois lead in siding with the British. The Shawnee of the

Ohio country and the Cherokee of the upper South allied to attack the encroaching Virginians even before the Continental Congress declared independence. "From being a great nation," the Shawnee sorrowfully told the Cherokee in May 1776, "[we are now] reduced to a handful." Once they had "possessed lands almost to the seashore," but "red people who were once masters of the whole country [now] hardly possessed ground enough to stand on." Knowing that the white settlers intended to destroy them, the Shawnee argued that it was "better to die like men than to dwindle away by inches."[25]

Two months later, the Cherokee, led by Dragging Canoe, a young militant Cherokee chief from the Overhill (or western) Cherokee villages, fell upon white settlements on the frontier of Virginia, the Carolinas, and Georgia. The southern frontiersmen under attack had settled west of the Proclamation Line in defiance of royal decree on lands ceded by older or impoverished Cherokee chiefs who made separate cessions without the consent of the Cherokee nation. Now the frontiersmen felt the wrath of young Cherokee warriors sickened by the loss of prime hunting grounds. However, failing to obtain support from the powerful Creek nation to their south and far from British trade sources, the Cherokee found themselves short of ammunition and other supplies. This left them vulnerable to southern militia eager to "carry fire and sword into the very bowels of their country," to extirpate the Cherokee and drive them, as Jefferson recommended, beyond the Mississippi River.[26] In the summer and fall of 1776, four expeditions of southern militiamen, not yet engaged in the fight against the British, punished Cherokee towns severely.

During the winter of 1780–81, American militias once more ravaged Cherokee towns. The Cherokee and Shawnee raided sporadically throughout the war, but they never mounted a sustained assault on the Americans. The war deeply divided the Cherokees with Dragging Canoe leading the young Cherokees south and west to establish new towns along the Chickamauga Creek where they remained militantly anti-American through the 1780s. By the time the white revolutionaries were ratifying their new constitution in 1788, the Cherokees had lost three-quarters of their land and seen half their towns destroyed.

In the Ohio country, the heroics of the Indian-hating George Rogers Clark turned the tide against the Native American allies of the British. In early 1778, Clark led a ragtag body of Kentuckians through icy rivers and

[25]Quoted in Gregory Evans Dowd, *A Spirited Resistance: The North American Indian Struggle for Unity, 1745–1815* (Baltimore: Johns Hopkins University Press, 1992), p. 47.

[26]Quoted in Colin G. Calloway, *The American Revolution in Indian Country: Crisis and Diversity in Native American Communities* (New York: Cambridge University Press, 1995), p. 197.

across 180 miles of frozen terrain to attack an English outpost at Vin-
cennes, in present-day Indiana. Though outnumbered four to one by 500
British regulars and their Indian allies, Clark fooled the fort's defenders
into believing that his force was much larger. Convinced that he faced disaster, the British commander surrendered without a shot. This marked
the beginning of a momentous collapse of pan-Indian efforts, aided by the
British, to drive the white frontiersmen out of their ancient Kentucky,
Ohio, and Indiana homelands. For the Shawnee people, who had captured
Daniel Boone in the winter of 1777–78 and laid siege to the frontier town
of Boonesborough that threatened Shawnee territory between Kentucky
and Virginia, the war in the West brought terrible destruction. Some
Shawnee villages tried to remain neutral, and a few pledged allegiance to
the Americans; but most villages gravitated toward the British. George
Rogers Clark's invasion of Shawnee country in the summer of 1780 began
an annual cycle of search and destroy missions to burn Shawnee crops
and villages, deeply disrupting the Indian cycles of subsistence farming and
hunting. Supplied by the British from their Detroit fort, the Shawnee, like
the Iroquois, were shocked when the British sued for peace in 1783 and
abandoned their Shawnee allies to the victorious Americans. At an exchange of prisoners in July 1783, a gloating American officer taunted the
Shawnee: "Your fathers the English have made Peace with us for themselves, but forgot you their Children, who Fought with them, and neglected
you like Bastards."[27]

Some Indian tribes, mostly small ones surrounded by white colonists
and greatly reduced in population by disease and earlier wars, fought with
the Americans. The Passamaquoddy and Penobscot in Maine, who had sustained bitter losses in the Seven Years War in fighting with New Hampshire
rangers, now fought alongside these rangers against the British. The Stockbridge in Massachusetts, an amalgam of remnant Indians from the Hudson River Valley in western Massachusetts who had fought alongside
Robert Rogers' Rangers in the Seven Years War, served with Washington's
troops at Boston in 1775 and later in New York, New Jersey, and Canada.
The Oneida in New York, and the Tuscarora and Catawba in North Carolina all signed allegiance to the Americans and contributed scouts
and warriors to the revolutionary cause. But the Indians who pledged support, usually because they were dependent on American trade and surrounded by a sea of white settlers, reaped little benefit from their efforts.
Although grateful state governments compensated a number of Indian
warriors after the war, this did little to protect the tribes from the land-
hungry Americans, well equipped and battle toughened, in the postwar
rush for more land.

[27]Quoted in *ibid.*, p. 174.

In the end, the Indians were disastrous losers in the war of the American Revolution. This was partly because they were less successful than the thirteen white tribes in overcoming intratribal and intertribal factionalism; partly because the supplies of European trade goods on which they depended—especially guns, powder, and shot—were seriously disrupted during the war; and partly because they were abandoned to the Americans by their British allies at war's end. Facing a white society in 1783 that was heavily armed and obsessed with the vision of western lands, nations such as the Iroquois and Cherokee were forced to cede most of their land. The American victory over the British was "the greatest blow that could have been dealt us," heard the Spanish governor of St. Louis from the Indian chiefs in 1784.[28] The prewar white population buildup, which had caused worsening economic conditions in many older communities along the coastal plain, was relieved as thousands of settlers spilled across the mountains after 1783, frequently in violation of treaties contracted by their own elected governments. Aiding these frontiersmen, many of them war veterans, were state and national governments that understood that the western lands, once the native inhabitants had been driven away, were the new nation's most valuable resource. The salve of western lands would provide the revenue both to liquidate the huge war debt and to underwrite the expenses of a nation of tax-shy people.

Such a policy required the newly independent American republic to sacrifice the sanctity of its own laws and treaty obligations and to abandon the revolutionary ideal of just and equitable relations among men. Some white leaders, such as George Morgan, were troubled by this. Morgan, a former Indian trader and agent for the Continental Congress, wrote in 1793:

> At what time do a People violate the Law of Nations, as the U[nited] S[tates] have done, with regard to the N[orth]W[estern] Indians? Only when they think they can do it with Impunity. Justice between Nations is founded on reciprocal Fear. Rome whilst weak was equitable; become more strong than her Neighbors, she ceased to be just. The ambitious & powerful are always unjust. To them the Laws of Nations are mere Chimeras.[29]

But most Americans were no more willing to apply the principles emblazoned on the revolutionary banners to relations with the Indian inhabitants

---

[28]Quoted in *ibid.*, p. xv.
[29]Quoted in Randolph C. Downes, *Council Fires on the Upper Ohio: A Narrative of Indian Affairs in the Upper Ohio Valley Until 1795* (Pittsburgh, Pa.: University of Pittsburgh Press, 1940. Reprint 1969), p. 249.

of the trans-Allegheny region than they were to fulfill the revolutionary ideal of abolishing slavery. Indian land, like black slave labor, was one of the new republic's preeminently important resources. The white Americans' revolution was fought in the East for release from the British Empire but was also fought in the West to create an empire of their own.

The pro-British stance of the Native Americans cannot be counted as a failure of judgment on their part. Had they sided with the Americans they would have fared no better, as the dismal postwar experience of several pro-American tribes, such as the Tuscaroras and Oneidas, demonstrates.

More to the point, the interior Indian nations, by the eve of the Revolution, had witnessed a flood of American settlers, perhaps as many as 50,000, who by clandestine purchase and defiance of royal authority had swept across the Appalachians. General Gage could not control them. If they were "too Numerous, too Lawless and Licentious to be restrained," as he explained, how could the Shawnee, Cherokee, Miami, or Iroquois further their struggle to retain their lands and independence by siding with the American revolutionaries?[30] The wartime pro-British attempts at intertribal confederation, though they could not prevent an American victory, played a large role in mounting the next great Indian resistance movement, from about 1783 to 1815, when white Americans, having won a war of national liberation, now embarked on a war of national expansion. Thayendanegea's wartime exertions and his efforts, after another trip to London in 1785, to foster intertribal cooperation, led to fierce Indian resistance in the Old Northwest. Similarly, in the Old Southwest, Hoboi-Hili Miko (known by whites as Alexander McGillivray), a Creek headman whose Scots-Irish father had married a Creek woman, galvanized Creek resistance to land-hungry South Carolinians and Georgians. "Our lands are our life and breath," he wrote; "if we part with them, we part with our blood. We must fight them."[31] Fearing assassination at the hands of Georgian officials, McGillivray told a friend:

> If I fall by the hand of such [assassins], I shall fall a victim in the noblest of causes—that of falling in maintaining the just rights of my country. I aspire to the honest ambition of meriting the appellation of preserver of my country, equally with those chiefs among you, whom from acting on such principles, you have exalted to the highest pitch of glory; and if, after every peaceable mode of obtaining a redress of

[30]Quoted in Richard White, *The Middle Ground: Indians, Empires, and Republics in the Great Lakes Region* (Cambridge and New York: Cambridge University Press, 1991), p. 340.

[31]McGillivray to James White [Superintendent of Indian Affairs for the United States], April 8, 1791, *American State Papers, Indian Affairs* (Washington, 1832), VII, 18.

grievances having proved fruitless, then having recourse to arms to obtain it, be marks of the savage, and not of the soldier, what savages must the Americans be. . . .[32]

Thayendanegea and McGillivray were the exemplars of pan-Indian resistance. From the work of a host of such war-tempered Indian leaders arose a new generation of resistance leaders—Black Hawk, Tecumseh, and others. The tribes of the Ohio Valley fought desperately in the postwar era to protect their homelands, only to lose against overwhelming odds when state militias and federal armies, whom they had defeated in the late 1780s and early 1790s, returned with larger and larger forces to invade their land. By this time the humanitarian language of the Northwest Ordinance of 1787 had been all but forgotten. "The utmost good faith," promised the Continental Congress in its last significant act, "shall always be observed towards the Indians; their lands and property shall never be taken from them without their consent; and in their property, rights and liberty, they never shall be invaded or disturbed, unless in just and lawful wars authorized by Congress; but laws founded in justice and humanity shall from time to time be made, for preventing wrongs being done to them, and for preserving peace and friendship with them."[33] As the strengthening of state militias and the creation of a national army progressed in the 1790s, Indian societies learned how hollow were the phrases of the Northwest Ordinance. Armed conflict replaced "utmost good faith." The republic's greatest wartime hero, now its first president, captured the national mood when he wrote, "The gradual extension of our settlements will as certainly cause the Savage as the Wolf to retire; both being beasts of prey tho' they differ in shape."[34]

In studying the Revolution, we need to broaden our perspective by recognizing that the conflict—fought by white Americans for life, liberty, and the pursuit of happiness—compelled most nonwhite Americans to take the British side in quest of the same goals. The red and black people were animated by the doctrine of natural rights as surely as were the Minutemen at Concord Bridge or the signers of the Declaration of Independence; and they were as moved by self-interest as were white revolutionaries. Most of them took the other side to gain or preserve these rights and to pursue their own interests, which had been defined by generations of interaction among red, white, and black people in North America. In their struggle against the white revolutionaries, most of them lost at least in the proximate sense. *Their* colonial experience would not be

[32]McGillivray to James White, *American State Papers*, VII, 18.
[33]Quoted in Horsman, "American Indian Policy in the Old Northwest, 1732–1812." *William and Mary Quarterly*, 3d Ser., 18 (1961), 40.
[34]Washington to James Duane, Sept. 7, 1783, quoted in *ibid.*, p. 38.

over when white Americans overthrew their colonial master. What they won, however, was a piece of history, for they kept lit the lamp of liberty and passed on their own revolutionary heritage to their children and their children's children. The founding principles of the American Revolution lived on in the nineteenth-century struggles of Denmark Vesey, Nat Turner, Frederick Douglass, Black Hawk, Tecumseh, Sequoyah, and a host of other black and red leaders.

12

The Mixing of Peoples

While Indians, Africans, Europeans, and Americans worked out their destinies in a complicated setting of tribal and imperial rivalry, economic growth, population change, and social and political transformation, they also interacted with each other at the most intimate and personal levels. This sexual mixing of individuals of different genetic stocks is usually called *miscegenation,* a word invented 135 years ago by Negrophobic journalists to discredit Abraham Lincoln's position on the plight of African-Americans. For many decades racial crossing was mostly the concern of those attempting to prove inherent qualitative differences of various "racial" groups in a society. This pseudoscientific exercise then used these findings to warn against racial mixing. For historians, anthropologists, and sociologists, however, miscegenation is important in another way. By studying racial mingling they document the process of acculturation and assimilation—the mixing of cultural elements and the absorption of one culture into another.

Most thinking on the subject of racial intermingling in North America starts with the arresting notion that Europeans on this continent did not intermix with Africans and Indians with anywhere near the same frequency as in colonial Latin American societies. Nor did Africans and Indians mix to the same degree. Latin America is known as the area of the world where the most extensive blending of the races in human history has taken place.

North America, where Europeans, Indians, and Africans also converged during roughly the same period of time, is noted for the general absence of any such intermixture. The census figures of modern North and South America seem to confirm this belief. They show, for example, that only 20 percent of the Venezuelans are classified as white, that only 11 percent of Panamanians are white, that mulattoes in Brazil make up a much larger portion of the population than in the United States, and so forth. Although the criteria for defining membership in a particular racial group vary greatly from place to place and are never exact, it is not necessary to be precise about the racial composition of any of the New World societies since the principal point is not in dispute—that widely practiced interracial sexual liaisons produced a dramatically larger proportion of mestizos (European-Indian), mulattoes (European-African), and mustees (African-Indian) in the southern half of the New World than in the northern half.

Two explanations are commonly advanced for this. First, before the European colonization of the New World the Spanish and Portuguese had a history of interacting with people of different cultures, particularly with dark-skinned people, whereas the English did not. Through centuries of war and trade with the Berbers, Moors, and other peoples of the Middle East and North Africa, Iberian society had already absorbed new cultural and genetic elements and developed flexible attitudes about the sexual mixing of peoples. The English, by contrast, had remained within their island fortress, sheltered from other cultures and therefore predisposed toward viewing interracial contacts with suspicion and even alarm.

A corollary to this argument is that the permissive attitudes of the Catholic church toward non-Christian people, the Roman system of law (which protected the slave), and the paternalistic attitudes of the Iberian governments combined to make racial intermixture acceptable and therefore common in the New World, where Spain and Portugal were confronting Indians and Africans in large numbers. By contrast, English Protestantism was unusually rigid in admitting "savage" people to the church. English law had nothing to say on the subject of enslavement, leaving colonists free to create the most rigid institutions to contain their bound laborers. And the English government exercised much less authority in its colonies, especially in the matter of the treatment of subordinate non-English groups. Given these differences in prior experience, in institutions and attitudes, and in governmental policy, it was not surprising that the history of interracial mixing should be so different in the colonies of Spain and Portugal and the colonies of England.

Such arguments have lost much of their explanatory force in recent years as historians have analyzed the social and demographic conditions underlying the history of cultural interaction in various parts of the New World. The differences in the degree and nature of interracial mixing in North and South America now seem to have been deeply related to conditions

At least a dozen Mexican painters in the eighteenth century openly acknowledged the mixing of Europeans, Africans, and Native Americans in panels such
as the one shown here. Each panel represents how intermixing produced children with various degrees of Spanish, African, and Indian blood. A new vocabulary, displayed in the captions for each panel, evolved to describe the degrees
of mixing. *(Courtesy Museo del Virreinato, Mexico)*

encountered in the New World rather than attitudes developed in the Old
World. The availability of white women; the ratio of Europeans, Africans,
and Native Americans in a given area; the extent to which Indians could be
pressed into forced labor systems; and the need to employ non-Europeans
in positions of importance—all of these had a role in shaping the pattern
of intercultural mixing. Thus it made sense that in areas where European

women were in short supply, white men overcame the racial prejudices they had brought to the New World to consort with women of another race. Similarly, where Indians or Africans were relatively numerous, intermixture was far more common than where they were relatively scarce. In New England, where Indians had been devastated by epidemics in the early years of European settlement, little red–white mixing occurred. In Mexico, where Spanish men were engulfed by the densely settled Indians, a great deal of mingling occurred.

INDIAN–EUROPEAN CONTACT

Contact between Indians and Europeans preceded all other contacts and influenced what later occurred, so it is best to begin with it. In New England, and later in the mid-Atlantic colonies of New York, New Jersey, Pennsylvania, and Delaware, sexual mixing between Europeans and Indians was extremely limited. Englishmen had immigrated to these regions with their families, or, if they were single men, found enough single women to satisfy their needs for marriage partners. Parity between the sexes was established quickly and continued throughout the colonial period, except following periods of war, when women sometimes outnumbered men by a small margin. Reinforcing this demographic situation was a strong cultural factor. Immigration by family ensured the rerouting of an entire cultural superstructure to which racial mingling was highly threatening, especially given the view, almost universal among whites, that their culture was superior to that of Native Americans and Africans. Cotton Mather, the pillar of early eighteenth-century Puritan society, shrank in horror at the "half Frenchified Indians" and "half Indianized French" who raided pure-blooded New England villages.[1]

In the northern colonies red-white mixing was also limited by the relatively small number of Indians. Epidemics and war rapidly reduced the coastal Indian societies during the initial period of contact, and those remaining were generally inaccessible. Intercultural marriage was a rarity. A number of fur traders operating on the frontier took Indian wives, and almost all of them had frequent sexual contact with Indian women. One notable case of intermarriage in the settled regions involved William Johnson, the Northern Superintendent of Indian Affairs, who took a Mohawk wife. Later knighted for his military exploits, Johnson gained great influence with the Mohawk, who renamed him Warraghiyagey, meaning "man who undertakes great things." This high tribute was conferred in large part because Johnson had deviated so radically from the white norm by dressing in Mohawk garb,

[1]Quoted in Colin Calloway, *New Worlds for All: Indians, Europeans and the Remaking of America* (Baltimore, Md.: Johns Hopkins University Press, 1997), p. 179.

accepting Mohawk customs, and learning their language, as few white men cared to do. "Something in his natural temper," wrote a contemporary, "responds to Indian ways."[2] However, few cared to follow the example of even a high imperial official when it came to matrimony, so long as there were European women to be found. It was said that Johnson's precedent-shattering marriage, noteworthy enough to attract the attention of the London newspapers, led to eighteen other red–white unions, but even so the number is insignificant.

In the Chesapeake colonies a different demographic pattern prevailed in the first few decades. With few exceptions, white women were unavailable in Virginia until about 1620. Yet white men had little recourse to Indian women. Several early eighteenth-century Virginia commentators believed that this was because the early colonizers found Indian women distasteful. William Byrd, no stranger to the pleasures of the flesh with women of different skin colors, claimed the English were imbued with a "false delicacy" in the early years and thus could not bring themselves to sleep with Indian women. Byrd believed that the Chesapeake tribes had been offended by this rejection and could never "perswade themselves that the English were heartily their Friends, so long as they disdained to intermarry with them." Robert Beverley, author of *The History and Present State of Virginia,* took a similar view, regretting that intermarriage had never occurred and convinced that the Indians had been eager for it.[3]

The limited evidence bearing on this question does not support such views, however. A large part of the predominantly male Virginia colony was composed of representatives of the English lower class, including many who had military experience in Ireland, the Spanish Netherlands, and other parts of the world. They were not known for squeamishness, and their later willingness to consort with African women suggests that the real cause of infrequent sexual contact with Indian women is to be found in Indian rather than European desires. The English did not establish themselves as conquerors in the early years, as had the Spanish and Portuguese. Therefore the Chesapeake tribes were under no compulsion to yield up their women. As for Indian women, they had little reason to admire white men, who could hardly keep themselves alive in the early years and who launched attacks on Indian villages once they had gathered strength.

The one case of intermarriage within the white community involved John Rolfe and Pocahontas. While their love for each other was apparently genuine, this was a political marriage. It is sometimes claimed that the King's council, by deliberating whether Rolfe had not committed high treason in

[2]Quoted in *ibid.,* p. 154.
[3]William Byrd, *Histories of the Dividing Line Betwixt Virginia and North Carolina,* ed., William K. Boyd (Raleigh: North Carolina Historical Commission, 1929), p. 3; Robert Beverley, *The History and Present State of Virginia,* ed. Louis B. Wright (Chapel Hill: University of North Carolina Press, 1960), pp. 38–39.

marrying an Indian princess, discouraged any further intermarriage. But the charge under consideration was high treason for marrying the daughter of a quasi-enemy, and Pocahontas and Rolfe were feted in London wherever they went, including the royal court. By the early eighteenth century the Board of Trade was pushing an official policy of intermarriage in the American colonies, indication enough that moral scruples were not offended in England by thoughts of the commingling of red and white blood.

By the end of the second Indian war in 1644 the native population in the tidewater area was only a small fraction of the white population; by the conclusion of Bacon's Rebellion in 1675, when white women were much more available, only a few Indians remained within the areas of white settlement. This puts in perspective Governor Spotswood's claim in 1717 that the "inclinations of our people are not the same with those of [the French] Nation" regarding intermarriage, as evidenced by the fact that not one such marriage was known in Virginia at that time.[4] Racial prejudice no doubt would have limited such partnerships. But neither the need nor the opportunity for Indian–white marriages remained. French "inclinations" in New France were different not so much because of variations in national character as because of different needs. Even along the St. Lawrence, where Frenchmen commonly took Indian wives and mistresses, European women were much preferred. But Indian women remained preferable to no women at all. The same was true in Spanish Florida where "Spanish–Indian marriage began immediately and continued persistently through two centuries of Spanish occupation."[5]

The only English area in which the demographic profile even roughly paralleled that in the Spanish and French North American colonies was the Southeast—the Carolinas and Georgia. In the early years white women were relatively unavailable but Indian women could easily be found. The result was a considerable contact between Englishmen and Indian women, much as in French Canada and the Spanish Southwest. Conspicuously absent from the records are indications of reticence when it came to intercultural sexual liaisons. Unembarrassed sexual relations between the two peoples seem to have been the rule. This was especially true of the fur traders who operated in the interior regions and would not give up the satisfactions of Indian "She-Bed-Fellows," as one eighteenth-century commentator called them. Women were specifically designated by the tribes as "Trading Girls" and were given special haircuts to denote that their role was to satisfy the traders while getting money "by their Natural Parts." Only these women were available to white men, however, for Indian males "are desirous (if

[4]R. A. Brock, ed., *The Official Letters of Alexander Spotswood. . .* , Virginia Historical Society *Collections,* (Richmond: Virginia Historical Society, 1885), 2: 227.

[5]Kathleen Deagan, "Accommodation and Resistance: The Process and Impact of Spanish Colonization in the Southeast," in David H. Thomas, ed., *Columbian Consequences,* vol. 2 (1990), p. 305.

possible) to keep their Wives to themselves, as well as those in other Parts of the World."[6]

While traders consorted with Indian women in the interior, white Carolinians confronted Indian women sold into slavery in the coastal settlements. After the Yamasee War of 1715, the enslavement of Indians in Carolina diminished. But during the first half century of the colony's history, the large number of children of Indian mothers and white fathers in Charleston testified to the extensive European–Indian sexual encounters there. White men outnumbered white women in South Carolina by more than 13 to 9 as late as 1708, and womanless men were not reluctant to avail themselves of Indian women. In Georgia no less a figure than Thomas Bosomworth, chaplain of Oglethorpe's utopian colony, found it respectable to marry a Creek woman in the early years of settlement, and many others followed his example, including John McDonald and Alexander Cameron, Deputy Indian Commissioners to the Cherokees in the late colonial period.

Interracial mixing between Indians and Europeans, then, was limited both by population ratios and by prior attitudes of both Europeans and Native Americans. It is also clear in the laws passed by all the colonies during the colonial period that attitudes differed toward black-skinned Africans and tawny-skinned Indians. Laws proscribing interracial marriage were aimed almost exclusively at white–black mating. Only North Carolina and Virginia forbade marriage between Indians and whites (though Massachusetts debated such a law), and no colonies applied special penalties for red–white fornication as they often did for cases involving blacks and whites. Many transplanted Europeans, applying their own standards of beauty, described Indian women as beautiful, whereas no such descriptions can be found of African women. Indian women, wrote Robert Beverley in 1705, were "generally Beautiful, possessing uncommon delicacy of shape and Features, and wanting no Charm but that of a fair complexion."[7]

The general lack of red–white sexual intermingling forecast the overall failure of the two cultures to merge, though the porous boundaries between the two peoples led to incessant interaction. The amalgamation of Indians and whites never proceeded very far in eighteenth-century North America because Indians were seldom eager to trade their culture for one they found inferior, and because the colonists found the Indians useful only as trappers of furs, consumers of European trade goods, and military allies. All these functions were best performed outside the white communities. This is a striking contrast to the Spanish colonies in the Americas where the lack of white women and the subjugation of Indian laborers brought the two peoples into intimate contact and produced a large mestizo population.

---

[6]John Lawson, *A New Voyage to Carolina,* ed., Hugh Lefler (Chapel Hill: University of North Carolina Press, 1967), pp. 189–90.
[7]Beverley, *History and Present State of Virginia,* ed. Wright, p. 159.

Even the most conservative estimates show that the mestizo population reached 25 percent of the whole in early nineteenth-century Spanish America. Many of these individuals rose to positions of artisan, foreman on the *encomiendas,* militiaman, and even collector of tithes and taxes. But in colonial America the half-Indian, half-white person, usually the product of a liaison between a white fur trader and an Indian woman, remained in almost all cases within Indian society. A considerable number of the male offspring became fur traders themselves or intermediaries between English and Indian society. Others, such as Joseph Brant of the Mohawks and Alexander McGillivray of the Creeks, became noted leaders of Indian resistance in the second half of the eighteenth century. Although historians have not yet systematically studied the American mestizo, who revealingly was called by the derogatory term "half-breed," there are indications that these persons, who white colonists recognized only as Indians, were the most alienated of all people from white society. One Virginian gave explicit expression to this in 1757 when he wrote that traders who consorted with Indian "squaws" left their offspring "like bulls or bears to be provided for at random by their mothers. . . . As might be expected," he pointed out, "some of these bastards have been the leading men or war captains that have done us so much mischief."[8]

The one case in which transculturation between Indians and Europeans did occur involved the Indianization of whites rather than the Europeanization of Indians. Throughout the colonial period, much to the horror of the leaders of white society, small numbers of colonists ran away to Indian settlements, or, when they were captured in war and had lived with a tribe for a few years, often refused to return to white society. This "reversion to savagery," as those who insisted on the superiority of white culture regarded it, has attracted the attention of American novelists since the late eighteenth century. For white colonists the prospect of their own people preferring the Indian way of life was a disturbing anomaly. "None can imagine what it is to be captivated, and enslaved to such atheistical, proud, wild, cruel, barbarous, brutish (in one word) diabolical creatures as these, the worst of the heathen," wrote a seventeenth-century Puritan.[9]

In spite of such fantasy characterizations, the colonizers were obliged to live with the notion that some of their own kind found life in Indian communities preferable to life in Anglo-American culture. To make matters worse, virtually no Indians took the reverse route, choosing to remain in white society after exposure to it. "By what power does it come to pass," asked Crèvecoeur, the famous Frenchman who lived in America for more

[8]Quoted in James Hugo Johnston, *Race Relations in Virginia and Miscegenation in the South, 1776–1860* (Amherst: University of Massachusetts Press, 1970), p. 169.
[9]Quoted in Roy Harvey Pearce, "The 'Ruines of Mankind': The Indian and the Puritan Mind," *Journal of the History of Ideas,* 13 (1952): 205.

than a decade in the late colonial period, in his celebrated *Letters from an American Farmer,*

> that children who have been adopted when young among these people, can never be prevailed on to readopt European manners? Many an anxious parent I have seen after the last war [Seven Years War], who at the return of peace, went to the Indian villages where they knew their children had been carried in captivity; when to their inexpressible sorrow, they found them so perfectly Indianised, that many knew them no longer, and those whose more advanced ages permitted them to recollect their fathers and mothers, absolutely refused to follow them, and ran to their adopted parents for protection against the effusions of love their unhappy real parents lavished on them! . . . There must be in their social bond something singularly captivating, and far superior to anything to be boasted of among us; for thousands of Europeans are Indians, and we have no examples of even one of those Aborigines having from choice become Europeans.[10]

The phenomenon of the "white Indians" is partially explained by the Indian custom of adopting into their communities as full-fledged members any persons captured in war. This practice became more important as disease and intensified warfare depleted the population of many tribes in the century after the Europeans arrived. In many instances a bereaved Indian family adopted a European captive to replace a lost child or other relative. This integration of newcomers into the kinship system and into the community at large, without judgmental comparisons of the superiority of the captor's culture, made it easy for the captured "outsider" to make a rapid personal adjustment. A white child taken into Indian society was treated on equal terms and prepared for any role open to others of his or her age. That a number of whites and Negroes who had fled to Indian communities or had been captured by them became chiefs is the most dramatic evidence of the receptiveness of Indian cultures to "outsiders."

The most talked about and troubling cultural conversion in New England was that of Eunice Williams. In 1704, when she was eight, Eunice and her minister father's family was captured when a Mohawk party allied to the French descended on Deerfield, Massachusetts, and overpowered the entire village. Dozens of the Deerfield captives perished on the punishing march of more than 300 miles through snow to the Mohawk village of Kahnawahe, north of Montreal. Here Eunice spent the rest of her life. Growing up Mohawk, she became Catholic. At sixteen she married a young Mohawk. Repeatedly she refused to return to her family, who were sent back to Massachusetts as part of a prisoner exchange. She forgot English, forgot

---

[10]J. Hector St. John Crèvecoeur, *Letters from an American Farmer* (New York: E. P. Dutton & Co., 1957), pp. 208–09.

Protestantism, and forgot her biological family. In many churches of New England, Puritans prayed for her "redemption" from "captivity." But Eunice had found a faithful and loving husband and had raised two daughters (who would later marry Mohawk men). Margurite Aronsen, Eunice Williams' Mohawk name, thought of a return to her Deerfield home as captivity rather than redemption.

European colonists differed sharply in incorporating the "other" from a different culture. Though a number of Indian children were adopted into white families, the general pattern was to isolate the newcomer socially. "It was not that the Indian could not be raised 'up' to the level of civilization," writes one student of the subject, "but rather the lack of an equivalent desire on the part of whites to welcome and assimilate the Indian, and the absence of any established cultural means that would mediate the transition from one culture to the other in a manner that was psychologically sound."[11] Even Christianized Indians trained in white schools, such as the Mohegan Samson Occum (1723–92), were expected to return to Indian society rather than occupy a place of dignity among whites. White colonists always regarded Native Americans as aliens and rarely allowed them to live within white society except as servants or dependents. Operating from their small communities and surrounded by a culture they regarded not only as inferior but as barbaric, the colonizers "erected a defensive wall of heightened consciousness of superiority" in order to keep out those who seemed so threatening.[12] This inability to develop the mentality or social mechanisms for incorporating Indians into their midst created a powerful block to a merging of two cultures. By contrast, Florida's Spanish governor described how the Indians were "settled amongst our Plantations . . . and are as it were a People interwoven with us."[13]

WHITE–BLACK INTERMIXTURE

White–black intermixture in colonial America is a more complicated phenomenon because whites and blacks were always in close proximity, both where white women were plentiful and where they were scarce. This physical and psychological closeness led to widespread sexual contact, but it rarely involved intermarriage. At first glance, one might imagine that the rarity of racial intermarriage stemmed from a deep-seated white aversion to blackness itself, but if this was the case it would be difficult to explain what countless observers of eighteenth-century society claimed to see—that "the country

---

[11]A. Irving Hallowell, "American Indians, White and Black: The Phenomenon of Transculturation," *Current Anthropology,* 4 (1963): 527.

[12]*Ibid.,* p. 528.

[13]Quoted in Calloway, *New Worlds for All,* p. 185.

swarms with mulatto bastards," as one Virginian crudely put it.[14] Such comments do nothing to define interracial mingling with statistical precision, but eighteenth-century censuses help to clarify the point. In Maryland in 1755 a special census showed that 8 percent of the Negroes in the colony were mulatto. In Rhode Island the census of 1783 revealed that 16.5 percent of the Negroes were of mixed blood. A register of slaves for Chester County, Pennsylvania, in 1780 listed 20 percent of the Negroes as mulattoes.[15] In all three areas white females were almost as numerous as white men, indicating that even when white women were available, white men frequently had sexual relations with black women.

These contacts would probably have been even more extensive if black women had been available in the period when white women were in short supply. Slaves did not begin to enter the English colonies in significant numbers until the end of the seventeenth century, and by that time the number of white women in all but the infant colony of South Carolina nearly equaled the number of white men. In the southern plantations in 1720, the slave population was about 50,000; not more than about 10,000 of these could have been adult black females. At the same time some 70,000 adult white colonists inhabited the southern colonies, of whom almost half were women. This is in stark contrast to the situation in Portuguese Brazil, Spanish Peru, Spanish and French North American colonies, and even the English islands in the West Indies. In all of these zones of contact European women were relatively unavailable for much longer periods of time.

The example of the English Caribbean colonies provides further evidence for the case against prior attitudes determining the nature and degree of racial intermixture. English women were not present in roughly equal numbers with white men until the second century of settlement, so African women were unhesitatingly exploited to fill the gap. Even married white plantation owners "keep a Mulatto or Black Girl in the house or at lodgings for certain purposes," reported one traveler, and a famous eighteenth-century historian of the English sugar islands colorfully pronounced that "He who should presume to shew any displeasure against such a thing as simple fornication, would for his pains be accounted a simple blockhead."[16]

In the mainland colonies, however, interracial sex brought private pleasure but public condemnation. The latter was mainly an eighteenth-century development. Not until 1662, when Virginia passed a law imposing a fine for fornication between white and black partners that was twice the

[14]Quoted in Johnston, *Race Relations in Virginia,* p. 170.
[15]Edward B. Reuter, *The Mulatto in the United States* (rpr. New York: Negro Universities Press, 1969), pp. 112–14; Evarts B. Greene and Virginia D. Harrington, *American Population before the Federal Census of 1790* (New York: Columbia University Press, 1932), pp. 69–70.
[16]Quoted in Winthrop Jordan, *White Over Black: American Attitudes Toward the Negro, 1550–1812* (Chapel Hill: University of North Carolina Press, 1968), p. 140.

usual amount, did an unambiguous law appear on the books that expressed public distaste for racial intermixture. White legislators banned interracial marriage in Virginia in 1691, in Massachusetts in 1705, in Maryland in 1715, and thereafter in Delaware, Pennsylvania, North Carolina, and Georgia.

The key change in the eighteenth century was not a marked increase in miscegenation, reflecting heightened private urges, but a shifting of public attitudes toward racial mixing. "By the turn of the century," writes Winthrop Jordan, "it was clear in many continental colonies that the English settlers felt genuine revulsion for interracial sexual union, at least in principle."[17] The grand jury in Charleston, South Carolina, for example, inveighed against "The Too Common Practice of Criminal Conversation with Negro and other Slave Wenches in this Province" in 1743.[18] Similar comments can be found in other colonies. But with the black population growing rapidly and slavery becoming deeply rooted in colonial society, lawmakers discovered that, while they could not manage biology, they could at least keep pure the bloodlines of the dominant group through laws prohibiting interracial marriage. Under these laws mulattoes could never be legitimate and would always be classified as black.

With slavery touching the lives of most inhabitants, white colonists found it necessary to contain the black population in a tight web of authority and to assert repeatedly their dominance. One way of accomplishing this was to emphasize the heathen or "savage" condition of the slave, which justified slavery on the one hand and made sexual contact legally impermissible on the other. A variety of laws and public statements described the offspring of white–black copulation as "spurious" or "mongrel." Moreover, mulattoes received no higher standing than pureblood blacks and in law were regarded as fully black. This contrasted sharply with the situation of the mulatto in almost every other part of the New World, where three-tiered racial systems had evolved. But sexual relations with black women went on and on. Desire could not be legislated out of the white psyche, and if the laws and public pronouncements did not correspond with private urges, little harm was done so long as laws preserved the domination of whites by disowning children of mixed racial inheritance.

By the early eighteenth century racial attitudes toward Indians and African-Americans began to diverge sharply. This divergence was closely tied to striking differences in the nature and degree of sexual contact that characterized red–white and black–white relationships. White attitudes toward the black man cannot be dissociated from the fact that sexual relations, especially between white men and black women, were frequent and usually coercive throughout the eighteenth century. White men banned interracial marriage as a way of stating with legal finality that the African-American,

---

[17]*Ibid.*, p. 139.
[18]Quoted in *ibid.*, p. 140.

even when free, was not the equal of the white man. But white power was also served by sexually exploiting black women outside of marriage—a method of white domination. Racial intermingling, so long as it involved free white men and slave black women, was a way of intimately and brutally proclaiming the superior rights and strength of white society.

Sexual contact of this character had no parallel in the case of Indian women. When she was accessible, for example to fur traders, she was not in the hapless position of a slave woman, nearly defenseless to resist the advances of a master with power of life and death over her. If an Indian woman chose to submit to a white man, it was usually on mutually agreeable terms. Furthermore, Indian men rarely molested female prisoners, believing that intercourse with a potential clan member was incest. In these differences we can find the source and meaning of a fear that has preoccupied white Americans for more than a century—the fear of the black male lusting after the white woman. This vision of the "black rapist" seems to have emerged during and after the Civil War. It endures in contemporary attitudes and literature. This fear of black men, who are seen rising not in quest of their freedom but in pursuit of white women, seems to stem from feelings of guilt originating in the sexual exploitation of black women and an associated fear of the black avenger, presumably filled with anger and poised to retaliate against those who first enslaved him and then plundered his woman.

This element of sexual fear is only rarely expressed in the literature concerning the Indian. Because little guilt could have been aroused by the occasional and noncoercive contacts with Indian women, white men, when they encountered hostile Indian males, rarely pictured them as sexual avengers. In the eighteenth century the Indian was almost never caricatured as the frenzied rapist, lurking in the bush or stalking white women. Indeed, the Indian was sometimes viewed as a peculiarly asexual creature. This in turn created a confused image in the white mind of a hostile, and yet sexually passive, "savage." His hostility was not doubted; but the hostile Indian was commonly regarded as a man with knife in hand, bent on obtaining the scalp of the white encroacher. It was imagined that hostile black men had focused on a different part of the anatomy in their quest for revenge.

The contrast with the sexual dynamics of Spanish–Indian contact is striking. The Spanish brought enslaved Africans to their New World colonies much earlier than the English and brought them in larger numbers proportionate to their European masters. What is more, with not enough colonists to serve all the middle-range occupational niches in their societies, the Spanish used Africans as craftsmen, supervisors of enslaved Indians, and even as militiamen. This gave many African males a status far above that of field laborer. No doubt, status-seeking Spaniards avoided marriage with Africans, and some colonial officials tried to obtain a royal ban on African–Spanish intermarriage. But all such attempts were doomed. Nobody, as one historian puts it, "was successful in keeping Spaniards, Indians, and Africans

This family portrait shows how a Spanish husband and mulatto wife produced a *morisca* daughter. The most important clientele for "caste" paintings such as this were Spanish visitors to the Americas who wanted to take back to Europe exotic Mexican souvenirs that reflected what seemed to be, in the Spanish view, the natural human mingling when three large cultural groups converged in the New World. *(Sir Edward Hulse, Breamore House, Hampshire, England)*

out of each other's gene pools."[19] This racial fusion did not stymie racial prejudice, though it modulated it. The offspring of Spanish mixed-race marriages faced a life of discrimination and thwarted ambition, and those with African ancestry had more limited chances than those of Indian ancestry. Not for many generations would Mexicans, for example, celebrate the creation of "the cosmic race" produced by the mingling of African, Indian, and Spanish blood. But if prejudice remained, the fusion continued.

In the North American colonies, Englishmen emphatically rejected racial fusion, objecting strongly not to sexual relations with dark-skinned women but to conferring status on blacks by accepting such intermingling as legitimate or by admitting its biological product to white society. Determined to prohibit a rise in the social status of those who labored at the

[19]Jorge Klor de Alva, "*Mestizaje* from Spain to Aztlan," in *New World Orders: Casta Painting and Colonial Latin America* (New York: America Society Art Gallery, 1996), p. 60.

bottom of society, those defined as inferior, white colonizers blocked the mulatto from occupying a position midway between white and black. The smallest portion of African blood classified a person as black; and to be black was almost always to be a slave. The "mulatto escape hatch" that Carl Degler has described in Latin American society hardly existed in British North America, for there was little need to call upon Africans or mulattoes for important, status-conferring services, and the well-rooted institution of the white family, an outgrowth of a family pattern of settlement, gave special reasons for excluding the living evidence of a sexual congress that threatened the purity of white culture. The single exception was South Carolina, which maintained the social-sexual system of the West Indies, where so many of its planters had originated and where white women were in short supply.

In England's North American colonies, then, Africans served the primary need for plantation labor. A secondary need was for occasional sex partners with whom one could act out sexual fantasies, heightened by the definition of black women as lascivious by nature. By prohibiting racial intermarriage, winking at interracial sex, and defining all mixed offspring as black, white society found the answer to its labor needs, its submerged sexual desires, its compulsion to maintain its culture purebred, and the problem of maintaining, at least in theory, absolute social control.

That calculus of sexual politics was the peculiar legacy of British North America, linked not so much to the national prejudices of Englishmen as to the historical circumstances of English settlement in North America, is demonstrated by the status of the mulatto in English Jamaica. By the mid-eighteenth century more than 90 percent of the Jamaica population was black, and white men greatly outnumbered white women. Such a distorted demographic history demanded a system in which black women were available to white men without scruple and where mulatto offspring could rise to places of importance. This is precisely what happened. Miscegenation occurred on a massive scale, and by 1733 the white legislature conferred privileges and property on mulattoes. The same was true in South Carolina, which never banned interracial marriage and conferred higher status on mulattoes.

AFRICAN–INDIAN CONTACT

The convergence of African and Indian peoples is the least studied chapter in the history of race relations in early America. Moreover, the terminology and institutions created by white Americans have disguised the degree of red–black intermixing by defining the children of mixed red–black ancestry as black and using the term mulatto in many cases to define half-African, half-Indian persons.

Naturally it is useless to look for this kind of acculturation in places where Indians and Africans did not meet in substantial numbers. Thus in

New England, where the coastal tribes had been killed off before more than a trickle of Africans had arrived, little cross-fertilization was possible. It is notable, however, that in the few places, such as Cape Cod, where Indians did survive, their mixture with a small number of free Negroes was extensive by the late eighteenth century. This also occurred in a number of New England towns, especially along the coast, where many Indian slaves from South Carolina had been imported in the early eighteenth century. A census in South Kingston, Rhode Island, in 1730 showed 333 Negro slaves and 223 Indian slaves; the resulting intermixture of blood is not to be wondered at. A report in Massachusetts in 1795 stated that the blacks of Massachusetts "have generally . . . left the country and resorted to the maritime towns. Some are incorporated, and their breed is mixed with the Indians of Cape-Cod and Martha's Vineyard."[20] Years later Herman Melville wrote of the African-Indian whalers who went to sea from Nantucket Island.

In New York, which contained the largest slave population north of the Chesapeake, intermixture of slaves and Indians, though unquantifiable, was far from unusual. Negro and Indian slaves had formed a blood bond in 1712 when they joined hands in an insurrection in New York City. Thereafter, provincial officials knew that the best place to look for escaped slaves was among the small local tribes that remained on Long Island and in the Hudson River valley. It was in the cities of the North, however, that black slaves were concentrated, and these were precisely the places where Indians in the second half of the eighteenth century were only occasionally to be found.

In the Chesapeake colonies, the possibility of African-Indian fusion was also reduced by the sheer force of circumstances. When Indians were relatively numerous in the tidewater region of Maryland and Virginia, slaves were present only in small numbers. In 1670, fewer than 2,000 slaves inhabited the Chesapeake region, and by the end of Bacon's Rebellion in 1676 the Indian population in the regions settled by whites was insignificant. Nonetheless, many small coastal tribes gave refuge to runaway slaves. Their descendants, mixed with whites as well, formed isolated tri-ethnic communities in Delaware, Maryland, Virginia, and North Carolina. The Wesorts of Maryland are one example. The name Wesort came to differentiate "we-sort-of-people" from "you-sort-of-people." Baptismal and marriage records tell the story of seven families that made up the core of this mixed race of people. One family traces back to the 1670s, when an enslaved African married an Irish maid-servant. Since then, black, red, and white bloodlines blended into one group, creating distinctive physical features. The majority of Wesorts have straight brown or black hair. Some have Indian facial features, but blue eyes are not uncommon. Today, other tri-racial societies such

[20]Quoted in Kenneth W. Porter, "Relations between Negroes and Indians within the Present Limits of the United States," *Journal of Negro History,* 17 (1932): 311.

as the Lumbees, Red Bones, and Brass Ankles maintain their distinctive identities from Alabama to New York.

Only in North Carolina, South Carolina, and Georgia did Indians and Africans in substantial numbers find themselves confronting Europeans simultaneously. Here was the one area in English America where the situation mirrored that prevailing in most regions of Spanish and French colonization.

The colonizers' position of numerical inferiority led to gnawing fears that Indians and slaves would combine forces and overpower them. Keeping Africans and Indians apart, therefore, became a necessity. Such fears were well grounded, for during the pre-Revolutionary period the Indians of the Southeast remained numerous in white areas of settlement and, combined with the black slaves, greatly exceeded the white population. White South Carolinians, for example, were outnumbered by their black and Indian slaves and by free Indians surrounding them by ratios of three or four to one throughout most of the early period of colonization. Even by the mid-eighteenth century, only about 25,000 whites inhabited the colony along with some 40,000 black slaves and 60,000 Indians gathered in the Creek, Cherokee, Choctaw, Chickasaw, and subsidiary tribes. Twenty years later, on the eve of the Revolution, the white population had increased to some 50,000 but the slave population had increased even faster, to about 80,000. South Carolinians lived surrounded by those who, if they could find a means for concerted action, might overwhelm them at any moment. Indian uprisings that punctuated the colonial period and a succession of slave uprisings and insurrectionary plots that were nipped in the bud kept South Carolinians sickeningly aware that only through the greatest vigilance and through policies designed to keep their enemies divided could they hope to remain in control of the situation.

That the white Carolinians were able to retain a hold on the situation testifies to their ability to play one Indian tribe against another and to their partial success in keeping Indians and Negro slaves divided. The policy, as one Carolinian put it, was "to make Indians & Negro's a checque upon each other least by their Vastly Superior Numbers we should be crushed by one or the other."[21] White officials devised various methods to accomplish this, for example prohibiting African-Americans, whether slave or free, from traveling in Indian country as traders or traders' helpers. Indian tribes were repeatedly asked to return fugitive slaves, and treaties signed with Creeks, Cherokees, and other tribes almost always included a clause stipulating that escaped slaves must be turned over to the Carolina government. White authorities offered bounties to Indians for the capture and return of escaped slaves and used patrols in frontier areas to prevent slaves from reaching Indian country. Fostering suspicion of blacks among the Indians was another

[21]Quoted in William S. Willis, Jr., "Divide and Rule: Red, White, and Black in the Southeast," *Journal of Negro History,* 48 (1963): 165.

way to keep mutual aid between them to a minimum. "It has been allways the policy of this government," wrote Governor Lyttelton in 1738, "to create an aversion in them [Indians] to Negroes."[22]

Incorporating black slaves into the South Carolina militia during Indian wars served a double purpose. Without them, the Carolinians would have been hard pressed to defeat their Tuscarora, Yamasee, or Cherokee enemies; second, the use of black soldiers helped to remind the Indians that Africans were not their friends. Half the Carolinian force that Governor Craven led against the Yamasee in 1715 was black, and another black company marched with Captain Pight in the same campaign. When these forces proved incapable of defeating the Yamasees, the Assembly called for a "standing army" of 1,200 men, including "400 negroes or other slaves."[23] This was merely an implementation of the policy begun in 1708 to compose the militia of equal numbers of blacks and whites. In the 1740 expedition against St. Augustine seventy-three slaves were included. By 1747 the militia law was changed to allow for no more than one-third of the soldiers to be black, a sign of a growing fear of black insurgency. In the campaigns against the Cherokee in 1760 a small number of black Carolinians again fought against Indian enemies of the white government. How precariously the Carolinians were suspended between red revolt and black insurrection was indicated in the Cherokee War. More blacks were needed to fight against the Indian enemy, but in an era of large slave importations the anxiety concerning black rebellion was also great. Thus a motion to equip 500 slaves "to serve against the savages" failed by a single vote in the South Carolina assembly.

Just as white colonists used slaves to quash Indian uprisings, they employed Indians to put down black rebellions. In the most spectacular black insurrection in the South, the Stono Revolt of 1739, the South Carolina government recruited "settlement" Indians to pursue the slaves, who had eluded white militiamen and were fleeing to Spanish Florida. The assembly equipped the Indians with clothes, guns, and ammunition and promised £50 for each slave brought back alive or £25 for each slave returned dead. Other attempts were made at warding off black rebellions by relocating Indian tribes into areas where large numbers of slaves were developing the rice and indigo plantations. This policy originated in the early eighteenth century and was pursued with special vigor in the 1730s, when the buildup of the slave population kept Carolina vibrating with fears of black rebellion. In 1737 white leaders requested Cherokee warriors "to come down to the settlements to be an awe to the negroes."[24]

In spite of these efforts to promote hatred between Indians and Africans, a surprising number of slaves were harbored within the Indian

[22] *Ibid.*

[23] David D. Wallace, *South Carolina: A Short History, 1520–1948* (Chapel Hill: University of North Carolina Press, 1951), p. 88.

[24] Willis, "Divide and Rule," p. 175.

communities throughout the colonial period. Measuring this phenomenon precisely is impossible, but the persistent inclusion in Indian treaties of a clause providing for the return of escaped slaves demonstrates that the bounties offered Indians for slave catching often produced little response. The Tuscarora tribe, for example, gave refuge to a large number of slaves in the period before the outbreak of war in 1711. When war came, these Africans fought with the Tuscaroras and one of them, named Harry, was said to have designed the Tuscarora fortress on a tributary of the Neuse River. Four years later, during the Yamasee uprising, fugitive slaves were also active in the raids on white settlements. Even after the Yamasee had given up their struggle, they refused to return their black allies, which, according to one Carolina official, "has encouraged a great many more [slaves] lately to run away to that Place."[25]

Because the Yamasees were located along the coast between the English settlements and the Spanish outposts in Florida, slaves had additional reason to flee in this direction. As early as 1699 the Spanish issued a royal decree promising protection to all fugitive English slaves and they repeated this offer periodically during the first half of the eighteenth century. Even after the Yamasee War, the Indians not only encouraged Carolina slaves to join them but also engaged in slave-stealing raids on outlying plantations. In 1738, 23 slaves escaped from Port Royal and made their way to St. Augustine. They joined an enclave of free Negroes where 38 escaped slave men, many with families, were already settled. These were the free blacks whose community of about one hundred slaves rose along the Stono River in 1739 in an attempt to kill slave masters and reach Spanish Florida. When Governor Oglethorpe of Georgia launched his attack on St. Augustine in 1740, he was met with the combined resistance of Spanish, Indians, and ex-Carolina slaves, who had no difficulty repulsing the expedition in which the Carolinians invested more than £7,000. Two years later the Spaniards retaliated with an attack on Georgia; among the invasion forces was a regiment whose Negro commanders "were clothed in lace, bore the same rank as the white officers, and with equal freedom and familiarity walked and conversed with their comrades and chief."[26] An eighteenth-century historian of South Carolina revealed how precarious the hold of white slave masters was in the tri-racial world they inhabited when he conjectured that if the Spanish expedition had attacked South Carolina rather than Georgia, the English would have been lost, for in South Carolina there were "such numbers of negroes, they would soon have acquired such a force, as must have rendered all opposition fruitless and ineffectual."[27]

[25]Quoted in Chapman J. Milling, *Red Carolinians* (Chapel Hill: University of North Carolina Press, 1940), p. 153.
[26]Kenneth W. Porter, "Negroes on the Southern Frontier, 1670–1763," *Journal of Negro History*, 33 (1948): 68.
[27]Quoted by Dr. Hewat, *The Territory of Florida* in *ibid.*, p. 68.

Southern slaves fled not only up and down the coast but to the interior. As early as 1725 a prominent South Carolina slaveholder reported with concern that the slaves had become well acquainted with the hill country of the Cherokees and were becoming fluent not only in English but also in the Cherokee language.

The Creeks also harbored runaway slaves in their towns. In 1725, a Spanish delegation arrived at Coweta, the principal town of the Lower Creeks, with an escaped Carolina slave who served as interpreter between the Creeks and Spanish. Still another refugee slave was an interpreter between the French and the Creeks during this period. Runaway slaves, concludes one student of red–black contacts in the Southeast, "operated to an unknown extent, but evidently with considerable effectiveness, as French and Spanish agents among Indian tribes bordering on the English settlements."[28] The threat of losing slaves to the Creeks was great enough in 1722 for the governor of South Carolina to issue a proclamation prohibiting Creeks from entering the white settlements, since their visits, purportedly for the purpose of trade, were encouraging large numbers of slaves to follow them back into the interior. As late as the 1760s the Carolinians were pressing the Creeks hard for the return of runaway slaves, and, although blacks were occasionally handed over, hundreds remained in the Indian territory, blending their cultures with those of the Creeks, Cherokees, and others.

By fashioning the harshest slave code of any of the colonies, by paying dearly for Indian support at critical moments, and by militarizing their society, white Carolinians were able to restrict the flow of black slaves into the backcountry. The Cherokee hill country never became the equivalent of the Maroon mountain hideaways in Jamaica or the Brazilian *quilombos* as a refuge for runaway slaves. But neither was the policy of fostering hatred between the two groups entirely successful. Throughout the eighteenth century slaves ran away and joined Indian settlements. On occasion, when the price was high enough or the need to propitiate the Carolinians great enough, Indians returned black runaways to their white masters. But in most cases the fugitive slaves disappeared into Indian society, where they took Indian wives, produced children of mixed race, and contributed to African–Indian acculturation in the same fashion as those slaves who lived with settlement Indians in the coastal region. So common was African–Indian contact in the southern colonies that the term *mustee* entered the southern vocabulary in order to categorize the offspring of African and Indian parents.

In spite of the considerable contact between Indians and Africans, it is historically inaccurate and politically simplistic to assume that their relations prove a natural affinity of oppressed peoples to unite against their oppressors. At no time in the colonial period did Creeks, Cherokees, and other

[28] *Ibid.,* p. 77.

southern tribes work in a concerted way to unite with slaves. The problems of communication, language, and cultural differences made this difficult. But more important, Indian groups, especially after the Yamasee War of 1715, were more intent on using white society for their own ends than eliminating it altogether. In their steadfast adherence to self-interest they acted variously toward Africans. Sometimes they held them as slaves; sometimes they gave them refuge and adopted them into their villages; sometimes they returned enough of them to satisfy white demands; and sometimes they hunted them down for pay. Only when an Indian tribe had a firm trading connection outside the English orbit, such as the Apalachees of Spanish Florida, were the slaves of English colonists welcomed without qualification.

In the final analysis the mixing of peoples in eighteenth-century America depended on both demographic and historical circumstances. By 1770 some 2.3 million persons lived east of the Allegheny Mountains, but of these 1.75 million were white, 450,000 were black, and only 100,000 or less were Indian. Such a preponderance of whites stood in stark contrast to almost every other part of the New World where Europeans had settled and, all other factors aside, would have guaranteed a fairly low level of racial mixing.

Where people of different colors did live in close proximity, considerable interracial contact occurred. White colonists did not sanction interracial liaisons, as in many European colonies, but this reflected not only a difference in settlement patterns but also the special concern for the preservation of family-centered "civilized society" in English North America. Whatever prior attitudes may have been brought by the Spanish to New Mexico, the French to Canada, or the English to the West Indies, these colonists represented small minorities of the population in their New World environments. Short of defeating their own purposes, they could not have implemented the strict ethnocentric social attitudes and laws that the English legislated in North America. What is surprising is that the color line was so often crossed in a society where the dominant group was making such strenuous claims for keeping its bloodstream pure. The gap between public pronouncements, as expressed in laws prohibiting miscegenation, and actual social practice, as visible in the large mixed-blood population, can only be explained in terms of the desire of white men to maintain social control while at the same time straying across the color line for casual sexual relations.

CULTURAL INTERACTION OF RED, WHITE, AND BLACK

By the end of the eighteenth century, American society, some four million strong, was far from a homogeneous culture. More than two hundred years of European colonization and the continuous interaction of three large and internally diverse cultural groups had left a conglomeration of cultural entities. Each cultural bloc was rich with experiences, varying traditions, and folkways.

The complex interaction of the three cultural groups was filled with paradoxes. English newcomers to the Americas claimed that they wished to assimilate Indians and Africans, but they found that the most effective way to exploit the land of one and the labor of the other was to follow a non-assimilationist policy. Bringing Christianity to non-Christians was an expensive and time-consuming enterprise, best left to men of the cloth. But Protestant England had only a pale version of the black- and brown-robed Jesuits and Franciscans who brought the "true message" to Native Americans. Puritan, Anglican, Presbyterian, and Quaker churchmen made only minimal efforts to instruct Indian tribes in Christian doctrine, and most of the efforts were inspired by the expectation that conversion would go hand in hand with pacification and political control. To be sure, in the Great Awakening a small wave of missionizing attempts made evangelical inroads among Indian tribes and enslaved Africans, especially in the North, but it is worth noting that the Awakeners themselves were regarded by polite society as disruptive and dangerous in their attempts to dissolve social, sexual, and racial boundaries. In the late colonial period and even more so after the American Revolution, Christian doctrine spread among slaves in the upper South, where the threat of slave revolt was not so keenly felt. But throughout most of South Carolina and Georgia planters carefully shielded slaves from the potentially radical message of Christianity, and a large majority of slaves died strangers to Christian religion. Slaves in the North were broadly inculcated with Protestantism but this would probably not have happened if slaves had not been vastly outnumbered by whites. In education it was the same: Slaves were educated in those things that enabled them to function in their work more effectively; but education as a process of inquiry was shunned, for it promised only to cultivate aspirations that were inappropriate to those whose servitude was lifelong.

A handful of reformers and churchmen kept alive the humanitarian impulse, based on the belief that by uplifting Africans and Indians from heathenism they could be assimilated into Anglo-American society. But most eighteenth-century whites regarded the two cultural minorities in their midst as unassimilable, as was to be revealed when the emancipation of slaves in the revolutionary era brought cries for their repatriation to Africa. So far as the assimilation of Indians was concerned, nothing could have been less desirable to European settlers, who coveted Indian land but not land with Indians on it.

Also working against assimilation was the inner need of white colonists to justify the exploitation of Africans and Indians by insisting on the wide gap that separated "savagery" from "civilization." By definition, assimilation would narrow this gap, making Africans and Indians more like Europeans. But when mighty master and lowly slave, or "rational European" and "unreasoning savage" were admitted to be alike, either in outward manners or inner capacity, then the entire rationale of domination and exploitation would crumble. This need to deny a likeness and to oppose any measures that would increase the similarity of peoples in colonial society was an important reason for resisting the Christianization of slaves. It also worked to convince white colonists that Indians were unassimilable. One of the mistaken notions about colonial Americans that endured in England was that the settlers would happily receive the missionaries of the Anglican Society for the Propagation of the Gospel, which hoped to convert both slaves and Indians to the word of Christ. The Bishop of London summed up this misconception of the colonial desire for assimilation when he "referred to Negroes as 'truly a Part of our own Nation'—which was just what the colonists were sure Negroes were not."[29] The same was true for Indians.

A second paradox was that white American culture developed the most pervasively negative attitudes toward the cultural minority in its midst that was most valuable to it—the African-Americans—and held the more positive attitudes toward the cultural minority that stood only as an obstacle to white society once their military assistance was no longer needed—the Indians. Colonial society grew in size and strength in direct relationship to an increase in slaves and a decrease in "land-cluttering" Indians. Yet it was the black African upon whom the colonists fastened the most indelibly negative images. The key to this irony was that the colonist almost always encountered Africans as slaves and thus came to think of them as abject and less than human creatures. But the English settlers met Indians as adversaries or half-trusted allies. The Indian maintained the freedom to come and go, to attack and kill, to give and withhold support, and to retain political sovereignty. Though he was hated for many of these things, they earned him a grudging respect. The Anglo–Indian relationship in the eighteenth century was rarely that of master and slave with all rights and power concentrated on one side. Instead, when Indian and European colonizer met, they were involved in a set of power relationships in which each side, with something to offer the other, maneuvered for the superior position. The Indian was the ultimate loser in most of these interchanges but that cannot obscure the fact that for several hundred years Anglo-Americans confronted Indians as formidable adversaries rather than as chattels. Though they were exploited, excluded, and often decimated in their contacts with European civilization, Indians usually maneuvered from a position of strength.

Africans in America, by contrast, were rarely a part of any political or business equation. Mostly they had their labor to offer and even that was not subject to contractual agreement. Slaves were not powerless in their dealings with white society, but they were deeply disadvantaged as compared with Indians. This uneven distribution of power in black–white relations could

[29]Jordan, *White Over Black*, p. 208.

not help but affect attitudes. Unlike the Indians, the Africans were rarely able to win the respect of the European settlers because their situation was rarely one where respect was required or even possible. Tightly trapped in an authoritarian relationship where most of the power was on the other side, Africans, as they became more and more important to the colonizers' economy, sank lower and lower in the white settlers' estimation. Meanwhile the male Indian, though hated, was respected for his fighting ability, his dignity, his ability as interpreter, and even his oratorical skill, while the female Indian was important as consort and cultural intermediary. American colonists sometimes scoffed at the efforts of the Enlightenment philosophers to depict the American native as a "noble savage," the archetype of natural beauty and virtue, uncorrupted by materialistic Western civilization; but their image of the Indian came to have a positive side. The sociology of red–white and black–white relations had differed greatly over many generations. From these variations evolved distinct white attitudes, in both cases adverse but in significantly different ways.

A third paradox in the convergence of cultures was that the group that was enslaved, degraded, and despised survived and flourished in North America, while the group that maintained more freedom, power, and European respect suffered a ghastly depopulation and cultural malaise. It does not minimize the pain, humiliation, and brutality of slavery to point out that Africans in North America were remarkably successful in a demographic sense, particularly in contrast to most other areas of the New World. The available data suggest that while black mortality was substantially higher than white mortality, black fertility was close to the white norm. It can be stated with certainty that slave mortality in eighteenth-century North America was far lower than anywhere else in the Americas. This does not necessarily reflect more humane treatment on American plantations. More important was the more favorable disease and climatic environment of North America. The Caribbean islands were known as graveyards for white and black alike, and in the Latin American countries tropical diseases swept away African slaves like leaves in a windstorm.

A comparison of slave life in Virginia and Jamaica illustrates the point. The slave populations of the two colonies were almost equal in 1775, with Virginians owning about 200,000 slaves and the Jamaicans about 193,000. But between 1700 and 1775, Virginia had imported not more than 100,000 slaves by the most liberal estimates, while in Jamaica importations were more than three and a half times as great. Life for enslaved Africans on eighteenth-century southern plantations, however brutal, was healthier than in other parts of the Americas and, because of a more favorable sex ratio than in other plantation areas, the chances of family life were much greater.

By contrast, the Indian tribes east of the Appalachian Mountains, and in the Spanish Southwest and Florida as well, suffered disastrous population losses in the first two centuries of contact with Europeans. Although they were not struck down in the same catastrophic proportions as the indigenous people of Mexico and most parts of Latin America, their mortality rate and natural decline stood in stark contrast to the natural increase of enslaved Africans. In areas of white settlement along the coastal plain, only remnants of the Indian population remained on the eve of the Revolution. Connecticut, for example, counted only 930 Indians in a census in 1762; Massachusetts found 1,681 in 1764; Virginia listed only 130 in 1774; and Rhode Island tabulated 1,482 in the same year.

Several factors explain the different demographic histories of Africans and Native Americans. First, Africans were far more resistant than Indians to European epidemic diseases and by the mid-eighteenth century were being immunized, like whites, against smallpox, the biggest killer of all. Hardly an Indian tribe in the eastern part of the continent escaped the dread disease. The European's invisible ally had decimated the eastern Massachusetts tribes even before the Puritans arrived and struck hard again in the early years of white settlement. The Iroquois were scourged several times in the seventeenth and eighteenth centuries. A raging smallpox epidemic hit the Cherokees so severely in 1738 that they lost nearly half their population, and the Catawba population of North Carolina was similarly reduced by half during a single epidemic in 1759. Smallpox swept the Creeks in the last years of the seventeenth century and continued to diminish their numbers in the following decades. Far less important as a killer were the wars tribes fought with European settlers and with each other at the instigation of their trading partners. But these too took a toll on life that was not duplicated in the slave experience. Still another cause of depopulation was alcohol, which, though it killed slowly in contrast to smallpox and other epidemic diseases, also counted victims by the thousands.

All the lethal factors that decimated Indian villages throughout eastern North America touched slaves only lightly. This was not coincidental. White colonists did not possess direct control over bacteriological and demographic factors, but they eagerly sought to increase the black slave population while reducing the Indian population. To this end they instituted policies that influenced, if they did not control, population curves. Blacks, for example, were inoculated against smallpox and given medical treatment in case of sickness. For a plantation owner to do this was only to preserve his property, just as he would attempt to maintain the health of his horses and other farm animals. If Indians, however, contracted an epidemic disease, the colonist could only give thanks that God had seen fit to diminish their numbers in order to make more room for "civilized" persons. European colonists consciously waged bacteriological warfare only occasionally by spreading smallpox through infected trade goods, but they were uninterested in arresting epidemic disease among the Indians in contrast to their slaves. With alcohol it was the same. The rum that masters rationed out to slaves at holiday time and sometimes at week's end as a reward for work accomplished, was distributed by traders among Indian tribes in order to create not only dependency but addiction. Rum was a liquid form of control used by white colonists in their dealings with both Africans and Indians. But it was intended to sustain life among blacks while destroying life among Indians.

War was the third killer and was also controlled to some extent by whites. Black rebellion, of course, was quelled as quickly as possible, for it directly threatened the labor system and social dominance by whites. But white colonists often artfully encouraged war with Indians and war among Indians. As soon as they had determined that they could outmatch local tribes, colonists in the seventeenth century found reasons for making war on coastal tribes. For example, Emanuel Downing, John Winthrop's brother-in-law, thought a war with the Narragansett Indians would be of "verie considerable" advantage to the colony because it would be a sin in God's eyes for the Puritans, "having power in our hands, to suffer them to maynteyne the worship of the devill which their paw wawes often doe." He then predicted the history of the next century by pointing out that "If upon a Just warre the Lord should deliver them [the Narragansetts] into our hands, wee might easily have men, women, and children enough to exchange for Moores [Africans], which wilbe more gaynefull pilladge for us than wee conceive."[30]

Downing's willingness to please God while serving the colonists' material needs was a typical seventeenth-century mode of justifying war against local tribes. In the eighteenth century white leaders couched such arguments in purely secular language and then applied them to strong interior tribes rather than to small coastal societies. In this changed context, the policy shifted to creating animosities between Indian groups. "If we cannot destroy one nation of Indians by another," wrote South Carolina's governor in 1717, "our country must be lost."[31] This was not only the most effective deterrent to pan-Indian uprisings against the Europeans but also contributed to the general population decline of Indians.

Thus, while escaping slavery in most cases, Native Americans found themselves confronting a mushrooming European population that sought the land they occupied and found Indians useful mostly as auxiliaries in the destruction of other Indians. This had not been true for most of the colonial period, for so long as the European population was small, so long as it was divided among Spanish, French, and English contenders for continental supremacy, and so long as the fur and skin trade was a major factor in the colonial economy, Indians had been indispensable to the colonizers. By the mid-eighteenth century, however, the Indian trade had become a minor part of the colonial economy. Fishing and shipbuilding in New England, grain and livestock production in the Middle Colonies, and tobacco, rice,

---

[30]Quoted in Almon E. Lauber, *Indian Slavery in Colonial Times Within the Present Limits of the United States* (New York: Columbia University Press, 1913), p. 311.
[31]Quoted in Wallace, *South Carolina: A Short History, 1520–1948,* pp. 91–92.

and indigo production on southern plantations had become the principal forms of economic activity. By 1763 the elimination of France as an imperial rival eliminated the need for Indian military support. The tremendous growth of population in the two generations before the Revolution made acquisition of the interior river valleys of the continent the preoccupation of both eastern speculators, for whom population growth had created a new source of wealth far greater than the fur trade, and the swarming settlers who poured through the mountain gaps into the trans-Appalachian region. Finally, with American victory in the war for independence, Indians east of the Mississippi River were nearly out of options in a chess game tilted ominously against them.

A final paradox was that Indian societies treasured many of the values that English settlers and other Europeans had braved the Atlantic to reestablish in the New World. Idealistic Europeans saw the "wilderness" of North America as a place where tired, corrupt, materialistic, self-seeking Europeans might begin a new life centered around the frayed but vital values of reciprocity, spirituality, and community. From John Winthrop to William Penn to John Woolman, the notion of transplanted Europeans building a virtuous society in the New World coursed through the dream-life of the newcomers. Yet as time passed and Europeans became more numerous, it occurred to some philosophically inclined whites that the people in North America who best upheld these values were the people being driven from the land.

Even hard-bitten, unsentimental colonists often recognized that Indian society, though by no means without its problems and its own disreputable characters, put white society to shame. The English Commissioners investigating Bacon's Rebellion in 1676 wrote a scorching letter to the government of Virginia asking them to stop the land grabbing of settlers who already had title to all the land they could use but "still Covett & seek to deprive them [the Indians] of more, out of meer Itch of Luxurie rather than any reall lack of it, which shames us and makes us become a Reproach and a by-word to those more Morall heathens."[32] Three-quarters of a century later, Thomas Pownall, governor of Massachusetts, lambasted the colonists for violating their own principles, writing that "the frauds, abuses, and deceits that these poor people have been treated with and suffered under have had no bounds."[33] Edmond Atkin, an Indian trader of South Carolina who knew Indians not from drawing-room accounts but from years of intimate contact, wrote in 1755 that

> No people in the World understand and pursue their true National Interest, better than the Indians. . . . Yet in their publick Treaties no

[32] *Virginia Magazine of History and Biography*, 14 (1906–07): 274.
[33] Quoted in Georgiana C. Nammack, *Fraud, Politics and the Dispossession of the Indians: The Iroquois Land Frontier in the Colonial Period* (Norman: University of Oklahoma Press, 1969), p. 31.

People on earth are more open, explicit, and Direct. Nor are they excelled by any in the observance of them. . . . With respect to . . . all Ruptures of Consequence between the Indians & the white People, and the Massacres that ensued. . . . the latter were first the Aggressors; the Indians being driven thereto under Oppressions and Abuses, and to vindicate their Natural Rights.[34]

Many European observers stood in admiration of the Indian traits of morality, generosity, bravery, and the spirit of mutual caring. Indians seemed to embody these Christian virtues almost without effort while colonizing Europeans, attempting to build a society with similar characteristics, were pulled in the opposite direction by the natural abundance around them— toward individualism, disputatiousness, aggrandizement of wealth, and the exploitation of other humans. Many eighteenth-century colonial moralists made the point that Indians hewed closer to the precepts of Christianity than most of the settlers. "As a nation," John Brickell wrote of the Delawares, "they may be considered fit examples for many of us Christians to follow. They certainly follow what they are taught to believe more closely, and I might say more honestly, in general, than we Christians do the divine precepts of our Redeemer."[35]

By embodying some of the virtues around which Europeans had hoped to reorganize their cultural system, the Indian was a disturbing reminder of the retrogression of Europeans in their New World setting. English, Germans, Scots-Irish, Swedes, Spanish, Dutch, French Huguenots, and others might congratulate themselves for "taming the wilderness"; for building thriving seaports where none had previously existed; for raising towns, churches, schools, and governments along a thousand miles of coastal plain from Maine to Florida. They had chosen productivity and acquisitiveness, but these had been pursued at the cost of principles earlier regarded as central to the colonizers' dreams for life in the New World.

In the complex interaction of Native Americans, Europeans, and Africans the distribution of power between dominant and subordinate groups must always be kept in mind. It largely dictated the formal outcome of the cultural confrontation. Laws, institutions, boundary lines, trade agreements, settlement patterns, and much else emerged as they did because white colonizers were ultimately stronger than native occupiers of the land or Africans brought to the Americas in chains. All social, economic, and political relations had to be mediated, however, because the power available to Europeans was anything but absolute. Still, the colonizers' power grew in

---

[34]Wilbur Jacobs, ed., *Indians of the Southern Colonial Frontier: The Edmund Atkin Report and Plan of 1755* (Columbia: University of South Carolina Press, 1954), p. 38.
[35]"John Brickell's Captivity," *American Pioneer*, 1 (1842): 47–48, quoted in James Axtell, "The White Indians of Colonial America," *William and Mary Quarterly*, 32 (1975): 86.

terms of raw numbers and political cohesiveness. Both of these rose sharply in the eighteenth century.

Yet the pathways of power did not strictly dictate the history of cultural interchange—a point that is obscured if we mistakenly assume that under conditions of oppression and exploitation acculturation occurs in only one direction. The culture of Africans and Indians—their agricultural techniques, modes of behavior, styles of speech and dress, food preferences, music, dance, and other aspects of daily existence—became commingled with European culture in ways not automatically determined by the status differences of the three groups. For example, "the status of the master's child vis-a-vis his slave governess," write Mintz and Price, "would surely affect his learning of a style of command in dealing with slaves. But his speech, his food preferences, his imagery, his earliest ideas about men and women, and a good deal more of what would become in time his characteristic quality as an individual would be learned from someone far below him in status, but otherwise very much in control of him."[36] Most of this Africanization of European culture occurred within the intimate personal encounters of slaves and masters and their families—relationships that took place daily within the context of work, domestic service, and interracial sex.

The Indianization of European culture occurred within a different context. Expanding rapidly and pushing west across the Appalachian Mountains after their successful revolution against their colonial British master, white Americans saw themselves as a new people—an amalgam of European settlers toughened in the North American "wilderness." But foreign travelers, while also picturing them as a "new" people, discerned an amalgam that bore the stamp of generations of contact with Native Americans. Even before the American Revolution, the Swedish visitor Peter Kalm believed that "the French, English, Germans, Dutch, and other Europeans who have lived for several years . . . near and among the Indians, grow so like them in their behavior and thought that they can only be distinguished by the difference of their color." Traveling through the United States at the end of the eighteenth century, the Frenchman Moreau de Saint-Mery believed "the American is the perfect mean between the European and Indian."[37]

"New World it is," we are reminded, "for those who became its peoples remade it, and in the process they remade themselves," whether red, white, or black.[38]

[36]Sidney W. Mintz and Richard Price, *An Anthropological Approach to the Afro-American Past: A Caribbean Perspective* (Philadelphia: Institute for the Study of Human Issues, 1976), p. 16.

[37]Quoted in Calloway, *New Worlds for All*, pp. 6, 2.

[38]Mintz and Price, *An Anthropological Approach to the Afro-American Past*, p. 44.

Bibliographical Essay

Students who wish to deepen their understanding of the interaction among ethnic and cultural groups in early America will soon learn that many of the books and journals they need to consult are not shelved in the American history section of their library but in the areas devoted to anthropology, ethnography, African history, and even music and folklore. In the bibliography that follows, particular attention is given to identifying these less familiar works of scholarship and relatively little attention is given to the immense historical literature concerning English colonists and other Europeans in North America during the colonial period.

INDIAN CULTURE

A few general histories of Indian history and culture in North America are worth consulting by those who are making their first acquaintance with "the first Americans." Excellent overviews are provided by Peter C. Mancall, "Native Americans and Europeans in English America, 1500–1700," *The Oxford History of the British Empire*, vol. 1, *The Origins of Empire* (Oxford, 1998), pp. 328–50 and Daniel Richter, "Native Peoples of North America and the Eighteenth Century British Empire" in William Roger Louis, ed., *The Oxford*

History of the British Empire, vol. 2: *The Eighteenth Century,* ed., P. J. Marshall (Oxford, 1998), pp. 347–71. More extensive treatments are Harold E. Driver, *Indians of North America* (Chicago, 1961); Fred Eggan, *The American Indian: Perspectives for the Study of Social Change* (Chicago, 1967); Harold Fey and D'Arcy McNickle, *Indians and Other Americans: Two Ways of Life Meet* (New York, 1959); Frederick Hodge, ed., *Handbook of American Indians North of Mexico* (New York, 1960); Francis Jennings, ed., *The Newberry Library Center for the History of the American Indian Bibliographical Series,* (30 vols., Bloomington, Ind., 1976–1983); Alvin M. Josephy, Jr., *The Indian Heritage of America* (New York, 1968); Frederick E. Hoxie, ed., *Indians in American History* (1988); D'Arcy McNickle, *They Came Here First: The Epic of the American Indians* (New York, 1949); Robert Spencer and Jesse Jennings, *The Native Americans: Prehistory and Ethnology of the North American Indians* (New York, 1965); W. W. Newcomb, Jr., *American Indian History: An Anthropological Perspective* (Pacific Palisades, Cal., 1974); Ruth M. Underhill, *Red Man's America: A History of Indians in the United States* (Chicago, 1953); Deward E. Walker, Jr., *The Emergent Native Americans: A Reader in Culture Contact* (Boston, 1972).

Of signal importance are four volumes of essays by James Axtell. *The European and The Indian: Essays in the Ethnohistory of Colonial North America* (New York, 1981); *The Invasion Within: The Contest of Cultures in Colonial North America* (New York, 1985); *Beyond 1492: Encounters in Colonial North America* (New York, 1992); *The Indians' New South: Cultural Change in the Colonial Southeast* (Baton Rouge, 1997). A provocative overview is Francis Jennings, *The Founders of America: How Indians Discovered the Land, Pioneered in It, and Created Great Classical Civilizations; How They Were Plunged into a Dark Age by Invasion and Conquest; and How They Are Reviving* (New York, 1993).

More detailed accounts of Indian life in North America before the arrival of Europeans are numerous, but students should be aware that new findings by archaeologists and new conceptual approaches by anthropologists are continually changing our understanding of how long human life has existed in North America, how societies changed, and how cultural diffusion took place. Some general works on the "prehistory" of North America are Jesse Jennings, *Prehistory of North America* (New York, 1968); Jesse Jennings and Edward Norbeck, eds., *Prehistoric Man in the New World* (Chicago, 1964); Alvin M. Josephy, Jr., ed., *America in 1492: The World of Indian Peoples before the Arrival of Columbus* (New York, 1992); Brian M. Fagan, *The Great Journey: The Peopling of Ancient America* (New York, 1987); Kenneth Macgowan and Joseph A. Hester, Jr., *Early Man in the New World* (Garden City, N.Y., 1962); William T. Sanders and Joseph Marino, *New World Prehistory: Archaeology of the American Indian* (Englewood Cliffs, N.J.: 1970).

Several topics concerning Indian life before European colonization deserve special attention. The development of agriculture, which is of critical importance in the evolution of all societies, is discussed in Richard S. MacNeish, "The Origins of New World Agriculture," *Scientific American* 211

(1964), 29–37. As to the population of the Americas before European arrival—a question fraught with implications for the study of later European–Indian contacts—students should consult the long-standard work of James Mooney, *The Aboriginal Population of America North of Mexico* (Washington, D.C., 1928) and then read the revisionist literature and ongoing debates: Henry F. Dobyns, "Estimating Aboriginal American Population: An Appraisal of Techniques with a New Hemispheric Estimate," *Current Anthropology* 7 (1966), 395–416; Wilbur R. Jacobs, "The Tip of the Iceberg: Pre-Columbian Indian Demography and Some Implications for Revisionism," *William and Mary Quarterly* 31 (1972), 23–32; Alfred W. Crosby, "Virgin Soil Epidemics as a Factor in the Aboriginal Depopulation in America," *William and Mary Quarterly* 34 (1976), 176–207; William M. Denevan, *The Native Population of the Americas in 1492* (Madison, Wis., 1976); Ann F. Ramenofsky, *Vectors of Death: The Archaeology of European Contact* (Albuquerque, 1987); Russell Thornton, *American Indian Holocaust and Survival: A Population History since 1492* (Norman, Ok., 1987); Douglas H. Ubelaker, "North American Indian Population Size, A.D. 1500–1985," *American Journal of Physical Anthropology* 77 (1988), 289–94; the roundtable discussion by Dobyns, Snow, Lanphear, and Henige, in "Commentary on Native American Demography," *Ethnohistory* 36 (1989), 285–307; and John W. Veran and Douglas H. Ubelaker, eds., *Disease and Demography in the Americas* (Washington, D.C., 1992).

EUROPEAN–INDIAN CONTACT

After gaining some understanding of the peoples of North America before Europeans "discovered" the ancient "New World," students will be better able to comprehend the early stages of European–Indian contact. Books are legion on the early voyages of discovery, but a good place to start is with Carlo M. Cipolla, *Guns, Sails and Empires: Technological Innovations and the Early Phases of European Expansion, 1400–1700* (New York, 1966); David B. Quinn, *England and the Discovery of America, 1481–1620: From Bristol Voyages of the Fifteenth Century to the Pilgrim Settlement at Plymouth* (London, 1973); Kenneth R. Andrews, *Trade, Plunder and Settlement: Maritime Enterprise and the Genesis of the British Empire, 1480–1630* (New York, 1985); and Samuel E. Morison, *The European Discovery of America* (2 vols., New York, 1971–74).

For Europeans, the exploration of North America was not only geographical but psychic, for the native inhabitants had a profound impact on the European mind—an impact that was later to play an important role in the character of intercultural relations. The reverse—what Native Americans thought about Europeans—is equally important. Only an interdisciplinary approach will fully reveal what Europeans and Indians thought about each other. Thus the following books represent the work of scholars in a half dozen disciplines: Karen O. Kupperman, ed., *America in European Consciousness,*

1493–1750 (Chapel Hill, N.C., 1995); Roger Schlesinger, *In the Wake of Columbus: The Impact of the New World on Europe, 1492–1650* (Arlington Heights, Ill., 1996); Henri Baudet, *Paradise on Earth: Thoughts on European Images of Non-European Man,* trans. Elizabeth Wentholt (New Haven, 1965); David Bidney, "The Idea of the Savage in North American Ethnohistory," *Journal of the History of Ideas* 15 (1954), 322–27; Olive P. Dickason, *The Myth of the Savage and the Beginnings of French Colonialism in the Americas* (Edmonton, Canada, 1984); Edward Dudley and Maximillian E. Novak, eds., *The Wild Man Within: An Image in Western Thought from the Renaissance to Romanticism* (Pittsburgh, 1972); Leslie A. Fiedler, *The Return of the Vanishing American* (New York, 1968); Carolyn T. Foreman, *Indians Abroad, 1493–1938* (Norman, Okla., 1943); Reginald Horsman, *Race and Manifest Destiny: The Origins of American Racial Anglo-Saxonism* (Cambridge, Mass., 1981); Lee E. Huddleston, *Origins of the American Indians: European Concepts, 1492–1729* (Austin, Tex., 1967); Nancy Shoemaker, "How Indians Got to Be Red," *American Historical Review* 102 (1997), 625–44; Alden Vaughan, "From White Man to Red Skin: Changing Anglo-American Perceptions of the American Indian," *American Historical Review* 87 (1982), 917–53; special issue on "Constructing Race" in *William and Mary Quarterly* 54 (January, 1997); Fredi Chiapelli, ed., *First Images of America: The Impact of the New World on the Old* (Berkeley and Los Angeles, 1976); Robert F. Berkhofer, Jr., *The White Man's Indian: Images of the American Indian from Columbus to the Present* (New York, 1978); Karen O. Kupperman, *Settling with the Indians: The Meeting of English and Indian Cultures in America, 1580–1640* (Totowa, N.J., 1980); Thomas D. Matijasic, "Reflected Values: Sixteenth-Century Europeans View the Indians of North America," *American Indian Culture and Research Journal* 11 (1987), 31–50; Gary B. Nash, "The Image of the Indian in the Southern Colonial Mind," *William and Mary Quarterly* 29 (1972), 197–230; Roy H. Pearce, *The Savages of America: A Study of the Indian and the Idea of Civilization* (Baltimore, 1953); and "The Metaphysics of Indian-Hating," *Ethnohistory* 4 (1957), 27–40; Edmundo O'Gorman, *The Invention of America* (Bloomington, Ind., 1961); and Carl O. Sauer, *Sixteenth-Century North America: The Land and the People as Seen by Europeans* (Berkeley, 1971).

The study of early European–Indian relations in North America begins not with English colonists and native peoples but with the arrival of the Spanish, Dutch, and French on the continent. It is important to study this interaction of non-English people with Indian tribes because it allows for a comparative perspective on the later English experience. A general introduction to a comparative study of European–Indian relations is provided in Howard Peckham and Charles Gibson, eds., *Attitudes of Colonial Powers Toward the American Indian* (Salt Lake City, 1969); William W. Fitzhugh, ed., *Cultures in Contact: The European Impact on Native Cultural Institutions in Eastern North America, A.D. 1000–1800* (Washington, D.C., 1985).

More detailed analyses of French–Indian relations in Canada by both historians and anthropologists are: Richard White, *The Middle Ground: Indians,*

Empires, and Republics in the Great Lakes Region, 1650–1815 (Cambridge, 1991); Alfred G. Bailey, *The Conflict of European and Eastern Algonkian Cultures, 1504–1700* (St. John, New Brunswick, 1937); John Webster Grant, *Moon of Wintertime: Missionaries and the Indians of Canada in Encounter since 1534* (Toronto, 1984); William J. Eccles, *The Canadian Frontier, 1534–1760* (New York, 1969); Robert Goldstein, *French–Iroquois Diplomatic and Military Relations, 1609–1701* (The Hague, 1969); John H. Kennedy, *Jesuit and Savage in New France* (New Haven, 1950); Conrad Heidenreich, *Huronia: A History and Geography of the Huron Indians, 1600–1650* (Toronto, 1971); Cornelius Jaenen, *Friend and Foe: Aspects of French–Amerindian Cultural Contact in the Sixteenth and Seventeenth Centuries* (Toronto, 1976) and *The French Relationship with Native Peoples of New France and Acadia* (Ottawa, 1984); Denys Delâge, *Bitter Feast* (Vancouver, 1993); and Bruce G. Trigger, *The Children of Aataentsic* (Montreal, 1976) and *Natives and Newcomers: Canada's "Heroic Age" Reconsidered* (Kingston, Ont., 1985). For French relations with Indian tribes on the Lower Mississippi, a case of culture contact that stands in vivid contrast to the Canadian experience, see Jean Delanglez, *The French Jesuits in Lower Louisiana, 1700–63* (New Orleans, 1935); Charles E. O'Neill, *Church and State in French Colonial Louisiana: Policy and Politics to 1732* (New Haven, 1966); and Patricia D. Woods, *French–Indian Relations on the Southern Frontier, 1699–1762* (Ann Arbor, Mich., 1980).

Spanish–Indian interaction in North America, which affected what followed in the English period of settlement, can be followed in Kathleen Deagan, *Spanish St. Augustine: The Archaeology of a Creole Community* (New York, 1983); Charles Gibson, *Spain in America* (New York, 1966); Elizabeth A. H. John, *Storms Brewed in Other Men's Worlds: The Confrontation of Indians, Spanish, and French in the Southwest, 1540–1795* (College Station, Tex., 1975); David J. Weber, *The Spanish Frontier in North America* (New Haven, 1992); Andrew L. Knaut, *The Pueblo Revolt of 1680: Conquest and Resistance in Seventeenth-Century New Mexico* (Norman, Ok., 1995); Jerald T. Milanich, *Florida Indians and the Invasion from Europe* (Gainesville, 1995); Ramón A. Gutiérrez, *When Jesus Came, the Corn Mothers Went Away: Sexuality and Power in New Mexico, 1500–1846* (Stanford, 1991); Robert H. Jackson and Edward Castillo, *Indians, Franciscans, and Spanish Colonization: The Impact of the Mission System on California Indians* (Albuquerque, 1995); Marc Simmons, *Coronado's Land: Essays on Daily Life in Colonial New Mexico* (Albuquerque, 1991); Charles Hudson, *Knights of Spain, Warriors of the Sun: Hernando de Soto and the South's Ancient Chiefdoms* (Athens, Ga., 1997); David Ewing Duncan, *Hernando de Soto: A Savage Quest in the Americas* (New York, 1995); D.W. Meinig, *Southwest: Three Peoples in Geographical Change, 1600–1970* (New York, 1971); William C. Sturtevant, "Spanish-Indian Relations in Southeastern North America," *Ethnohistory* 9 (1962), 41–94; Edward Spicer, *Cycles of Conquest: The Impact of Spain, Mexico, and the United States on the Indians of the Southwest, 1533–1960* (Tucson, 1962); and Steven W. Hackel, "The Stuff of Leadership: Indian

Authority in the Missions of Alta California," *William and Mary Quarterly,* 54 (1997), 347–76.

For the Dutch record in New Netherland the best studies are Allen W. Trelease, *Indian Affairs in Colonial New York: The Seventeenth Century* (Ithaca, N.Y., 1960); Ted J. Brasser, *Riding on the Frontier's Crest: Mahican Indian Culture and Culture Change,* National Museum of Man, Mercury Series, #13 (Ottawa, 1974); and Oliver A. Rink, *Holland on the Hudson: An Economic and Social History of Dutch New York* (Ithaca, N.Y., 1986).

Extending the scope of European–Indian relations to other parts of the New World is a valuable way of establishing the special character of cultural interaction in North America. Magnus Mörner's *Race Mixture in the History of Latin America* (Boston, 1967) is an excellent place to begin. Regarding Spanish colonization, see Lewis Hanke, *Aristotle and the American Indian: A Study in Race Prejudice in the Modern World* (London, 1959); Lewis Hanke, *The Spanish Struggle for Justice in the Conquest of America* (Philadelphia, 1949); Murdo J. MacLeod, *Spanish Central America: A Socio-economic History, 1420–1720* (Berkeley, 1973); and Inga Clendinnen, *Ambivalent Conquests: Maya and Spaniard in Yucatan, 1517–1570* (Cambridge, 1987). The Portuguese case is carefully examined in Charles R. Boxer, *Race Relations in the Portuguese Colonial Empire, 1415–1825* (Oxford, 1963); Mathias C. Kiemen, *The Indian Policy of Portugal in the Amazon Region, 1614–1693* (Washington, D.C., 1954); Alexander N. Marchant, *From Barter to Slavery: The Economic Relations of Portuguese and Indians in the Settlement of Brazil, 1500–1580* (Baltimore, 1942); and John Hemming, *Red Gold: The Conquest of the Brazilian Indians, 1500–1760* (Cambridge, Mass., 1978). Charles R. Boxer's *The Dutch Seaborne Empire, 1600–1800* (New York, 1965) includes material on Dutch relations with Indian peoples.

Before embarking on a more detailed investigation of English–Indian interaction in early America, students can profit by assaying the ideas of various historians on how this subject can—and ought to be—approached. In the order of their publication the most important of these are: William N. Fenton, *American Indian and White Relations to 1830: Needs and Opportunities for Study* (Chapel Hill, N.C., 1957); Stanley Pargellis, "The Problem of American Indian History," *Ethnohistory* 4 (1957–58), 113–24: Wilcomb E. Washburn, "A Moral History of Indian–White Relations: Needs and Opportunities for Study," *Ethnohistory* 4 (1957–58), 47–61; Bernard W. Sheehan, "Indian–White Relations in Early America: A Review Essay," *William and Mary Quarterly* 26 (1969), 267–86; Robert F. Berkhofer, Jr., "The Political Context of a New Indian History," *Pacific Historical Review* 40 (1971), 375–82; Robert M. Carmack, "Ethnohistory: A Review of Its Development, Definition, Methods, and Aims," *Annual Review of Anthropology* 1 (1972), 227–46; James Axtell, "The Ethnohistory of Early America," *William and Mary Quarterly* 35 (1978), 110–44; *After Columbus: Essays in the Ethnohistory of Colonial North America* (New York, 1988); and "Colonial America without the Indians: Counterfactual Reflections," *Journal of American History* 73 (1986–1987), 981–96; Daniel

K. Richter, "Whose Indian History?" *Journal of American History,* 50 (1993), 379–93; James H. Merrell, "Some Thoughts on Colonial Historians and American Indians," *William and Mary Quarterly,* 46 (1989), 94–119; Neal Salisbury, "The Indians' Old World: Native Americans and the Coming of Europeans," *William and Mary Quarterly,* 53 (1996), 435–58; Kenneth M. Morrison, "Native American History: The Issue of Values," *Journal of Ethnic Studies* 5 (1978), 80–89; and Calvin Martin, ed., *The American Indian and the Problem of History* (New York, 1987).

Another prerequisite for studying English–Indian relations is acquiring an understanding of tribal cultures at the time of contact. It is particularly important to comprehend how Native Americans differed from Europeans in their attitude toward land, their economies, their social and political organization, their values and religious beliefs, and their methods of diplomacy and warfare. For a stimulating discussion see Neal Salisbury, "The Indians' Old World: Native Americans and the Coming of Europeans," *William and Mary Quarterly,* 53 (1996), 435–58. On land, see A. Irving Hallowell, "The Nature and Function of Property as a Social Institution," in *Culture and Experience* (Philadelphia, 1955), 236–49; Ralph M. Linton, "Land Tenure in Aboriginal America," in Oliver La Farge, ed., *The Changing Indian* (Norman, Okla., 1942), 42–54; George S. Snyderman, "Concepts of Land Ownership among the Iroquois and Their Neighbors," in William N. Fenton, ed., *Symposium on Local Diversity in Iroquois Culture* (Washington, D.C., 1951), 13–34; A. L. Kroeber, "Nature of the Land-Holding Group," *Ethnohistory* 2 (1955), 303–14; and Anthony F. C. Wallace, "Political Organization and Land Tenure among the Northeastern Indians, 1600–1830," *Southwestern Journal of Anthropology* 13 (1957), 301–21.

The most comprehensive work on the economic organization of American Indian societies is Marshall Sahlins, *Stone Age Economics* (Chicago, 1972). Other useful essays are David Hurst Thomas, ed., *Columbian Consequences,* vol. 2 (Washington, 1990), 139–51; Nelson Foster and Linda S. Cordell, eds., *Chilies to Chocolate: Food the Americas Gave the World* (Tucson, 1992); Merrill K. Bennett, "The Food Economy of the New England Indians, 1605–1675," *Journal of Political Economy* 63 (1955), 369–97; Judith Brown, "Economic Organization and the Position of Women Among the Iroquois," *Ethnohistory* 17 (1970), 151–67; and George S. Snyderman, "The Functions of Wampum," *Proceedings of the American Philosophical Society* 98 (1954), 469–94.

Related to economic behavior is the fascinating and hotly debated issue of Indians' environmental values and behavior. Important contributions to this topic are William Cronon, *Changes in the Land: Indians, Colonists, and the Ecology of New England* (New York, 1983); Calvin Martin, *Keepers of the Game: Indian–Animal Relationships and the Fur Trade* (Berkeley and Los Angeles, 1979); and Shepard Krech III, ed., *Indians, Animals, and the Fur Trade: A Critique of "Keepers of the Game"* (Athens, Ga., 1981); Timothy Silver, *A New Face on the Countryside: Indians, Colonists and Slaves in South Atlantic Forests, 1500–1800* (Cambridge, Mass., 1990); Carolyn Merchant, *Ecological Revolutions: Nature, Gender, and Science in New England* (Chapel Hill, N.C., 1989); Alfred W. Crosby, *Ecological Imperialism: The Biological Expansion of Europe, 900–1900* (Cambridge, Mass., 1986); and Christopher Vecsey and Robert W. Venables, eds., *American Indian Environments: Ecological Issues in Native American History* (Syracuse, N.Y., 1980).

On social organization it is especially important to study the role of women in Native American societies. Among the most important works are John R. Swanton, *Social Organization and Social Usages in the Southeast* (Washington, D.C., 1928); Anthony F. C. Wallace, "Women, Land, and Society: Three Aspects of Colonial Delaware Life," *Pennsylvania Archaeologist* 17 (1947), 1–35; Karen Anderson, *Chain Her by One Foot: The Subjugation of Native Women in Seventeenth-Century New France* (New York, 1991); Nancy Shoemaker, ed., *Negotiators of Change: Historical Perspectives on Native American Women* (New York, 1995); Judith K. Brown, "Iroquois Women: An Ethnohistoric Note," in Rayna R. Reiter, *Toward an Anthropology of Women* (New York, 1975); James Axtell, ed., *The Indian Peoples of Eastern America: A Documentary History of the Sexes* (New York, 1981); John Upton Terrell and Donna M. Terrell, *Indian Women of the Western Morning: Their Life in Early America* (New York, 1974); and Natalie Z. Davis, "Iroquois Women, European Women," in Margo Hendricks and Patricia Parker, eds., *Women, "Race," and Writing* (London, 1994).

Political organization, including the much misunderstood problem of factionalism among American Indians, is studied in: Elizabeth Tooker, "Clans and Moieties in North America," *Current Anthropology* 12 (1971), 357–76; William N. Fenton, "Factionalism in American Indian Society," *Tirage a part: Actes du IVe Congres International des Sciences Anthropologiques et Ethnologiques,* II (Vienna, 1952), 330–40; P. Richard Metcalf, "Who Should Rule at Home: Native American Politics and Indian–White Relations," *Journal of American History* 61 (1974–75), 651–65; and Ralph W. Nicholas, "Factions: A Comparative Approach," in Michael Banton, ed., *Political Systems and the Distribution of Power* (London, 1965).

Indian–white relations cannot be understood without appreciation of the value system and religious beliefs of Native Americans. A good place to begin is with Ruth M. Underhill's *Red Man's Religion: Beliefs and Practices of the Indians North of Mexico* (Chicago, 1965). Also valuable are: Ake Hultkrantz, *The Religions of the American Indians,* trans. Monica Setterwall (Berkeley and Los Angeles, 1979); Claude Levi-Strauss, *The Savage Mind* (Chicago, 1966); Dennis Tedlock and Barbara Tedlock, eds., *Teachings From the American Earth: Indian Religion and Philosophy* (New York, 1975); Elizabeth Tooker, ed., *Native North American Spirituality of the Eastern Woodlands: Sacred Myths, Dreams, Speeches, Healing Formulas, Rituals and Ceremonies* (New York, 1979); and Walter H. Capps, ed., *Seeing with a Native Eye: Essays on Native American Religion* (New York, 1976).

On Indian diplomacy and warfare a number of essays and books are valuable. On diplomacy see James H. Merrell, *Into the American Woods: Negotiators on the Pennsylvania Frontier* (New York, 1999); Wilbur R. Jacobs, *Wilderness Politics and Indian Gifts: The Northern Colonial Frontier, 1748–1763* (Lincoln, Neb., rev. ed., 1966); Dorothy Jones, *License for Empire: Colonialism by Treaty in Early America* (Chicago, 1982); Nancy L. Hagedorn, "A Friend to Go Between Them: The Interpreter as Cultural Broker During Anglo-Iroquois Councils, 1740–1770," *Ethnohistory* 35 (1988), 60–80; Francis Jennings et al., eds., *The History and Culture of Iroquois Diplomacy: An Interdisciplinary Guide to the Treaties of the Six Nations and Their Leagues* (Syracuse, N.Y., 1985); and Fredrika J. Tente and Andrew R. L. Cayton, eds., *Contact Points: American Frontiers from the Mohawk Valley to the Mississippi, 1750–1830* (Chapel Hill, N.C., 1998).

Indian warfare is analyzed in George S. Snyderman, "Behind the Tree of Peace: A Sociological Analysis of Iroquois Warfare," *Pennsylvania Archaeologist* 18 (1948), 2–93; Patricia Seed, *Ceremonies of Possession in Europe's Conquest of the New World, 1492–1640* (Cambridge, Mass., 1995); John Phillip Reid, *A Better Kind of Hatchet: The Law, Trade, and Diplomacy in the Cherokee Nation during the Early Years of European Contact* (University Park, Pa., 1976); Inga Clendinnen, "Fierce and Unnatural Cruelty: Cortés and the Conquest of Mexico," *Representations* 33 (1991), 65–100; Patricia M. Malone, *The Skulking Way of War: Technology and Tactics among the New England Indians* (Lanham, Md., 1991); Daniel K. Richter, "War and Culture: The Iroquois Experience," *William and Mary Quarterly* 40(1983), 529–37; Marian W. Smith, "American Indian Warfare," *New York Academy of Sciences, Transactions,* 2d Ser. 13 (1951), 348–65; Wendell S. Hadlock, "War among the Northeastern Woodland Indians," *American Anthropologist,* n.s. 49 (1947), 204–21; Nathaniel Knowles, "The Torture of Captives of the Indians of Eastern North America," *American Philosophical Society Proceedings* 82 (1940), 151–225; James Axtell and William C. Sturtevant, "The Unkindest Cut of All, or Who Invented Scalping?" *William and Mary Quarterly* 37 (1980), 451–72; Patrick M. Malone, "The Changing Military Technology Among the Indians of Southern New England, 1600–1677," *American Quarterly* 25 (1973), 48–63; Adam J. Hirsch, "The Collision of Military Cultures in Seventeenth-Century New England," *Journal of American History* 74 (1988), 1187–1212; and J. Frederick Fausz, "Fighting 'Fire' With Firearms: The Anglo–Powhatan Arms Race in Early Virginia," *American Indian Culture and Research Journal* 3 (1979), 33–50.

After studying the characteristics of broad cultural groups, one can turn to examining individual cases of European-Indian contact. These should be considered within a general understanding of "acculturation," a concept that has its own history. See, for example, Melville J. Herskovits, *Acculturation: The Study of Culture Contacts* (New York, 1938); Ralph Linton, ed., *Acculturation in Seven American Indian Tribes* (New York, 1940); Homer G. Barnett, et al., "Acculturation: An Exploratory Formulation," *American Anthropologist,* n.s. 56 (1954), 972–1002; Edward H. Spicer, ed., *Perspectives in American Indian Culture Change* (Chicago, 1961); and Frederik Barth, ed., *Ethnic Groups and Boundaries: The Social Organization of Culture Difference* (London, 1969).

In studying the first major Indian-English confrontation—in the Chesapeake area of Virginia—students must sort through a maze of books and articles written from a variety of approaches. From the historians have come important works, such as Wesley Frank Craven, *White, Red and Black: The Seventeenth-Century Virginian* (Charlottesville, Va., 1971); Bernard Sheehan, *Savagism and Civility: Indians and Englishmen in Colonial Virginia* (Cambridge, Mass., 1980); J. Frederick Fausz, "Merging and Emerging Worlds: Anglo–Indian Interest Groups and the Development of the Seventeenth-Century Chesapeake," in Lois Green Carr, Philip D. Morgan, and Jean B. Russo, eds., *Colonial Chesapeake Society* (Chapel Hill, N.C., 1988); Helen C. Rountree, *Pocahontas's People: The Powhatan Indians of Virginia through Four Centuries* (Norman, Ok., 1990) and *The Powhatan Indians of Virginia: Their Traditional Culture* (Norman, Ok., 1989); W. Stitt Robinson, Jr., "The Legal Status of the Indian in Colonial Virginia," *Virginia Magazine of History and Biography* 61 (1953), 249–59; David D. Smits, "'Abominable Mixture': Toward the Repudiation of Anglo–Indian Intermarriage in Seventeenth-Century Virginia," *Virginia Magazine of History and Biography* 95 (1987), 157–92; Alden T. Vaughan, "'Expulsion of the Savages': English Policy and the Virginia Massacre of 1622," *William and Mary Quarterly* 35 (1978), 57–84; William S. Powell, "Aftermath of the Massacre: The First Indian War, 1622–1632," *Virginia Magazine of History and Biography* 66 (1958), 44–75; Carl Bridenbaugh, *Jamestown, 1544–1699* (New York, 1980); J. Frederick Fausz, "The Invasion of Virginia—Indians, Colonialism, and the Conquest of Cant: A Review Essay on Anglo–Indian Relations in the Chesapeake," *Virginia Magazine of History and Biography* 95 (1987), 132–156; Wilcomb E. Washburn, *The Governor and the Rebel: A History of Bacon's Rebellion in Virginia* (Chapel Hill, N.C., 1957); and three accounts of Pocahontas, whose acceptance of the English colonists and marriage to one of them suggests why she, rather than her father Powhatan, has captured the American imagination: Philip L. Barbour, *Pocahontas and Her World* (Boston, 1970); J. A. Leo LeMay, *Did Pocahontas Save Captain John Smith?* (Athens, Ga., 1992); and Grace Woodward, *Pocahontas* (Norman, Okla., 1969).

From the anthropologists and ethnohistorians of early Virginia the following are particularly worthy of attention: Lewis R. Binford, "An Ethnohistory of the Nottoway, Meherran and Weanock Indians of Southeastern Virginia," *Ethnohistory* 14 (1967), 104–218; David I. Bushnell, Jr., "Virginia before Jamestown," in *Essays in Historical Anthropology of North America* (Washington, D.C., 1940); Christian F. Feest, "Powhatan: A Study in Political Organization," *Wiener Völkerkundliche Mitteilungen* (1966), 69–83; J. Frederick Fausz, "Opechancanough: Indian Resistance Leader," in David W. Sweet and Gary B. Nash, eds., *Struggle and Survival in Colonial America* (Berkeley and Los Angeles, 1981); Nancy O. Lurie, "Indian Cultural Adjustment to European Civilization," in James M. Smith, ed., *Seventeenth-Century America: Essays in Colonial History* (Chapel Hill, N.C., 1959); Ben C. McCary,

Indians in Seventeenth-Century Virginia (Williamsburg, Va., 1957); and Theodore Stern, "Chickahominy: The Changing Culture of a Virginia Indian Community," *Proceedings of the American Philosophical Society* 96 (1952), 152–225.

To the immediate north and south of the Virginian–Powhatan encounter, the story of Anglo–Indian relations can be followed in Francis Jennings, "Glory, Death, and Transfiguration: The Susquehannock Indians in the Seventeenth Century," *Proceedings of the American Philosophical Society* 112 (1968), 15–53; Jane Henry, "The Choptank Indians of Maryland Under the Proprietary Government," *Maryland Historical Magazine* 65 (1970), 171–80; James H. Merrell, "Cultural Continuity among the Piscataway Indians of Colonial Maryland," *William and Mary Quarterly* 36 (1979), 548–70; and Douglas Rights, *The American Indian in North Carolina* (Durham, N.C., 1947).

The second major case of culture contact between Englishmen and native North Americans in the seventeenth century came in New England. Of special importance in understanding cultural interaction are recent works that probe the Puritan mind for characteristics that imparted a special quality to the Puritan approach to Indian affairs: James Axtell, "The Scholastic Philosophy of the Wilderness," *William and Mary Quarterly* 29 (1972), 335–66; Peter N. Carroll, *Puritanism and the Wilderness: The Intellectual Significance of the New England Frontier, 1629–1700* (New York, 1969); Roy H. Pearce, "The 'Ruines of Mankind': The Indian and the Puritan Mind," *Journal of the History of Ideas* 13 (1952), 200–17; Richard Slotkin, *Regeneration through Violence: The Mythology of the American Frontier, 1600–1860* (Middletown, Conn., 1973); William S. Simmons, "Cultural Bias in the New England Puritans' Perception of Indians," *William and Mary Quarterly* 38 (1981), 56–72; and David D. Smits, "'We Are Not to Grow Wild': Seventeenth-Century New England's Repudiation of Anglo–Indian Intermarriage," *American Indian Culture and Research Journal* 11 (1987), 1–32.

Widely divergent opinions are held by historians on Puritan–Indian relations. The labels "coexistence" and "coercion" can stand for the two approaches that historians have discerned. Both interpretations are well amplified in the following works: Laurence Hauptman and James D. Wherry, eds., *The Pequots in Southern New England: The Rise and Fall of an American Indian Nation* (Norman, Ok., 1990); William S. Simmons, *Spirit of New England Tribes: Indian History and Folklore, 1620–1984* (Hanover, N.H., 1986); Alfred Cave, *The Pequot War* (Amherst, Mass., 1996); George F. Willison, *Saints and Strangers* (New York, 1945); Alden T. Vaughan, *New England Frontier: Puritans and Indians, 1620–1675* (Boston, 1965); Alden T. Vaughan and Daniel K. Richter, "Crossing the Cultural Divide: Indians and New Englanders, 1605–1763," *Proceedings of the American Antiquarian Society* 90 (1980), 23–99; Francis Jennings, *The Invasion of America: Indians, Colonialism, and the Cant of Conquest* (Chapel Hill, N.C., 1975); Kenneth M. Morrison, *The Embattled Northeast: The Elusive Ideal of Alliance in Abenaki-Euramerican Relations* (Berkeley and Los Angeles, 1984); Neal E. Salisbury, *Manitou and*

Providence: Indians, Europeans, and the Beginnings of New England (New York, 1982); Douglas E. Leach, *Flintlock and Tomahawk: New England in King Philip's War* (New York, 1958); Philip Ranlet, "Another Look at the Causes of King Philip's War," *New England Quarterly* 61 (1988), 79–100; Russell Bourne, *The Red King's Rebellion: Racial Politics in New England, 1675–1678* (New York, 1991); Jill Lepore, *The Name of War: King Philip's War and the Origins of American Identity* (New York, 1998); James Drake, "Restraining Atrocity: The Conduct of King Philip's War," *New England Quarterly,* 70 (1997), 33–56 and "Symbol of a Failed Strategy: The Sassamon Trial, Political Culture and the Outbreak of King Philip's War," *American Indian Culture and Research Journal,* 19, (1995), 111–41; Virginia DeJohn Anderson, "King Philip's Herds: Indians, Colonists, and the Problem of Livestock in Early New England," *William and Mary Quarterly,* 3d Ser., 51 (1994), 601–24; Daniel R. Mandell, *Behind the Frontier: Indians in Eighteenth-Century Eastern Massachusetts* (Lincoln, Neb., 1996).

More specialized studies are Leonard A. Adolf, "Squanto's Role in Pilgrim Diplomacy," *Ethnohistory* 11 (1964), 247–61; David Bushnell, "The Treatment of the Indians in Plymouth Colony," *New England Quarterly* 26 (1953), 193–218; Jack L. Davis, "Roger Williams among the Narragansett Indians," *New England Quarterly* 43 (1970), 593–604; Richard R. Johnson, "The Search for a Usable Indian: An Aspect of the Defense of Colonial New England," *Journal of American History* 64 (1977–78), 623–50; M. K. Bennett, "The Food Economy of the New England Indians, 1605–75," *Journal of Political Economy* 63 (1955), 369–97; Peter A. Thomas, "Contrastive Subsistence Strategies and Land Use as Factors for Understanding Indian-White Relations in New England," *Ethnohistory* 23 (1976), 1–18; Yasu Kawashima, *Puritan Justice and the Indian: White Man's Law in Massachusetts, 1630–1763* (Middletown, Conn., 1986); James P. Ronda, "Red and White at the Bench: Indians and the Law in Plymouth County, 1620–1691," *Essex Institute Historical Collections* 110 (1974), 200–15; Lyle Koehler, "Red–White Relations and Justice in the Courts of Seventeenth-Century New England," *American Indian Culture and Research Journal* 3 (1979), 1–31; Colin G. Calloway, *The Western Abenakis of Vermont, 1600–1800: War, Migration, and the Survival of an Indian People* (Norman, Ok., 1990); G. E. Thomas, "Puritans, Indians, and the Concept of Race," *New England Quarterly* 48 (1975), 3–27; and William Burton and Richard Lowenthal, "Uncas: The First of the Mohegans," *American Ethnologist* 1 (1974), 589–99.

No Indian group in eastern North America has been more studied by historians and anthropologists than the Iroquois, whose geographical position placed them in close contact for two centuries with European settlers from France, Holland, and England. Both anthropologists and historians are represented in the following selection, which represents only an introduction to Iroquois studies: Dean Snow, *The Iroquois* (Oxford, 1996); William N. Fenton, "Problems Arising from the Historic Northeastern

Position of the Iroquois," in *Essays in Historical Anthropology of North America* (Washington, D.C., 1940); Michael K. Foster, Jack Campisi, and Marianne Mithun, eds., *Extending the Rafters: Interdisciplinary Approaches to Iroquoian Studies* (Albany, N.Y., 1984); George T. Hunt, *The Wars of the Iroquois: A Study in Intertribal Relations* (Madison, Wis., 1940); Daniel K. Richter and James H. Merrell, eds., *Beyond the Covenant Chain: The Iroquois and Their Neighbors in Indian North America, 1600–1800* (Syracuse, N.Y., 1987); José António Brandão, *"Your Fyre Shall Burn No More:" Iroquois Policy Toward New France and Its Allies to 1701* (Lincoln, Neb., 1997); Daniel Richter, *The Ordeal of the Longhouse: The Peoples of the Iroquois League in the Era of European Colonization* (Chapel Hill, N.C., 1992); James W. Bradley, *Evolution of the Onondaga Iroquois: Accommodating Change, 1500–1655* (New York, 1987); Karl H. Schleiger, "Epidemics and Indian Middlemen: Rethinking the Wars of the Iroquois, 1609–1653," *Ethnohistory* 23 (1976), 129–45; Allen W. Trelease, *Indian Affairs in Colonial New York: The Seventeenth Century* (Ithaca, N.Y., 1960); Richard Aquila, *The Iroquois Restoration: Iroquois Diplomacy on the Colonial Frontier, 1701–1754* (Detroit, 1983); Anthony F. C. Wallace, *The Death and Rebirth of the Seneca* (New York, 1969); William N. Fenton, "The Lore of the Longhouse: Myth, Ritual, and Red Power," *Anthropological Quarterly* 48 (1975), 131–47; James T. Flexner, *Mohawk Baronet: Sir William Johnson of New York* (New York, 1959); Francis Jennings, "The Constitutional Evolution of the Covenant Chain," *Proceedings of the American Philosophical Society* 115 (1971), 88–96; *The Ambiguous Iroquois Empire: The Covenant Chain Confederation of Indian Tribes with English Colonies from Its Beginnings to the Lancaster Treaty of 1744* (New York, 1984); Francis Jennings, ed., *The History and Culture of Iroquois Diplomacy: An Interdisciplinary Guide to the Treaties of the Six Nations and Their League* (Syracuse, N.Y., 1985); Isabel Thompson Kelsay, *Joseph Brant, 1743–1807, Man of Two Worlds* (Syracuse, N.Y., 1984); Georgiana C. Nammack, *Fraud, Politics, and the Dispossession of the Indians: The Iroquois Land Frontier in the Colonial Period* (Norman, Ok., 1969); Patrick Frazier, *The Mohicans of Stockbridge* (Lincoln, Neb., 1992); and Arthur C. Parker, *History of the Seneca Indians* (Port Washington, N.Y., 1967).

Of special interest to students of Indian–European relations, because it casts grave doubts on the widely enunciated thesis that conflict was inevitable between cultural groups as widely separate as Algonquians and Europeans, is the interaction of the Pennsylvania Quakers and the Delaware (Lenni Lenape) Indians. Both the early Quaker contacts with the Delawares and the subsequent breakdown of amicable relations are detailed in the following selections: Thomas E. Drake, "Penn's Experiment in Race Relations," *Pennsylvania Magazine of History and Biography* 68 (1944), 372–87; Francis Jennings, "The Delaware Interregnum," *Pennsylvania Magazine of History and Biography* 89 (1965), 174–98; W. W. Newcomb, Jr., *The Culture and Acculturation of the Delaware Indians* (Ann Arbor, 1956); Theodore G. Thayer, "The Friendly Association," *Pennsylvania Magazine of History and Biography* 67

(1943), 356–76; Frederick B. Tolles, "Nonviolent Contact: The Quakers and the Indians," *Proceedings of the American Philosophical Society* 107 (1963), 93–101; Sherman P. Uhler, *Pennsylvania's Indian Relations to 1754* (Allentown, Pa., 1951); Anthony F. C. Wallace, *King of the Delawares: Teedyuscung, 1700–1763* (Philadelphia, 1949); Paul A. W. Wallace, *Indians in Pennsylvania* (Harrisburg, Pa., 1961); C. A. Weslager, *The Delaware Indians: A History* (New Brunswick, N.J., 1972); Charles E. Hunter, "The Delaware Nativist Revival of the Mid-Eighteenth Century," *Ethnohistory* 18 (1971), 39–50; and Peter C. Mancall, *Valley of Opportunity: Economic Culture along the Upper Susquehanna, 1700–1800* (Ithaca, N.Y., 1991).

Because it was not settled until the last third of the seventeenth century the Southeast was the last zone of Anglo–Indian contact in the colonization of North America. But interaction between the English settlers of the Carolinas and Georgia with the Creeks and Cherokees, the two most powerful tribes of this region, is among the most instructive examples of culture contact, because these powerful tribes, like the Iroquois, maintained their political power and cultural integrity long after the small coastal tribes had been decimated or subordinated. This complex confrontation, which involved shifting alliances between the three European powers contending for advantage in the area and the two Indian powers seeking preeminence, must be followed in both historical and anthropological accounts. The best are: David H. Corkran, *The Cherokee Frontier: Conflict and Survival, 1740–62* (Norman, Ok., 1962); and *The Creek Frontier, 1540–1783* (Norman, Ok., 1967); James Axtell, *The Indians' New South: Cultural Change in the Colonial Southeast* (Baton Rouge, La., 1997); R. S. Cotterill, *The Southern Indians: The Story of the Civilized Tribes before Removal* (Norman, Ok., 1954); Charles Hudson and Carmen Chaves Tesser, eds., *The Forgotten Centuries: Indians and Europeans in the American South, 1521–1704* (Athens, Ga., 1994); Verner W. Crane, *The Southern Frontier, 1670–1732* (Ann Arbor, Mich., 1929); Frederick Gearing, *Priests and Warriors: Social Structures for Cherokee Politics in the 18th Century* (Menasha, Wis., 1962); Joel Martin, *Sacred Revolt: The Muskogees' Struggle for a New World* (Boston, 1991); Charles M. Hudson, ed., *Red, White and Black: Symposium on Indians in the Old South* (Athens, Ga., 1971); Chapman J. Milling, *Red Carolinians* (Chapel Hill, N.C., 1940); Carolyn Keller Reeves, ed., *The Choctaw Before Removal* (Jackson, Miss., 1985); Patricia Galloway, *Choctaw Genesis, 1500–1700* (Lincoln, Neb., 1995); Hale G. Smith, *The European and the Indian: European–Indian Contacts in Georgia and Florida* (Gainesville, Fla., 1956); Alexander Spoehr, *Changing Kinship Systems: A Study in the Acculturation of the Creeks, Cherokees, and Choctaws* (Chicago, 1947); Peter H. Wood, et al., *Powhatan's Mantle: Indians in the Colonial Southeast* (Lincoln, Neb., 1991); Charles Hudson, *The Southeastern Indians* (Knoxville, Tenn., 1976); Philip Reid, *A Law of Blood: The Primitive Law of the Cherokee Nation* (New York, 1970), and *A Better Kind of Hatchet: Law, Trade, and Diplomacy in the Cherokee Nation during the Early Years of European Contact* (State College,

Pa., 1976); Rennard Strickland, *Fire and the Spirits: Cherokee Law From Clan to Court* (Norman, Ok., 1975); and J. Leitch Wright, Jr., *The Only Land They Knew: The Tragic Story of the American Indians in the Old South* (New York, 1981), and *Creeks and Seminoles: Destruction and Regeneration of the Muscogulge People* (Lincoln, Neb., 1986).

Valuable accounts of smaller coastal tribes in the South include John T. Juricek, "The Westo Indians," *Ethnohistory* 11 (1964), 134–73; James W. Covington, "Apalachee Indians, 1704–1763," *Florida Historical Quarterly* 50 (1972), 366–84; William C. Sturtevant, "Spanish–Indian Relations in Southeastern North America," *Ethnohistory* 9 (1962), 41–94; George L. Hicks, "Cultural Persistence Versus Local Adaptation: Frank G. Speck's Catawba Indians," *Ethnohistory* 12 (1965), 343–54; Charles M. Hudson, *The Catawba Nation* (Athens, Ga., 1970); and James H. Merrell, *The Indians' New World: Catawbas and Their Neighbors from European Contact through the Era of Removal* (Chapel Hill, N.C., 1989).

In the national imagination and in popular history warfare has always stood out as the crucial element in Indian–white relations. But three aspects of the acculturative process—disease, trade, and religion—deserve much greater emphasis. Of the three, trade is especially important, for along the trade routes went not only material goods but also microorganisms and ideology. For various aspects of the Indian trade and for different assessments of its conduct the following are significant: Carolyn Gilman, ed., *Where Two Worlds Meet: The Great Lakes Fur Trade* (St. Paul, Minn., 1982); Harold A. Innis, *The Fur Trade in Canada* (New Haven, 1930); Francis X. Moloney, *The Fur Trade in New England, 1620–1676* (Cambridge, Mass., 1931); Walter O'Meara, *Daughters of the Country: The Women of the Fur Traders and Mountain Men* (New York, 1959); Lewis O. Saum, *The Fur Trader and the Indian* (Seattle, 1965); Malvina Bolus, ed., *People and Pelts: Second North American Fur Trade Conference* (Winnipeg, 1972); *Aspects of the Fur Trade: Selected Papers* (St. Paul, Minn., 1967); Conrad Heidenreich and Arthur J. Ray, *The Early Fur Trade: A Study in Cultural Interaction* (Toronto, 1976); Thomas E. Norton, *The Fur Trade in Colonial New York, 1686–1776* (Madison, Wis., 1974); Christopher L. Miller and George R. Hamell, "A New Perspective on Indian-White Contact: Cultural Symbols and Colonial Trade," *Journal of American History* 73 (1986), 311–28; and Kathryn E. Holland Braund, *Deerskins and Duffels: Creek Indian Trade with Anglo-America, 1685–1815* (Lincoln, Neb., 1993). More specialized studies include Allen W. Trelease, "The Iroquois and the Western Fur Trade: A Problem of Interpretation," *Mississippi Valley Historical Review* 49 (1962), 32–51; Bruce Trigger, "The Jesuits and the Fur Trade," *Ethnohistory* 12 (1965), 30–53; Francis Jennings, "The Indian Trade of the Susquehanna Valley," *Proceedings of the American Philosophical Society* 110 (1966), 406–24; John C. McManus, "An Economic Analysis of Indian Behavior in the North American Fur Trade," *Journal of Economic History* 32 (1972), 36–53; Harold Hickerson,

"Fur Trade Colonialism and the North American Indians," *Ethnohistory* 1 (1973), 15–44; George I. Quimby, *Indian Culture and European Trade Goods: The Archaeology of the Historic Period in the Western Great Lakes Region* (Madison, 1966); and W. J. Eccles, "The Fur Trade and Eighteenth-Century Imperialism," *William and Mary Quarterly* 40 (1983), 341–62.

On the role of disease in Indian–European relations, see P. M. Ashburn, *The Ranks of Death: A Medical History of the Conquest of America*, ed. Frank D. Ashburn (New York, 1947); Alfred W. Crosby, *The Columbian Exchange: Biological and Cultural Consequences of 1492* (Westport, Conn., 1972); Henry F. Dobyns, *Their Number Become Thinned: Native Population Dynamics in Eastern North America* (Knoxville, Tenn., 1983); John Duffy, "Smallpox and the Indians in the American Colonies," *Bulletin of the History of Medicine* 25 (1951), 324–41; E. Wagner and Allen E. Stearn, *The Effect of Smallpox on the Destiny of the Amerindian* (Boston, 1945); and Sherburne F. Cook, "The Significance of Disease in the Extinction of the New England Indians," *Human Biology* 45 (1973), 485–508. Alcohol, another form of disease brought by Europeans to Indian societies in the view of many historians and anthropologists, is re-examined in Nancy Oestreich Lurie, "The World's Oldest On-Going Protest Demonstration: North American Indian Drinking Patterns," *Pacific Historical Review* 40 (1971), 311–32; Peter C. Mancall, *Deadly Medicine: Indians and Alcohol in Early America* (Ithaca, N.Y., 1995); and Craig MacAndrew and Robert B. Edgerton, *Drunken Comportment: A Social Explanation* (Chicago, 1969).

English missionary activity, which must be seen in a political as well as religious context, is analyzed in Elma Gray, *Wilderness Christians: The Moravian Mission to the Delaware Indians* (Ithaca, N.Y., 1956); Frank J. Klingberg, *Anglican Humanitarianism in Colonial New York* (Philadelphia, 1940); W. Stitt Robinson, "Indian Education and Missions in Colonial Virginia," *Journal of Southern History* 18 (1952): 152–68; Neal Salisbury, "Red Indians: The 'Praying Indians' of Massachusetts Bay and John Eliot," *William and Mary Quarterly* 31 (1974), 27–54, and "Prospero in New England: The Puritan Missionary as Colonist," in William Cowan, ed., *Papers of the Sixth Algonquian Conference,* 1974 National Museum of Man, *Mercury Series* (Ottawa, 1975), 253–73; Francis Jennings, "Goals and Functions of the Puritan Missions to the Indians," *Ethnohistory* 18 (1971), 197–212; Harold W. van Lonkhuyzen, "A Reappraisal of the Praying Indians: Acculturation, Conversion, and Identity in Natick, Massachusetts, 1646–1730," *New England Quarterly,* 63 (1990), 396–428; James P. Ronda, "The European Indian: Jesuit Civilization Planning in New France," *Church History* 41 (1972), 385–95; "Generations of Faith: The Christian Indians of Martha's Vineyard," *William and Mary Quarterly* 38 (1981), 369–94, and "'We Are Well As We Are': An Indian Critique of Seventeenth-Century Christian Missions," *William and Mary Quarterly* 34 (1977), 66–82; Nancy Bonvillain, "The Iroquois and the Jesuits: Strategies of Influence and Resistance," *American Indian Culture and Research Journal* 10 (1986), 29–42; George Tinker,

Missionary Conquest: The Gospel and Native American Genocide (Minneapolis, 1993); Robert Conkling, "Legitimacy and Conversion in Social Change: The Case of the French Missionaries and the Northeastern Algonkian," *Ethnohistory* 21 (1974), 1–24; James Axtell, "The European Failure to Convert the Indians: An Autopsy," *Ethnohistory*, 274–90; and Kenneth M. Morrison, "Towards a History of Intimate Encounters: Algonkian Folklore, Jesuit Missionaries, and Kiwakwe, The Cannibal Giant," *American Indian Culture and Research Journal* 3 (1979), 51–80, "That Art of Coyning Christians: John Eliot and the Praying Indians of Massachusetts," *Ethnohistory* 21 (1974), 77–92, and "Montaignais Missionization in Early New France: The Syncretic Imperative," *American Indian Culture and Research Journal* 10 (1986), 1–23.

Acculturation, of course, was a two-way process. On "Indianization" of European colonists, some especially valuable works are: Alden T. Vaughan and Daniel K. Richter, "Crossing the Cultural Divide: Indians and New Englanders, 1605–1763," *Proceedings of the American Antiquarian Society* 90 (1980), 33–35; John Demos, *The Unredeemed Captive: A Family Story from Early America* (New York, 1995); June Namias, *White Captives: Gender and Ethnicity on American Frontiers* (Chapel Hill, 1993); Erwin H. Ackerknecht, "White Indians," *Bulletin of the History of Medicine* 15 (1944), 18–35; Marius Barbeau, "Indian Captivities," *Proceedings of the American Philosophical Society* 94 (1950), 522–48; Thomas A. Boyd, *Simon Girty: The White Savage* (New York, 1928); Felix S. Cohen, "Americanizing the White Man," in Lucy Kramer Cohen, ed., *The Legal Conscience: Selected Papers of Felix S. Cohen* (New Haven, 1960); A. Irving Hallowell, "The Backwash of the Frontier: The Impact of the Indian on American Culture," in Walker D. Wyman and Clifton B. Kroeber, eds., *The Frontier in Perspective* (Madison, Wis., 1957); A. Irving Hallowell, "American Indians, White and Black: The Phenomenon of Transculturalization," *Current Anthropology* 4 (1963), 519–31; J. Norman Heard, *White into Red: A Study of the Assimilation of White Persons Captured by Indians* (Metuchen, N.J., 1973); Roy H. Pearce, "The Significance of the Captivity Narrative," *American Literature* 19 (1947), 1–20, and *Savagism and Civilization: A Study of the Indian and the American Mind* (Baltimore, 1965); James Axtell, "The White Indians of Colonial America," *William and Mary Quarterly* 32 (1975), 55–88, and *The Invasion Within: The Contest of Cultures in Colonial North America* (New York, 1985).

AFRICAN-AMERICAN HISTORY

African-American history begins in Africa, and students who wish to learn more about the Atlantic slave trade and the initial phases of the enslavement process should first gain a basic understanding of African cultures at the time of initial contact with Europeans. A good place to begin is with Basil Davidson, *The African Genius: An Introduction to African Social and Cultural History* (Boston, 1969) and *A History of West Africa, 1000–1800,* new revised ed.

(London, 1977); John Thornton, *Africa and Africans in the Making of the Atlantic World, 1400–1680* (Cambridge, Mass., 1992); F. K. Buah, *A History of West Africa from* A.D. *1000* (London, 1986); J. F. A. Ajayi and Michael Crowder, eds., *History of West Africa,* 3rd ed. (London, 1985); J. D. Fage, *A History of West Africa,* 4th ed. (London, 1969); G. T. Stride and Caroline Ifeka, *Peoples and Empires of West Africa: West Africa in History, 1000–1800* (New York, 1971); and Richard Gray, ed., *The Cambridge History of Africa: Vol. 4: From c. 1600 to c. 1790* (Cambridge, Mass., 1975).

The slave trade should be considered in an international context. Among the many contributions to the literature of this commerce, which was to play such a crucial role in the development of colonial societies in the New World, the following are especially important: Basil Davidson, *The African Slave Trade: Pre-Colonial History, 1450–1850* (Boston, 1961); Philip D. Curtin, *The Atlantic Slave Trade: A Census* (Madison, Wis., 1969); Walter Rodney, *West Africa and the Atlantic Slave Trade* (Nairobi, 1969); Richard N. Bean, *The British Transatlantic Slave Trade, 1650–1775* (New York, 1975); Richard S. Sheridan, "Africa and the Caribbean in the Atlantic Slave Trade," *American Historical Review* 77 (1972), 15–35; Herbert Klein, *The Middle Passage: Comparative Studies in the Atlantic Slave Trade* (Princeton, N.J., 1978); Henry A. Gemery and Jan S. Hoogendorn, eds., *The Uncommon Market: Essays in the Economic History of the Atlantic Slave Trade* (New York, 1979); Paul E. Lovejoy, "The Impact of the Atlantic Slave Trade on Africa: A Review of the Literature," *Journal of African History* 30 (1989), 365–94; David Henige, "Measuring the Immeasurable: the Atlantic Slave Trade, West African Population and the Pyrrhonian Critic," *Journal of African History* 27 (1986), 295–313; Joseph C. Miller, *Way of Death: Merchant Capitalism and the Angolan Slave Trade, 1730–1830* (Madison, Wis., 1988); Harvey M. Feinberg, *Africans and Europeans in West Africa: Elminans and Dutchmen on the Gold Coast during the Eighteenth Century,* American Philosophical Society, *Transactions,* 79, No. 7 (Philadelphia, 1989); John Thornton, *Africa and Africans in the Making of the Atlantic World, 1400–1680* (Cambridge, Mass., 1992); David Eltis and Stanley L. Engerman, "Was the Slave Trade Dominated by Men?" *Journal of Interdisciplinary History,* 23 (1992); David Eltis and David Richardson, "The Numbers Game and Routes to Slavery," *Slavery and Abolition,* 18 (1997), 1–15; and "West Africa and the Transatlantic Slave Trade: New Evidence of Long-Run Trends," *Slavery and Abolition,* 18 (1997), 16–35; Philip D. Morgan, "The Cultural Implications of the Atlantic Slave Trade: African Regional Origins, American Destinations and New World Developments," *Slavery and Abolition,* 18 (1997), 122–45; Peter Caron, "Of a Nation Which Others Do Not Understand: Bambara Slaves and African Ethnicity in Colonial Louisiana, 1718–60," *Slavery and Abolition,* 18 (1997), 98–121. A comprehensive bibliographical discussion of the slave trade can be found in Joseph C. Miller, ed., *Slavery: A Worldwide Bibliography, 1900–1982* (White Plains, N.Y., 1985).

Some general works on slavery that deal with the origins of the labor system in the New World are Eric Williams, *Capitalism and Slavery* (Chapel Hill, N.C., 1944); Roger T. Anstey, "Capitalism and Slavery: A Critique," *Economic History Review* 21 (1968), 307–20; Philip D. Curtin, *The Rise and Fall of the Plantation Complex: Essays in Atlantic History* (Cambridge, Mass., 1990); David Brion Davis, *The Problem of Slavery in Western Culture* (Ithaca, N.Y., 1966); Stanley M. Elkins, *Slavery: A Problem in American Institutional and Intellectual Life* (Chicago, 1959); Oscar and Mary F. Handlin, "Origins of the Southern Labor System," *William and Mary Quarterly* 7 (1950), 199–222; C. L. R. James, "The Atlantic Slave Trade and Slavery: Some Interpretations of Their Significance in the Development of the United States and the Western World," *Amistad* 1 (1970), 119–64; Evsey D. Domar, "The Causes of Slavery and Serfdom: A Hypothesis," *Journal of Economic History* 30 (1970), 18–32; Stanley L. Engerman, "Some Considerations Relating to Property Rights in Man," *ibid.* 33 (1973), 43–65; Carville Earle, "A Staple Interpretation of Slavery and Free Labor," *Geographical Review* 68 (1978), 51–65; and Barbara L. Solow, ed., *Slavery and the Rise of the Atlantic System* (Cambridge, Mass., 1991).

General histories of slavery in the United States are legion, but most of them focus on nineteenth-century slavery in the South and do not trace the evolution of slavery from the colonial period. A general framework for studying slavery can be gained from studying the work of U. B. Phillips, Kenneth Stampp, John W. Blassingame, and Eugene Genovese. A general corrective to their indifference to geographical and temporal variations in the history of slavery is provided by Ira Berlin, "Time, Space, and the Evolution of African American Society on British Mainland North America," *American Historical Review* 85 (1980), 44–78 and is spelled out in five landmark books: Ira Berlin and Philip D. Morgan, eds., *The Slaves' Economy: Independent Production by Slaves in the Americas* (London, 1991), and *Cultivation and Culture: Labor and the Shaping of Slave Life in the Americas* (Charlottesville, Va., 1993); Ira Berlin, *Many Thousands Gone: The First Two Centuries of Slavery in North America* (Cambridge, Mass., 1998); Philip D. Morgan, *Slave Counterpoint: Black Culture in the Eighteenth-Century Chesapeake and Lowcountry* (Chapel Hill, N.C., 1998); Larry E. Hudson, ed., *Working Toward Freedom: Slave Society and the Domestic Economy in the American South* (Rochester, N.Y., 1994). A short general account is Donald R. Wright, *African Americans in the Colonial Era: From African Origins through the American Revolution* (Arlington Heights, Ill., 1990); and Michael A. Gomez, *Exchanging Our Country Marks: The Transformation of African Identities in the Colonial and Antebellum South* (Chapel Hill, N.C., 1998).

Since slavery differed significantly, depending on geography, ecology, settlement patterns, and other factors, regional studies of the institution are invaluable. The Chesapeake colonies of Maryland and Virginia are especially important because it was there that slavery took deepest root in colonial soil in the seventeenth century. A great burst of scholarship is now adding greatly to our understanding of the evolution of Chesapeake slavery delineated in older works, such as Thad W. Tate, Jr., *The Negro in Eighteenth-Century Williamsburg* (Williamsburg, Va., 1965); Wesley F. Craven, *White, Red, and Black: The Seventeenth-Century Virginian* (Charlottesville, Va., 1971); T. H. Breen, "A Changing Labor Force and Race Relations in Virginia 1660–1710," *Journal of Social History* 7 (1973), 3–25; and Jonathan L. Alpert, "The Origin of Slavery in the United States: The Maryland Precedent," *American Journal of Legal History* 14 (1970), 189–221. Among the rich new work of demographic and social historians is Carville V. Earle, *The Evolution of a Tidewater Settlement System: All Hallow's Parish, Maryland, 1650–1783* (Chicago, 1975); Allan Kulikoff, *Tobacco and Slaves: The Development of Southern Cultures in the Chesapeake, 1680–1800* (Chapel Hill, N.C., 1986); Jean Butenhoff Lee, "The Problem of Slave Community in the Eighteenth-Century Chesapeake," *William and Mary Quarterly* 43 (1986), 333–61; Russell Menard, "The Maryland Slave Population, 1658–1730: A Demographic Profile of Blacks in Four Counties," *William and Mary Quarterly* 32 (1975), 29–54; and "From Servants to Slaves: The Transformation of the Chesapeake Labor System," *Southern Studies* 16 (1977), 355–90; Walter Minchinton, Celia King and Peter Waite, eds., *Virginia Slave Trade Statistics, 1698–1775* (Richmond, Va., 1984); Carole Shammas, "Black Women's Work and the Evolution of Plantation Society in Virginia," *Labor History* 26 (1985), 5–28; Ronald L. Lewis, "Slavery on Chesapeake Iron Plantations before the American Revolution," *Journal of Negro History* 59 (1974), 242–54; and "The Use and Extent of Slave Labor in the Chesapeake Iron Industry: The Colonial Era," *Labor History* 17 (1976), 388–412; J. Douglas Deal, *Race and Class in Colonial Virginia: Indians, Englishmen, and Africans on the Eastern Shore, 1640–1676* (New York, 1980); Kathleen M. Brown, *Good Wives, Nasty Wenches and Anxious Patriarchs: Gender, Race and Power in Colonial Virginia* (Chapel Hill, N.C. 1996); Lois Green Carr, Russell R. Menard, and Lorena S. Walsh, *Robert S. Cole's World: Agriculture and Society in Early Maryland* (Chapel Hill, N.C., 1991); Lorena S. Walsh, *From Calabar to Carter's Grove: A History of a Virginia Slave Community* (Charlottesville, Va., 1997); and Mechal Sobel, *The World They Made Together: Black and White Values in Eighteenth-Century Virginia* (Princeton, N.J., 1987).

Slavery south of the Chesapeake colonies has also attracted the attention of a new generation of scholars. Most important are Peter H. Wood, *Black Majority: Negroes in Colonial South Carolina from 1670 through the Stono Rebellion* (New York, 1974); Robert Olwell, *Masters, Slaves, and Subjects: The Culture of Power in Carolina Low Country, 1740–1790* (Ithaca, N.Y., 1998); Betty Wood, *Slavery in Colonial Georgia, 1730–1775* (Athens, Ga., 1984); Russell R. Menard, "Slave Demography in the Low-country, 1670–1740: From Frontier to Plantation," *South Carolina Historical Magazine,* 96 (1995); Daniel C. Littlefield, *Rice and Slaves: Ethnicity and the Slave Trade in Colonial South*

Carolina (Baton Rouge, La., 1981); Philip Morgan, "Black Society in the Lowcountry, 1760–1810," in Ira Berlin and Ronald Hoffman, eds., *Slavery and Freedom in the Revolutionary Era* (Charlottesville, Va., 1982), and "Colonial South Carolina Runaways: Their Significance for Slave Culture," *Slavery and Abolition* 6 (1985), 57–78; Peter A. Coclanis, *The Shadow of a Dream: Economic Life and Death in the South Carolina Low Country: 1670–1820* (New York, 1988); Marvin L. Michael Kay and Lorin Lee Cary, *Slavery in North Carolina: 1748–1775* (Chapel Hill, N.C., 1995); Julia Floyd Smith, *Slavery and Rice Culture in Low Country Georgia, 1750–1860* (Knoxville, Tenn., 1985); Joyce E. Chaplin, *An Anxious Pursuit: Agricultural Innovation and Modernity in the Lower South, 1730–1815* (Chapel Hill, N.C., 1993); Allan Gallay, *The Formation of a Planter Elite: Jonathan Bryan and Southern Colonial Frontier* (Athens, Ga., 1989); Betty Wood, *Women's Work, Men's Work: The Informal Slave Economies of Lowcountry Georgia* (Athens, Ga., 1995); David R. Colburn and Jane L. Landers, ed., *The African American Heritage of Florida* (Gainesville, Fla., 1995); Gwendolyn Midlow Hall, *Africans in Colonial Louisiana: The Development of Afro-Creole Culture in the Eighteenth Century* (Baton Rouge, La., 1982); and Thomas N. Ingersoll, *Mammon and Manon Early New Orleans: The First Slave Society in the Deep South, 1718–1819* (Knoxville, Tenn., 1999).

Among the studies of northern slavery in the colonial period, the most important are Lorenzo J. Greene, *The Negro in Colonial New England, 1620–1776* (New York, 1942); William D. Piersen, *Black Yankees: The Development of an Afro-American Subculture in Eighteenth-Century New England* (Amherst, Mass., 1988); Edgar J. McManus, *Black Bondage in the North* (Syracuse, N.Y., 1973), and *Negro Slavery in New York* (Syracuse, N.Y., 1966); Graham Russell Hodges, *Slavery and Freedom in the Rural North: African Americans in Monmouth County, New Jersey, 1665–1865* (Madison, Wis., 1996); Gary B. Nash, "Slaves and Slaveholders in Colonial Philadelphia," *William and Mary Quarterly* 30 (1973), 223–56; Edward R. Turner, *The Negro in Pennsylvania: Slavery, Servitude, Freedom, 1639–1861* (Washington, D.C., 1911); Richard C. Twombly and Robert H. Moore, "Black Puritans: The Negro in Seventeenth-Century Massachusetts," *William and Mary Quarterly* 24 (1967), 224–42; Joyce D. Goodfriend, "Burghers and Blacks: The Evolution of a Slave Society at New Amsterdam," *New York History* 59 (1978), 125–44; and Joseph P. Reidy, "'Negro Election Day' and Black Community Life in New England, 1750–1860," *Marxist Perspectives* 1 (1978), 102–17.

Comparative studies of slavery in the last generation have done more to increase our understanding of American slavery than almost any other conceptual approach to the history of this institution. Thus students will want to examine slavery outside of North America, both in English colonies in the West Indies and in the colonies of Spain, Portugal, France, and Holland. The field of comparative slave studies is growing enormously, and only a fraction of the many studies can be mentioned here. But of special importance are studies that compare two or more slave societies, such as Frank Tannenbaum's pioneering *Slave and Citizen: The Negro in the Americas* (New York, 1956); Marvin Harris, *Patterns of Race in the Americas* (New York, 1964); Herbert S. Klein, *Slavery in the Americas: A Comparative Study of Virginia and Cuba* (Chicago, 1967); Carl N. Degler, *Neither Black Nor White: Slavery and Race Relations in Brazil and the United States* (New York, 1971); H. Hoetink, *Slavery and Race Relations in the Americas* (New York, 1973); Stanley L. Engerman and Eugene Genovese, *Race and Slavery in the Western Hemisphere: Quantitative Studies* (Princeton, N.J., 1975); Ann M. Pescatello, ed., *Old Roots in New Lands: Historical and Anthropological Perspectives on Black Experiences in the Americas* (Westport, Conn., 1977); Peter Kolchin, *Unfree Labor: American Slavery and Russian Serfdom* (Cambridge, Mass., 1987); Vera Rubin and Arthur Tuden, eds., *Comparative Perspectives on Slavery in New World Plantation Societies*, Annals of the New York Academy of Sciences, 292 (New York, 1977); and Michael Mullin, *Africa in America: Slave Acculturation and Resistance in the American South and the British Caribbean, 1737–1831* (Urbana, Ill., 1992).

Valuable studies of seventeenth- and eighteenth-century slavery in the British West Indies are Virginia Bernhard, "Bermuda and Virginia in the Seventeenth Century: A Comparative View," *Journal of Social History* 19 (1985), 57–70; Harry J. Bennett, *Bondsmen and Bishops: Slavery and Apprenticeship on the Codrington Plantations of Barbados, 1710–1838* (Berkeley, Cal., 1958); Robert Dirks, *The Black Saturnalia: Conflict and Its Ritual Expression on British West Indian Slave Plantations* (Gainesville, Fla., 1987); Richard S. Dunn, *Sugar and Slaves: The Rise of the Planter Class in the British West Indies, 1624–1713* (Chapel Hill, N.C., 1972); David Barry Gaspar, *Bondsmen and Rebels: A Study of Master–Slave Relations in Antigua with Implications for Colonial British America* (Baltimore, 1985); Elsa V. Goveia, *Slave Society in the British Leeward Islands at the End of the Eighteenth Century* (New Haven, 1965); Orlando Patterson, *The Sociology of Slavery: An Analysis of the Origins, Development and Structure of Negro Slave Society in Jamaica* (London, 1967); Frank W. Pitman, "Slavery on the British West India Plantations in the Eighteenth Century," *Journal of Negro History* 11 (1926), 584–668; Michael Craton and James Walvin, *A Jamaican Plantation: A History of Worthy Park, 1670–1970* (Toronto, 1970); Michael Craton, *Searching for the Invisible Man: Slaves and Plantation Life in Jamaica* (Cambridge, Mass., 1978); Richard B. Sheridan, *Sugar and Slavery: An Economic History of the British West Indies, 1623–1775* (Baltimore, 1974), and *Doctors and Slaves: A Medical and Demographic History of Slavery in the British West Indies, 1680–1834* (New York, 1985); Edward Brathwaite, *The Development of Creole Society in Jamaica, 1770–1820* (Oxford, 1971).

Slavery in Portuguese and Spanish colonies is treated in Ronald H. Chilcote, ed., *Protest and Resistance in Angola and Brazil* (Berkeley, Cal., 1972); Colin A. Palmer, *Slaves of the White God: Blacks in Mexico, 1570–1650* (Cambridge, Mass., 1976); Florestan Fernandes, *The Negro in Brazilian Society* (New

York, 1969); Gwendolyn M. Hall, *Social Control in Slave Plantation Societies: A Comparison of St. Domingue and Cuba* (Baltimore, 1971); David R. Colburn and Jane L. Landers, eds., *The African American Heritage of Florida* (Gainesville, Fla., 1959); Jane L. Landers, "Gracia Real de Santa Teresa de Moses: A Free Black Town in Spanish Colonial Florida," *American Historical Review* 95 (1990), 9–30; and Daniel Usner, Jr., *Indians, Settlers and Slaves in a Frontier Exchange Economy: The Lower Mississippi Valley Before 1783* (Chapel Hill, N.C., 1992).

The connections between racism and slavery are intimate. The major work in this area is Winthrop D. Jordan, *White Over Black: American Attitudes Toward the Negro, 1550–1812* (Chapel Hill, N.C., 1968). Jordan's book can be supplemented by Milton Cantor, "The Image of the Negro in Colonial Literature," *New England Quarterly* 36 (1963), 452–77; Carl N. Degler, "Slavery and the Genesis of American Race Prejudice," *Comparative Studies in History and Society* 2 (1959), 49–66; Roger Bastide, "Color, Racism, and Christianity," *Daedalus* 96 (1967), 312–27; and Ronald Sanders, *Lost Tribes and Promised Lands: The Origins of American Racism* (Boston, 1978). Also profitable are the psychoanalytical and anthropological approaches of Erik H. Erikson, "The Concept of Identity in Race Relations," *Daedalus* 95 (1966), 145–71 and Jennifer L. Morgan, "Some Could Suckle over their Shoulder: Male Travelers, Female Bodies, and the Gendering of Racial Ideology," *William and Mary Quarterly*, 54 (1997), 167–92.

A number of special topics concerning the evolution of African-American society in colonial America deserve attention. Miscegenation and the status of mixed race people are of great importance. They are thoroughly treated in the previously mentioned work of Winthrop Jordan and Carl Degler and also in Carter G. Woodson, "The Beginnings of Miscegenation of the Whites and Blacks," *Journal of Negro History* 3 (1918), 335–53; Winthrop D. Jordan, "American Chiaroscuro: The Status and Definition of Mulattoes in the British Colonies," *William and Mary Quarterly* 19 (1962), 183–200; Edward B. Reuter, *The Mulatto in the United States* (Boston, 1918); Joel Williamson, *New People: Miscegenation and Mulattoes in the United States* (New York, 1980); Donald L. Horowitz, "Color Differentiation in the American Systems of Slavery," *Journal of Interdisciplinary History* 3 (1973), 509–41; A. Leon Higgenbotham, Jr., *In the Matter of Color: Race and the American Legal Process: The Colonial Period* (New York, 1978); and William M. Wiecek, "The Statutory Law of Slavery and Race in the Thirteen Mainland Colonies of British America," *William and Mary Quarterly* 34 (1977), 258–80. For an overview that continues into the nineteenth and twentieth centuries see Gary B. Nash, *Forbidden Love: The Secret History of Mixed-Race America* (New York, 1999).

Slave resistance is studied in many of the works already mentioned, but is the special concern of the following studies: Raymond A. Bauer and Alice H. Bauer, "Day to Day Resistance to Slavery," *Journal of Negro History* 27

(1942), 388–419; Michael Craton, *Testing the Chains: Resistance to Slavery in the British West Indies* (Ithaca, N.Y., 1983); Thomas J. Davis, *A Rumor of Revolt: The "Great Negro Plot" in Colonial New York* (New York, 1985); Mary Ellison, "Resistance to Oppression: Black Women's Response to Slavery in the United States," *Slavery and Abolition* 4 (1983), 56–63; Marvin L. Michael Kay and Lorin Lee Cary, "'They are Indeed the Constant Plague of Their Tyrants': Slave Defence of a Moral Economy in Colonial North Carolina, 1748–1772," *Slavery and Abolition* 6 (1985), 37–56; Gerald W. Mullin, *Flight and Rebellion: Slave Resistance in Eighteenth-Century Virginia* (New York, 1972); Ferenc M. Szasz, "The New York Slave Revolt of 1741: A Re-Examination," *New York History* 48 (1967), 215–30; Darold D. Wax, "Negro Resistance to the Early American Slave Trade," *Journal of Negro History* 51 (1966), 1–15; Richard Price, ed., *Maroon Societies: Rebel Slave Communities in the Americas* (Garden City, N.Y., 1973); Edward A. Pearson, "A Countryside Full of Flames: A Reconsideration of the Stono Rebellion and Slave Rebelliousness in the Early Eighteenth-Century South Carolina Low Country," *Slavery and Abolition,* 17 (1996) 22–50; and John K. Thornton, "African Dimensions of the Stono Rebellion," *American Historical Review* 96 (1991), 1101–13.

Important studies on the manumission of slaves and the role of the free black in colonial society are included in many of the more general histories mentioned above. Specialized studies for the South and the Caribbean include James H. Brewer, "Negro Property Owners in Seventeenth-Century Virginia," *William and Mary Quarterly* 12 (1955), 575–80; Thomas N. Ingersoll, "Free Blacks in a Slave Society: New Orleans, 1718–1812," *William and Mary Quarterly* 48 (1991), 173–200; Kimberly S. Hanger, *Bounded Lives, Bounded Places: Free Black Society in Colonial New Orleans, 1769–1803* (Durham, N.C., 1997); Marina Wikramanayake, *A World in Shadow: The Free Black in Antebellum South Carolina* (Columbia, S.C., 1973); Robert Olwell, "Becoming Free: Manumission and the Genesis of a Free Black Community in South Carolina, 1740–90," *Slavery and Abolition* 17 (1996), 1–19; David W. Cohen and Jack P. Greene, eds., *Neither Slave Nor Free: The Freedman of African Descent in the Slave Societies of the New World* (Baltimore, 1972); Mary Turner, ed., *From Chattel Slaves to Wage Slaves: The Dynamics of Labor Bargaining in the Americas* (Kingston, 1995); C. Ashley Ellefson, "Free Jupiter and the Rest of the World: The Problems of a Free Negro in Colonial Maryland," *Maryland Historical Magazine* 66 (1971), 1–13; Ross M. Kimmell, "Free Blacks in Seventeenth-Century Maryland," *Maryland Historical Magazine* 71 (1976), 19–25; T. H. Breen and Stephen Innes, *"Myne Owne Ground": Race and Freedom on Virginia's Eastern Shore, 1640–1676* (New York, 1980); Ira Berlin, *Slaves Without Masters: The Free Negro in the Antebellum South* (New York, 1974); Michael L. Nicholls, "Passing Through This Troublesome World: Free Blacks in the Early Southside," *Virginia Magazine of History and Biography,* 92 (1984), 50–70.

For the North see Gary B. Nash and Jean R. Soderlund, *Freedom by Degrees: Emancipation in Pennsylvania and its Aftermath* (New York, 1991); Gary B. Nash, *Forging Freedom: The Formation of Philadelphia's Black Community, 1720–1840* (Cambridge, Mass., 1988); Shane White, *Somewhat More Independent: The End of Slavery in New York City, 1770–1810* (Athens, Ga., 1991); and James Oliver Horton and Lois E. Horton, *In Hope of Liberty: Culture, Community and Protest Among Northern Free Blacks, 1700–1860* (New York, 1997).

The best studies of early abolitionist thought are David B. Davis, *The Problem of Slavery in Western Culture* (Ithaca, N.Y., 1966) and *The Problem of Slavery in the Era of Revolution* (Ithaca, N.Y., 1975). Also valuable are Thomas E. Drake, *Quakers and Slavery in America* (New Haven, 1950); W. E .B. DuBois, *The Suppression of the African Slave Trade* (New York, 1896); Arthur Zilversmit, *The First Emancipation: The Abolition of Slavery in the North* (Chicago, 1967); James D. Essig, *The Bonds of Wilderness: American Evangelicals against Slavery, 1770–1808* (Philadelphia, 1983); and Jean R. Soderlund, *Quakers and Slavery: A Divided Spirit* (Princeton, N.J., 1985).

The conversion of the African slave to the Christian religion, an important element in the acculturative experience, is studied in Denzil T. Clifton, "Anglicanism and Negro Slavery in Colonial America," *Historical Magazine of the Protestant-Episcopal Church* 39 (1970), 29–70; Alan Gallay, "The Origins of Slaveholders' Paternalism: George Whitefield, the Bryan Family, and the Great Awakening in the South," *Journal of Southern History* 53 (1987), 369–94; and Edgar L. Pennington, "Thomas Bray's Associates and Their Work Among the Negroes," *American Antiquarian Society Proceedings*, n.s. 48 (1938), 311–403.

Slave religion should be considered not only from the viewpoint of white proselytizing efforts but also from the vantage point of the forging by slaves of Black Christianity. This requires studying the cultural characteristics of African societies from which slaves were taken and the adaptation of these cultural traits in a new environment. For a valuable study of the formation of black culture across the Atlantic, see Paul Gilroy, *The Black Atlantic: Modernity and Double Consciousness* (Cambridge, Mass., 1993). A particularly valuable essay on this approach is Sidney W. Mintz and Richard Price, *An Anthropological Approach to the Afro-American Past: A Caribbean Perspective* (Philadelphia, 1976). Among the works by anthropologists, ethnomusicologists, and historians that students can profitably consult are: Melville J. Herskovits, *The Myth of the Negro Past* (Boston, 1941) and *The New World Negro* (Bloomington, Ind., 1966); John S. Mbiti, *African Religions and Philosophy* (New York, 1969); Roger Bastide, *African Civilizations in the New World* (New York, 1971); Margaret W. Creel, *A Peculiar People: Slave Religion and Community-Culture Among the Gullahs* (New York, 1988); Lawrence W. Levine, "Slave Songs and Slave Consciousness: An Exploration in Neglected Sources," in Tamara K. Hareven, ed., *Anonymous Americans: Explorations in Nineteenth-Century*

Social History (Englewood Cliffs, N.J., 1971); John Lovell, Jr., *Black Song: The Forge and the Flame* (New York, 1972); John Rublowsky, *Black Music in America* (New York, 1971); Eileen Southern, *The Music of Black Americans: A History* (New York, 1971); Lorenzo D. Turner, "African Survivals in the New World with Special Emphasis on the Arts," in John A. Davis, ed., *Africa from the Point of View of American Negro Scholars* (Paris, 1958); John M. Vlach, *The Afro-American Tradition in Decorative Arts* (Cleveland, 1978); Norman E. Whitten, Jr., and John F. Szwed, eds., *Afro-American Anthropology: Contemporary Perspectives* (New York, 1970); Leland Ferguson, *Uncommon Ground: Archaeology and Early African America, 1650–1800* (Washington, D.C., 1992); Dale Rosengarten, *Row Upon Row: Sea Grass Baskets of the South Carolina Lowcountry* (Columbia, S.C., 1986); William D. Piersen, *Black Legacy: America's Hidden Heritage* (Amherst, Mass., 1993); Leonard Barrett, *Soul-Force: African Heritage in Afro-American Religion* (New York, 1974); Henry Mitchell, *Black Belief: Folk Beliefs of Blacks in America and West Africa* (New York, 1975); Mechal Sobel, *Trabelin' On: The Slave Journey to an Afro-Baptist Faith* (Westport, Conn., 1978); Albert Raboteau, *Slave Religion* (New York, 1978); John B. Boles, *Master & Slave in the House of the Lord: Race and Religion in the American South, 1740–1861* (Columbia, S.C., 1988); and Christine Leigh Heyrman, *Southern Cross: The Beginnings of the Bible Belt* (New York, 1997).

The slave family has been the subject of several important works. Most important are: The new books by Ira Berlin and Philip Morgan cited earlier; Herbert Gutman, *The Black Family in Slavery and Freedom* (New York, 1976); Allan Kulikoff, "The Beginnings of the Afro-American Family in Maryland," in Aubrey C. Land, et al., eds. *Law, Society, and Politics in Early Maryland* (Baltimore, 1977); Cheryll Ann Cody, "Naming, Kinship, and Estate Dispersal: Notes on Slave Family Life on a South Carolina Plantation, 1786 to 1833," *William and Mary Quarterly* 39 (1982), 192; Stanley Engerman, "Studying the Black Family," *Journal of Family History* 3 (1978), 78–101; and Mary Beth Norton, et al., "The Afro-American Family in the Age of Revolution," in Ira Berlin and Ronald Hoffman, eds., *Slavery and Freedom in the Revolutionary Era* (Charlottesville, Va., 1981).

Another aspect of intercultural contact in early America was that between African and Indians. Much remains to be done in this area, but some glimpses into this are available in Laurence Foster, *Negro–Indian Relationships in the Southeast* (Philadelphia, 1935); Peter B. Hammond, "Afro-Americans, Indians, and Afro-Asians: Cultural Contacts Between Africa and the Peoples of Asia and Aboriginal America," in Gwendolyn M. Carter and Ann Paden, eds., *Expanding Horizons in African Studies* (Evanston, Ill., 1969); John M. Lofton, Jr., "White, Indian, and Negro Contacts in Colonial South Carolina," *Southern Indian Studies* 1 (1949), 3–12; James H. Merrell, "The Racial Education of the Catawba Indians," *Journal of Southern History* 50 (1984), 363–384; Kenneth W. Porter, *The Negro on the American Frontier* (New York, 1971); Richard Halliburton, Jr., *Red Over Black: Black Slavery Among the*

Cherokee Indians (Westport, Conn., 1977); Theda Perdue, *Slavery and the Evolution of Cherokee Society, 1540–1866* (Knoxville, Tenn., 1979); William S. Willis, Jr., "Divide and Rule: Red, White and Black in the Southeast," *Journal of Negro History* 48 (1963), 157–76; Daniel F. Littlefield, *Africans and Creeks From the Colonial Period to the Civil War* (Westport, Conn., 1976); Jack Forbes, *Black Africans and Native Americans: Color, Race, and Caste in the Evolution of Red-Black Peoples* (New York, 1988); and *Africans and Native Americans; The Language of Race and the Evolution of Red–Black Peoples*, 2d ed., (Urbana, Ill., 1993); and Jane L. Landers, "Black–Indian Interaction in Spanish Florida," *Colonial Latin American Historical Review* 2, (1993), 141–62.

RIVALRY FOR NORTH AMERICA

International rivalry for the North American continent has been the subject of a vast literature, mostly cast in the genre of political or military history. For a detailed English account see volumes 6–7 of Lawrence Henry Gipson, *The British Empire Before the American Revolution*, 14 vols. (New York, 1958–69). Works that deal primarily with the role of Indian societies in this struggle for the eastern half of the continent and that have importance for social and cultural as well as political and military history are John R. Alden, *John Stuart and the Southern Colonial Frontier: A Study of Indian Relations, War, Trade, and Land Problems in the Southern Wilderness, 1754–1775* (Ann Arbor, Mich., 1944); Richmond P. Bond, *Queen Anne's American Kings* (Oxford, 1952); Julian P. Boyd, ed., *Indian Treaties Printed by Benjamin Franklin, 1736–1762* (Philadelphia, 1938); Louis DeVorsey, Jr., *The Indian Boundary in the Southern Colonies, 1763–75* (Chapel Hill, N.C., 1966); Randolph C. Downes, *Council Fires on the Upper Ohio: A Narrative of Indian Affairs in the Upper Ohio Valley Until 1795* (Pittsburgh, 1940); R. Brian Ferguson and Neil L. Whitehead, eds., *War in the Tribal Zone: Expanding States and Indigenous Warfare* (Santa Fe, N.M., 1992); Wilbur R. Jacobs, *Diplomacy and Indian Gifts: Anglo–French Rivalry along the Ohio and Northwest Frontiers, 1748–1763* (Stanford, 1950); and *Indians of the Southern Colonial Frontier: The Edmond Atkin Report and Plan of 1755* (Columbia, S.C., 1954); Michael N. McConnell, *A Country Between: The Upper Ohio Valley and Its Peoples, 1724–1774* (Lincoln, Neb., 1992); Francis Jennings, *Empire of Fortune: Crowns, Colonies, and Tribes in the Seven Years War in America* (New York, 1988); Douglas E. Leach, *The Northern Colonial Frontier, 1607–1763* (New York, 1966); Ian K. Steele, *Betrayal: Fort William Henry and the "Massacre"* (New York, 1990); Peter Marshall, "Sir William Johnson and the Treaty of Fort Stanwix, 1768," *Journal of American Studies* 1 (1967), 149–79; David C. Skaggs, ed., *The Old Northwest in the American Revolution* (Madison, Wis., 1977); Howard H. Peckham, *Pontiac and the Indian Uprising* (Princeton, N.J., 1947); Jack M. Sosin, *Whitehall and the Wilderness: The Middle West in British Colonial Policy, 1760–1775* (Lincoln, Neb., 1961); Paul A. W. Wallace,

Conrad Weiser, 1696–1760: Friend of Colonist and Mohawk (Philadelphia, 1945); and Nicholas B. Wainwright, *George Croghan: Wilderness Diplomat* (Chapel Hill, N.C., 1959). For nativistic movements, which were an important part of the eighteenth-century Indian response to changing conditions of contact with European colonizers, see Ralph Linton, "Nativistic Movements," *American Anthropologist* 45 (1943), 230–40; Anthony F. C. Wallace, "Revitalization Movements: Some Theoretical Considerations for Their Comparative Study," *American Anthropologist* 58 (1956), 264–81; Charles E. Hunter, "The Delaware Nativist Revival of the Mid-Eighteenth Century," *Ethnohistory* 18 (1971), 39–50; and Gregory Dowd, *A Spirited Resistance: The North American Struggle for Unity, 1745–1815* (Baltimore, Md., 1992).

SOCIAL AND POLITICAL CHANGE

An excellent overview of social and political change in the eighteenth-century colonies is James A. Henretta and Gregory H. Nobles, *Evolution and Revolution: American Society, 1600–1820* (Lexington, Mass., 1987). In addition, there are a number of more specialized studies, many of them based on close examination of individual communities.

Four pathbreaking community studies, published more than three decades ago, are: Richard L. Bushman, *From Puritan to Yankee: Character and the Social Order in Connecticut, 1690–1765* (Cambridge, Mass., 1967); John Demos, *A Little Commonwealth: Family Life in Plymouth Colony* (New York, 1970); Philip J. Greven, Jr., *Four Generations: Population, Land, and Family in Colonial Andover, Massachusetts* (Ithaca, N.Y., 1970); and Kenneth A. Lockridge, *A New England Town: The First Hundred Years*, rev. ed. (New York, 1985).

More recent contributions to the social history of New England are: David G. Allen, *In English Ways: The Movement of Societies and the Transferral of English Local Law and Custom to Massachusetts Bay in the Seventeenth Century* (Chapel Hill, N.C., 1980); Paul Boyer and Steven Nissenbaum, *Salem Possessed: The Social Origins of Witchcraft* (Cambridge, Mass., 1974); T. H. Breen, *Puritans and Adventurers: Change and Persistence in Early America* (New York, 1980); Bruce Daniels, *The Connecticut Town: Growth and Development, 1635–1790* (Middletown, Conn., 1979); John Demos, *Entertaining Satan: Witchcraft and the Culture of Early New England* (New York, 1982); Richard P. Gildrie, Salem, *Massachusetts, 1626–1683: A Covenant Community* (Charlottesville, Va., 1977); Robert A. Gross, *The Minutemen and Their World* (New York, 1976); Christine Leigh Heyrman, *Commerce and Culture: The Maritime Communities of Colonial Massachusetts, 1690–1750* (New York, 1984); Daniel Vickers, *Farmers and Fishermen: Two Centuries of Work in Essex County, Massachusetts* (Chapel Hill, N.C., 1994); Stephen Innes, *Labor in a New Land: Economy and Society in Seventeenth-Century Springfield* (Princeton, N.J., 1983); Christopher M. Jedrey, *The World of John Cleaveland: Family and Community in*

Eighteenth-Century New England (New York, 1979); Carol F. Karlsen, *The Devil in the Shape of a Woman: Witchcraft in Colonial New England* (New York, 1987); Laurel Thatcher Ulrich *Good Wives: Image and Reality in the Lives of Women in Northern New England, 1650–1750* (New York, 1982); and Paul R. Lucas, *Valley of Discord: Church and Society Along the Connecticut River, 1636–1725* (Hanover, N.H., 1976).

Social change in the Middle Colonies has been illuminated by Douglas Greenberg, *Crime and Law Enforcement in the Colony of New York, 1691–1776* (Ithaca, N.Y., 1976); Sung Bok Kim, *Landlord and Tenant in Colonial New York: Manorial Society, 1664–1775* (Chapel Hill, N.C., 1978); James T. Lemon, *The Best Poor Man's Country: A Geographical Study of Early Southeastern Pennsylvania* (Baltimore, 1972); Robert C. Ritchie, *The Duke's Province: A Study of New York Politics and Society, 1664–1691* (Chapel Hill, N.C., 1977); Alan Tully, *William Penn's Legacy: Politics and Social Structure in Provincial Pennsylvania, 1726–1755* (Baltimore, 1978); Philip L. White, *Beekmantown, New York: Forest Frontier to Farm Community* (Austin, Tex., 1979); Jerome H. Wood, Jr., *Conestoga Crossroads: Lancaster, Pennsylvania, 1730–1790* (Harrisburg, Pa., 1979); and Stephanie G. Wolf, *Urban Village: Population, Community, and Family Structure in Germantown, Pennsylvania, 1683–1800* (Princeton, N.J., 1977).

In addition to the references in the section on African-American history, the following are important in tracing social change in the colonial South: Richard R. Beeman, "Social Change and Cultural Conflict in Virginia: Lunenburg County, 1746 to 1774," *William and Mary Quarterly* 35 (1978), 455–76; Paul G. E. Clemens, *The Atlantic Economy and Colonial Maryland's Eastern Shore: From Tobacco to Grain* (Ithaca, N.Y., 1980); Carville Earle and Ronald Hoffman, "Urban Development in the Eighteenth-Century South," *Perspectives in American History* 10 (1976), 7–78; Alan Gallay, *The Formation of a Planter Elite : Jonathan Bryan and the Southern Colonial Frontier,* (Athens, Ga., 1989); Rachel N. Klein, *Unification of a Slave State: The Rise of the Planter Class in the South Carolina Backcountry, 1760–1808* (Chapel Hill, N.C., 1990); Thad W. Tate and David L. Ammerman, eds., *The Chesapeake in the Seventeenth Century: Essays on Anglo-American Society* (Chapel Hill, N.C., 1979); David C. Skaggs, *Roots of Maryland Democracy, 1753–1776* (Westport, Conn., 1973); and Gregory A. Stiverson, *Poverty in a Land of Plenty: Tenancy in Eighteenth-Century Maryland* (Baltimore, 1978).

European immigration to British North America, including the traffic in servants and convicts, is analyzed in the following: Bernard Bailyn, *Voyagers to the West: A Passage in the Peopling of America on the Eve of the Revolution* (New York, 1986); A. Roger Ekirch, *Bound for America: The Transportation of British Convicts to the Colonies, 1718–1775* (New York, 1987); David W. Galenson, *White Servitude in Colonial America: An Economic Analysis* (New York, 1982); Sharon V. Salinger, *"To Serve Well and Faithfully": Labor and Indentured Servants in Pennsylvania, 1682–1800* (New York, 1987); John Van der Zee, *Bound Over: Indentured Servitude and American Conscience* (New York, 1985);

and A. G. Roeber, *Palatines, Liberty and Property* (Baltimore, 1993); Alan J. Karras, *Sojourners in the Sun: Scottish Migrants in Jamaica and the Chesapeake* (Ithaca, 1992); and Aaron S. Fogleman, *Hopeful Journeys: German Immigration, Settlement, and Political Culture, 1717–1775* (Philadelphia, 1996).

For economic life and values, see J. E. Crowley, *This Sheba Self: The Conceptualization of Economic Life in Eighteenth-Century America* (Baltimore, 1974); David W. Galenson, *Traders, Planters, and Slaves: Market Behavior in Early British America* (New York, 1986); John J. McCusker and Russell R. Menard, *The Economy of British America, 1607–1789* (Chapel Hill, N.C., 1985); Joyce E. Chaplin, *An Anxious Pursuit: Agricultural Innovation and Modernity in the Lower South, 1730–1815* (Chapel Hill, 1993); James A. Henretta, "Families and Farms: Mentalité in Pre-Industrial America," *William and Mary Quarterly* 35 (1978), 3–32; and Stephen Innes, ed., *Work and Labor in Early America* (Chapel Hill, N.C., 1988). The cities are studied in Gary B. Nash, *The Urban Crucible: Social Change, Political Consciousness, and the Origins of the American Revolution* (Cambridge, Mass., 1979); Thomas M. Doerflinger, *A Vigorous Spirit of Enterprise: Merchants and Economic Development in Revolutionary Philadelphia* (Chapel Hill, N.C., 1986); Jacob M. Price, "Economic Function and the Growth of American Port Towns in the Eighteenth Century," *Perspectives in American History* 8 (1974), 7–78; and Carville Earle, "The First English Towns of North America," *Geographical Review* 67 (1977), 34–50.

The Great Awakening is examined in J.M. Bumsted and John Van de Wetering, *What Must I Do to Be Saved? The Great Awakening in Colonial America* (Hinsdale, Ill., 1976); Alan Heimert, *Religion and the American Mind from the Great Awakening to the Revolution* (Cambridge, Mass., 1966); Harry S. Stout, "Religion, Communications, and the Ideological Origins of the American Revolution," *William and Mary Quarterly* 34 (1977) 519–41 and *The New England Soul: Preaching and Religious Culture in Colonial New England* (New York, 1986); Rhys Isaac, *The Transformation of Virginia, 1740–1790* (Chapel Hill, N.C., 1982); Patricia J. Tracy, *Jonathan Edwards, Pastor: Religion and Society in Eighteenth-Century Northampton* (New York, 1979); Milton J. Coalter, *Gilbert Tennent, Son of Thunder: A Case Study of Continental Pietism's Impact on the First Great Awakening in the Middle Colonies* (New York, 1986); W. R. Ward, *The Protestant Evangelical Awakening* (New York, 1992); and Frank J. Lambert, *Pedlar in Divinity: George Whitefield and the Transatlantic Revivals, 1737–1770* (Princeton, 1994).

THE TRI-COLORED AMERICAN REVOLUTION

A good short history of the American Revolution that partially treats the involvement of African-Americans and Native Americans is Edward Countryman, *The American Revolution* (New York, 1985).

A few older histories, such as Philip M. Hamer, "John Stuart's Indian Policy During the Early Months of the American Revolution," *Mississippi Valley Historical Review*, 17 (1930–31), 351–66; Thomas P. Abernathy, *Western Lands and the American Revolution* (New York, 1937), Randolph Downes, *Council Fires on the Upper Ohio: A Narrative of Indian Affairs in the Upper Ohio Valley until 1795* (Pittsburgh, 1940), Randolph Downes, "Creek-American Relations, 1782–90," *Georgia Historical Quarterly*, 21 (1937), 142–84; Randolph Downes, "Cherokee–American Indian Relations in the Upper Tennessee Valley, 1776–1791," *East Tennessee Historical Society Publications*, 8 (1936), 35–53; and John W. Caughey, *McGillivray of the Creeks* (Norman, Ok., 1938) broke ground on showing how important American Indians were to the conduct of the war and how much they suffered from its results.

A new generation of books has greatly increased our understanding of this topic. Among the most important are Ronald Hoffman, et al., eds., *Native Americans and the Early Republic* (Charlottesville, Va. in press); Colin Calloway, *Crown and Calumet: British–Indian Relations, 1783–1815* (Norman, Ok., 1987) and *The American Revolution in Indian Country: Crisis and Diversity in Native American Communities* (Cambridge, 1995); Francis Jennings, "The Indians' Revolution," in Alfred F. Young, ed., *The American Revolution: Essays in the History of American Radicalism* (DeKalb, Ill., 1976), 319–48; and James Merrell, "Declarations of Independence: Indian–White Relations in the New Nation," in Jack P. Greene, ed., *The American Revolution: Its Character and Limits* (New York, 1987).

More specialized studies are Barbara Graymont, *The Iroquois in the American Revolution* (Syracuse, N.Y., 1972); Anthony F. C. Wallace, *The Death and Rebirth of the Seneca* (New York, 1972); Isabel Thompson Kelsay, *Joseph Brant, 1743–1807: Man of Two Worlds* (Syracuse, N.Y., 1984); James H. O'Donnell, *Southern Indians in the American Revolution* (Knoxville, Tenn., 1973), David Corkran, *The Creek Frontier, 1540–1783* (Norman, Ok., 1967); James Merrell, *The Indians' New World: Catawbas and Their Neighbors from European Contact through the Era of Removal* (Chapel Hill, N.C., 1989); Thomas Hatley, *Dividing Paths: Cherokees and South Carolinians through the Era of Revolution* (New York, 1993); Joel Martin, *Sacred Revolt: Muskogees and the Struggle for a New World* (Boston, 1991); Gregory E. Dowd, *A Spirited Resistance: The North American Indian Struggle for Unity, 1745–1815* (Baltimore, Md., 1992); Richard White, *The Middle Ground: Indians, Empires, and Republics in the Great Lakes Region, 1650–1815* (Cambridge, 1991); and Wiley Sword, *President Washington's Indian War: The Struggle for the Old Northwest, 1790–1795* (Norman, Ok., 1985).

For the fiery argument over contributions of the Iroquois to the American concept of confederation and constitution-making, see Donald Grinde, *The Iroquois and the Founding of the American Nation* (San Francisco, 1977); Bruce E. Johansen, *Forgotten Founders: Benjamin Franklin, the Iroquois, and the Rationale for the American Revolution* (Ipswich, Mass., 1982); Donald Grinde and Bruce Johansen, eds., *Exemplar of Liberty: Native America and the Evolution of Democracy* (Los Angeles, 1991); Elisabeth Tooker, "The United States Constitution and the Iroquois League," *Ethnohistory* 35 (1988), 305–36; Bruce Johansen, "Native American Societies and the Evolution of Democracy in America, 1600–1800," *Ethnohistory* 37 (1990), 279–90; Elisabeth Tooker, "Reply to Johansen," *ibid.* 37 (1990), 291–97; Bruce Johansen and Donald Grinde, "The Debate Regarding American Precedents for Democracy: A Recent Historiography," *American Indian Culture and Research Journal* 14, no. 1 (1990), 61–88; Forum: The "Iroquois Influence Thesis—Con and Pro," *William and Mary Quarterly*, 3d Ser., 53 (1996), 587–636; and Oren R. Lyons et al., *Exiled in the Land of the Free: Democracy, Indian Nations and the U.S. Constitution* (Santa Fe, N. Mex., 1992).

The study of African-Americans in the American Revolution began many generations ago with the work of William C. Nell, *The Colored Patriots of the American Revolution* (Boston, 1855). But modern scholarship begins with Benjamin Quarles, *The Negro in the American Revolution* (Chapel Hill, N.C., 1961; new edition with foreword by Gary B. Nash, Chapel Hill, N.C., 1996). A beautifully illustrated book with poignant mini-biographies is Sidney Kaplan, *The Black Presence in the Era of the American Revolution, 1770–1800* (New York, 1973). Very important is Ira Berlin, "The Revolution in Black Life," in Alfred F. Young, ed., *The American Revolution: Essays in the History of American Radicalism* (DeKalb, Ill., 1976); Peter H. Wood, "'The Dream Deferred'. Black Freedom Struggles on the Eve of White Independence," in Gary Y. Okihiro, ed., *In Resistance: Studies in African, Caribbean, and Afro-American History* (Amherst, Mass., 1986); and the essays in Ira Berlin and Ronald Hoffman, eds., *Slavery and Freedom in the Era of the American Revolution* (Charlottesville, Va., 1982).

More geographically specific studies are Jeffrey J. Crow, *The Black Experience in Revolutionary North Carolina* (Raleigh, N.C., 1977); Peter H. Wood, "'Taking Care of Business' in Revolutionary South Carolina: Republicanism and the Slave Society," in Jeffrey J. Crow and Larry E. Tise., eds., *The Southern Experience in the American Revolution* (Chapel Hill, N. C., 1978); Sylvia Frey, *Water From the Rock: Black Resistance in a Revolutionary Age* (Princeton, N.J., 1991); Gary B. Nash, *Forging Freedom: The Formation of Philadelphia's Black Community, 1720–1840* (Cambridge, Mass., 1988); Billy G. Smith, "Runaway Slaves in the Mid-Atlantic Region during the Revolutionary Era," in Ronald Hoffman and Peter J. Albert, eds., *The Transforming Hand of Revolution* (Charlottesville, Va., 1995); Gary B. Nash and Jean Soderlund, *Freedom by Degrees: Emancipation and Its Aftermath in Pennsylvania, 1690–1840* (New York, 1991); Graham Hodges, *African-Americans in Monmouth County During the Age of the American Revolution* (Lincroft, N.J., 1990); Shane White, *Somewhat More Independent: The End of Slavery in New York City, 1770–1810* (Athens, Ga., 1991); Carol V. R. George, *Segregated Sabbaths: Richard Allen and the Rise of Independent Black Churches, 1760–1840* (New York, 1973).

Valuable recent work on black Americans who joined the British includes Mary Beth Norton, "The Fate of Some Black Loyalists of the American Revolution," *Journal of Negro History* 58 (1973), 402–26; James W. St. G. Walker, *The Black Loyalists: The Search for a Promised Land in Nova Scotia and Sierra Leone, 1783–1870* (New York, 1976), Ellen Wilson, *The Loyal Blacks* (New York, 1976); and Gary B. Nash, "Thomas Peters: Millwright and Deliverer," in David Sweet and Gary B. Nash, eds., *Struggle and Survival in Colonial America* (Berkeley and Los Angeles, 1979).

For the rise of the antislavery movement in the revolutionary era and resistance to it see Arthur Zilversmit, *The First Emancipation: The Abolition of Slavery in the North* (Chicago, 1967); Donald L. Robinson, *Slavery in the Structure of American Politics, 1765–1820* (New York, 1971); Duncan J. MacLeod, *Slavery, Race, and the American Revolution* (Cambridge, Mass., 1974); Winthrop D. Jordan, *White Over Black: American Attitudes toward the Negro, 1550–1812* (Chapel Hill, N.C., 1968); David Brion Davis, *The Problem of Slavery in the Era of Revolution, 1770–1823* (Ithaca, N.Y., 1975); Jean Soderlund, *Quakers and Slavery: A Divided Spirit* (Princeton, N.J., 1985); Gary B. Nash, *Race and Revolution* (Madison, Wis., 1990); and Paul Finkelman, *Slavery and the Founders: Race and Liberty in the Age of Jefferson* (Armonk, N.Y., 1996).

Index